T0329586

Managing a Family Fixed-Income Portfolio

Aaron S. Gurwitz

Published by Frank J. Fabozzi Associates

To my Family

ISBN: 1-883249-71-6

Table of Contents

About the Author

Aaron S. Gurwitz is Fixed Income Research Strategist for Private Wealth Management at Goldman, Sachs & Co. In that capacity he advises Goldman's high net worth clients regarding investment opportunities and risks in bond markets worldwide.

Dr. Gurwitz has been at Goldman Sachs for 12 years serving as Senior Economist, Fixed Income Portfolio Strategist for institutional clients, and Manager of the Firm's Municipal Capital Markets Group. He was twice elected First Team All-American Municipal Portfolio Strategist by *Institutional Investor* magazine.

Before joining Goldman, Dr. Gurwitz held positions as Manager of Domestic Bond Market Research at Salomon Brothers, as Senior Economist at the Federal Reserve Bank of New York and the Rand Corporation, and as Assistant Professor of Economics at Michigan State University. Before attending graduate school, he served for three years as a Peace Corps Volunteer in the Republic of Korea.

Dr. Gurwitz holds a bachelor's degree from the State University of New York at Binghamton, masters degrees from Adelphi University and Stanford University, and a Ph.D. in economics from Stanford. He is the husband of Dr. Susan Abramowitz and the father of Beatrice and Zev Gurwitz.

Preface

This book does not contain many footnotes. This is not because the ideas presented in this volume are new or because I invented them. Quite the contrary. Citations of the "literature" on fixed-income investments are sparse in this book because the concepts presented here are so much a part of the climate of opinion in the bond market that no one thinks about where the ideas first came from. Filling these pages with footnotes would be like citing Copernicus in a junior high school science textbook when explaining that the Earth revolves around the sun.

My own understanding of the concepts presented in this book comes from two primary sources. First, the bulk of what I've learned has been absorbed from the atmosphere of the fixed-income departments in which I've been employed since 1985: first at Salomon Brothers, Inc., and, for the past 12 years, at Goldman, Sachs & Co. Most of the concepts presented in this book were first explained to me by colleagues or clients. The explanations of these concepts have evolved over the years through a process of trial and error. In retrospect, I have a great deal of sympathy for and gratitude to the clients or colleagues who, I'm sure, were thoroughly confused by my first clumsy attempts to explain things like yield to maturity or duration.

The second source, notwithstanding the absence of footnotes, has been my reading publications on fixed-income securities and markets. Much of the literature on fixed-income securities and markets has appeared in the form of publications prepared exclusively for the employees and clients of broker-dealer firms. It has been my privilege to have access to much of the best of this material. But not all of the fixed-income literature has been proprietary. The symbiotic relationship between the "free lance" and academic communities on the one hand, and the "street" on the other, has been particularly fruitful. The publisher of this book, Frank Fabozzi, has played a central role in this interaction as both an independent contributor of innovative ideas and as a catalyst for others' collaboration. Readers who wish to move beyond the material presented in this book and deepen their understanding of fixed-income securities and markets should look to Dr. Fabozzi's publication list.

Almost everyone I've worked with and a large number of the clients I've served over the past 15 years deserve some note of gratitude for making it possible for me to write this book. However, a number of my colleagues at Goldman Sachs have provided a great deal of specific help recently. I would never have started this project without the support of Scott Pinkus, David Henle, Bill Buckley, and Vic Simone. Fortunately, all four were enthusiastic about the idea of producing this book, and all four have continued to support the effort in numerous ways.

I have relied extensively on help and advice from my colleagues in the Research Department of the Goldman Sachs Fixed Income, Commodities, and Currencies Division. With the enthusiastic blessing of the head of that Department, Armen Avanessians, the following people provided extensive and very helpful comments on earlier drafts of various chapters: Ron Krieger, Hayley Boesky, Mimi Duff, Paul Young, Alan Brazil, Jean Paul Calamaro, Paul Frean, Katherine Oakley, Marcus Huie, Mika Toikka, Matt Jozoff, and Scott McDermott. Steve Bunson and Reinhard Zechner of the Goldman Sachs Tax Department and Andy Carlson of the Goldman Repo Trading Desk were also very helpful in spotting errors and suggesting better explanations.

I have also received the most extensive help and constant support from two of the finest alumnae of the Barnard College Chemistry Department. My friend and colleague, Robin Hochberg, carefully reviewed every chapter, discovered many mistakes, and demanded clarification of numerous unnecessarily obscure passages in earlier drafts. Finally, my wife, Dr. Susan Abramowitz, devoted the better part of a beach vacation to reading and annotating a draft manuscript. Her extensive and detailed suggestions give me some confidence that the material is accessible to an interested non-specialist.

Aaron Gurwitz

Part I

[1764]

CHAPTER 1

Introduction

B onds don't get the attention they deserve. The nightly business report on net-work news inevitably headlines the change in the Dow Jones Industrial Aver-age, and then proceeds to report on the most actively traded companies. Then there is the obligatory sentence about whether the price of gold "at the London fixing" rose or fell by 50¢. At most, the day's action in the bond market is summarized with a sentence like, "The price of long-term government bonds rose by 5/8s of a percent, bringing the yield down to 6.42%." More often, there is no mention of bonds at all.

The popular press barely mentions the bond market, and the general financial press usually confines its coverage to a back-page column filled with boilerplate, clichés, and opaque quotations from the usual suspects. Browse through the shelves of the business section of the typical shopping mall bookstore and you find, at most, a few dusty volumes on bonds sandwiched in between an array devoted to every aspect of stock picking and stock market timing strategies. A bond market professional can see that much of the accurate information is two decades out-of-date, and some of the content is downright wrong.

To be sure, a great deal is written about the bond market every day in the trade press, and a student of the field has a choice among many excellent detailed and accurate texts on fixed-income securities and markets. But, most of this mate-rial is aimed at full-time bond market professionals.

It is inevitable that stocks will get somewhat greater attention from the general investing public than bonds. Stocks inherently have more human interest, and most families (in the U.S., at least) hold more of their investment portfolio in stocks than in bonds. But the extreme imbalance in popular attention does a dis-service to family investors who hold a substantial proportion of their financial assets as fixed-income securities.

At the end of 1996, bonds accounted for about 27% of the average U.S. household's securities portfolios. The average Japanese family's asset allocation in its securities portfolio is roughly similar; bonds constitute about 25% of directly held securities. In other countries, families' commitment to the bond market is more pronounced. In Germany, for example, the portfolio allocations are almost exactly reversed; bonds account for 75% of the average German household's securities portfolio.[1]

This book is intended to redress the balance in bond information. Its aim is to provide independent investors and financial generalists with the tools needed to build and manage serviceable bond portfolios.

TOOLS OF BOND PORTFOLIO MANAGEMENT

Bond portfolio management tools include a variety of quantitative measures and techniques developed over the past fifteen years. It isn't surprising that the bond markets should have gone through a technological revolution over the past fifteen years. First, bonds and other fixed-income instruments are more readily subject to rigorous quantitative analysis than other assets such as common stocks or real estate. Second, between 1982 and 1996, the size of the U.S. bond market more than doubled in real (inflation-adjusted) terms, while the power of desktop computers increased even faster. More bonds created a demand for more sophisticated portfolio management techniques, and increased computational power enabled financial professionals to meet this need.

A few of these new quantitative tools rely on mid-level undergraduate mathematics, but most of what goes by the name of "rocket science" in the bond markets is readily accessible by anyone with three years of high school math and reasonable quantitative common sense.

What, then, do these fixed-income portfolio management "tools" do? Their most important function is to help the investor avoid surprises. No one knows for sure what financial market conditions will be in the future. But we do have a pretty good idea how fixed-income investments and portfolios are likely to perform under given market conditions. The concepts and techniques presented in this book are designed to assure that the investor will not be surprised by changes in the market value of his or her portfolio or changes in the amount of investment income generated by the portfolio, regardless of how market conditions evolve.

Suppose an investor has a liquid net worth of US$10 million and wants to develop an investment strategy that is likely to increase portfolio market value by 25% over a period of five years while producing a minimum of $400,000 in after-tax investment income to be spent per year for at least ten years. The tools we present will help the investor assess whether these objectives are reasonable and, if they are, select securities that are likely to achieve these goals. The tools will also tell the investor the types of market conditions that will cause this portfolio to lose market value or fail to produce the requisite level of income.

---

[1] Sources: Board of Governors, Federal Reserve System, Flow of Funds Accounts, First Quarter, 1999; Bank of Japan, Flow of Funds Accounts, 1st Quarter 1999, July 1999; and Deutsche Bundesbank, Financial Accounts for Germany: 1980-1998, July 1999.

The tools presented in this book have another application; they can help investors cut through the smoke screen that sometimes surrounds fixed-income investments. Not all registered representatives of securities firms are as informed as they should be about fixed-income instruments, and, as in any market, a few firms or salespeople may be disreputable. Anyone who reads this book should be able to ask the right questions about any fixed-income security offered and understand the right answer. If a bond dealer's representative can't answer the questions this book suggests or gives an answer that is incomprehensible in terms of the concepts presented here, don't take the offering, and consider finding another provider of fixed-income investments.

In addition to providing the reader with an understanding of modern bond mathematics, this book is also intended to introduce family portfolio managers to the workings of the world's bond markets. Just as the sophistication of portfolio management techniques has increased over the past decade and a half, so have the size and variety of bond markets around the world. As recently as 20 years ago, the market for mortgage-backed securities in the United States was in its infancy, there was simply no way for private investors to tap into the markets in developing countries, and many of the countries issuing investment-grade government bonds today didn't even exist. This continuing expansion creates opportunities for investors; there are now new ways to increase returns and diversify risks by investing in new markets and new types of bonds.

But each of these new markets and new types of securities has its own peculiarities and is subject to its own unique risks. Family investors will want to pick and choose carefully among these new markets and varieties of bonds. The aim of this book is *not* to offer the final word on, for example, the valuation of French municipals or the ins and outs of the Brazilian corporate bond market, but to provide a broad introduction to the range of markets and types of bonds that are available to the family investor.

WHAT'S IN THIS BOOK

This text is divided into three parts. The first two should prove useful to all readers, while Part III is aimed at financial professionals and investors who aim to build "high-performance" fixed-income portfolios and to spend a considerable amount of time and attention on the task.

Part I focuses on the general characteristics shared by all fixed-income investment instruments and portfolios. Individual chapters in this section introduce the basic concepts of bond mathematics and portfolio theory. Because, by their nature, fixed-income investments are intimately connected with interest rates, we also devote attention to the process by which financial markets determine the "price of money." The concluding chapter of Part I ties this material together by providing guidance on how to determine the right general structure for a family bond portfolio.

Once a family or its financial advisor has targeted a general structure, the next step in building a portfolio involves purchasing specific bonds in real bond markets. Part II begins with descriptions of the various types of bonds: various countries' government bonds, corporate bonds, municipals, mortgage-backed securities, and so on. In these descriptions, we pay the most attention to securities and markets that generally make the most sense in family portfolios. Thus, we devote considerable attention to municipal bonds in the U.S. markets and to commercial bank obligations in the European markets. These chapters also describe the ways in which the markets for these bonds work, with particular focus on how family portfolio managers can operate successfully in markets dominated by large institutional investors.

Fleshing out the general structure of a bond portfolio also involves tax considerations, and, while this book is not intended as a definitive guide to the taxation of fixed-income investments, one chapter in Part II discusses the ways an investor's tax situation should influence the choice of specific bonds and the management of the portfolio over time. In Chapter 13 we provide a detailed illustration of the process of building a bond portfolio, using real bonds offered in real markets and, then, of managing that portfolio as time goes on and as market conditions change.

Part III covers more advanced topics related to bond portfolio management. In particular, the concluding chapters of the book offer a fuller view of fixed-income mathematics, with the aim of enabling the reader to understand fixed-income derivatives. These include leveraged purchases and short sales, forward purchases and sales of bonds, puts and calls on fixed-income investments, interest rate swap contracts, and interest rate futures. The material in these chapters will be essential to readers who anticipate making use of these types of transactions in building and managing their bond portfolios. Even those investors who never make use of derivatives may find this material helpful in that it provides a deeper understanding of bond valuation and interest rate dynamics. Chapter 19 illustrates how the concepts and tools presented can be used to manage a fixed-income portfolio.

THE AUDIENCE

This book will be of most use to two broad audiences: substantial, involved, private investors, and generalist financial professionals who serve wealthy families. The material in this book, particularly in the first two parts, should also be of interest to members of families deciding to turn over the day-to-day management of their fixed-income portfolios to professional investment advisors. It can be very difficult to sort out the claims of competing investment advisors or to determine whether a particular manager has done a good job over a period of years. Turning a few million dollars or euros or a few hundred million yen over to a particular portfolio manager is, in and of itself, an important investment decision, and even a cursory review of this book should turn the reader into a better-informed consumer.

CHAPTER 2

Fixed-Income Basics

T his book is about fixed-income portfolios. A fixed-income portfolio is a collection of fixed-income securities held by an individual household or institution. A fixed-income security is a *negotiable* contract between an *issuer* and an investor (or "purchaser") through which the investor advances funds to the issuer, and the issuer undertakes, among other things, to make a series of payments to the purchaser. The fact that fixed-income securities contracts are "negotiable" — the initial purchaser may transfer his or her rights under the contract to any third party without the consent of the issuer — distinguishes fixed-income investments from loans.

As with any contract between two parties, the interesting features of fixed-income securities fall into two categories: the specific terms of the contract, and the economic value of the contract.

THE TERMS OF BOND INDENTURES

Fixed-income securities contracts are most commonly referred to as *bond indentures* or *bond trust indentures*. Typical terms of bond indentures include:

1. The identities of the issuer and obligor.
2. The amount and timing of cash flows the issuer undertakes to pay to the investor.
3. Any contingencies on which those cash flows may depend.
4. *Events of default*, which specify the circumstances under which the issuer may be deemed to have violated the terms of the contract.
5. Actions investors may take in the event of default by the issuer.

Identifying the Obligor

The Issuer

The official name of the company, government, or government agency in whose name the securities are issued; for example, the United States Treasury, the Republic of Korea, The Ford Motor Credit Corporation, or the Dormitory Authority of the State of New York.

The Obligor(s)

Usually the obligor — the entity that receives the principal amount and is responsible for providing the cash flows under the contract — is the same as the issuer. Occasionally, however, the issuer of the bonds is not responsible for providing the funds needed to meet the payments due on the securities but, instead, does no more than pass payments made by another party, the obligor, to the purchaser. For example, a trustee, acting under the terms of a *"trust agreement"* on behalf of a legal entity referred to as a *"trust,"* might pass payments on a collection of commercial real estate mortgages through to purchasers of an issue of mortgage-backed securities. In this case, the trust would be the issuer, but the obligors would be the mortgagees. Or the Dormitory Authority of the State of New York might issue tax-exempt bonds secured solely by payments to the Authority by Cornell University. In this case, the Authority is the issuer, but the University is the obligor.

Defining Cash Flows

Denominations

Fixed-income securities are offered by issuers in specified denominations. In the United States, the most common denomination is $1,000 of principal amount. This unit of denomination is so common that bond traders will, for example, refer to an investment with a principal value of $50,000 as, "50 bonds." There are some exceptions to this generalization, though. For example, particularly complex securities targeted at highly sophisticated investors may be issued in denominations of $1 million or more. The principal value of a bond investment is also referred to as the "face amount" or the "par value."

Payment Frequency

Unless it is otherwise specified, it is safe to assume that bonds issued in the United States, the United Kingdom, Italy, and Japan make semiannual payments, while most bonds issued by continental European issuers pay annually. Many floating-rate notes pay coupons monthly.

Coupon

Today almost all bonds are issued in "book entry" form; that is, the investor's ownership interest in the bond is reflected only in the records of a participant in a securities industry depository. For family portfolios, the depository participant is usually one of the broker-dealer firms acting as custodian for the household's investments.

Before the advent of this system of depositories and custodians, bonds were issued as "bearer" securities, in which case the investor's ownership of the security was evidenced by an engraved document. These bearer bonds consisted of a single large certificate representing the principal amount of the security and a number of small "coupons," each representing a particular interest payment. For example, a 10-year bond with semiannual payments would be issued with 20 coupons attached. When an interest payment came due, the investor would "clip" the particular coupon and submit it to the payment agent in exchange for cash. When the bond's principal came due, the investor would submit the body of the certificate, along with the last coupon, and receive the final payment. Although clipping coupons is no longer a physical event, periodic payments on bonds are still called coupons.

The coupon of a fixed-income security is expressed as a percentage and specifies the periodic — annual, semiannual, monthly — payment that will be made by the issuer to the purchaser. The term "fixed income" notwithstanding, coupon payments need not necessarily be constant, nor need they be fully specified at the time the security is first sold by the issuer to a purchaser. The payments may also vary from period to period depending on a predetermined formula. Thus, a "floating-rate note" is a variety of fixed-income security.

In the case of a fixed-rate bond, the coupon is a single number. For example, each coupon payment of a $5,000 6.00% semiannual pay bond will equal $150. Some fixed-rate bonds pay no periodic coupons but make a single payment at maturity. These are referred to as zero-coupon bonds.

In the case of a variable-rate bond, the coupon is expressed as a formula. For example, a variable-rate bond might pay a monthly coupon equal to 25 basis points above the most recently reported 30-day U.S. dollar-London Interbank Offer Rate (LIBOR).[1] In this case, if the par amount of the floating-rate note were $100,000 and 30-day US$-LIBOR were pegged at 5.00%, the monthly coupon would be:

$437.50 (= $100,000 × 5.25%/12)

If the next month 30-day US$-LIBOR were reset to 4.50%, the coupon on this bond would decline to $375.00.

Day Count

Because calendar months are of different lengths, fixed-income contracts must specify the *day count convention* to be used in computing coupon payments. Day

---

[1] LIBOR is the rate at which international banks in London offer to lend each other funds for specified periods of time. LIBOR has become the most common interest rate benchmark in global financial markets. Examples of LIBOR include 30-day US$-LIBOR and 6-month J¥-LIBOR.

count conventions are also used to compute the "accrued" interest a buyer must pay to the seller of a bond if the purchase–sale transaction takes place between interest payment dates. Day count conventions differ across sectors of the bond market. For example, U.S. Treasury notes and bonds pay semiannual coupons according to an actual/actual day count convention. By contrast, the day count convention for U.S. Government agency coupon-paying notes is 30/360. Under this convention all monthly or semiannual payments will be identical.

Maturity

The maturity is the last date on which a cash flow payment is due. In many cases all principal and the last coupon payment are due on the maturity date, but there are also many exceptions to this generalization.

Sinking Funds

The maturity date is the last date on which cash flows are due on a bond, but it is not necessarily the case that the entire principal amount is due to be paid on the maturity date. Frequently bond contracts will provide for scheduled principal payments before the maturity date. Such contract terms are called "sinking fund" or amortization provisions. Sinking fund provisions used to be very common among corporate bonds in the United States. Currently, sinking fund and other amortization provisions are typical only for municipal bonds with initial maturities longer than 20 years and for some asset-backed securities.

For example, a bond issued with a total principal amount of $100 million and maturing on January 1, 2020, might provide the sinking fund schedule found in Exhibit 1.

The terms of sinking fund provisions vary widely across bonds. Sometimes the sinking fund payments are mandatory for the issuer; sometimes they are optional. Sometimes issuers can satisfy sinking fund requirements by purchasing bonds in the open market; sometimes they cannot. Most frequently, specific bonds are selected for redemption through a lottery process. In such cases, the purchaser will not know exactly when within the last five years before maturity the particular bonds will be redeemed. In all cases, information about sinking fund provisions, if any, is part of the standard description of a bond.

Exhibit 1: Hypothetical Sinking Fund Schedule for a 20-Year Bond

Date	Payment Due
January 1, 2016	$20,000,000
January 1, 2017	20,000,000
January 1, 2018	20,000,000
January 1, 2019	20,000,000
January 1, 2020	20,000,000

Contingencies

Early redemption provisions are the most common type of contingency that affect bond cash flows. While the maturity of a bond is the date on which the last cash flow payment is due, in many cases payments can cease well before that date. For example, many bond indentures provide that under certain circumstances the issuer either must or may redeem the security early by repaying at least the principal amount of the bond to the purchaser plus any coupon payments that have accrued but not been paid. In some cases, the issuer must pay an additional amount to the investor if the bond is redeemed before maturity.

Other common types of contingency are caps and floors on floating-rate bonds. In addition, coupon payments on a small proportion of bonds are contingent on the issuer's financial condition.

Call Provisions

A "call provision" is a term of a bond indenture that identifies the circumstances under which the issuer can redeem up to the full principal amount of the bond at some time before maturity. Some call provisions limit the circumstances under which a bond may be redeemed early to circumstances that are beyond the control of the issuer. For example, some bonds secured by real property must be called if the property suffers some irreparable casualty damage. Mandatory early redemption is also common for bonds whose source of cash flows is a collection, or "pool" of single-family home mortgages. Such securities must be redeemed early in the event that the mortgagees prepay their loans early. The impact of prepayments on mortgage-related securities is discussed in more detail later.

In the case of most callable bonds, however, early redemption is not mandatory. Instead, the issuer has the option to redeem the bonds early. Sometimes the right to call the bonds early is limited to cases in which the issuer uses cash on hand to redeem the securities. In most cases, though, the issuer may issue new bonds and use the proceeds of the new sale to redeem outstanding bonds.

We discuss the circumstances under which issuers might decide to call the bonds and the impact such early redemptions have on investors who own callable bonds in subsequent chapters. At this point, it suffices to define the terms used in specifying call provisions. A bond that can be redeemed early at the issuer's option will include a complete "call schedule." This schedule lists the dates on which the issuer may exercise its option to redeem the bonds (the call dates), and the premium, if any, that the issuer must pay over and above the principal amount plus any accrued but unpaid coupons (the call prices or call premiums).

For example, a bond issued on January 1, 2000, that matures on January 1, 2020, might provide for the call schedule shown in Exhibit 2. The first date on which the issuer could redeem the bonds at its option would be January 1, 2005. If it does so, it would have to pay investors 102% of the principal amount of the bonds plus the coupon that was due on that date. If the issuer redeems the bonds after January 1, 2007, the call price will equal 100% of the principal amount of the bonds plus accrued coupon.

Exhibit 2: Hypothetical Call Schedule for a 20-Year Bond

Date	Call Price
January 1, 2000–December 31, 2004	not callable
January 1, 2005–June 30, 2005	102.00
July 1, 2005–December 31, 2005	101.50
January 1, 2006–June 30, 2006	101.00
July 1, 2006–December 31, 2006	100.50
January 1, 2007–December 31, 2019	100.00

Caps, Floors, and Collars

Coupon payments on floating-rate notes vary from period to period, depending on the level of an interest rate index such as LIBOR. The coupon on most FRNs floats freely, regardless of the level of the index. Thus, if the coupon on a particular FRN is set at LIBOR + 100 basis points (or 1 percentage point), and if LIBOR for the period is 23.50%, the coupon on the security will be 24.50%. The coupons on a significant minority of FRNs are subject to maximum and/or minimum levels (caps and floors). Thus, a capped FRN might pay a coupon of 8.00% or LIBOR + 50 basis points, whichever is lower. If LIBOR is 6.25%, this note will pay 6.75% for the period. If LIBOR is 8.75%, the note will pay 8.00%. An FRN subject to a 3.00% floor would pay 3.00% if LIBOR for the period were set at 2.25%.

Financial Condition Contingencies

Issuers of a small but growing minority of corporate bonds retain the right to suspend cash coupon payments for a period of years if the company is experiencing serious financial distress. During any such period, interest due on the bond would continue to accrue, and the issuer would have to make good on all coupon and principal payments (plus interest on suspended coupons) by the time the bond matures. Such bonds — many of which have been issued by commercial banks — are discussed in more detail in Chapter 8.

Events of Default

A *default* on a fixed-income instrument is a violation by the issuer of one or more of the terms of a bond indenture. The most obvious variety of default is failure to make scheduled coupon or principal payments in a timely manner. Indentures may also include additional provisions with which issuers must comply. For example, if the proceeds of a bond issue are used to construct a specific facility the indenture may require the issuer to purchase a casualty insurance policy on the property and/or to maintain the physical condition of the facility. Other indentures may limit the issuer's ability to sell additional bond issues. Many municipal bond indentures require that the issuer hold specific amounts of money in *debt service accounts* or *debt service reserves* held by the bond trustee.

Failure to comply with any of these provisions would be events of default under bond indentures. Some events of default are more serious than others. Failure to make a scheduled coupon payment would be very serious. Making a deposit into a debt service account one day late would be much less problematical. Such relatively trivial events of default are referred to as *technical defaults*. Such defaults are usually "cured" very quickly and have no economic impact on investors or issuers.

Remedies

As an integral part of the process of bringing new bonds to market, the issuer will appoint a *trustee*. The trustee, usually the trust department of a commercial bank, is appointed and paid by the issuer, but is instructed to represent the interests of bondholders. Subsequent to any event of default — other than a quickly cured technical default — the trustee will immediately take legal actions to protect bondholders.

Some of these actions will involve legal remedies available to all creditors vis-à-vis deadbeat debtors. Other post-default actions that may be taken by trustees will be specified in the indenture. For example, many indentures specify that, subsequent to an event of default the trustee has the right to demand immediate payment of the principal amount to the bondholders. Other indentures allow the trustee, acting on behalf of the bondholders, to seize control of specified real property of the issuer.

Not all the bonds of a given issuer are necessarily created equal with respect to post-default remedies. Some municipalities and corporations offer bonds under several different "liens," some more senior than others. The trustee representing holders of senior lien bonds may be able to seize property and/or demand acceleration of principal payments. Trustees representing junior lien bondholders may have no specific remedies under the bond indenture other than rights available to all creditors under general commercial codes. Further, default on junior lien obligations may also be a specific event of default under the senior lien bond indenture; the opposite may not be the case. In other words, the bond indentures may provide senior lien bondholders an opportunity to assert their claims ahead of those of investors holding junior lien bonds. A more complete discussion of bond liens appears in Chapter 10.

THE ECONOMIC VALUE OF FIXED-INCOME CONTRACTS

A dealer offering a bond for sale to an investor will provide a complete description of the security in question, including all the relevant provisions of the bond indentures and will then indicate an "offering price" or "offering yield." The price of a bond is quoted as a percentage of the par (face, principal) amount of the security. Thus, typical bond prices are 99.50, 100.65625, or 103.375.

In the United States, bond prices are commonly quoted in even fractions: 8ths, 16ths, 32nds, or 64ths. Thus, a price of 99.50 might be represented as 99-16, indicating 99 and 16/32nds. In practice the sample prices listed here would be quoted as "99 and a half," "par and 20 32nds," or "one-oh-three and three-eighths." A 64th of a point is represented by appending a plus sign to the price indication. Thus, 107-30+ is equivalent to 107 and 61 64ths or 107.953125. Most non-U.S. bond prices are quoted as decimals.

The descriptive characteristics will, for the most part, remain constant over the life of the security. The price and yield will change from day to day, even from hour to hour, depending on conditions in the marketplace.

What is Yield?

"Yield" is one of the most common and most useful terms in the fixed-income markets. It is also one of the most commonly misused and misunderstood concepts we will deal with in this book. One reason for this confusion is that several different definitions of yield are used for different purposes in the market. When someone asks, "What is the yield on this bond?" several different correct answers could be given, and the meaning of the answer will be ambiguous unless the query specifically calls for "current yield," "yield to maturity," "yield to call," "yield to worst," "after-tax yield," "taxable-equivalent yield," or "option-adjusted yield." All these alternative uses of the term "yield" are touched upon in this book; in this chapter the discussion is limited to the first four.

This discussion in this chapter refers only to the concept of yield as it applies to *fixed-rate* bonds. The appendix discusses the terminology appropriate for floating-rate notes.

The concept of yield is used to differentiate among bonds with the same maturity but with different coupons and prices. Consider three different bond investments, all of the same lien of the same obligor, none either callable or subject to sinking funds, all issued on January 1, 2000, all maturing on January 1, 2010, all paying semiannual coupons, and all having a principal value of $100,000. The investments pay the coupons and are offered for sale at the prices listed in Exhibit 3.

The concept of yield is intended as a way of determining which of these three bonds is the "best" and which is the "worst" for the investor to buy. All three will return $100,000 on January 1, 2010, but they provide different semiannual coupon payments — $3,000 for A, $2,500 for B, and $3,500 for C — and they are offered at different prices.

We compare two measures of yield — current yield and yield to maturity — show how they produce different rankings, and then explain why the latter is the right yield concept to use when ranking these bonds.

Exhibit 3: Three Hypothetical 10-Year Bonds

Bond	Coupon	Price
A	6.00%	$100,000
B	5.00%	91,855
C	7.00%	108,221

Current Yield

Current yield is the easiest of these concepts to define and to understand. Current yield is defined as coupon divided by purchase price. The current yield on Bond A is the easiest to calculate; the current yield is the same as the coupon because the price is equal to par. The current yield on Bond C is:

$$6.47\% = 7.00\% \times \$100,000 \div \$108,211$$

That of Bond B is 5.44%. By this measure, Bond C is the best, with a 6.47% current yield; Bond A follows at 6.00%; and Bond B looks worst.

Yield to Maturity

Unfortunately, comparing investments solely on the basis of current yield can lead to bad decisions. A more complex concept, yield to maturity, is the right basis for comparison.

Let's begin with the formal definition of yield to maturity, and then explain the terms in the definition. *The yield to maturity of a bond* is the discount rate, *expressed as an annual percentage rate, that, when applied to all the scheduled cash flows, results in a present value equal to the price of the bond.* The two terms in this definition that need further explanation are "discount rate" and "present value."

The best way to introduce the concept of present value is with a "good news, bad news" example. The good news is that you've just won a million dollars in a lottery. The bad news is that this lottery pays one dollar a year for a million years. Almost everyone can see this, because it is intuitively obvious that it is better to receive any given amount of money immediately than to receive the same amount of money over a period of time. That much is easy to understand. The next step is to find a way to answer some more specific questions about a series of cash flow payments.

For example, one might ask, "How many U.S. dollars should I be willing to pay today for a stream of payments of $100,000 per year for a period of ten years?" Or, "Which of the three streams of payments presented in Exhibit 4 is worth the most?" Note that the series of payments mirror those of Bonds A, B, and C in Exhibit 3.

First we explore this simpler question: "What is the value today of ten annual $100,000 payments?" We can break this question into ten separate questions. "How much should I be willing to invest today to receive $100,000 one year from now"; "How much should I be willing to pay today to receive $100,000 two years from now"; and so on. For the present we will assume that the annual interest rate for each of these periods is the same, 6.00%. If so, in order to receive $100,000 one year from now, I would have to invest an amount $M, where

$$\$M + (0.06 \times \$M) = \$100,000$$

Exhibit 4: Three Hypothetical 10-Year Annual Cash Flow Streams

Date	Stream A	Stream B	Stream C
7/1/00	6,000	5,000	7,000
7/1/01	6,000	5,000	7,000
7/1/02	6,000	5,000	7,000
7/1/03	6,000	5,000	7,000
7/1/04	6,000	5,000	7,000
7/1/05	6,000	5,000	7,000
7/1/06	6,000	5,000	7,000
7/1/07	6,000	5,000	7,000
7/1/08	6,000	5,000	7,000
7/1/09	6,000	5,000	7,000
7/1/10	106,000	105,000	107,000

or $\$M \times (1.06) = \$100,000$

or $\$M = \$100,000/1.06$

so $\$M = \$94,340$

We can ask the same question about the payment due at the end of the second year, but in answering it we must recognize that interest on these "loans" compounds. That is, during the second year interest is paid on the full value of the investment, including both the original principal amount invested *and* interest earned during the first year. Thus, the amount one would have to put up initially in order to receive $100,000 at the end of two years would be:

$\$M_2 +$ Principal

$(0.06 \times \$M_2) +$ + First Year's Interest

$\{0.06 \times [\$M_2 + (0.06 \times \$M_2)]\}$ + Second Year's Interest

$= \$100,000$

or $[\$M_2 \times (1.06)] + \{0.06 \times [\$M_2 \times (1.06)]\} = \$100,000$

or $1.06\$M_2(1.06) = \$100,000$

or $\$M_2 \times (1.06)^2 = \$100,000$

or $\$M_2 = \$100,000/(1.06)^2$

so $\$M_2 = \$100,000/1.1236$

and $\$M_2 = \$89,000$

We can repeat this process for each $100,000 payment. For example, in order to receive $100,000 seven years from now, one would have to lend

$M_7 = \$100,000/(1.06)^7$

or $M_7 = \$100,000/1.5036$

and $M_7 = \$66,506$

The amount one should be willing to pay today to receive the series of ten $100,000 payments in an environment of 6.00% interest rates would simply be the sum of these individual amounts. Specifically this amount would be:

$= [\$100,000/(1.06)^1] + [\$100,000/(1.06)^2] + [\$100,000/(1.06)^3] +$
$[\$100,000/(1.06)^4] + [\$100,000/(1.06)^5] + [\$100,000/(1.06)^6] +$
$[\$100,000/(1.06)^7] + [\$100,000/(1.06)^8] + [\$100,000/(1.06)^9] +$
$[\$100,000/(1.06)^{10}]$

or $= \$94,340 + \$89,000 + \$83,962 + \$79,209 + \$74,726 + \$70,496 +$
$\$66,506 + \$62,741 + \$59,190 + \$55,840$

or $= \$736,010$

So, if the interest rate on loans is 6.00%, the present value of a stream of ten annual $100,000 payments is $736,010. We refer to the interest rate in present value calculations, 6.00% in this example, as the "discount rate."

Using standard mathematical notation, the general formula for the present value of a series of cash flows is:

$$PV = \sum_{t=1}^{T} F_t/(1+r_t)^t$$

where

F_t = the cash flow paid at period t, and
r_t = the interest (or discount) rate applicable to cash flows received during period t.

Observe also that this formula can be used to solve either for the present value, given the cash flows and the discount rate, or for the discount rate, given the cash flows and the present value. For example, one could be asked what single discount rate produces a present value of $650,000 for a series of ten annual $100,000 payments. Any financial calculator will provide the answer, which is 8.71%.

Exhibit 5: Present Values of Three Hypothetical Cash Flow Streams

Stream	Present Value @ 6.00% Discount Rate
A	$100,000.00
B	92,561.26
C	107,438.74

Let's return now to the question about the three alternative payment streams, and assume that all three derive from the same obligor and that all loans to this issuer pay 6.00% interest. If we apply a 6.00% semiannual discount rate (that is, each semiannual payment is discounted at 3.00%), we find that the three cash flow series have three different present values. (See Exhibit 5.)

So our present value concept provides a way of evaluating different cash flows, provided we are comfortable with the assumption that the same interest, or discount, rate is applicable in each case.

We can now return to the definition of yield to maturity. If we know the coupon and principal value of a non-callable fixed-rate bond with no sinking fund payments, we can determine the series of cash flows generated by the bond. If, in addition, we know the price of the bond, we can find the single discount rate that, if applied to all these cash flows produces a present value equal to the price. This discount rate — usually converted into annual terms — is the yield to maturity of the bond.

To illustrate this calculation, we use the 5.00% ten-year bond priced on January 1, 2000, at 91.855% of par. The cash flows generated by this bond are listed in Exhibit 4 as "Stream B." We want to find the discount rate that produces a present value for these cash flows equal to $91,855. In other words, we want to solve the equation for YTM:

$$\$91{,}855 = \$100{,}000/[1 + (YTM/2)]^{10} + \sum_{t=1}^{10} \$2{,}500/[1 + (YTM/2)]^{t}$$

This is not an easy equation to solve; with pencil and paper it might take all day. Thirty years ago bond traders would look up the answer in a fat book of tables called a "basis book," so-called because the yield to maturity used to calculate a bond's price was referred to as the bond's "basis." This term has gone out of customary use, as has the basis book itself. The basis book was replaced initially by desktop bond calculators that allowed a trader to input coupon, maturity, and price, and calculate yield; or input coupon, maturity, and yield, and calculate price. These functions are now available on inexpensive pocket-sized electronic calculators. Software programs are also available for use on personal computers that perform these and a wide variety of other fixed-income calculations. Using any one of these devices, we can quickly calculate that the yield to maturity for a ten-year 5.00% coupon bond priced at 91.855% of par is 6.10%.

Exhibit 6: ns and Yields of Three Hypothetical Bonds

Bond	Coupon	Price	Current Yield	Yield to Maturity
A	6.00%	$100,000	6.00%	6.00%
B	5.00%	92,561	5.40%	6.10%
C	7.00%	107,438	6.52%	5.90%

Having developed the definition of yield to maturity, we can now compare the two concepts of yield presented so far. Exhibit 6 lists the current yields and yields to maturity of the three hypothetical ten-year bonds.

An inspection of these numbers reveals two characteristics immediately. First, the current yield and the yield to maturity are identical only for the bond priced at par. Second, current yield and yield to maturity result in very different rankings of the bonds. The 7.00% bond looks best by the current yield criterion and worst on the basis of yield to maturity. The yield to maturity measure makes the 5.00% bond look best, and the current yield yardstick makes it look worst.

Yield to maturity is the better measure of bond value. The current yield calculation does not take into account all of the cash flows associated with the bond; it takes into account only the purchase price and the coupon. In particular, it does not recognize the fact that, on the 5.00% bond the investor puts up $92,561 and gets back $100,000 ten years later, while the investor purchasing the 7.00% bond puts up $7,438 more than is received when the bond matures. Any measure of a bond's value that does not take into account such important information is inadequate. In this regard, yield to maturity is the superior measure because it does take into account all of the cash flows associated with a non-callable bond with no sinking fund.

The standard practice in the bond market is to quote the yield to maturity of a non-callable bond. Although the practice is standard, it is best to check that the yield quoted on any non-callable bond offered at a premium price is, in fact, the yield to maturity.

Alternatives to Yield to Maturity for Specific Types of Bonds

The illustrations of the concept of yield to this point have dealt with non-callable bonds without sinking funds. Such securities are usually referred to as "bullet bonds." We must modify the yield concept somewhat to deal with bonds that do have sinking funds and/or bonds that can be redeemed early at the issuer's option. We will consider sinking fund bonds first.

For bonds subject to mandatory sinking funds, the appropriate yield measure is not yield to maturity but yield to average life. The latter calculation takes into account the fact that the investor will (or expects to) receive some principal returned before the stated maturity date of the bond. For example, let's consider the 20-year 6.00% bond maturing on January 1, 2020, with four equal sinking fund payments prior to maturity beginning on January 1, 2016. We will assume that the purchase price of the bond on January 1, 2000, is 95.00% of par.

There are two ways of calculating yield to average life. The first is to find the discount rate such that the present value of the actual cash flows generated by the bond is equal to the purchase price. The cash flows for the bond are listed in Exhibit 7. For the first 16 years, the payment stream is the same as that of a bullet bond, but then the investor may begin receiving sinking fund payments. As the bond "sinks," the amount of principal outstanding decreases, as does the dollar amount of each coupon payment. The discount rate that sets the present value of these cash flows to 95.00% of par is 6.475%, and this is the precise yield to average life.

The second method for calculating yield to average life is an approximation that assumes that the final maturity of the bond is equal to the average life of the bond. In the example above, we would set the maturity at 17.5 years after the pricing date; that is, on July 1, 2017. Then we would use a bond calculator to find the yield to maturity of a bond with a 6.00% coupon maturing on July 1, 2017, and priced at 95.00% of par. In this case, the result would be 6.482%. This is slightly different from the precise figure derived from the calculation based on the actual cash flows, but bond traders frequently use this second method as a convenient, acceptably accurate approximation.

Information regarding the yield to average life of a sinking fund bond should be used with caution. For any individual holder of a sinking fund bond, the cash flow figures in Exhibit 7 are an exact representation of what the investor will receive only under certain circumstances. First, the sinking fund must be mandatory. Further, one of two specific circumstances must hold: Either each bond must be retired pro rata by sinking fund payments, or the investor must hold all of the outstanding bonds subject to the sinking fund.

While most recently issued sinking funds are, in fact, mandatory, the latter two conditions do not apply in most cases. In the more typical case in which bonds are selected by a lottery for sinking fund redemption and in which each investor holds a relatively small proportion of the total bond issue, the yield to average life will represent an "expected" yield. The cash flows each investor actually receives and the investor's actual realized yield will depend, literally, on the luck of the draw.

We will return to this discussion of the yield on sinking fund bonds below. At this point it is useful to focus on the way yields are quoted for bonds subject to early redemption at the option of the issuer.

Yield to Call

Consider a 6.00% bond paying annual coupons and maturing on January 1, 2010. Assume that the issuer may opt to redeem the bond on any interest payment date after January 1, 2005, at call prices listed in the schedule presented in Exhibit 8. A bond with this structure would be referred to as a "6.00% ten-year, non-call five-year bond," or as "ten non-call five."

Exhibit 7: Cash Flows on a 20-Year Bond with a 5-Year Mandatory Sinking Fund

Date	Sinking Fund	Principal Outstanding	Coupon	Total Cash Flow
07/01/00	–	100.00	3.00	3.00
01/01/01	–	100.00	3.00	3.00
07/01/01	–	100.00	3.00	3.00
01/01/02	–	100.00	3.00	3.00
07/01/02	–	100.00	3.00	3.00
01/01/03	–	100.00	3.00	3.00
07/01/03	–	100.00	3.00	3.00
01/01/04	–	100.00	3.00	3.00
07/01/04	–	100.00	3.00	3.00
01/01/05	–	100.00	3.00	3.00
07/01/05	–	100.00	3.00	3.00
01/01/06	–	100.00	3.00	3.00
07/01/06	–	100.00	3.00	3.00
01/01/07	–	100.00	3.00	3.00
07/01/07	–	100.00	3.00	3.00
01/01/08	–	100.00	3.00	3.00
07/01/08	–	100.00	3.00	3.00
01/01/09	–	100.00	3.00	3.00
07/01/09	–	100.00	3.00	3.00
01/01/10	–	100.00	3.00	3.00
07/01/10	–	100.00	3.00	3.00
01/01/11	–	100.00	3.00	3.00
07/01/11	–	100.00	3.00	3.00
01/01/12	–	100.00	3.00	3.00
07/01/12	–	100.00	3.00	3.00
01/01/13	–	100.00	3.00	3.00
07/01/13	–	100.00	3.00	3.00
01/01/14	–	100.00	3.00	3.00
07/01/14	–	100.00	3.00	3.00
01/01/15	–	100.00	3.00	3.00
07/01/15	–	100.00	3.00	3.00
01/01/16	20.00	100.00	3.00	23.00
07/01/16	–	80.00	2.40	2.40
01/01/17	20.00	80.00	2.40	22.40
07/01/17	–	60.00	1.80	1.80
01/01/18		60.00	1.80	21.80
07/01/18	–	40.00	1.20	1.20
01/01/19	20.00	40.00	1.20	21.20
07/01/19	–	20.00	0.60	0.60
01/01/20	20.00	20.00	0.60	20.60

Exhibit 8: Hypothetical Call Schedule

Date	Call Price (% of Par)
Jan. 1, 2005	105
Jan. 1, 2006	104
Jan. 1, 2007	103
Jan. 1, 2008	102
Jan. 1, 2009	101

Exhibit 9: Cash Flows on a Hypothetical Callable Bond and Yields to Final Cash Flow at Various Prices

Date	Cash Flow I	Cash Flow II	Cash Flow III	Cash Flow IV	Cash Flow V	Cash Flow VI
1/1/01	6.00	6.00	6.00	6.00	6.00	6.00
1/1/02	6.00	6.00	6.00	6.00	6.00	6.00
1/1/03	6.00	6.00	6.00	6.00	6.00	6.00
1/1/04	6.00	6.00	6.00	6.00	6.00	6.00
1/1/05	6.00	111.00	6.00	6.00	6.00	6.00
1/1/06	6.00	0	110.00	6.00	6.00	6.00
1/1/07	6.00	0	0	109.00	6.00	6.00
1/1/08	6.00	0	0	0	108.00	6.00
1/1/09	6.00	0	0	0	0	107.00
1/1/10	106.00	0	0	0	0	0

Purchase Price	Yield to Last Cash Flow					
98.00	6.275%	7.356%	6.979%	6.717%	6.527%	6.385%
100.00	6.000%	6.872%	6.565%	6.354%	6.201%	6.087%
102.00	5.732%	6.400%	6.162%	5.999%	5.882%	5.796%
108.00	4.966%	5.053%	5.011%	4.987%	4.973%	4.967%
108.50	4.904%	4.946%	4.919%	4.906%	4.900%	4.900%
109.00	4.843%	4.838%	4.827%	4.825%	4.828%	4.834%
109.50	4.783%	4.732%	4.736%	4.745%	4.756%	4.769%
110.00	4.722%	4.626%	4.645%	4.665%	4.684%	4.703%

An investor who purchases this bond on, say, January 1, 2000, might receive any one of the six payment series listed in the top panel of Exhibit 9. The bond might remain outstanding to maturity (Cash Flow I). Or the issuer might call the bond on January 1, 2005 (Cash Flow II), in which case the investor would receive the call price, 105% of par, plus a final coupon payment for a total of 111% of par. Or the issue might be called on the second call date, January 1, 2006 (Cash Flow III), and so on.

For any given purchase price, the yield will depend on when the bond is redeemed. The lower panel of Exhibit 9 lists all the possible yields on the bond for purchase prices ranging from 98% to 110% of par and the yields on each cash flow series associated with that purchase price.

As these representations of cash flows indicate, a callable bond purchased at any given price could have several different yields, depending on whether and when the issuer decides to redeem the bond before maturity.

Yield to Worst

It would not be useful to quote every possible yield associated with a given price when offering a bond to an investor. Therefore, the bond market has adopted the convention of quoting the *lowest* among all the yields — the "yield to worst" — associated with the bond's price and to identify the date of the final cash flow associated with that yield.

In the case of our ten non-call five 6.00% structure at a $109.00 price, the lowest yield associated with that price is 4.825%, which will be realized if the bond is redeemed on January 1, 2007, at 103% of par. Thus, if a dealer were offering the bond at a price of 109.00, the conventional yield quotation would be 4.825% to the '07 call. If the price were 98, the yield to worst would be 6.275% to maturity, and for prices of about 109.5 and higher, the yield to worst is the yield to the first call date.

The yields to worst are shaded in the lower panel of Exhibit 9. The pattern of the shading reflects the fact that in most cases the yield to worst will be either the yield to maturity or the yield to the first call date. For any callable bond, there will also be a range of prices for which the yield to worst is the yield to a call date subsequent to the first call date.

The concept of yield to worst can also apply to a sinking fund bond. The worst outcome for an investor who purchases a sinking fund bond at a price below par is that all of the principal will be returned on the last possible date, the maturity date. Therefore, a dealer offering a sinking fund bond at a discount price to par should quote the yield to maturity as the yield to worst. If the bond is priced at a premium to par, the worst-case outcome is that the investment will be redeemed on the first sinking fund date. The yield to worst in this case would be the yield to the first possible redemption date.

In the case of sinking fund bonds, there is no standard way of quoting yield; any given number might be yield to average life or yield to worst. Fixed-income portfolio managers should make it a practice to find out whether any given bond is subject to a sinking fund redemption schedule and to ascertain which convention for quoting yields the dealer is using.

APPENDIX: THE YIELD OF FLOATING-RATE NOTES

The coupon paid on a floating-rate note varies over the life of an instrument. For example, the coupon on a ten-year FRN paying six-month U.K. sterling LIBOR + 50 bp issued on January 1, 1988, would have varied between 5.75% and 16.01% over the life of the security. At any given time, however, the rate at which an FRN-owner is accruing interest can be calculated with reference to the current level of the note's interest rate index. As with most other bonds, the initial offering price of newly issued FRNs is usually very close to par. Again, as with other bonds, the market price of an FRN may fluctuate over time. Because we can always calculate the current coupon accrual rate, if we know the market price of an FRN, we can also compute the *current yield* on the instrument.

Thus, if euro LIBOR were 3.55% and the price of a note paying euro LIBOR + 25 bp were 97.50, then the current yield on the instrument would be

$$3.897\% = [(3.55\% + 0.25\%) \div 0.9750]$$

Current yield is not an adequate measure of the value of a floating-rate note because it does not take into account the fact that the principal amount received by the investor at maturity will be different from the amount used to purchase the instrument. In the discussion of fixed-rate bonds, we compared three hypothetical securities of the same issuer with identical maturities, but different coupons and dollar prices. That example highlights the fact that the bond with the highest current yield is not necessarily the most attractive one to buy.

Investors considering FRNs may face the same quandary. Suppose an investor is choosing among the three hypothetical semiannual pay FRNs of the same issuer listed in Exhibit A-1 for purchase on January 1, 2000. Assume that LIBOR at the time is 4.50%.

The relevant question here, as it was in the case of the fixed-rate bonds, is, "Which of these three offerings is the most attractive." The current yield figure probably is not the best indicator because it does not take into account the fact that, with securities A and C, the investor will receive, respectively, less and more than the purchase price when the bond matures. In the case of fixed-rate bonds, we concluded that the yield to maturity is the best measure of the value when comparing bonds of the same issuer with similar maturities but different coupons. To calculate yield to maturity, however, we must know all of the cash flows paid by the bond. Since future coupon payments on FRNs depend on the unknowable future levels of an interest rate index, *the yield to maturity concept does not apply to these securities.*

Exhibit A-1: Coupons, Prices, and Current Yield on Three Hypothetical Floating Rate Notes

Bond	Coupon	Maturity	Price	Current Yield
A	LIBOR + 75 bp	1/1/10	103.90	5.053%
B	LIBOR + 25	1/1/10	100.00	4.750%
C	LIBOR - 25	1/1/10	96.10	4.420%

Because yield to maturity has no meaning with respect to FRNs, and current yield may be misleading, participants in this market have developed an alternative measure of a bond's value. We see from the data in Exhibit A–1 that a ten-year FRN of this issuer paying a coupon of LIBOR + 25 bp has a market value of par. Bond A, an otherwise identical obligation of the same issuer, pays a coupon of LIBOR + 75 bp. Clearly Bond A should command a higher price than Bond B. But how much higher? The difference between these two bonds is equal to the present value of a series of 20 semiannual payments of 25 basis points each. Thus, a question about the price of Bond A turns into a question about the right discount rate to use when calculating the present value of a series of payments from the security's issuer.

The convention is to calculate the present value of these cash flows using as the discount rate the yield on a fixed-rate bond of the issuer with the same maturity as the FRN. Suppose, for example, that the issuer of this bond has ten-year fixed-rate bonds outstanding that yield 5.75%. Using this figure we could calculate the present value of 20 semiannual payments of 0.25%, each discounted at a rate of 2.875% (= 5.75%/2). A simple way of computing the same figure is to find the price of a ten-year semiannual pay bond with a 6.25% coupon priced to yield 5.75%. The price of such a security would be 103.763.

Thus, the present value of 25 bp paid semiannually for ten years by this issuer is 3.763% of the principal amount on which the 25 bp is paid. This also means that the price of the FRN paying LIBOR + 75 bp that is consistent with the pricing of the issuer's fixed-rate bonds is 103.763. Observe that the hypothetical price quoted in Exhibit A-1, 103.90, is a little higher than the 103.763 that is consistent with both the par price on the LIBOR + 25 bp bond and the 5.75% yield on the issuer's fixed-rate bonds. This indicates that, at the market prices, the bond paying LIBOR + 75 bp is a little "expensive" compared to the par bond, so that an investor should unambiguously prefer Bond B to Bond A.

We can go through a similar process for the bond paying LIBOR – 25 bp. In this case, we want to find the price of a ten-year fixed-rate, semiannual bond with a 5.25% coupon priced to yield 5.75%. The price of such a bond — and of Bond C in Exhibit A-1 — would be 96.237. According to this analysis, the hypothetical market price of Bond C is a little lower than the level that would be consistent with the LIBOR + 25 bp coupon on the FRN priced at par and the 5.75% yield on ten-year fixed-rate bonds. By this criterion, therefore, Bond C is the most attractively priced of the three hypothetical offerings, even though its current yield is the lowest.

The relative value of Bond C stands out even more clearly if we calculate the discount margin of these bonds. The discount margin of an FRN is the spread over (or below) the index implied by the note's coupon and market price. For an FRN priced at par, the discount margin is simply the floating coupon spread over (or below) the index: 25 bp in the case of Bond B. If we know that a ten-year fixed-rate bond of the issuer yields 5.75%, then we can calculate the discount margin associated with the price of any comparable-maturity FRN.

Exhibit A-2: Coupons, Prices, and Discount Margin on Three Hypothetical Floating-Rate Notes

Bond	Coupon	Maturity	Price	Discount Margin
A	LIBOR + 75 bp	1/1/10	103.90	23.2 bp
B	LIBOR + 25	1/1/10	100.00	25 bp
C	LIBOR - 25	1/1/10	96.10	26.8 bp

For example, consider Bond A. At a dollar price of 103.90, the yield on a ten-year bond with a 5.75% coupon would be 6.268%. This is 51.8 bp above the coupon on the ten-year, fixed-rate par bond. Therefore, the 3.9% premium on Bond C's price is the present value of a semiannual 51.8 bp. To put it differently, the buyer of Bond A is receiving LIBOR + 75 bp, but 51.8 bp of this coupon amounts to an amortization of the premium purchase price. Therefore, the investor is netting LIBOR + 23.2 bp (= 75 bp – 51.8 bp), and the discount margin on this bond is 23.2 bp.

We can work through the same calculation for Bond C. If we do so, we find that the coupon associated with a dollar price of 96.10 on a ten-year fixed-rate bond yielding 5.75% would be 5.232%. Again, the present value of 3.9% of par is 51.8 bp. In this case, the investor will be receiving LIBOR – 25 bp in coupon income *plus* a 51.8 bp amortization of the discount purchase price. The all-in yield will be LIBOR + 26.8 bp (= –25 bp + 51.8 bp), and the discount margin will be 26.8 bp.

Typically FRN yields are quoted in terms of discount margin. Thus, an offering of Bonds A, B, and C would look like Exhibit A-2. Faced with these offerings, and considering that the bonds are identical in most respects, there would be no good reason not to prefer Bond C.

Calculating the discount margin on a floating-rate note requires a lot of information. Suppose we are offered a choice between one bond paying a coupon of LIBOR + 37.5 bp at a price of 101.75 and another with the same maturity paying LIBOR + 65 bp priced at 103.50. In order to calculate the discount margin on these securities, we need to know the coupon on an FRN of the same issuer with the same maturity priced at par and the yield on a fixed-rate bond of the same issuer with the same maturity. If such bonds are actively quoted in the market, it will be possible to find this information. In many cases there will be no comparable-maturity fixed- or floating-rate obligations of the same issuer outstanding. In these cases, it will be necessary to estimate the relevant yield and coupon levels from other information available in the market. The task is even more complicated if the two FRNs under consideration have somewhat different maturities and/or different payment or coupon reset frequencies.

For these reasons, yield quotations on FRNs are somewhat more subjective than those on fixed-rate bonds. Investors considering a purchase of FRNs should routinely ask about each offering's discount margin and the assumptions used to calculate that figure.

CHAPTER 3

The Big Picture: Portfolios, Returns, and the Role of Fixed-Income Assets

Over long periods of time, returns on stocks have exceeded returns on bonds by a wide margin. One dollar invested in the S&P 500 in 1953, with all returns reinvested in the stock market, would have grown to nearly $200 by the end of 1997, while $1 invested in corporate bonds would have increased only 16 times.[1] It does not necessarily follow, however, that investors should only hold equities. Even in light of the long history of relatively high stock returns and relatively low bond returns, the average U.S. family's allocation of 27% of its securities portfolio to the fixed-income market is perfectly rational. Indeed, even the average German household's 75% allocation to bonds is rational, although any allocation to fixed-income assets greater than about 75% would probably be a mistake.

This chapter presents the basic financial concepts that justify these assertions: the concepts of investment returns, return volatility, and asset return correlation, the concepts of risk and of portfolio efficiency, and the implications of all these concepts for a family's "big picture" investment decisions. Some basic knowledge of statistics will be necessary in understanding the concepts discussed in this chapter. A quick review of some basic terms will be helpful at this point.

QUICK REVIEW OF STATISTICAL CONCEPTS

The discussion of portfolio theory presented in this chapter will make use of five statistical concepts: mean or average, variance, standard deviation, covariance, and correlation. Readers who are familiar with these concepts should skip to the next section of this chapter. We will illustrate these concepts by considering hypothetical data on the daily prices of two bonds over a period of one month. The hypothetical data are presented in Exhibit 1.

---

[1] Aaron S. Gurwitz, "The Case for Bonds," Goldman, Sachs & Co., New York, January 1999, p. 1.

27

Exhibit 1: Yields on Two Hypothetical Bonds

Day of the Month	Bond A	Bond B
1	97.500	97.027
2	97.745	98.586
3	98.629	99.702
4	97.667	96.963
5	95.878	96.641
8	96.808	98.945
9	96.131	97.121
10	95.484	97.905
11	96.067	98.430
12	95.016	96.756
15	93.878	96.689
16	95.355	97.730
17	94.600	94.652
18	94.909	97.375
19	94.011	95.715
22	95.028	96.877
23	96.144	98.741
24	97.879	101.349
25	98.290	99.860
26	98.547	97.958
29	99.768	99.975
30	100.202	100.338
31	99.872	100.295
Mean	**96.757**	**98.071**
Variance	3.583	2.733
Standard Deviation	1.893	1.653
Covariance	**2.342**	
Correlation	0.782	

The mean of a series of prices (or yields or investment returns) is simply the average: the sum of the daily price observations over the period divided by the number of observations in the period. For Bond A, the mean or average price for this one-month period is 96.757, and for Bond B it is 98.071.

The variance and standard deviation of a series of prices are related measures of the dispersion of observed prices around the average. If the price does not change over a period of time, both the variance and the standard deviation of the price series are zero. Variance is the average of the squared deviations from the mean of the observed prices.

To see how variance is calculated, consider the price of Bond A on the first day of the month, 97.500. The mean price for Bond A for the period is 96.757, so the deviation of Bond A's price from the mean price on day one is 0.743 (= 97.500 − 96.757), and the squared deviation from the mean for this observation is 0.552 (= 0.743^2). To calculate the variance, we would take the sum of these squared differences and divide by the number of observations in the series minus one.[2] In these examples, the variance of Bond A's price is 3.583, and that of Bond B is 2.733. Thus, Bond A exhibits wider dispersion around the mean than does Bond B.

In calculating variance we take the sum of the squared deviations from the mean. This is because a large "deviation" can be either positive or negative, and the square of either a positive or negative number is positive. Yet because the deviations are squared, the variance of a series of prices is in different units from the prices themselves (dollars squared versus dollars). The most commonly used dispersion measure that has the same units as the series itself is the "standard deviation," which is simply the square root of the variance. In our example, the standard deviations are 1.893 and 1.653 for Bonds A and B, respectively.

In addition to having the same units as the series itself, the standard deviation of a series has another interesting property. If the observations in question resemble a normal, bell-shaped, frequency distribution, then we expect that approximately two-thirds of the observed prices in a series will fall in a range of values between one standard deviation below the mean and one standard deviation above the mean. For the relatively short series of prices in our example, this is approximately true. The price of Bond A, for example, falls in the range between 94.864 and 98.650 (96.757 ± 1.893) for 17 out of 23 observation, or 73.4% of the time. This is somewhat more than two-thirds of the time, but if our sample were larger the characteristic of standard deviation in this regard would be more clearly reflected in the data.

Correlation and covariance are statistics that reflect the relationship between two or more series of observations. The price of (yield of, return on) Bond B would be positively correlated with that of Bond A if, when the price of (yield of, return on) A is above its mean, that of B is also likely to be above its own mean. The prices would be negatively correlated, if when A's price is above the mean, B's price tends to be below its own mean, and vice versa.

The correlation of two series can be illustrated effectively by graphs called scatter diagrams. Exhibit 2 is a scatter diagram depicting the relationship between the prices of Bonds A and B. Each point in the diagram represents a particular day of the month and the price of each bond on that day. Different types of correlation are illustrated in Exhibit 3.

As the figures illustrate, correlations may be either positive or negative. If two series are perfectly correlated, either positively or negatively, and if we know the value of one price (yield, return), we also know the value of the other with certainty. If two series are completely uncorrelated, then information about the value of one price (yield, return) provides no information at all about the value of the other.

Two financial data series are seldomly either perfectly correlated or totally uncorrelated. They will usually exhibit some degree of either positive or negative correlation. Our two hypothetical price series are somewhat positively

---

[2] Why this "average" squared deviation is calculated using the number of observations minus one rather than the number of observations is interesting mathematically, but not relevant to the discussion here.

correlated, for example. As this chapter progresses, you will see why the degree of positive or negative correlation between two series can be of crucial importance to a portfolio manager.

The covariance of two series is the average product of the two variables' deviations from their respective means for each time period. For example, consider the first time period of our hypothetical series. The first price of Bond A is 97.500, which represents a deviation from its mean of 0.743. For Bond B, the first price is 97.027, which represents a deviation from its mean of −1.044. The product of these two deviations is −0.776. The covariance of two series is the sum of these products divided by the number of days (weeks, months) for which observations are available. In the case of our two hypothetical bond prices, the covariance is 2.341.

We use the covariance of two or more series in some applications in this book, but as a general indicator of the degree of "relatedness" of two series, the usefulness of this statistic is limited. The problem is that the size of the covariance depends on the units involved in measuring the series. For example, covariance of two series of bond yields will be different, depending on whether yield is measured in percent or basis points. For this reason, correlation is used more often than covariance as a measure of the relatedness of series. The correlation between two series always lies between −1.00 and +1.00, with the extremes representing perfect negative and perfect positive correlation. A correlation of zero would indicate that two series are perfectly uncorrelated.

Formally, the correlation of two series is defined as

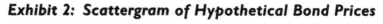

$$\text{Correlation}(X, Y) = \frac{\text{Covariance}(X, Y)}{\text{Standard Deviation of } X \times \text{Standard Deviation of } Y} \quad (1)$$

In our example, the correlation is +0.782.

Exhibit 2: Scattergram of Hypothetical Bond Prices

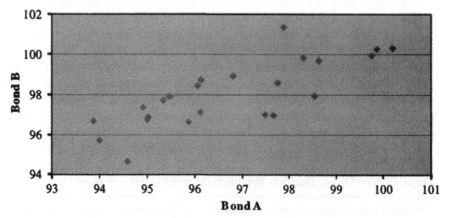

Exhibit 3: Various Degrees of Correlation

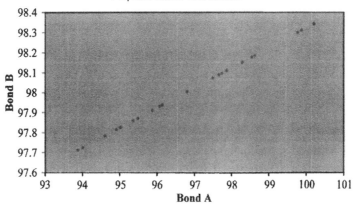

Perfect Positive Correlation

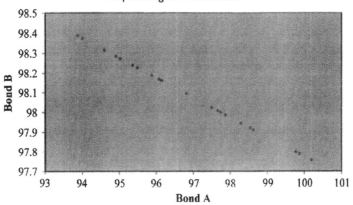

Perfect Negative Correlation

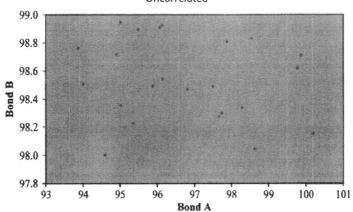

Uncorrelated

RETURN AND RISK

The basic job of a portfolio manager is to make trade-offs between expected return and risk. These two terms have very specific meanings in financial analysis.

The Concept of Return

The return on any investment for any period of time is the sum of two components:

1. The income paid by the issuer to the holder of the investment during the period.
2. The change in the market value of the investment over the period.

The sum of these two numbers is also sometimes referred to as the "total return" on the investment for the period. In the case of fixed-income investments, the first of these components is the coupon income paid on the security. The second component reflects two influences. The price of a bond may change from period to period either because its yield has changed, or because any premium or discount to par in the investor's original purchase price will diminish over time.

A few examples will help clarify this concept. Let's return to the bond purchased on January 1, 2000, and maturing on January 1, 2010. Suppose first that the bond pays a 6.00% coupon, and the investor buys the security at par (100.00) with a total purchase price of $100,000. Six months goes by, and the investor receives a coupon payment of $3,000, but suppose now that the market yield on a nine-year bond is 5.75%. If so, the price of the bond as of July 1, 2000, will be 101.810, and the market value of the investment will be $101,810. Therefore, the total return over the six-month period would be $4,810.[3] As a percentage of the amount invested, the standard way of quoting a total return, this would be 4.81%.

Assume that the coupon on the bond purchased on January 1, 2000, is 7.00%, and that the investor paid $107,438 to buy bonds with a par value of $100,000 at a yield to maturity of 6.00%. If there were no change in the bond's yield over the ensuing six months, the market value of the bond would be $107,163. The $275 difference between these two prices represents the amortization of the premium purchase price over the six-month period. In other words, the investor should not treat the full 7.00% coupon received on this bond as "interest income" because, if the investor spent the full amount, the amount of principal left when the bond matured would be less than the initial investment. Part of the coupon payment on a premium bond is, in effect, a return of principal, and should be accounted for as such as in Exhibit 4.

Now, if we assume that the yield on this bond, like that of the 6.00% coupon bond, declines to 5.75% over the six-month period, the market value of the bond will be 109.052 and that of the investment will be $109,052. On July 1, 2000, the investor will receive $3,500 in coupon payments. Exhibit 4 presents the components of the total return on this bond over the six-month period.

---

[3] This is the sum of the interest income for the period ($3,000) and the change in market value ($1,810).

Exhibit 4: Components of Total Return on a Bond Purchased at a Premium

Item	Dollar Amount	Percent of Investment
Coupon	$3,500	3.258%
Amortization of Premium/Accretion of Discount	($275)	(0.226%)
Gain/Loss Due to Yield Change	$1,889	1.758%
Total	$5,114	4.760%

Exhibit 5: Components of Total Return on a Bond Purchased at a Discount

Item	Dollar Amount	Percent of Investment
Coupon	$2,500	2.701%
Amortization of Premium/Accretion of Discount	277	0.299%
Gain/Loss Due to Yield Change	1,731	1.870%
Total	$4,508	4.870%

Now suppose that all the facts are the same, except that the investor will now be paying $92,561 on January 1, 2000, to purchase a ten-year bond with a 5.00% coupon at yield to maturity of 6.00%. On July 1, 2000, the bond has a yield to maturity of 5.75% and a market value of $94,569. The components of total return in this case are presented in Exhibit 5.

Note that the total returns for the three bonds are slightly different even though they all have the same maturity and were purchased at the same yield to maturity and evaluated at the same yield to maturity at the end of the period. Why this is so is the subject matter of Chapter 5. At this point, our aim is to illustrate the application of the concept of total return to fixed-income securities.

To this point the illustrations have been for six-month returns on a semi-annual pay bond. If the evaluation horizon is shorter than the interest payment period, the calculation would simply include interest that is accrued but unpaid. For example, if the assumptions were exactly the same about initial and final market price but we are calculating total return as of April 1, 2000, the numbers would be exactly the same, except that the coupon figures would be only half the size.

Things get a little more complicated if the evaluation horizon is longer than the interest payment period so that some cash flows are received between the initial purchase date and the date on which the return is being calculated. Again, let's look at the example of the 6.00% par bond purchased on January 1, 2000, under the scenario in which the yield to maturity of the bond declines over the period to 5.75%. In this case, however, we want to calculate the total return on the investment to January 1, 2001. The cash flows and values that relate to this calculation are listed in Exhibit 6.

The total return on the investment over this horizon is the discount rate such that the present value of the cash flows at the purchase date equals the purchase price of the bond. In this case, we are looking for the discount rate that produces a present value of $100,000 as of January 1, 2000, for payments of $3,000 on July 1, 2000, and of $104,737 on January 1, 2001. In this case, the return, expressed as an annual percentage, is 7.704%.

The discount rate calculated this way is also referred to as the "internal rate of return" or "IRR" of the cash flows and valuations associated with the investment. The IRR is the precise way of measuring the total return on an investment over a period during which various payments may be received. Unlike such terms as "yield to maturity" or "yield to worst," there is no standard convention used for calculating total return. We will report IRR as total return, unless it is otherwise specified. Portfolio managers should be familiar with one other common way of reporting portfolio return. Faced with the same facts as presented in Exhibit 6, we might calculate the one-year total return on this investment by assuming that the July 1 coupon payment of $3,000 is reinvested at the final yield to maturity of the bond (i.e., 5.75% in this example). Thus, the total cash available to the investor on January 1, 2001, would be the sum of: (1) the market value of the bond ($101,737); (2) the semiannual coupon payment received on that date ($3,000); (3) plus the coupon payment received on July 1, 2000 ($3,000); and (4) six months of interest on that coupon payment at 5.75% ($86.25). The total funds available at the end of the year under these assumptions are $107,823.25. We then compare the total funds at the end of the period with the amount invested initially and calculate the percentage change. By this method, the one-year total return on the investment would be 7.823%.

The internal rate of return is the preferred way of reporting total return because its calculation does not require any assumptions. The second method requires an assumption about reinvestment. In the example, we assume that the reinvestment rate is the yield on the bond at the end of the period, but other assumptions would be equally reasonable or unreasonable. Nevertheless, the second method described here is commonly used and is not wrong. The point is that when a dealer or investment advisor quotes a total return on an investment over a period of time, the investor should be careful to ask what method and what reinvestment assumptions were used in calculating that return.

Expected Return and the Concept of Investment Risk

In the discussion and examples above we deal with the calculation of total return once all the required information is available; that is, after the fact. Calculating the actual performance of a bond or portfolio one already owns can be useful; it is nice to know how well one has done. Yet the purpose of this book, and the reason for introducing the concept of total return, is to aid in the selection of fixed-income investments before we know how they will perform.

Exhibit 6: Cash Flows and Valuations of a 10-Year Bond Over a One-Year Period

Date	Coupon Payment	Principal Transaction	Total
July 1, 2000	$3,000		$3,000
January 1, 2001	$3,000	$101,737	$104,737

The return an investment will produce is almost always subject to uncertainty. The sole exception to this rule might be the return on the note of a sound national government denominated in that country's currency and maturing on the horizon date of the return analysis. But even in this case, unless the country's rate of inflation is always constant, the real (after-inflation) return would still be uncertain. In an uncertain world, decisions must be made on the basis of expectations about the future. In particular, investments for a portfolio must be selected on the basis of expectations about the returns those investments will produce. Later in the chapter we discuss various ways a portfolio manager might reasonably form such expectations. At this point, the goal is to explore the ways in which expectations regarding returns translate into investment decisions.

When asked why a portfolio manager purchased a particular investment the answer might be, "Because I thought it would do well," or "Because my downside was limited," or "Because it was a hedge against some of my other investments." These three everyday observations about investment decisions correspond to the three quantitative characteristics of any security:

1. Its expected return over an investment horizon; the higher, the better.
2. The degree of uncertainty with respect to its return at the horizon; the lower, the better.
3. The relationship between uncertainties with regard to this investment and uncertainties with respect to other investments available in the market; the less correlated, the better.

These beliefs are not usually quantified precisely, nor do we expect that family portfolio managers will want to turn their investment decisions over to some sort of quantitative investment decision machine. The reason for quantifying these commonsense concepts is to highlight the logical relationship among the three motivations for selecting an investment.

The three characteristics are related to the statistical concepts presented earlier in this chapter: average, standard deviation, and correlation. A portfolio manager anticipates a range of returns from an investment over a period of time and each outcome has some probability. The expected return is the probability-weighted average of the possible outcomes. For example, if the investor believes that the one-year total return on an investment might range between –4.00% and +6.00% and that all outcomes within that range are equally likely, the expected return would be +2.00%. More typically the investor might anticipate that the likelihood of different returns on an investment would have a normal, bell shaped distribution.

Exhibit 7 shows the return probabilities, assuming a normal distribution for two hypothetical bonds, both with expected returns of 6.00%. However, the returns on Bond B are subject to more uncertainty than those on Bond A. At this point, we will also assume that the returns on the two bonds are completely uncorrelated. That is, if we knew what the return on Bond A was going to be, this would provide no information about what the return on Bond B would be.

Exhibit 7: Two Bonds with Normally Distributed Returns, Equal Expected Returns, and Different Return Variances

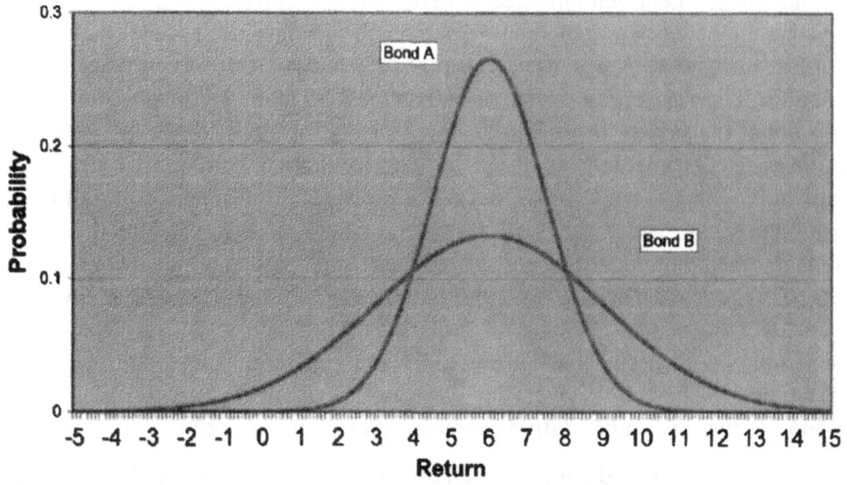

Risk of Loss

We have been measuring risk by the variance or standard deviation of a return distribution. Another way of summarizing the data may be more intuitively appealing to some investors. In particular, information about the mean and standard deviation (or variance) of a return distribution for an investment or a portfolio can be translated into a probability that the return on the investment will be below some given level. For example, suppose we believe that the expected annual return on an investment is 4.00%, that the standard deviation of the return distribution is 3.00% and that the distribution is normal. With this information, we can use a table of the normal distribution and find that there is a 0.16 (16.00%) probability that the annual return on this investment will be less than 1.00% and a 0.05 (5.00%) probability that the annual return will be at or above 9.00%.

Frequently investors will ask about an investment, "what is my chance of losing money on this?" Losing money means experiencing a total return of less than 0%. As illustrated in Exhibit 8, the probability of a loss is equal to the proportion of the area under a normal bell-shaped curve that falls to the left of the 0% return marker. In the case of the investment with a 4.00% expected annual return and a 3.00% return standard deviation, the risk of loss is about 9.00%.

The different degrees of uncertainty with respect to the two bonds' returns are expressed as different standard deviations of the distribution of returns; in Exhibit 7 the standard deviation of Bond A's return distribution is 1.50% while Bond B's is 3.00%. In other words, the investor believes that there is a 66⅔% chance that the return on Bond A will be between 4.50% and 7.50%, while for Bond B, there is a 66⅔% chance that the return will be between 3.00% and 9.00%.

Exhibit 8: Risk of Loss on an Investment with 4% Expected Return and 3% Return Standard Deviation

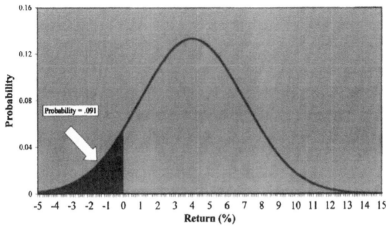

Exhibit 9: Two Bonds with Different Expected Returns and the Same Return Variances

Bond	Expected Return	Standard Deviation of Return Distribution
A	6.00%	1.50%
C	8.00%	1.50%

It is reasonable to assume that no investor would prefer Bond B to Bond A. Both have the same expected return, but the return on B is subject to greater uncertainty than the return on A. Bond B offers no "good" in compensation for the "bad" of greater uncertainty. Any additional "upside" provided by Bond B relative to Bond A is exactly matched by additional "downside."

The case is less clear with respect to a comparison of Bond A and Bond C, as illustrated in Exhibit 10. In this example, the return distribution for Bond C shows both a higher expected return than Bond A (8.00% versus 6.00%) and a higher standard deviation (3.00% versus 1.50%). In this example two rational investors could disagree about which bond to buy; there can be different answers to the question: "Is the 2.00% additional expected return enough compensation for the 1.50% of additional uncertainty?" There is no right answer to this question for all investors.

The analytical tools designed to help investors build portfolios are aimed at distinguishing between two types of situations:

1. Those in which the rational choices are obvious — Bond A is unambiguously a better investment than Bond B.
2. Those in which rational investors with different attitudes toward return and risk could make different choices.

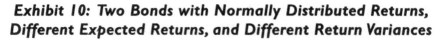

Exhibit 10: Two Bonds with Normally Distributed Returns, Different Expected Returns, and Different Return Variances

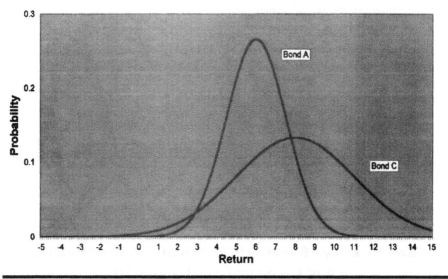

CORRELATIONS AMONG RETURNS AND PORTFOLIO DIVERSIFICATION

Up to this point, we have been discussing returns on individual bonds. We now consider the impact on the distribution of portfolio returns of correlations among portfolio assets. In order to discuss this topic, we need to introduce one more statistical concept: the variance of the sum of two series (of prices, yields, or returns) is equal to the sum of the variances of the two series plus two times the covariance of the two series.[4]

More generally, if we have a_1% of the portfolio invested in investment S with return distribution having a variance of Var(S) and a_2% invested in investment T with return distribution having a variance of Var(T), and if return distributions of the two investments have a covariance of Cov(S, T), the return distribution of the portfolio will have a variance of:

$$\text{Var}(a_1 S + a_2 T) = a_1^2 \text{Var}(S) + a_2^2 \text{Var}(T) + 2\, a_1\, a_2 \text{Cov}(S, T) \qquad (2)$$

For example, suppose we were considering a portfolio with 65.00% of its market value invested in Bond A (expected return of 6.00%, standard deviation of 1.50%

---

[4] This formula can be extended to deal with more than two series. That is, the variance of a sum of series is equal to the sum of the variances of the individual series plus two times the sum of the covariances of all pairs of two series.

or variance of $1.5\%^2 = 0.0225\%$) and 35.00% invested in Bond E with the same expected return and standard deviation of the return distribution. Suppose, now, that the correlation between the returns on the two assets is 0.70, so that their covariance is 0.01575% (see formula (1)). Under these assumptions and using formula (2), we can calculate that the variance of the portfolio's return distribution is 0.000194, and its standard deviation is 1.39%.

Notice that the standard deviation of returns for the portfolio is lower than the (equal) standard deviations of the two assets in question. This reflects one of the most important principles of portfolio management; *diversification of investments across assets that are less than perfectly positively correlated decreases risk.* If the two assets were perfectly correlated — i.e., if the correlation coefficient were equal to 1.00 — then the uncertainty with respect to the portfolio's returns would be the same as that of each of the individual assets. If the correlation coefficient were –1.00, then the standard deviation of the portfolio's return would be very small. In fact, if the return distribution of the two assets is perfectly negatively correlated, if the assets have the same standard deviation, and if the portfolio is equally divided between the two assets, there will be no uncertainty about the portfolio's return; the standard deviation of the return distribution will be zero.

These relationships are illustrated in Exhibit 11, where we plot the standard deviation of a portfolio's return distribution against the correlation between the assets' returns for three different portfolios. The greater the diversification and the lower the correlation, the less the uncertainty.

Exhibit 11: Standard Deviation of Portfolio Returns by Asset Return Correlation and Portfolio Composition

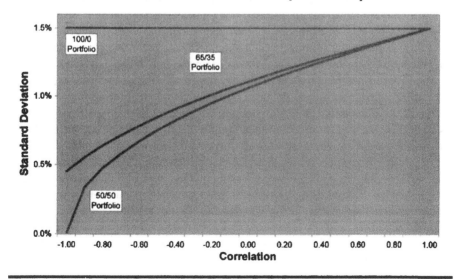

Let's return now to a point made earlier. In discussing the distribution of asset returns, we observed that a rational investor faced with two assets that produce the same returns with varying degrees of uncertainty always chooses the less risky asset. We can apply the same observation to portfolios. All three portfolios depicted in Exhibit 11 offer the same 6.00% expected return. Yet, unless the returns on the two assets in the portfolio are perfectly positively correlated, one of the portfolios will be subject to less uncertainty than the other two. Specifically, the portfolio consisting of 50.00% of investment S and 50.00% of investment T dominates any other possible portfolio in a world where these two bonds are the only available assets. The portfolio consisting of 100.00% of one asset and the portfolio consisting of 65.00% of one and 35.00% are *inefficient* in the sense that the investor could reduce uncertainty without reducing expected return by moving toward the 50/50 portfolio.

This conclusion is *theoretical*. Diversification is important, but it is not the only consideration that needs to be taken into account in building a portfolio. The benefits of diversification must be applied in a world in which there are many more than two assets; expected returns and uncertainty with respect to returns on different assets are unequal; and increasing diversification beyond a reasonable point can lead to other problems in a portfolio. The challenge now is to apply these concepts of total return, expected return, standard deviation of return distributions, and correlations among returns to issues involved in building real-world investment portfolios.

FORMING EXPECTATIONS

Methods for selecting investments on the basis of their expected returns, the variance of their return distributions, and the correlations among their returns presuppose some way of estimating these statistics. In fact, a portfolio manager can never be sure that the return distributions — their means, variances, and correlations — used to inform investment decisions are the right ones. The best a portfolio manager can do and the least a serious investor should do is to use all the available information about investments and markets in a systematic, logically consistent way.

Fixed-income analysts have developed three broad ways of translating available information into estimates of distributions of future asset returns. All three of these approaches are in common use today. Other chapters of this book will discuss each of these techniques in more detail. At this point, it is sufficient to describe them in general terms and illustrate their use in an example.

The first approach is to use *historical data* to estimate return distributions. The examples so far, where we estimate the mean, variance, and covariance of two series of bond prices, illustrate this technique. If our data were for total returns rather than prices, and if we use data for a much broader array of investment alternatives, and if our data cover a very long period of time, we could estimate a complete set of average returns and a "variance-covariance matrix." The matrix would list the variances for the return on each asset and the covariances between each pair of investments.

There is no guarantee, of course, that future return distributions will resemble historical experience. A portfolio manager can gain confidence in statistical analysis only to the extent that the historical data cover a long period of time characterized by a wide range of economic and financial market conditions. In addition, because some return distributions tend to be more stable than others, another way in which an investor can gain confidence about using historical data is to calculate return distributions — means, variances, and covariances — for groups of assets over different historical periods. For example, an analyst might estimate return statistics for U.K. Gilts and U.S. Treasuries for three periods, 1985-1989, 1990-1994, and 1995-2000. A portfolio manager should gain confidence in using historical data for these asset classes, if the three periods produce similar estimates of some or all of the statistics. Conversely, if the statistics estimated for the three periods differ radically, an investor should probably look to other ways of estimating return distributions.

The second approach is *forecasting*. The next chapter describes the forces that drive interest rates and interest rate changes. These forces include the rates of global and domestic economic growth, monetary policy, fiscal policy, and investor expectations about all of these. Because interest rate changes exert an important influence over the returns on fixed-income assets, forecasts of interest rates can translate into estimates of return distributions. Forecasting interest rates is difficult at best, and may in fact be impossible. Any very specific prediction — e.g., that yields on ten-year benchmark Japanese government bonds (JGBs) will be below 2.75% by the end of 2001 — should be taken with more than a grain of salt. Yet an investor should be willing to listen to a well-reasoned argument that Japanese bond yields are more likely to fall than rise over the next year, and, if the argument is convincing, expect a higher return on JGBs than historical patterns would suggest.

Finally, one can form expectations about return distributions through *inference from current market prices*. Parts of Chapters 4 and 15 will demonstrate how the relationships between the current market yields of various fixed-income investments can be used for inferring consistent expected returns, variances, and covariances of asset returns.

Regardless of how they are derived, precise numerical estimates of expected returns, return variances, or return correlations should be viewed skeptically. At the same time, all three approaches to formulating expectations, applied separately or in combination, can and do provide useful insights into how different portfolios are likely to perform.

FIXED-INCOME ASSETS AND RETURN DISTRIBUTIONS

The techniques described in this chapter relate to fixed-income assets in two ways. First, estimates of return distributions can be used to make informed decisions on the overall allocation among large-capitalization stocks, small-cap stocks, bonds, real estate, commodities, and other "asset classes" for a family's portfolio. Second, the same concepts can help decide allocations within the fixed-income market among the various types of bonds to be discussed in Part II. We consider the first of these questions in this chapter. The allocation question is, in a sense, the subject of the rest of this book.

Return Distributions for U.S. Stocks and Bonds

Exhibit 12 depicts the raw data on monthly returns on U.S. common stocks and U.S. government bonds over the 25-year period from mid-1972 through mid-1997. An inspection of the numbers immediately suggests that stock returns are somewhat more volatile than bond returns. In order to use these data effectively, however, we must first compute the basic statistics for the two return series. These are presented in Exhibit 13.

These statistics reflect the performance of the S&P 500 and U.S. government bonds over a 25-year period. How appropriate would it be to use the return distributions derived from these historical statistics to inform investment decisions today? Remember that we noted two criteria by which one can evaluate the usefulness of historical data. Specifically, the data need to cover a long period of time during which economic and financial market conditions vary over a wide range. Second, the statistics describing asset returns need to be relatively stable over various historical periods.

Exhibit 12: Historical Returns on U.S. Stocks and Bonds

Asset	S&P 500	U.S. Government Bonds
Mean	1.130%	0.770%
Variance	19.691	9.918
Standard Deviation	4.404%	3.149%
Covariance	5.098	
Correlation	0.369	

Source: Aaron S. Gurwitz, "The Case for Bonds," Goldman, Sachs & Co., New York, January 1999.

Exhibit 13: Monthly Returns on Stocks and U.S. Government Bonds

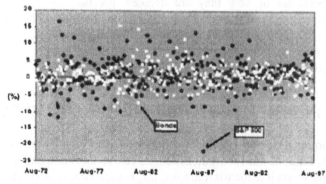

Source: Aaron S. Gurwitz, "The Case for Bonds," Goldman, Sachs & Co., New York, January 1999.

Exhibit 14: S&P 500 and U.S. Government Bond Return Distribution Statistics by Five-Year Periods

Period	S&P 500 Mean	Gov't Bonds Mean	S&P 500 Std. Dev.	Gov't. Bonds Std. Dev.	Correl.
Aug-72 - Jul-77	0.31%	0.50%	5.01%	2.10%	0.308
Aug-77 - Jul-82	0.67	0.19	4.22	4.23	0.327
Aug-82 - Jul-87	2.28	1.43	4.31	3.79	0.509
Aug-87 - Jul-92	0.89	0.98	5.07	2.50	0.261
Aug-92 - Jul-97	1.62	0.81	2.85	2.52	0.507

Source: Aaron S. Gurwitz, "The Case for Bonds," Goldman, Sachs & Co., New York, January 1999.

Our data on stock and bond returns do pass the first test; 25 years is a long time in financial markets, and the period between 1972 and 1997 in particular witnessed both the highest inflation and interest rates ever seen in the U.S. and the worst recession since the great depression of the 1930s, and both the second-worst one-day percentage drop in the Dow Jones Industrial Average, and the most dramatic financial market rally on record. By the second criterion, however, the historical statistics appear to be a less reliable guide to decisions. Exhibit 14 compares the monthly return statistics for the two asset classes for sequential five-year periods. These comparisons suggest that the return distributions of these asset classes are not stable over time. This does not mean that historical data are useless, but just that one should not take the results of an analysis based on these statistics as the sole guide for investment decision making.

With this caveat in mind, let's consider the implications of the return distribution statistics estimated using data from the full 25-year period.

If we take each asset's mean return over the last 25 years as our indicator of expected returns and assume the historical variances and covariances for the same period, we can use formula (2) to calculate the expected return and standard deviation of portfolios holding varying proportions of stocks and bonds. For example, consider a portfolio consisting of 60% S&P 500 stocks and 40% U.S. government bonds. The average return on stocks over the 25-year period is 1.13% monthly or 14.4% annualized. For bonds, the monthly and annual figures are 0.8% and 9.6%, respectively. The expected return of this portfolio is simply the weighted average of the expected returns of the two asset classes or 12.5% (= [0.6 × 14.4%] + [0.4 × 9.6%]). The historical variance of monthly stock returns was 19.7 and that of bond returns is 9.9, while the covariance between the two monthly return series was 5.1. So, by formula (2), the variance of the 60/40 portfolio's monthly returns would be

Portfolio Monthly Return Variance

$$= (0.6^2 \times 19.7) + (0.4^2 \times 9.9) + (2 \times 0.6 \times 0.4 \times 5.1) = 11.1$$

We can annualize this number by multiplying it by 12 to get 133.5, and calculate the standard deviation of the return by taking the square root to get 11.6%. We repeat the same process for each combination of stocks and bonds.

Exhibit 15: Expected Returns and Standard Deviations for Combinations of S&P 500 Stocks and Government Bonds

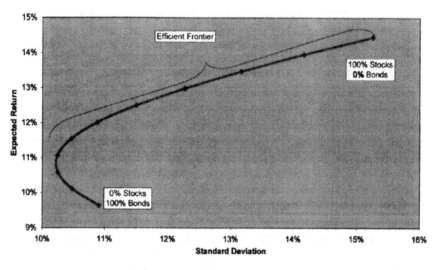

The results of these calculations are depicted in Exhibit 15. Each marker on the curve in the graph represents a different combination of stocks and bonds, ranging from 100% bonds to 100% stocks. Given the fact that over the 25 years between 1972 and 1997 government bonds have provided lower and less volatile returns than the S&P 500 stocks, it isn't surprising that the portfolios heavily weighted in fixed-income assets fall into the lower left-hand corner. Nor is it surprising that the curve is generally upward-sloping; adding stocks to the portfolio results in higher expected returns and, for the most part, higher portfolio return standard deviations.

The intriguing thing about this graph is that direction of the curve is not consistent over its entire length. The "twist" at the lower left-hand part of the curve indicates that increasing the proportion of the portfolio held in stocks from zero to 20% or 30% actually has the effect of *decreasing* the standard deviation of expected returns, even though stock returns are more volatile than bond returns! To understand why this happens, recall the conclusion presented earlier; unless the returns of two assets are perfectly positively correlated, returns on some portfolio of both assets will be subject to less uncertainty than a portfolio of only one asset. In the case presented earlier, when the return distributions on both assets have the same standard deviation, the diversified portfolio with the lowest variance of returns includes 50% of each asset. In the case of S&P 500 stocks and U.S. government bonds, the lowest-variance portfolio has more of the low-return volatility asset. Yet, because of the beneficial effect of diversification on portfolio return variance, adding some stocks to an all-bond portfolio does reduce expected return volatility.

Some Generalizations

Consideration of Exhibit 15 leads to an immediate conclusion. In a "two-asset world," to the extent that the use of historical data to estimate return distribution statistics is reliable, no rational investor would hold a portfolio of less than 25% stocks. With any less exposure to the equity market than that, it is possible to increase expected returns without increasing uncertainty regarding returns. To put it differently, given a world with these two and only these two assets and the return distributions based on the 25-year history, a portfolio holding less than 30% equities would be *inefficient*. Further, under these assumptions, portfolios holding between 30% and 100% equities are said to be "*on the efficient frontier.*"

The efficient frontier identifies all the portfolios it makes sense to hold. The most risk-averse investor might want to hold a portfolio consisting of 75% bonds, but reducing the equity allocation below 25% with the aim of reducing uncertainty even further could be self-defeating.

This analysis has little to say about choices among portfolios along the efficient frontier. Equity allocations greater than 25% reflect the portfolio manager's preferences with respect to uncertainty and expected returns; investors who are willing to accept more uncertainty in exchange for the expectation of better returns will gravitate to the upper right-hand end of the efficient frontier. Those with the opposite attitude will gravitate toward the lower left-hand end.

This analysis of returns on S&P 500 stocks and U.S. government bonds is intended to illustrate how estimates of return distributions can be used to guide investment decisions. Using only the estimates of expected returns and standard deviations illustrated in Exhibit 15 as a definitive guide to portfolio allocations would not be appropriate. After all, there are certainly more than these two asset classes in the world, and we have already seen that extrapolation from historical data is not necessarily the best way of estimating return distributions.

We can nevertheless use this analysis as a starting point for thinking about fixed-income portfolios, and will take it as a working assumption that a "rational" allocation to fixed-income investments will range between 0 and 75% of an investor's portfolio.

CHAPTER 4

The Level of Interest Rates and the Shape of the Yield Curve

T hinking about fixed-income investments requires thinking about interest rates. Fixed-income securities produce interest income. Changes in interest rates drive changes in bond prices, which, in turn, help determine total returns. Therefore, a fixed-income portfolio manager should have some understanding of the forces that affect the level of interest rates and the ways in which a bond's yield relates to its maturity.

THE LATE 1970s AND EARLY 1980s AND FIXED-INCOME PHOBIA

Attention to interest rates is especially important in any fixed-income book written after the extreme fluctuations in interest rate levels during the 1970s and 1980s. To see how dramatic these interest rate changes have been we need to look at a long history of comparable interest rates. Because fixed-income markets have evolved so rapidly in recent years, there are surprisingly few reliable interest rate time series that go back much more than 25 years.

One exception is the U.S. municipal bond market. High-quality general obligations of state governments with 20-year maturities have been available in the market for nearly 150 years, and since the beginning of the 20th century the municipal market's daily trade journal, *The Bond Buyer*, has published an index of yields on such securities. Exhibit 1 presents a chart tracking these data. After falling to their lowest levels of the century during World War II, rates rose until the early 1980s. The rate of increase became very rapid after 1969, when, for the first time, bond yields rose above 6.00%.

Wall Street legend has it that the increase in bond yields above 6.00% led to a technological revolution in the fixed-income markets. As we mentioned in Chapter 2, before that time bond traders would use thick volumes of tables called

47

a "basis book" to translate yield into price and vice versa. Because interest rates had never risen much above 5.00% before the late 1960s, the basis book yield tables only went up to 6.00%. When yields went above these levels, traders had, for the first time, to resort to the then-newly developed electronic calculators to price bonds.

The dramatic increase in interest rates in the late 1970s and early 1980s had more profound effects. As interest rates rose, bond prices decreased. A 20-year bond with a 6.00% coupon purchased at 100.00 in 1978, for example, would have fallen in market value to a price of less than 60.00 four years later.

INFLATION, REAL BOND RETURNS, AND THE BABY BOOMERS' WATERSHED

To make matters worse for the fixed-income investor, the rate of inflation was also high and increasing rapidly at the same time. Inflation is a major concern for all investors, but for fixed-income investors the impact of unanticipated decreases in the purchasing power of money can be devastating. The distinction between *nominal* (before inflation) bond returns and *real* (after inflation) returns is important enough to explore in some detail.

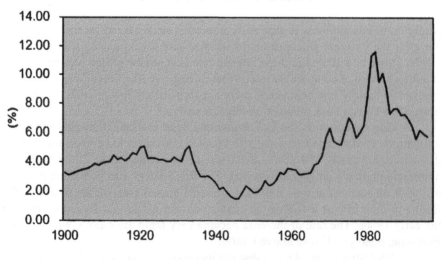

Exhibit 1: Bond Buyer Index of 20 High-Grade General Obligations

Source: *The Bond Buyer*

Money is not an end in and of itself. What matters are the goods and services that money can purchase. Inflation is a generalized increase in the total cost of a constant "market basket" of goods and services. The consumer price index (CPI) is one measure of inflation; it is the price of a fairly constant market basket of goods and services representing the average monthly expenditures of a typical household. For example, suppose the CPI was 1.00 in August 1983 and had reached 1.45 by August 1993. This means that the cost of the average family's average monthly market basket had increased by 45% over the ten-year period. This is equivalent to saying that the average annual rate of inflation — the percentage rate of increase of the CPI — had been about 3.8% over the decade.[1]

In the previous chapter we discussed the concept of investment returns on fixed-income securities. We now need to distinguish between *nominal* and *real* returns. The yield or return on a fixed-income investment measured in the amount of money in each cash flow is referred to as the *nominal return*: the return concept we have been dealing with up to this point. The yield or return on a fixed-income investment measured in the amount of goods and service each cash flow can buy — i.e., in terms of the purchasing power of each cash flow — is referred to as *real return* on the asset. Translating nominal cash flows into real cash flows is easy mathematically:

$$C_t = C_n \, (\text{CPI}_0/\text{CPI}_t)$$

where:

C_t = the real value of a cash flow received in period t;
C_n = the nominal value of the cash flow received in period t;
CPI_0 = the level of the price index on the evaluation date (usually the purchase date); and
CPI_t = the level of the price index in period t.

For example, the goods and services that could be purchased with a payment of $1,000 in 1983 would have cost $1,452 in 1993. Put differently, $1,000 "1993 dollars" had the same purchasing power as $689.66 (= $1,000/1.452) "1983 dollars."

With this as background we can examine the impact of inflation on an investor who purchased a ten-year bond with a coupon of 5.20% for $100,000 on January 1, 1973. The nominal and real cash flows produced by such an investment are listed in Exhibit 2. The impact of inflation is seen most clearly in the principal payment. The purchasing power of the $100,000 invested in 1973 had declined to $44,750 by 1983, a 65.25% decrease. Mostly for this reason, the total *real* rate of return on this investment is *negative*.

---

[1] $1.038^{10} = 1.452$

Exhibit 2: Nominal and Real Cash Flows on a 10-Year Bond Purchased in 1973

Date	Principal	Coupon	Nominal Cash Flow	CPI	Real Cash Flow 1973 Dollars
1/1/73	(100,000)		(100,000)	0.427	(100,000)
7/1/73		2,600	2,600	0.442	2,512
1/1/74		2,600	2,600	0.468	2,372
7/1/74		2,600	2,600	0.493	2,252
1/1/75		2,600	2,600	0.523	2,123
7/1/75		2,600	2,600	0.540	2,056
1/1/76		2,600	2,600	0.558	1,990
7/1/76		2,600	2,600	0.570	1,948
1/1/77		2,600	2,600	0.587	1,891
7/1/77		2,600	2,600	0.608	1,826
1/1/78		2,600	2,600	0.627	1,771
7/1/78		2,600	2,600	0.655	1,695
1/1/79		2,600	2,600	0.685	1,621
7/1/79		2,600	2,600	0.730	1,521
1/1/80		2,600	2,600	0.780	1,423
7/1/80		2,600	2,600	0.826	1,344
1/1/81		2,600	2,600	0.872	1,273
7/1/81		2,600	2,600	0.915	1,213
1/1/82		2,600	2,600	0.944	1,176
7/1/82		2,600	2,600	0.975	1,139
1/1/83	100,000	2,600	102,600	0.979	44,750
IRR			5.20%		−3.19%

THE HISTORY OF INFLATION IN THE 20TH CENTURY

Until the 1970s, severe inflation had been only a theoretical threat to fixed-income investors. As Exhibit 3 indicates, there had been some severe bouts of temporary wartime inflation in the U.S. earlier in the 20th century, but these periods had been followed by a rapid return to price stability or even, after the First World War, a period of rapid price decreases. Investors all over the world are well aware of Germany's devastating hyperinflation of the 1920s, but this also was seen as an aberration. These theoretical and historical concerns became very real, however, as the 1970s progressed and investors began to experience the impacts of a prolonged period of peacetime inflation.

As Exhibit 4 indicates, inflation in the 1970s was a worldwide problem. Even in West Germany, where, for historical reasons, inflation is anathema, the annual rate rose above 5.00%, and some monthly figures began pushing double digits. The problem for investors was not simply that inflation rates were high, but that the causes of this bout of inflation were not at all clear to professional economists, much less to the general investing public. For this reason, it was also unclear how long inflation rates would remain elevated. Indeed, at the time some social scientists were making the argument that permanently higher and rising inflation was inevitable in a "post-industrial democracy." To make matters worse, rapid inflation and rising interest rates — the two worst things that can happen to a fixed-income investor — became a vicious cycle. Investors who had purchased long-term bonds early in the 1970s saw the nominal market value of their investments drop sharply and the real value fall even more. Investors who lived through this period came out of it with the strong impression that fixed-income instruments are very risky, unattractive investments.

Exhibit 3: U.S. Consumer Price Index Inflation, 1913-1997

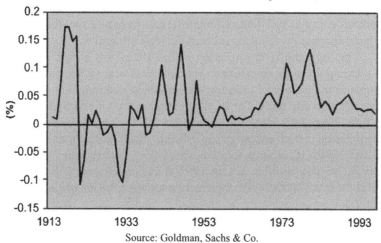

Source: Goldman, Sachs & Co.

Exhibit 4: Consumer Price Index Inflation in Three Large Economies

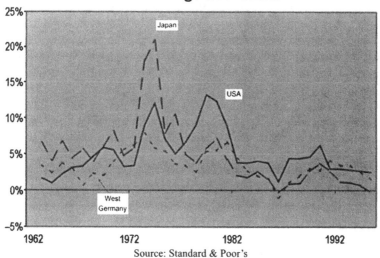

Source: Standard & Poor's

The dramatic developments in the fixed-income markets of the 1970s and early 1980s may be receding into history, but their effects are likely to linger for many years to come. The dominant economic events of an individual's early adult life seem to color a person's perceptions for many years. The generation that watched its parents sink into poverty through the Great Depression 1930s — the apparent result of stock market speculation in the 1920s — remained overly risk-averse with respect to equity investments for the rest of their lives. The baby boom generation may be at the other end of the attitude spectrum. The number of live births in the United States peaked at 4.3 million in 1957, and about 20 years after that date, the largest cohort of the "baby boom" generation began entering the workforce, just as inflation and interest rates were reaching their peak and just when fixed-income investments seemed the least attractive.

The high and rising inflation of the 1970s was a particularly dramatic event that had a profound effect on interest rates around the world. But, while inflation and the history of inflation are important determinants of interest rates, they are not the only ones. To see this, compare the United States and Japan in 1997. Both countries shared the experience of very high inflation in the 1970s, and the inflation in both countries had fallen to much more normal post-war levels by the late 1990s. If inflation told the whole story, interest rates in the two countries would be quite similar. Yet, in 1997 yields on ten-year U.S. Treasury notes remained close to 6.00% while Japanese government bonds offered yields of less than 2.00%.

This is not a macroeconomics textbook. An understanding of how economic conditions and government policies affect interest rates, however, is an essential tool of the trade for any fixed-income portfolio manager.

A QUICK REVIEW OF FINANCIAL MACROECONOMICS

An interest rate can be thought of as a price; it is the price at which a lender is willing to transfer the use of money to a specific borrower for a specified period of time. It is also the price the borrower is willing to pay for the use of money for the same period of time. Like any other price, interest rates are determined by supply and demand in an organized market. Therefore, understanding financial macroeconomics is the same as understanding the supply and demand for the use of money over time and the ways in which supply and demand are mediated in financial markets.

The Supply of Loans

In any country, the supply of funds from lenders comes from two sources: domestic savings, and net capital inflows from abroad. The aggregate volume of domestic savings depends mainly on the level and distribution of income in the country. The higher the level of income — that is, the larger the country's gross domestic product (GDP) — the more funds available to be saved. Further, higher-income households tend to save a larger proportion of their income than poorer families. Therefore, all else held equal, one can expect the volume of savings generated domestically to increase more than proportionally as a country's income grows.

A country's demographic characteristics — and the age distribution of its population in particular — also influence the proportion of the average household's income that is saved (the "savings rate"). People go through an economic cycle over the course of their lives. During their 20s and early 30s, individuals are forming households and starting families. The expenditures necessary for these activities and the fact that, at this stage, the household's income is just starting to increase combine to limit the family's ability to save. Later, as the heads of the household mature into their late 30s, 40s, 50s, and early 60s, income peaks while immediate spending needs begin to diminish and old age becomes more imminent. Consequently, the household's savings rate increases. Finally, as the household heads age into their late 60s and beyond, income decreases, and families begin to live on their savings. At this stage of the life cycle, net new savings will be minimal.

If a country's population were distributed evenly along the age spectrum, these life cycle patterns would have little impact on the overall savings rate. Uniform age distributions are rare, though. More often, some age cohorts will be much larger than others. For example, because of the global economic depression and the Second World War, relatively few people were born between 1930 and 1945. After the war, most countries experienced dramatic "baby booms," making up for 15 years of postponed fertility. As a result, an extremely large age group moved through its life cycle together. This tended to depress average savings rates when "baby boomers" were in their 20s and early 30s and to increase savings rates as this large age group entered their 40s and 50s.

With respect to the flow of capital from abroad, the main influences are: (1) the level of interest rates in the borrower country relative to those available elsewhere in the world; (2) the outlook for the exchange rate between the lender's currency and that of the borrower; and (3) the political stability of the borrower's country.

These underlying characteristics — the country's level of income, the age distribution of its population, and its ability to attract foreign investment — all influence the level of savings, regardless of the level of interest rates. At any given level of rates, savings will be greater to the extent that the country is wealthy, its population is predominantly middle-aged, and other countries wish to invest there. The actual volume of savings at any given time will reflect both these fundamental national characteristics *and* the price at which money is borrowed and lent. The higher the level of interest rates in a country, the more funds will be made available by domestic and foreign lenders, although the magnitude of the effect may be small.

The Demand for Loans

Demand for loans comes from both the private sector and the public sector. The private sector's demand for loans is influenced primarily by the pace of economic activity in a country and by expectations about the future level of activity. Consider, for instance, the demand for loans for home mortgages. Households will be willing to take out mortgage loans, or take out larger mortgage loans, to the extent that family members are well paid and anticipate pay increases. Likewise, companies will be inclined to borrow funds to purchase inventories or to expand productive capacity to the extent that business is good and expected to get even better.

Some public sector borrowing is also influenced positively by economic conditions. If times are good, roads will be congested and tax revenues will high and growing. Under these circumstances, local governments may be more willing than otherwise to borrow funds to build transportation infrastructure. In most countries, however, budget deficit financing accounts for the bulk of net public sector borrowing. If government expenditures exceed government revenues, the difference must be borrowed.

Budget deficits can be decomposed into structural deficits and cyclical deficits. Countries operate with structural deficits if there is some sustained mismatch between the level of government expenditures and the system by which the government raises revenues. Through most of the 1980s, the U.S. federal government ran a large structural deficit; the Treasury had to borrow large amounts of money each year, even when economic conditions were good and tax revenues were increasing robustly. There is no reason in principle why a government could not run a structural surplus for a long period of time. In fact, the United States did so consistently between 1823 and 1836. In the 20th century, however, there has been a marked tendency of governments to operate with structural deficits: occasional balanced budgets and very infrequent surpluses.

The level of a country's structural deficit is not related to economic conditions. A cyclical deficit, however, reflects slow or negative economic growth. In any given tax system, the volume of revenues a government collects will depend on the level of economic activity. Thus, tax revenues will generally decline in a recession. Government expenditures, by contrast, do not decline when the economy slows down or contracts. If anything, governments must spend more on social welfare programs when times are hard and unemployment rates are high. Therefore, when economic conditions are bad, the government's deficit, and its demand for borrowed funds, tends to increase. Note that a government's cyclical deficit is the only source of demand for borrowed funds that tends to increase when economic growth is slow or negative.

Private sector demand for credit is sensitive to interest rates. When interest rates are high, for example, home buyers will have to satisfy themselves with smaller mortgage loans and smaller houses than they might have chosen if rates were low and economic conditions otherwise unchanged. Likewise, when confronted with high interest rates, businesses might be less sanguine about financing large inventories or borrowing to add productive capacity. Governments, whether borrowing to finance infrastructure investments or to cover operating budget deficits are relatively insensitive to interest rates.

Exhibit 5: The Effect of a Large, Aging Population Cohort on Interest Rates

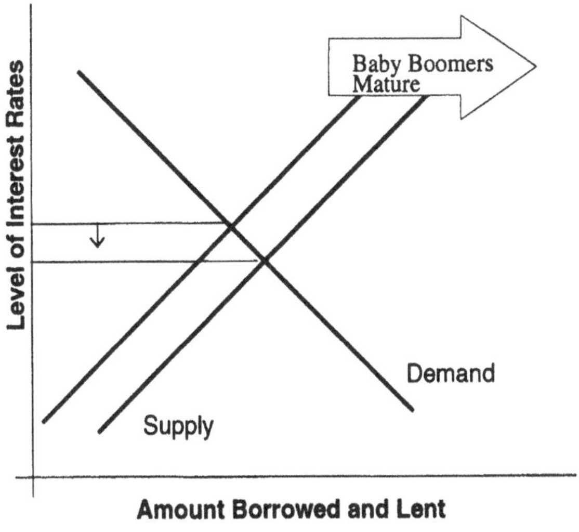

SUPPLY AND DEMAND

Economic activity, expectations about future activity, demographics, and interest rates combine to produce levels of aggregate supply and demand for borrowed (and lent) funds. The determinants of supply and demand and their aggregate effects can be summarized in a standard graph of price and quantity. The supply of credit tends to increase as interest rates rise, while the demand for credit is negatively related to interest rates. In this context, it is useful to work through some applications of the basic supply and demand concept.

Demographic and Social Effects

Suppose, for example, a large population cohort in a country begins to move into their peak savings years. This means that at any given level of interest rates, all else held equal, more savings will take place — that is, more credit will be supplied — than was the case previously. We can represent this development as a shift to the right of the supply curve with the effect, as illustrated in Exhibit 5, of lowering interest rates.

To take another example, suppose the central government of the Republic of X has had a balanced central government operating budget for a number of years. Then assume that a new party is elected to a parliamentary majority on a platform promising large tax cuts with minimal cuts in government spending. If the new government enacts its program, the effect will be to increase the aggregate demand for credit at any level of interest rates; that is, the demand curve in Exhibit 6 shifts to the right. Suppose further that foreign investors take this policy as a sign that the new government is fiscally irresponsible, making them less willing to lend money to the Republic at any given level of interest rates in X. This has the effect of shifting the supply curve in Exhibit 6 to the left. Both effects — an increased demand and a decreased supply — have the same effect: to raise interest rates in the Republic.

A more complete array of potential social and economic influences on the level of interest rates is summarized in Exhibit 7.

Exhibit 6: The Effect of an Increased Budget Deficit on Interest Rates

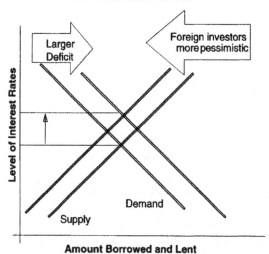

Exhibit 7: Broad Range of Influences on Credit Supply and Demand

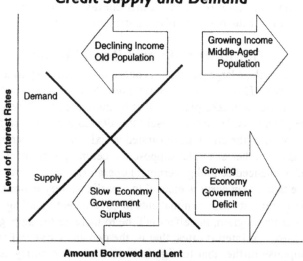

The Regulation of Credit Supply through Monetary Policy

As a practical matter, it makes no sense for each individual borrower to find an individual lender for each transaction. Instead, market mechanisms have evolved by which financial institutions act as intermediaries between borrowers as a group and lenders as a group.

Lessons learned slowly over the 250-year history of modern capitalism have taught us that a large economy incorporating free markets and financial intermediaries will, if left to its own devices, experience dramatic and socially disruptive business cycles. Instead of growing steadily, such economies tend to experience periods of extremely rapid economic growth and price inflation followed by severe depressions and widespread unemployment. For this reason, all countries have established central banks whose primary function is to regulate the supply of credit. By "tightening" the supply of credit during boom periods and "loosening" when the economy begins to slow, central banks aim to counteract the free market's tendency to generate sharp fluctuations in economic activity.

Central banks control the supply of credit in an economy by regulating financial institutions. As intermediaries in the capital markets, banks receive deposits from lenders and make loans to borrowers. Banks are not the sole financial intermediaries in modern economies. For example, a corporation wishing to finance inventory might either take out a bank loan or issue bonds. Similarly, a "lender" could deposit money in a bank or buy a company's commercial paper. Rates on bank loans do influence other interest rates available throughout the financial markets, and, by regulating credit supplied through the banking sector, central banks can influence the level of interest rates offered by all lenders.

HOW A BANKING SYSTEM EXPANDS CREDIT

The discussion of the effect of monetary policy on the supply of credit requires a brief digression into the way a banking system creates credit. To see how this works most easily, it is useful to think of a banking system as a single bank. The bank receives a deposit of, say, $100. The bank immediately seeks to find a borrower to whom to lend the money. Upon receipt of a loan of $100, the borrower immediately deposits the money in the bank or uses the money to purchase something, in which case the seller of the item deposits the money in the bank. In either case, the bank now has $200 of deposits and immediately starts looking for another borrower. The second borrower receives a $100 loan and that money, too, immediately finds its way back into the bank. This might go on indefinitely, and, if it did, credit would expand without limit until one of the depositors wanted to withdraw funds. With no reserves, the bank would not have the funds to meet the demand, and the bubble would burst.

Obviously the "one bank" model underlying this scenario is too simple. In an open multi-bank market, lenders would be unwilling to deposit money in a particular bank if they were aware that the institution was not keeping any reserves. Nevertheless, between the advent of capitalism and the development of the modern system of central banks, there were repeated episodes of uncontrolled credit expansion followed by "runs" on the banking system and subsequent financial collapse.

Bank regulation aims to prevent such credit explosions. To limit expansion of credit, central banks require that depository institutions maintain reserves equal to a fixed proportion of their deposits. Consider a simple example again from a one-bank world. Suppose the bank faces a reserve requirement of 50%. With an initial deposit of $100, the bank could make a $50 loan. When that $50 is deposited, the bank would be able to make another $25 loan, and then a $12.50 loan, and then a $6.25 loan, and so on. In this way, the imposition of a reserve requirement limits the expansion of credit. With a 50% reserve requirement, an initial deposit of $100 cannot generate bank lending in excess of $200.

Avoiding uncontrolled expansions of credit is not the only policy objective central banks pursue. They also aim to expand lending when the economy is growing too slowly and to reduce lending when growth is accelerating too rapidly. Central banks could make these adjustments in credit availability by changing reserve requirements: They might reduce the requirement when they want to expand credit and require larger reserves when they want to tighten lending conditions. Yet, central banks have learned that there are subtler and better ways to manage credit supply.

Banks' reserves are usually held as deposits in accounts at the central bank. A bank interested in expanding its deposits and loans must increase the reserves it has on deposit at the central bank. It can do so in three ways: (1) it may deposit funds directly; (2) it may borrow reserves from other banks; and (3) it may borrow reserves from the central bank itself. One way the central bank can influence banks' willingness to expand credit is to raise or lower the interest rate at which it lends reserves to financial institutions. In the United States, this interest rate is referred to as the Federal Reserve "discount rate." Some central banks use this mechanism frequently.

In other countries, including the United States, another method is preferred. The central bank can increase or decrease the aggregate level of reserves available to the banking system by trading government securities with banks. For instance, if the central bank buys Treasury bills from a bank, it pays for them by transferring cash to the bank's reserve account. This transfer increases the bank's reserves on deposit and enables the institution either to make more loans or to lend reserves to another bank. If the central bank sells government securities, bank payment for the purchase is made by a transfer of funds from the bank's reserve account. This reduces the bank's reserve levels, and the bank must then either reduce its level of borrowing and lending or borrow more from other banks.

The buying and selling of government securities — referred to as "open market operations" — is the primary way most central banks influence the availability of credit in an economy. If the central bank buys government securities over a period of time, reserves will become more plentiful, and banks will be more willing to make loans and accept deposits themselves or more willing to lend reserves to other banks. When the central bank is, on average, selling government securities, bank reserves will be scarcer, and banks will be less willing to expand credit.

Open market operations have a direct influence on the aggregate level of reserves on deposit at the central bank. These purchases and sales of securities by the central bank have an immediate, albeit indirect, effect on the interest rate at which banks are willing to lend each other reserves. This interest rate, which is determined in an active market among banks, is called the "Federal Funds rate" or "Fed Funds" in the United States. When market participants discuss United States Federal Reserve policy, they are more likely refer to changes in the Fed Funds rate than to the actual level of bank reserves. A rising Fed Funds rate is an indication that the U.S. central bank is making credit tighter by reduce the volume of reserves available for banks to lend to one another. A declining Fed Funds rate has the opposite implication.

The operation of monetary policy and the specific interest rates influenced by central bank policy differ from country to country. The basic objectives of monetary policy and the fundamental levers of open market operations, however, are the same in all industrialized countries.

Recall the fundamental economic forces that influence the supply of credit in an economy: the country's level of income, the population's propensity to save, and the country's attractiveness to foreign investors. We now see that a banking system can expand credit supply and that, by regulating this expansiveness, central banks can influence the rate at which household savings become loans to borrowers. This means we can add another element to the supply and demand diagram, as illustrated in Exhibit 8. With the demand for credit held constant, "easier" central bank policy increases the supply of credit, leading to lower interest rates and, therefore, to more borrowing. "Tighter" policy reduces the supply of credit, leads to higher rates, and curtails the amount borrowed.

WHAT DRIVES CENTRAL BANK POLICY?

Through open market operations or other mechanisms of monetary policy, central banks can increase or decrease the supply of credit in an economy and thereby influence the level of interest rates. For this reason, active participants in the fixed-income markets closely monitor central bank intentions. "Fed watching" is a time-old practice in the United States, and participants in the global markets will be examining the behavior of the new European Central Bank just as closely. Informed reading of the financial press requires some understanding of how central banks decide whether to ease or tighten credit conditions.

Exhibit 8: The Effects of Changes in Central Bank Policy

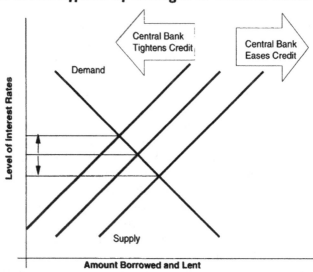

We begin with a central bank's fundamental policy objective. All central banks pursue two basic goals: steady economic growth, and price level stability. Unfortunately, however, these two objectives can be mutually contradictory. Statistical evidence from industrialized countries over the post-World War II period indicate that if an economy grows too rapidly for too long, to the point where the unemployment rate falls below some level, the inflation rate will rise. There is considerable disagreement as to what rate of economic growth is "too fast," what the non-accelerating inflation rate of unemployment or "NAIRU" is, what the lag in time might be between low unemployment rates and higher inflation, and to what degree all these relationships change over time.

These debates flared up with renewed vigor in the late 1990s when unemployment rates in the United States fell to 30-year lows while inflation essentially disappeared. Within any central bank at any given time, policymakers might be debating, for example, whether two years of real GDP growth in excess of 3.5% leading to an unemployment rate of 4.5% is sufficient reason to tighten monetary policy to head off an increase in inflation. Given these facts, and all the other economic and political considerations that need to be taken into account, the decision could go either way, and, once made, the decision could be right or wrong. Nevertheless, these are the economic indicators on which central bankers focus most closely.

Central bank officials get their information about the economy from the same sources as the general public: monthly or quarterly economic statistics indicating whether economic growth is accelerating or decelerating, whether the unemployment rate is rising or falling, and whether the inflation rate is increasing or decreasing. As an example of how the policymaking process works, let's return to the hypothetical policy debate about 3.5% growth and 4.5% unemployment.

While a central bank might be undecided as to how to respond to these conditions, new statistical releases indicating that growth was accelerating to 4.0% and the unemployment rate had dropped to 4.3% would likely resolve the debate on the side of tightening.

A staple of media reporting of fixed-income markets is to explain why news of strong or accelerating economic growth is treated as bad news for the bond market, while indications that the economy may be headed into recession is good news. The logic of this paradox should now be clear. Suppose the news comes over the wire that orders for durable goods placed with manufacturing firms increased sharply in the previous month. This would be good news for the economy, because it suggests that manufacturers will be selling more and looking to hire more workers. Yet, accelerating economic growth also makes it more likely that the central bank will feel called upon to tighten credit conditions in order to keep economic growth on an even keel. This will reduce the supply of credit in the economy, which, with the demand for credit held constant, will tend to increase interest rates. Higher interest rates mean lower bond prices. Thus, the headline: "Good News for Main Street, Bad News for Wall Street."

The logic also works in reverse. Suppose the news services report that total payroll employment in the country decreased by 50,000 the previous month. This would be taken as "bad news" for the economy, suggesting that economic growth might turn negative and the unemployment rate might rise. These trends, in turn, would worry the central bank and might lead policymakers to ease credit conditions. All else held equal, this would tend to reduce interest rates and increase bond prices.

Central bank actions can be inscrutable. It may not be obvious initially whether any given statistical release indicates that the economy is growing or slowing down. To get to central bank policymakers' "bottom line," it may be necessary to sift out the effects of special circumstances (e.g., a labor strike), unusual seasonal conditions (e.g., a mild winter), or changes in the way the government calculates certain economic statistics, but the objective of this analysis is always the same. The aim is to figure out whether the central bank will interpret new information as pointing toward a need for easier or tighter credit conditions.

THE YIELD CURVE

So far we have been discussing the determinants of "the general level of interest rates." Actually, however, there is no good single measure of the general level of interest rates. Lenders extend credit to specific borrowers for specified periods of time. Loans extended or bonds issued at the same time will bear different interest rates, depending on the term of loan, the creditworthiness of the borrower, and other considerations. The impact of borrower creditworthiness on bond yields is the subject of Chapter 10. For our purposes now, we want to focus on the relationship between bond maturity and bond yield. This relationship is referred to as "the yield curve," or the "the term structure of interest rates."

Exhibit 9: U.S. Treasury Yield Curve, July 1997

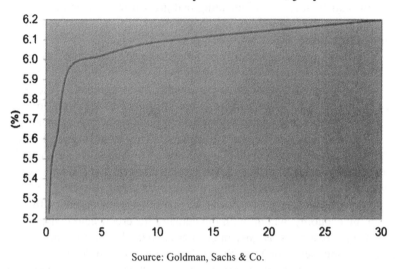

Source: Goldman, Sachs & Co.

Exhibit 10: Japanese Government Bond Yield Curve, July 1997

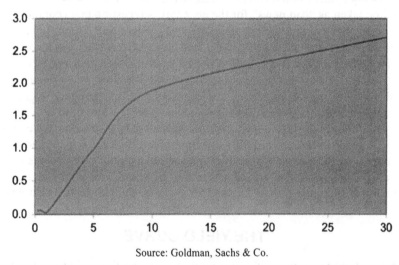

Source: Goldman, Sachs & Co.

Exhibits 9 and 10 depict the yield curves for U.S. treasury bonds (UST) and Japanese government bonds (JGB) on July 1, 1997. These curves are typical in that they are "upward-sloping" over all or most of their range; that is, yields generally increase with maturity.

The upward slope represents the typical shape of the yield curve. Occasionally, however, the yield curve will be "inverted," with yields declining with maturity over some or all maturity ranges. The yield differential between, for example, two-year and 30-year bonds can be used to represent the slope of the term structure as a whole. The history of this yield relationship for the United States is plotted in Exhibit 11. Most of the time, the yield on the 30-year U.S. Treasury is above that of the two-year. Occasionally, however, the two-year has the higher yield. Further, the spread between these two yields — "the slope of the yield curve" — varies over a wide range.

In Chapter 6 we will see how a change in the slope of the yield curve could affect the total return of a fixed-income portfolio even when the average "level of interest rates" remains unchanged. Such examples highlight the importance of understanding not only the forces that drive the level of rates, but also those that influence the slope of the yield curve.

Yield Curve Theory

Economists have developed several theories to explain changes in the shape of the yield curve. No one knows which, if any, of these theories is valid, but each of them provides insights into how fixed-income markets work that can be useful to a portfolio manager.

The first theory is referred to as the *expectations hypothesis,* which holds that the slope of the yield curve reflects market expectations about what bond yields will be in the future. Development of this theory begins with the assumption that the prices of any two securities must be such that the "marginal" investor (an investor who is completely indifferent between the two securities) expects the returns on these two securities to be equal over some horizon. If not, the marginal investor would buy the security offering the higher expected return and sell the security with the lower expected return until the prices reach levels where the expected returns are equal.

Exhibit 11: 30-Year and 2-Year U.S. Treasury Yields

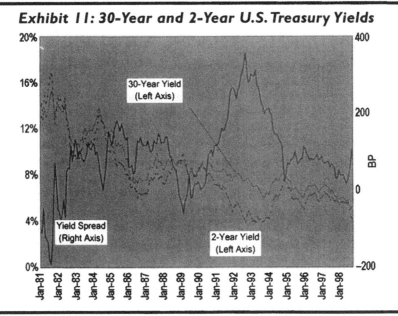

An example using two bonds will help clarify how this theory produces a yield curve. Suppose it is January 1, 2000, and the bond market includes many investors but only two bonds, both zero-coupon, one bond maturing on January 1, 2001, and the other maturing on January 1, 2002. Assume that the one-year bond yields 6.00% and the two-year bond yields 6.25% with initial market prices of 94.34 and 88.58, respectively. In other words, the two-period yield curve for this model world is upward-sloping. Finally, assume that all investors aim to earn maximum returns over a two-year horizon.

During the first year, buyers of the 2001 bond will earn 6.00% with certainty. The return on the 2002 bond over the first year is subject to some uncertainty because we don't know what the market price of this bond will be at the end of the year. We do know that the returns on the two bonds will be equal over the course of the first year if the market value of the 2002 bond is 93.90 (= 88.42 × [1.06]) on January 1, 2001. At a price of 93.90, the yield to maturity on the 2002 bond as of January 1, 2001, would be 6.50%.

Given these assumptions, on January 1, 2000, any investor who expects the yield of a one-year zero-coupon to be lower than 6.50% on January 1, 2001, would prefer to buy the bond maturing in 2002. Likewise, anyone who, as of January 1, 2000, expected the price of a one-year zero to be lower than 93.90 on January 1, 2001, would prefer the one-year bond. An investor who expects the one-year zero-coupon yield to be exactly 6.50% and its price to be exactly 93.90 on January 1, 2001, would be indifferent between the two securities. Therefore, according to this analysis, we can say that a 6.00% yield on a one-year zero and a 6.25% yield on a two-year zero reflects the expectation of the "indifferent" ("marginal") investor that one-year interest rates on one-year zero-coupon bonds will rise by 50 basis points over the next year.

As long as we assume that investors will buy whichever bond they expect to produce a higher return over any given horizon, this analysis could be generalized to reach the same conclusion about coupon-paying bonds or downward-sloping yield curves. Under this hypothesis, an upward-sloping curve reflects the expectation of the "marginal" investor that rates will rise in the future; a downward-sloping curve reflects the opposite expectations; and a flat curve reflects the expectation that rates will remain unchanged.

Fixed-income market analysts make frequent use of the expectations hypothesis. For example, after analyzing yields on yen-denominated certificates of deposit (CDs) with a range of maturities, an analyst might conclude that the market expects the Bank of Japan to tighten credit conditions, leading to a 100 basis point increase in three-month interest rates by the end of next year. Such insights can be very useful to a portfolio manager, but any conclusion about the direction of interest rates based solely on the expectations hypothesis are subject to two very important "warning labels."

First, market expectations as reflected in the slope of the yield curve are not always borne out. As Exhibit 11 indicates, the yield curve is almost invariably upward-sloping, but interest rates did *not* almost invariably go up between 1982 and 1997. Quite the contrary, in fact. Under the expectations hypothesis, the yield curve reflects market expectations about the direction of interest rates; the curve says nothing at all about the actual direction rates will take. Second, the expectations hypothesis is not the only widely accepted approach to analyzing the yield curve and explaining its slope.

A second theory on the yield curve is the *risk premium hypothesis,* or the *liquidity premium hypothesis.* This approach attempts to explain why the yield curve is generally upward-sloping. The longer the term of a loan, the greater the risk to the lender, in the sense that more things in the world can change over a long period of time than over a short period. For this reason, the difference between the yield on a 100-year bond and a one-year bond might reflect more than just market expectations about the yield on 99-year bonds one year from now. Entire economic systems can collapse over a 100-year period, and powerful nations and currencies can sink into oblivion. Investors advancing funds for 100 years may demand additional compensation in the form of higher yield, regardless of their expectations regarding the direction of interest rates over the foreseeable future. And, on the demand side of the credit market, borrowers may be willing to pay higher yields to avoid any near-term worry about access to credit markets for replacement financing.

Market analysts also make frequent use of the risk premium hypothesis. For example, after a period of geopolitical turmoil, a commentator might observe that the yield curve is likely to steepen as investors flee to quality.

The final approach to analyzing the yield curve is referred to as the *preferred habitat hypothesis.* This approach focuses on the fact that certain types of lenders, for reasons related to their specific investment objectives, tend to prefer certain bond maturities. For example, sponsors of employee retirement pension plans in industries with a large proportion of young workers might choose to buy very long-term bonds.

This hypothesis may be more useful in explaining certain anomalies in the shape of a yield curve than in analyzing the overall shape. For example, the yield curve for U.S. Treasury bonds usually has a "hump" at around 20 years the curve is inverted between the 25- and 30-year maturities. That is, even though the yield curve is generally upward sloping, 30-year bonds frequently yield less than 25 year bonds. This shape may reflect some of the unique features of the longest-term U.S. Treasury bonds as the most liquid, non-callable long-maturity security in the global capital markets.

Central Bank Policy and the Yield Curve

Under most circumstances, central banks regulate the supply of credit in an economy through open market operations that affect the interest rate at which banks lend reserves to one another. Most interbank loans are for very short terms; overnight transactions are the most common. Therefore, central bank policy has its most direct effect on short-term interest rates. Monetary policy also influences interest rates for longer-term loans and bonds, but the effect is less direct.

Central banks' influence on overnight interest rates in their home countries is most direct. Interest rates on loans that expire before the next regularly scheduled meeting of central bank policymakers are also affected directly by regulators' current monetary policy stance. Yields on loans and bonds that mature after the next policymaking meeting are affected both by the current level of rates on interbank loans and by expectations about whether the central bank will move to raise or lower these rates in the near future.

As the maturity of the loan or bond is farther out, the impacts of current central bank policy and expectations about future central bank policy diminish, and other influences assume more of a role. For example, investors buying bonds with maturities of ten or more years may be more concerned with the level of inflation in the distant future than they are with the direction of central bank policy in the near term. Yields on 10-year bonds will reflect expectations about central bank policy over the next year or two to some extent, but will also reflect beliefs about the direction of interest rates in the more distant future. Yields on longer-maturity bonds may also incorporate risk premiums of varying magnitudes and may reflect the specific requirements of investors for whom such bonds are a "preferred habitat."

In fact, yields on long-term bonds may move in the opposite direction from what expectations about central bank policy might lead one to expect. Suppose the economy is growing so strongly that investors begin to worry that higher inflation rates might lead to higher nominal interest rates in the future. Under these circumstances, the failure of the central bank to raise interest rates on short-term interbank loans to slow the economy could have the effect of exacerbating investors' worries, thereby *raising* yields on long-term bonds.

FINAL OBSERVATIONS

Building any investment portfolio requires judgments about expected returns and uncertainty regarding returns. For fixed-income investors, the distribution of returns in the future depends importantly on future changes in interest rates. We have discussed the main forces that influence the level of interest rates and the slope of the yield curve. These include the supply of and demand for loans, central bank policy, investors' expectations about future central bank policy, and so on.

The purpose of the presentation has *not* been to provide a guide for interest rate prognostication. Indeed, Chapter 7 will argue that, among the tools available to a fixed-income portfolio manager, interest rate forecasting should play, at most, a minor role. Recall that the purpose of fixed-income analysis is to help a manager anticipate the impact of economic and market events on portfolio performance.

Thus, the purpose of this chapter has been to empower a family portfolio manager to understand what is happening in fixed-income markets and how it will affect investments, not to predict what will happen in the future.

CHAPTER 5

Interest Rates, Bond Prices, and Portfolio Performance

I once knew a bond salesman who was very proud of the fact that his two-year-old daughter already knew the essentials of bond math. He would ask her, "What happens when price goes up?" She would cheerfully respond, "Yield goes down." "What happens when yield goes down?" "Price goes up." She knew all the possible permutations; you couldn't trip her up.

This two-year old's feat is indeed the essential fact of fixed-income mathematics; the rest is detail. The details involve answering questions like: "If a particular bond's yield rises by 10 basis points, how much will its price decrease?" Or "If interest rates along the U.S. Treasury yield curve decline by 25 bp, how much will the market value of my bond portfolio increase?" The answer to the more detailed question in all cases is, "It depends on the characteristics of the bond or of the portfolio in question."

AN EXAMPLE

To illustrate the essential fact of bond math and many of the details we begin with a very simple case and then elaborate. We start with the bond:

Evaluation (Settlement) Date:	February 15, 2000
Issuer:	U.S. Treasury
Maturity:	February 15, 2010
Coupon	6.00%
Par Amount	$100,000

Suppose an investor purchases this bond on the evaluation date at a price equal to par; that is, the present value of the coupon and principal payments on this investment discounted at 6.00% equals $100,000. Then suppose that yields on 10-year U.S. Treasury notes decrease by 50 basis points (0.50%) to 5.50% instantaneously.[1] In other words, the price of a 10-year Treasury note with a 5.50% coupon

---

[1] Treasury notes are one of three types of marketable securities offered by the U.S. Federal government. A more detailed discussion of these instruments appears in Chapter 9.

will now be 100.00, so a note paying a 6.00% coupon must be selling at more than par. Specifically, the market value of the 6.00% note will now be equal to the present value of the security's cash flows discounted at 5.50%, or $103,806 so that the note will now command a market value of 103.806. Yield goes down; price goes up.

Now suppose instead that on February 15, 2000, the same bond is quoted in the *Wall Street Journal* at a price of 98.375. The discount rate that produces a present value of $98,375 for this investment's cash flows is 6.221%, and this would be the new yield to maturity of the note. Price goes down; yield goes up.

That's the basic relationship. Now let's illustrate some of the details. Suppose all the characteristics of the bond remain the same except for the maturity, which will be set at 20 years.

Evaluation Date:	February 15, 2000
Maturity:	February 15, 2020
Coupon	6.00%
Par Amount	$100,000

Assume again that the yield on the bond instantaneously drops to 5.50%. In this case, given a 50 bp decrease, the bond's yield would lead to a price increase to 106.019. With a 20-year bond and a 50 bp decrease in the yield, we have a price increase of slightly more than 6%; with a 10-year bond with the same coupon and the same yield change, the price increase would be only about 3.8%. This comparison illustrates our first "detail": *All else held equal, the longer a bond's maturity, the greater the percentage price change for any given change in yield.* The actual numbers illustrate another point; although the maturity of the 20-year bond is twice that of the 10-year, the price of the longer bond does not increase twice as much as that of the shorter. That is, *the relationship between maturity and price sensitivity to yield changes is not linear.*

Now let's look at the impact of another bond characteristic, coupon, and its effect on price sensitivity to yield changes. Let's consider a 20-year bond with the initial characteristics.

Evaluation Date:	February 15, 2000
Maturity:	February 15, 2020
Coupon:	5.00%
Par Amount:	$100,000
Initial Yield:	6.00%
Purchase Price:	$88,442

Suppose again that the yield on this bond instantaneously decreases to 5.50%. If so, the dollar price of the bond would increase from 88.442 to 93.980. This would represent a market value increase of $5,538 on a position with an initial market value of $88,442, or a percentage increase of 6.26%. This compares with a 6.02% price increase for the same yield change on the 20-year bond with a 6.00% coupon. This illustrates the second "detail": *All else held equal, the lower a bond's coupon, the greater the percentage price change for any given change in yield.*

Finally, let's consider the case of a callable bond. To make the illustration a little simpler, we will assume that the yield curve is completely flat: Bonds of all maturities initially yield 6.00%, and after an instantaneous shift, they all yield 5.50%. Consider a bond as follows:

Evaluation Date:	February 15, 2000
Maturity:	February 1, 2020
Coupon:	5.75%
First Call Date:	February 15, 2005
First Call Price:	100.00
Par Amount:	$100,000
Initial Yield to Maturity:	6.00%
Purchase Price:	$97,110

Now suppose interest rates drop to 5.50% so that the price of the bond will be above 100.00. For an investor who purchases a bond with a coupon that is higher than current interest rate levels, the longer the security remains outstanding paying this high coupon, the better. Since the issuer has the right to call the bond at par and replace it with a lower coupon issue, however, investors should assume that, as a worst case outcome, the call will take place on the first opportunity. When all bonds are yielding 5.50% to their respective redemption dates, investors will be unwilling to pay a price higher than what will produce a yield of 5.50% if the bond is redeemed at par on the first call date: a yield to the first call of 5.50%. That is, the highest price that the bond might command would be 101.08, representing a 4.1% increase from the "preshock" level.

We saw previously that the price of a *non-callable* 20-year bond would increase by upward of 6% if interest rates decline by 50 bp. This illustrates the third "detail": *All else held equal, the price sensitivity of a callable bond to interest rate changes is lower than that of a non-callable bond with the same coupon and maturity.*

These examples illustrate how maturity, coupon, and call features all influence the sensitivity of a bond's price to yield changes. We have also seen that the relationship between price sensitivity and these three determinants is not linear. What's missing at this point is some useful way of measuring the price sensitivity to yield changes of any given bond or bond portfolio.

To meet this need, fixed-income analysts have developed two useful measures of bond and portfolio sensitivity: duration and convexity. These two concepts are the most commonly used tools of fixed-income portfolio management.

DURATION

Like many highly useful analytical tools, duration can be conceptualized in several different ways. In particular, the duration of a bond is:

- The percentage change in the price of the bond associated with a given percentage change in the yield on the bond, and

Exhibit 1: Cash Flows on a 10-Year 6.00% Bond

Period (A)	Date	Nominal Cash Flow (B)	Discounted Cash Flow (C)	Time Weighted Discounted Cash Flow (C × A)
0	1-Jan-00	0	0	0
1	1-Jan-01	6,000	5,660	5,660
2	1-Jan-02	6,000	5,340	10,680
3	1-Jan-03	6,000	5,038	15,113
4	1-Jan-04	6,000	4,753	19,010
5	1-Jan-05	6,000	4,484	22,418
6	1-Jan-06	6,000	4,230	25,379
7	1-Jan-07	6,000	3,990	27,932
8	1-Jan-08	6,000	3,764	30,116
9	1-Jan-09	6,000	3,551	31,963
10	1-Jan-10	106,000	59,190	591,898
Total		160,000	100,000	780,169

- The sum of the time-weighted discounted cash flows paid on the bond divided by the price of the bond.

The economist Frederick Macaulay first proved that these characteristics of a bond are related in the 1930s, and in his honor the concept defined in this way is referred to as *Macaulay duration*.[2] To illustrate Macaulay duration, let's return to a 10-year bond with a 6.00% coupon purchased at par for $100,000 on January 1, 2000. To make the example simpler, we have assumed that the bond pays annual interest rather than the semiannual interest typical of bonds in the United States. The cash flows produced by this bond are presented in Exhibit 1.

Column B lists the dollar value of the cash flows received every year. Column C shows these cash flows discounted to January 1, 2000, at the 6.00% yield on the bond. Thus, the first discounted cash flow of $5,660 equals $6,000 divided by 1.06; the discounted value of the second cash flow is $6,000 divided by 1.06^2, and so on. The last column weights these cash flows by the number of years until they are received. In this example the sum of the time-weighted discounted cash flows is $780,169, and we can calculate the Macaulay duration of the bond by dividing the sum by the price of the bond or $100,000. Thus the Macaulay duration of the bond is a bit more than 7.8.

The formula relating price change, yield change, and Macaulay duration is as follows:

[Macaulay Duration] × [Percentage Change in Discount Factor]
= [Percentage Change in Price]

---

[2] Frederick Macaulay, *Some Theoretical Problems Suggested by the Movements of Interest Rates, Bond Yields, and Stock Prices in the U.S. Since 1856* (New York: National Bureau of Economic Research, 1938).

Let's take this bond as an example. The duration of the bond is 7.80. The discount factor (1 + the initial yield) is 1.060. A 10% change in this discount factor would involve a yield increase (or decrease) of 10.6 basis points (0.106%). A 10% change in the discount factor on a bond with duration of 7.8 should translate into a 0.78% change in the price of the bond, and, indeed, the price of a 10-year 6.00% coupon bond at a yield of 6.106% is 99.22.

Modified Duration

Investors seldom think of percentage changes in discount factors; speaking in terms of absolute basis point changes is much more common. For this reason, an alternative expression, *modified duration*, is used more frequently than Macaulay duration. Modified duration is the percentage change in price associated with a given change in yield, and can be expressed as:

[Modified Duration] = [Macaulay Duration]/(1 + Periodic Yield)

The periodic yield is the same as the quoted yield for a bond paying an annual coupon; it is the quoted yield divided by two for a semiannual pay bond, and so on. In the case of our 10-year 6.00% bond paying an annual coupon, the modified duration is

7.36 = 7.80/(1.0600)

If we multiply this modified duration figure by a yield change of 10.6 bp, we get the same percentage yield change as in the previous example.

[Percentage Price Change] = 7.36 × 0.106% = 0.78%

A convenient way to understand modified duration is that it is the approximate percentage by which the market value of a bond (or portfolio) will change if interest rates change by 100 basis points, or one percentage point,. So in this example, if bond yields decline by 100 bp, this bond's price will increase by roughly 7.36%.

Some Applications

To see how duration can summarize information about the sensitivity of bond prices to yield changes let's return to the first three examples. The characteristics and durations of these three bonds are listed in Exhibit 2. Note that the Macaulay and modified durations of the 10-year 6.00% bond are slightly different from the numbers derived in the example above. That is because we have now switched to a semiannual interest payment schedule, the payment schedule most typical of bonds issued in the U.S., Japan, and the U.K. With semiannual payment bonds, the investor receives cash flows somewhat sooner on average, so the duration of a semiannual pay bond is a bit lower than that of an annual pay bond with the same maturity and coupon.

Exhibit 2: Durations of Bonds Evaluated on January 1, 2000

Maturity	1/1/10	1/1/20	1/1/20
Coupon	6.00%	6.00%	5.00%
Yield	6.00%	6.00%	6.00%
Macaulay Duration	7.662	11.904	12.372
Modified Duration	7.439	11.557	12.011

As the examples in the first part of this chapter led us to expect, the durations of the longer-maturity bonds are greater than that of the 10-year; although the 20-year is twice as long as the 10-year, however, the durations are not twice as great.

Further, the duration of the 5.00% 20-year coupon bond is greater than that of the 6.00% 20-year. Intuitively, this is because the principal payment at the end of the bond's cash flows accounts for a larger proportion of the bond's present value, the smaller the coupon payments. It is interesting to extrapolate from this coupon effect. The Macaulay duration of a zero-coupon bond is equal to the number of years to the bond's maturity and single cash flow. Thus, the Macaulay duration of a 10-year annually compounding zero-coupon bond, evaluated at a dollar price of 55.368 to yield 6.00% to maturity, is 10.00, and its modified duration is 9.43 (= 10/1.06).

The concept of duration can also be applied to callable bonds. Frequently fixed-income analysts speak of "duration to worst." For a bond trading at a price below par with a yield higher than its coupon, duration to worst is the duration calculated on the assumption that the bond will remain outstanding until maturity. For a bond trading above its first call price, duration to worst will be the duration calculated on the assumption that the bond will be called on its first call date.

To see how this might be applied, let's consider the example of a 20-year bond with 5.75% coupon callable at par in five years. If the bond's yield were 6.00% so that its price is below par, the worst-case outcome from the investor's point of view would be for the bond to remain outstanding to maturity. Thus, the bond's (modified) duration to worst is its (modified) duration to maturity, or 11.66. If the bond's yield declines to 5.50%, the investor's worst case would be for the bond to be redeemed at the first call date, and its (modified) duration to worst will be its (modified) duration to the par call in 2005, or 4.30.

This "duration to worst" approach to measuring the sensitivity of a bond's price to yield changes is of limited usefulness, particularly when one is looking at a single bond or a small number of bonds. One problem is that we are seeking a number that can characterize the sensitivity of a bond's price to yield changes. Here, however, we have two very different numbers for the same bond; one of them reflects the bond's price sensitivity to interest rate changes if it remains outstanding to maturity, the other if it is called at the first opportunity. It isn't clear which is the "right" way to characterize the interest rate sensitivity of this bond. To put it differently, the likelihood that any given bond will be called does not increase from 0% to 100% as soon as the market price rises above the call price.

A better measure of the duration of a callable bond would incorporate the fact that even if yields are low and the bond is trading at a premium price today, interest rates might rise before the call date and, if so, the bond will not be redeemed. So, even if the bond is priced at a premium, the duration to call may not be the right measure of the bond's interest rate sensitivity. Likewise, even if yields are high at present, it is not safe to assume that any given callable bond will necessarily still be outstanding after its call date.[3]

This initial discussion of the duration of callable securities highlights the fact that a bond's duration is not necessarily constant as interest rates change. A consideration of how a bond's duration changes as the market moves will help us understand the performance of callable bonds as well as several other interesting aspects of bond behavior.

How Duration Changes when Yields Change

The change in the duration to worst of a 20-year bond callable in five years and priced near par is a particularly dramatic illustration of the fact that, in general, the duration of a bond is not constant as its yield changes. Exhibit 3 illustrates the fact that the duration of a non-callable bond also changes as its yield shifts, albeit not as dramatically. For example, a non-callable 20-year bond with a 6% coupon priced at 144.874 to yield 3.00% to maturity would have a modified duration of 13.152, while the same bond if priced at 68.915 to yield 9.50% would have a modified duration of 9.735.

If we return to the basic fact that a bond's price is equal to the present value of its interest and principal payments and to the definition of duration, it is easy to see why this should be so. As bond yield decreases, the discounted value of each cash flow increases, but the discounted value of the later cash flows increases by more.

Consider the coupon payments on a $100,000 investment in a 20-year 6% bond. The discounted value of the first $3,000 semiannual coupon would be $2,913, if the bond's yield to maturity were 6%; and $2,955, if the yield is 3%. By contrast, the discounted value of the last coupon payment is $920 in the 6% yield environment and $1,653 if the yield is 3%.

Now recall that a bond's Macaulay duration is equal to the sum of the *time-weighted* discounted cash flows divided by the price. Price, in turn, is the sum of the *unweighted* cash flows. Since the numerator weights the later cash flows more, the numerator increases faster than the denominator, and the bond's Macaulay duration increases as the yield declines.

CONVEXITY

Notice the shape of the curve in Exhibit 3 that traces the price of the 6.00% 20-year bond as its yield changes. The line is not straight; it is bowed, or "convex". This

---

[3] Chapter 17 presents the methodology fixed-income analysts use to measure the "option-adjusted" duration of a callable bond.

"convexity" of the price yield curve — the convexity of the 20-year 6.00% bond — reflects the fact that the duration of the bond is not constant as interest rates change. Convexity is an attractive property for a bond. As the market rallies — that is, as interest rates decline — the duration of a convex bond will increase, and the bond's price will rise at increasing rates. Similarly, as interest rates rise, the duration of a convex bond will decrease, and the bond's price will decline at a decreasing rate. Thus the duration of a convex bond or portfolio of convex bonds will increase just when the investor wants it to and decrease just when the investor wants it to.

A bond's convexity is defined formally as the rate at which the bond's duration changes as interest rates change. Convexity can be either positive or negative. The duration of a bond with positive convexity will increase as the bond's price increases and decrease as the bond's price declines. Institutional investors may want to know the precise value of a bond's or a portfolio's convexity. For a family investor, however, it is more important to understand what makes a bond or portfolio convex and how convexity affects investment returns.

Bonds with very similar durations at their initial yield levels may perform quite differently if interest rates shift substantially. Consider, for example, the two bonds illustrated in Exhibit 4. Initially the two bonds have similar durations. If the yield on the two bonds changes by 10 basis points either way, the price changes on the two bonds will be nearly identical. Also, the positive percentage price change associated with a 10 basis point decrease in yields is slightly larger in absolute terms than the "downside" percentage change associated with a 10 bp increase in yields.

If yields change by 100 basis points, there is a much more marked difference between the performance of the two bonds; the coupon-paying bond outperforms the zero-coupon bond by more than 0.50% on the upside and underperforms by 0.20% on the downside. Again, however, for both bonds, the downside percentage change is smaller than the upside percentage change.

Exhibit 3: Prices and Yields of a Non-Callable 6.00% 20-Year Bond as its Yield Changes

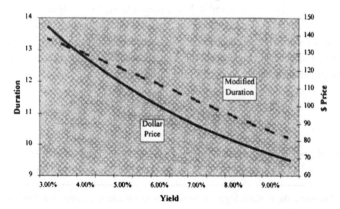

Exhibit 4: Performance Differences Between Bonds with Similar Durations

Settlement	1/1/00	
	Bond I	Bond II
Coupon	0%	6.30%
Maturity	1/1/10	5/15/15
Yield	6.00%	6.00%
Duration	9.43	9.42
Price	55.839	102.915
Price @ 5.90%	56.369	103.929
Percentage Price Difference	0.95%	0.98%
Price @ 6.10%	55.315	101.916
Percentage Price Difference	-0.94%	-0.97%
Price @ 5.00%	61.391	113.683
Percentage Price Difference	9.94%	10.46%
Price @ 7.00%	50.835	93.484
Percentage Price Difference	-8.96%	-9.16%

Exhibit 5: Prices of Callable and Non-Callable Bonds as Yields Change

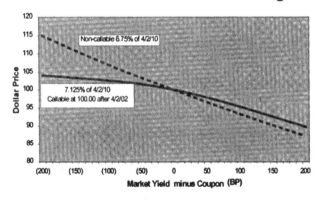

Thus, both bonds exhibit positive convexity; the percentage decline in price as rates increase is less than the percentage rise if rates drop by the same absolute amount. However, the coupon-paying bond is more convex than the equal-duration zero; its relative performance improves as interest rate moves get larger.

Callable bonds trading close to their call prices provide the most dramatic example of negative convexity. Exhibit 5 traces the expected prices as of January 1, 2000, of a hypothetical callable bond with a 7.125% coupon maturing on January 1, 2010. This bond is callable at par starting on January 1, 2002. The comparison security is a hypothetical non-callable bond with the same maturity and a 6.75% coupon. Both bonds are priced initially at par, and then the level of interest rates shifts upward and downward by 2.00% in 10 basis point increments. At each interest rate level, we estimate the market price of each bond. The results of these calculations are presented in the graph.

The price yield relationship for the non-callable bond — the dotted line in Exhibit 5 — has the same convex shape as the bond in Exhibit 3; as the price increases, the bond's duration increases as well. But the price yield curve for the callable bond is *negatively convex*; it is bowed downward. As this bond's yield decreases, its price increases at a *decreasing rate*; that is the bond's duration decreases as interest rates decline. Negative convexity is not a desirable characteristic because it always works against the investor. A negatively convex bond becomes less likely to be called, and it is therefore more exposed to interest rates just when the investor does not want it to be. It becomes more likely to be called, and therefore less sensitive to interest rate changes just when interest rates are declining, and the investor is wishing he had a longer duration security.

The fact that negative convexity, in and of itself, is not desirable does not necessarily mean that investors should avoid callable bonds. Note that the assumed coupon on the non-callable bond is 6.75% and that on the callable is 7.125%; both are initially priced at 100.00. This assumption reflects the fact that investors are usually compensated for purchasing negatively convex securities, and the compensation usually comes in the form of a higher yield on the callable bond than on the non-callable. As with most other things in efficient financial markets, selecting among negatively and positively convex bonds involves a trade-off. We discuss this trade-off in more detail in Chapter 7.

PORTFOLIO DURATION AND CONVEXITY

Information about the duration and convexity of individual bonds is useful to portfolio managers, but what really affects the investor's well-being as interest rates change are the *duration and the convexity of the portfolio as a whole*. In fact, the performance characteristics of individual bonds are important only to the extent that they affect the duration and convexity of the entire portfolio.

If we know the duration and the market value of each bond holding, it is easy to compute the duration of the portfolio as a whole. Portfolio duration is simply the weighted average of individual bond durations, where the weighting is based on each bond's market value. To illustrate this relationship, let's consider a portfolio consisting of equal par amounts of the first three bonds used as examples in this chapter. Exhibit 6 lists the performances of these bonds and of the portfolio as a whole, given 10 bp changes in interest rates.

The weighted modified duration of the portfolio is 10.3. Given an initial portfolio value of $288,443 and a yield change of 10 bp, the market value of the portfolio should rise or fall by a bit less than $3,000 (= 0.1% × $288,443 × 10.3), and the price changes of the individual bonds in fact sum to such a number.

Exhibit 6: Weighted Duration of a Three-Bond Portfolio

Bond	Par Amount (000)	Coupon	Maturity	Initial Yield	Initial Market Value	Mod. Dur.	Market Value +10 bp	Market Value –10 bp	Gain/ Loss +10 bp	Gain/ Loss –10 bp
1	$100	6.00%	1/1/10	6.00%	100,000	7.4	99,260	100,747	(740)	747
2	$100	6.00%	1/1/20	6.00%	100,000	11.6	98,854	101,165	(1,146)	1,165
3	$100	5.00%	1/1/20	6.00%	88,443	12.0	87,389	89,514	(1,054)	1,071
Total/ Weighted Average	$300	5.69%	7/13/16	6.00%	288,443	10.3	285,502	291,426	(2,941)	2,984

Exhibit 7: Equal-Duration Bullet and Barbell Portfolios

	Par Amount	Coupon	Maturity	Initial Yield	Duration	Purchase Price
Portfolio A	1,000,000	6.00%	01/01/10	6.00%	7.4	1,000,000
Portfolio B	1,257,971	0.00%	01/01/20	6.50%	19.4	350,000
	650,000	5.25%	01/01/01	5.25%	1.0	650,000
Total or Weighted Avg.	1,907,971	3.41%	08/26/07	5.69%	7.4	1,000,000

Just as two bonds with the same duration can exhibit different convexities, equal-duration portfolios will not necessarily be equally convex. We can illustrate this observation by considering two equal-duration portfolios (see Exhibit 7). These alternative types of portfolios are so common that they have their own names. A single-bond portfolio, or a portfolio consisting of bonds very close in maturity and duration, is referred to as a "bullet portfolio." A portfolio holding some low-duration bonds coupled with high-duration investments is called a "barbell portfolio." The example given here is of a particularly pronounced barbell in which the portfolio consists of some one-year securities and some 20-year zero-coupon bonds. It is, in fact, difficult to build a more "barbelled" portfolio.

We discuss the relative advantages and disadvantages of bullet and barbell portfolios in more detail in the chapters devoted to portfolio strategies. At this point, it suffices to show that the barbell portfolio is more convex than the equal-duration bullet.

This is illustrated in Exhibit 8, which traces the market values of the two portfolios as interest rates move up and down from their initial levels. As the graph indicates, the barbell portfolio is more convex; its market value rises more when interest rates decline and falls by less when rates rise.

Exhibit 8: Price Performance of Bullet and Barbell Portfolios as Interest Rates Change

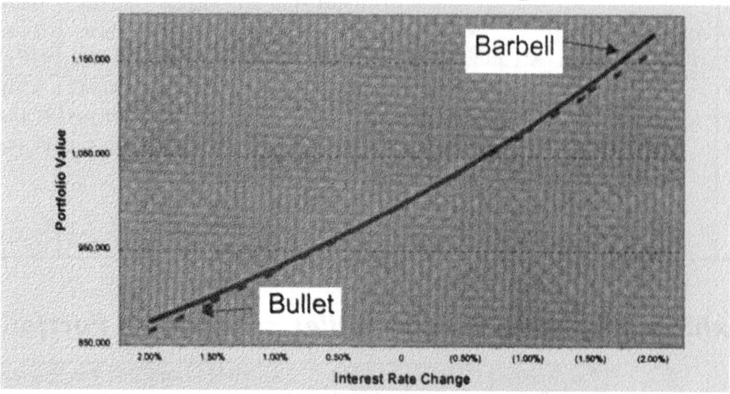

YIELD CURVE EXPOSURE

Duration and convexity are very useful tools for any bond portfolio manager. The manager of a family portfolio should always know what the duration of his or her portfolio is and by about how much its market value will change if interest rates move up or down by 50, 100, or 200 basis points. Decisions to buy or sell should always be made in light of how the addition or deletion of a particular bond will affect the overall characteristics of the portfolio. Yet, duration and convexity don't reveal everything about the risks and performance potential of a portfolio. In particular, the manager should keep track of the portfolio's exposure along the yield curve.

We have shown how two very different portfolios — a bullet coupon-paying bond, on the one hand, and a barbell of shorter-term notes and longer zeroes — could have the same durations but different convexities. These two portfolios also differ in how they respond to changes in the shape of the yield curve and to interest rate movements at different points along the yield curve. Some examples will illustrate how yield curve exposures can affect portfolio price changes.

Up to this point we have been assuming that when interest rates change they move by an equal number of basis points for bonds of all maturities. But this is not the way things usually happen.

Exhibit 9 tracks the history of yields on benchmark 2-year and 30-year U.S. Treasury securities from 1981 through 1998. The graph illustrates two facts about yield curve behavior. First, yields on the 2-year bond are more volatile than 30-year yields. During the final five years of the period represented in Exhibit 9, the yield on the 2-year ranges over 388 basis points, while the range for the 30-year is 300 basis points. Second, the slope of the yield curve is far from constant; over the full period depicted, the differential between 2- and 30-year yields ranges from as high as 357 basis points to as "inverted" as negative 88 basis points.

Exhibit 9: Yields on 2-Year and 30-Year U.S. Treasuries

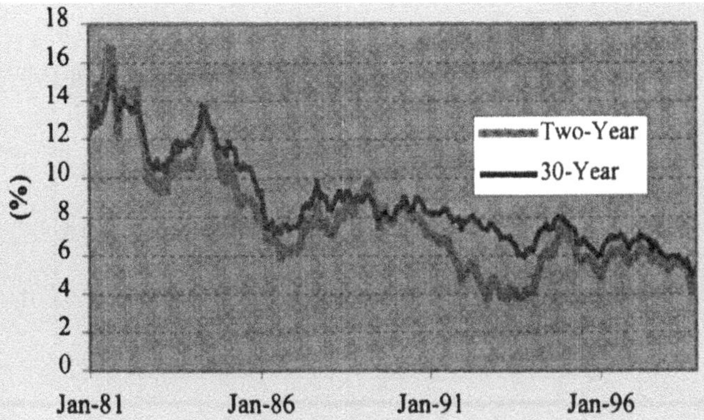

Source: Goldman, Sachs & Co.

Yield Volatility along the Curve

Both of these facts about the yield curve have implications for portfolio risk assessment. Consider first the relatively higher volatility of shorter-term bonds. We have already seen that bonds with longer maturities have longer durations; that is, the prices of longer-maturity bonds tend to change by more when interest rates change by any given number of basis points. Does this necessarily mean that longer-maturity bonds are riskier in terms of potential price changes than shorter-maturity bonds? The answer is: "Not necessarily."

To see why this is so, we make use of the concept of standard deviation. Between 1981 and 1998, the standard deviation of monthly yield changes for 2-year U.S. Treasuries was 47 basis points; that is, about 67% of the time yields on the 2-year Treasury at the end of any month were within 47 basis points, plus or minus, of where they had been at the end of the previous month. The corresponding statistic for 10-year Treasuries was 41 basis points.

Exhibit 10 compares the price changes on 2- and 10-year bonds that would be associated with one standard deviation yield changes. As the exhibit indicates, by this measure a 10-year bond is a bit more than three times "riskier" than a 2-year. A comparison of the durations of the bonds would have led to the conclusion that the 10-year was four times riskier. Further, if we had looked to an even more naive analysis of a bond's interest rate exposure, maturity, we would have concluded that a 10-year bond was five times riskier than a two-year.

Investors should draw two general lessons for this discussion. Extending a portfolio's average maturity or duration does not increase expected price volatility as much as a naive analysis might suggest. By the same token, shortening duration reduces potential price volatility, but not by as much as most "defensive" portfolio managers expect.

Exhibit 10: Impact of a One-Standard Deviation Yield Change on the Prices of 2- and 10-Year Bonds

Settlement	1/1/00		
	Bond I	Bond II	Ratio: Bond II
Over Bond I			
Coupon	0.05	0.06	
Maturity	1/1/02	1/1/10	5.0
Price	100	100	
Duration	1.9	7.4	4.0
Standard Deviation of			
Monthly Yield Changes	0.47%	0.41%	
One-Standard Deviation			
Price Change	0.9	3.0	3.4

The Slope of the Yield Curve and Portfolio Performance

Exhibit 9 indicates that the slope of the yield curve went through some substantial changes over the five-year period. The curve was very steep in 1992 and 1993. It then flattened substantially through 1994 until it was nearly flat by the end of that year; then it steepened somewhat, and finally remained stable through most of 1996 and 1997. Changes in the slope of the curve affect portfolio performance, and two portfolios of equal duration can perform very differently, depending on what happens to the shape of the curve.

To illustrate this point, we return to the equal-duration bullet and barbell portfolios. Assume that the yield on the bullet security remains unchanged in all scenarios, but that in Scenario A the curve flattens by 50 basis points, with the yield on the one-year note rising by 25 bp and that on the 20-year zero declining by 25 bp. In Scenario B the curve steepens by 50 bp, with the one-year yield declining by 25 bp and the 20-year yield rising by 25 bp. The price changes associated with these scenarios are presented in Exhibit 11.

The results illustrate one of the basic principles of fixed-income portfolio management. Barbells tend to perform better than bullet portfolios if the yield curve flattens and to perform worse than bullets if the yield curve steepens. This result makes common sense; in a flattening scenario, rates at the long-maturity end of the yield curve are declining by more or rising by less than yields at the short end or the middle of the curve. The barbell portfolio gives the investor more exposure to the part of the yield curve where yields are declining by the most or rising the least. Conversely, with a steepening curve, yields at the long end are increasing the most, and exposure to this sector of the yield curve hurts the relative performance of the barbell.

Exhibit 11: Bullet versus Barbell Portfolios: Market Value Changes in Steepening and Flattening Scenarios

	Par Amount	Coupon	Maturity	Initial Yield	Duration	Purchase Price	Flattening Scenario	Steepening Scenario
Portfolio A	$1,000,000	6.00%	01/01/10	6.00%	7.4	$1,000,000	$1,000,000	$1,000,000
Portfolio B	1,257,971	0.00%	01/01/20	6.50%	19.4	350,000	367,377	333,464
	650,000	5.25%	01/01/01	5.25%	1.0	650,000	648,440	651,566
Total or Weighted Avg.	1,907,971	3.41%	08/26/07	5.69%	7.4	1,000,000	1,015,817	985,030

CHAPTER 6

Currency Exchange Rates and Interest Rates

·······························

I nterest rate levels and interest rate changes are the primary determinant of how happy investors will be with their fixed-income portfolios. For many investors, currency exchange rates also affect fixed-income investment returns. In Chapter 3 we discussed the benefits of portfolio diversification; diversification allows investors to increase expected returns without increasing risk. One common way to diversify a portfolio is to include bonds denominated in something other than the investor's home currency. For this reason, a U.S. investor might buy a Japanese government bond denominated in yen, or an Italian investor might buy a Brazilian corporate bond denominated in U.S. dollars. Wealthy families in countries with small local bond markets may have no choice but to look abroad to build an internationally diversified fixed-income portfolio.

CURRENCY MATTERS

Portfolio returns are measured in the investor's base currency. British investors care about how many more pounds sterling their portfolios are worth at the end of the year than at the beginning. Thus, the total return on a portfolio that includes bonds denominated in more than one currency will depend on both the change in the price of the securities in terms of the currency in which they are denominated *and* the change in the relevant exchange rates over the measurement period.

For example, suppose that at the beginning of the year the exchange rate between Japanese yen and U.S. dollars is 135.00 ¥/$. Assume further that at that time a yen-based investor purchases the portfolio illustrated in Exhibit 1. Now suppose that by the end of one year the market yield on Bond A in the Japanese market has risen to 2.00%; the yield on the U.S. dollar bond has fallen to 5.00%; and the yen/dollar exchange rate has fallen to 120.00 ¥/$. If we make the further simplifying assumption that all coupon income is realized on the last day of the one-year period (or that interim coupon payments are simply held in non-interest-paying accounts), the portfolio's year-end value will be as listed in Exhibit 2.

As the table indicates, the net effect of interest accrual, local currency bond price changes, and the exchange rate change is to reduce the value of the portfolio from ¥283.217 million to ¥274.174 million, which translates into a return of −3.187%. The return has been affected by both the change in bond prices — a rally in the U.S. market and a sell-off in Japan — and the change in the exchange rate. In particular, the decline in the value of the U.S. dollar relative to the yen has substantially offset the price increase for the U.S. investment. Currency matters.

SELECTING A BASE CURRENCY

In most cases, the choice of a base currency is obvious; it is the national currency of the investor's primary residence. For a few wealthy international families with economic interests and residences in several countries the choice of a base currency will be more complicated. This may also be true of investors who live in small countries with underdeveloped capital markets. Most families who find themselves in one or the other of these situations will adopt one of the world's "big three" currencies as their base currency — U.S. dollars, euros, or, less frequently, Japanese yen. Occasionally families in very specific circumstances — a Saudi family with approximately equal business interests in Europe and North America, for example — will adopt two base currencies. In such cases, the investor might compute returns by comparing the average value of the portfolio in euros and U.S. dollars at the beginning of the year and the average value at the end.

Exhibit 1: Hypothetical Multi-Currency Bond Portfolio at Acquisition Prices

Bond	Par Amount (Millions)	Coupon	Maturity	Yield	Market Price	Local Currency Value (Millions)	Yen Value (Millions)
A	¥135	2.50%	6/20/07	1.532%	108.083	¥145.9	¥145.9
B	$1	5.50%	2/15/08	5.275%	101.708	$1.017	¥137.3
Total							¥283.2

Exhibit 2: Hypothetical Multi-Currency Bond Portfolio at Year-End Prices

Bond	Yield	Market Price	Local Currency Mkt. Val. (Millions)	Interest	Local Currency Value (Millions)	Yen Value (Millions)
A	2.00%	103.666	¥139.949	¥3,375,000	¥143.324	¥143.324
B	5.00%	103.541	$1.035	$55,000	$1.090	¥130.850
Total						¥274.174

Exhibit 3: Hypothetical Multi-Currency Bond Portfolio at Year-End Prices

Bond	Yield	Market Price	Local Currency Mkt. Val. (Millions)	Interest	Local Currency Value (Millions)	Yen Value (Millions)
A	2.00%	103.666	¥140.0	¥3,375,000	¥143.3	¥143.3
B	5.00%	103.541	$1.035	$55,000	$1.090	¥141.6
Total						¥284.9

SEPARATING INTEREST RATE RISK FROM CURRENCY RISK

Let's return to Exhibits 1 and 2 when the return in the Japanese investor's base currency was affected by changes in both the exchange rate and the interest rate. In particular, the price of the U.S. dollar bond rose by 1.80% in terms of its own currency. This price increase along with the 5.50% of coupon income translates into a total return in U.S. dollars on the original $1,017,080 investment of 7.18%. When the yen/dollar exchange rate decreases from 135 ¥/$ to 120 ¥/$, the loss on the currency more than offsets the gain on the price of the bond. The net impact of these two changes is a total return on the U.S. dollar investment in Japanese yen terms of −4.70%. Because the Japanese bond investment also lost money on the year, the result is a negative total return on the portfolio as a whole.

This result is not inevitable, even given the assumed changes in bond yields and exchange rates. The Japanese investor could have purchased the U.S. dollar bond at the beginning of the year without taking substantial currency risk; the investor could have *hedged* the currency risk associated with the position.

The Japanese investor, as in Exhibit 1, must buy US$1.017 million with ¥137.305 million at the beginning of the year. In Exhibits 1 and 2 this is the only currency transaction that took place until the end of the year when the portfolio is assumed liquidated. Suppose now that at the beginning of the year the investor enters into another currency transaction by agreeing to purchase yen with U.S. dollars 12 months in the future.

Such transactions are common, and, in fact, forward exchange rates for various currencies are reported daily in the financial press.

Let us assume for now that the investor can contract to buy yen for settlement in one year at an exchange rate of 130 ¥/$. Specifically, assume that the investor agrees to purchase ¥139,360,000 for $1,072,000 (= ¥139,360,000/130) for settlement at year-end, where the dollar amount is equal to the purchase price of the U.S. bond position plus interest income on that investment. Under these circumstances, and again assuming that the spot exchange rate at year end is 120 ¥/$, the results are as illustrated in Exhibit 3.

Everything in Exhibit 3 is the same as in Exhibit 2, except that the year-end yen value of the U.S. dollar bond position is ¥141.569 million in Exhibit 3 instead of ¥130.850 million. This difference has two components. At the end of the year the investor has US $1,090,000. Of this, $1,072,000 will be used to purchase ¥139,360,000 under the forward currency exchange agreement entered into at the beginning of the year. The remaining $18,000 will be exchanged into ¥2,160,000 at the year-end spot rate of 120 ¥/$. The effect of the forward purchase of yen is to convert what would have been an unhedged yen return on the portfolio of 3.187% into a hedged return of 0.60%.

Purchases of bonds denominated in non-base currencies provide two potential sources of risk diversification: performance differences among bond markets *in local currency terms* and exchange rate fluctuations. Both risk components provide diversification benefits. In this example, the U.S. dollar bond market rallied and Japanese bond prices declined, both in local currency terms, and the dollar depreciated against the yen. Returns are measured in terms of a base currency, however, and exchange rates tend to be relatively volatile, so a little bit of currency exposure can go a long way toward providing diversification; too much currency exposure can produce excessive volatility. For this reason, efficient portfolios frequently include investments in foreign bonds that are mostly, but not fully, currency-hedged. It may make sense for investors to leave some of their currency exposure unhedged. In Exhibit 3, the Japanese investor purchased yen one year forward with the full U.S. dollar value of the investment at year-end (assuming an unchanged bond price). An alternative might have been to purchase yen with, say, 75% of the anticipated year-end value of the U.S. dollar bond position.

The answer to the question "Should I add foreign bonds to my diversified fixed-income portfolio?" is unequivocal. For many investors, particularly for those who are not U.S. taxpayers, the answer is "Yes." The answer to the likely next question, "How much of the associated currency risk should I eliminate through a hedge?" is not so obvious. Selecting the right amount of currency exposure is as important a part of a portfolio manager's job as targeting the right level of interest rate and credit risk. Understanding the determinants of exchange rates is as important as understanding the dynamics of interest rates.

SPOT EXCHANGE RATES, FORWARD EXCHANGE RATES, AND INTEREST RATES

To understand the impact of exchange rates on investment returns, it is useful to begin by considering the relationships among spot exchange rates, forward exchange rates, and interest rates. The spot exchange rate between any two currencies is the rate at which one currency is exchanged for another with immediate settlement.

We begin with the observation that equally risky investments must produce equal returns. This is only approximately true, on average over time, in most financial markets. The market for short-term investments and short-term currency transactions, however, is as efficient as a market can be, and equally risky investments do, in fact, produce equal returns almost 100% of the time.

Compare two equally risky investments on the assumption that the initial spot exchange rate between U.S. dollars and U.K. pounds is US$1.6311 per UK£ (the value on March 6, 1998). The investments are as follows:

1. The purchase on March 6, 1998, of a 90-day £1,000,000 insured time deposit in global bank C at a yield of X%.
2. The combination of
   a. The purchase on March 6 of US$1,631,100 with £1,000,000 at the spot exchange rate.
   b. And the purchase on March 6 of a US$1,631,100 90-day insured time deposit in global bank C at a yield of Y%.
   c. And the sale for delivery on June 6, at an exchange rate contracted on March 6, of US$1,631,100 plus interest for UK£ at a forward exchange rate of US$$Z$ per UK£.

There are three unknowns in this example: the UK£ three-month deposit rate (X), the US$ three-month deposit rate (Y), and the forward exchange rate (Z). Because the market is highly efficient and the two investments will invariably produce the same returns, if we know any two of these we also know the third.

For example, suppose the UK£ three-month deposit rate is, as it closed on Friday, March 6, 1998, 7.578%. At the same time, the U.S. dollar three-month rate was 5.688%. At the spot exchange rate of March 6, UK£1 million could purchase US$1,631,100. At the end of 90 days the US$ deposit would be worth:

$1,654,294.24 = $1,631,100 \times [1 + (5.688\%/4)]$

and the sterling deposit would be worth:

£1,018,945.00 = £1,000,000 \times [1 + (7.578\%/4)]$

Since the two investments are equally risky, they must produce the same returns. For this to be so, the forward exchange rate between dollars and sterling on March 6, 1998, has to be:

1.6235 $/£ = $1,654,294.24/£1,018,945.00.

These calculations could be repeated with any two currencies and for any period of time. For example, suppose the one-year Japanese yen deposit rate is 0.692%, the one-year euro deposit rate is 3.75%, and the spot exchange rate is ¥115.38/€. The two investments following must produce identical euro returns:

1. €1,000,000 invested at 3.758% for one year, and
2. ¥69,650,000 invested at 0.70% for one year.

At the end of one year, the investments will be worth €1,037,580 and ¥70,131,978, respectively, and the one-year forward exchange rate that equalizes the returns is ¥67.5919/€.

By this method, we can calculate a series of forward exchange rates between two currencies for a range of dates in the future and use these forward rates to convert any set of cash flows from one currency into the other currency.

To illustrate this, we consider a two-year Japanese bond paying a semiannual coupon and "hedge" all the cash flows paid on this security into U.S. dollars. With information on yields of zero coupon investments in the two currencies, such as certificates of deposit, we can calculate the series of forward exchange rates for contracts entered into on April 1, 1998, listed in Exhibit 4. The calculations in the table illustrate how the yen cash flows on a two-year Japanese bond can be converted into U.S. dollar cash flows.

The return on the Japanese bond hedged into U.S. dollars will be nearly identical to that of a two-year dollar obligation of the same issuer if the two investments are held to maturity. If the two positions are liquidated before maturity, there is no guarantee that the sale proceeds will be the same. As we saw in the first example this will depend on what happens to bond yields in the U.S. and Japan in the interim. If, for example, yields in the U.S. rise, and yields in Japan decline, assuming no change in exchange rates, the investor would realize a gain on the Japanese position and a loss on the local currency bond. Indeed, the possibility that market values might move differently in different countries is the source of diversification in global fixed-income portfolios and one of the primary reasons for diversifying internationally on a currency-hedged basis.

For the three-month and one-year investments hedged into another currency, we said that the results of equally risky investments— one denominated in the investor's home currency and the other hedged into the investor's home currency— would be exactly the same. For the two-year investment, we now call the results "nearly identical." This is because the transaction costs associated with currency hedging rise as the forward term lengthens.

Exhibit 4: Cash Flows on a Two-Year Japanese Yen Investment Hedged Into U.S. Dollars

Date	Yen CD Rate	US$ CD Rate	Forward Exchange Rate Yen/$	Yen Cash Flows	US$ Cash Flows
Apr-98			128.0146	(100,000,000)	(781,161.08)
Nov-98	0.73%	5.77%	124.8830	390,000	3,122.92
Apr-99	0.71%	5.78%	121.8706	390,000	3,200.12
Nov-99	0.74%	5.81%	118.9240	390,000	3,279.40
Apr-00	0.83%	5.97%	115.8962	100,390,000	866,206.04
Yield				0.780%	5.834%

Investing in foreign currency-denominated securities on a hedged basis involves buying currency in the spot market and simultaneously selling that currency forward. Like any other market, the currency market has a bid-asked spread. This spread is very narrow for large ($1 million or more) transactions involving major currencies and settling a year or less in the future. The bid-asked spread for these transactions will not significantly affect the yield on a hedged fixed-income investment. For transactions involving more obscure currencies, of smaller size, or for settlement much more than one year forward, the bid-asked spread can become wider.

Now let's examine what happens to exchange rates when interest rates change. We will begin again with three-month deposits and the U.K./U.S. exchange rate. Recall that with sterling and U.S. dollar deposit rates of 7.578% and 5.688% and a spot exchange rate of 1.6311 $/£, the three-month forward exchange rate had to be 1.6235 $/£. Now suppose the Federal Reserve System acts to reduce short-term rates in the United States so that the three-month U.S. dollar deposit yield falls to 5.00%. At this point, the equations relating spot and forward dollar-sterling exchange rates no longer work. A bank could issue a U.S. dollar three-month CD, buy U.K. pounds with the proceeds, invest in a sterling three-month deposit, buy back the dollars at the three-month forward exchange rate of 1.6235 $/£, and make more than the cost of funds.

Such profitable risk-free investments should not be possible in an efficient market, and something must change. Unless the Bank of England changes its monetary policy, the sterling three-month deposit rate will not change. Therefore, either the spot or forward exchange rate between U.S. dollars and U.K. pound must change. Either (1) the forward rate would have to *increase* from 1.6235 $/£ to 1.6808 $/£; (2) the spot exchange rate would have to *decrease* from 1.6311 $/£ to 1.5755 $/£; or (3) some combination of the two changes must occur.

This discussion should show that exchange rates and interest rates are linked systematically and that changes in one almost invariably lead to changes in the other. It should also show that the relationship between interest rates and exchange rates is not simple. A decrease in U.S. interest rates, U.K. rates held constant, could lead to a decrease in the spot value of the dollar versus the pound, an increase in the forward value of the dollar against sterling, or some combination of the two effects. Which combination of outcomes occurs depends on why the Federal Reserve felt called upon to lower short-term interest rates; that is, on what else is going on at the same time in the U.S. and U.K. economies and financial markets.

THE MACROECONOMICS OF EXCHANGE RATES

Purchasing Power Parity

From time to time *The Economist*, a British weekly magazine covering business, economics, and politics, publishes a comparison of the prices of a McDonald's

Big Mac in various cities around the world quoted in both local currency terms and converted into U.S. dollars. The point is that the price of a uniform and freely traded commodity that uses about the same inputs wherever it is sold should be roughly uniform around the world. To put it differently, one would expect that exchange rates between various currencies and the U.S. dollar would reflect "purchasing power parity." That is, although there might be small differences in the U.S. dollar price of a Big Mac depending on differences in local rental prices for retail space or wages of high school students, substantial differences in the prices of the commodity should not be sustainable over time.

The Economist publishes its comparisons precisely because currency exchange rates hardly ever reflect purchasing power parity (PPP). In April 1996, for example, when the price of a Big Mac was US$2.36 in New York, the price in Germany, converted into dollars at the then-current exchange rate was $3.22. By 1999, the price was $2.43 in New York and $2.72 in Germany.

Economists differ as to whether international exchange rates tend to gravitate toward PPP as the "right" equilibrium rate. PPP believers would argue that if a Big Mac costs less in U.S. dollar terms in Tokyo than in New York, we should expect that the yen will eventually appreciate relative to the dollar.[1] Even analysts who expect such adjustments of exchange rates toward purchasing power parity acknowledge that any trend of exchange rates toward purchasing power parity can take a very long time. Further, adjustments in the "right" direction are as likely to overshoot the PPP target as to stop close to the right level.

This is not to say that analyses like *The Economist*'s Big Mac table are useless. Theoretical purchasing power parities provide useful information, but other influences that cause exchange rates to diverge from PPP substantially and for long periods of time are equally or more important for investors.

Exchange Markets and Exchange Rates

An exchange rate is a price — e.g., the price of a dollar in terms of yen or the price of a pound in terms of euros — and, like other prices, exchange rates are determined by supply and demand. Demand by residents of one country for another country's goods, services, and financial investments creates demand for a foreign currency.

The exchange market works like any other financial market; the dollar-yen exchange rate adjusts until U.S. consumers, firms, investors, and speculators want to exchange the same amount of their dollars for yen as Japanese consumers, firms, investors, and speculators want to exchange their yen for dollars. To illustrate how foreign exchange markets work, we will consider two simple scenarios involving changes in the exchange rate between U.S. dollars and Japanese yen.

---

[1] Analysts who use PPP to help predict exchange rate changes use much more sophisticated measures of purchasing power parity than the price of a single commodity. *The Economist's* Big Mac index is a caricature of much more sophisticated empirical concepts.

Scenario I: Suppose that, *all else held equal*, U.S. residents suddenly want to buy more Japanese goods and, consequently, seek to convert dollars into yen. For this to happen, Japanese consumers and investors must be willing to convert a like amount of yen into dollars. Since, by assumption, they are not inclined to do so at the *ex ante* exchange rate, the value of the dollar must depreciate relative to the yen, making U.S. goods or investments cheaper for the Japanese. Under these circumstances, the exchange rate might drop from 135 ¥/$ to 128 ¥/$.

Scenario II: Suppose that, *all else held equal,* Japanese investors suddenly decide to buy larger volumes of U.S. financial instruments and seek to sell yen and buy dollars. For this to happen, U.S. consumers and investors must be induced to purchase more Japanese-made goods or services or buy more yen-denominated investments. Since, by assumption, they are not inclined to do so, the exchange rate must rise — say, from 135 ¥/$ to 140 ¥/$ — to make Japanese products and assets less expensive for Americans.

The phrase "all else held equal" is emphasized in these scenarios for good reason; the mechanisms that influence bilateral exchange rates can be quite complex. If we combine the two simple examples — an increase in U.S. demand for Japanese-made goods and an increase in Japanese demand for U.S. investments — the net impact on the exchange rate might go either way. So an increase in the U.S. merchandise trade deficit with Japan will not necessarily lead to a depreciation of the dollar relative to the yen because the impact might be offset by increased demand from Japanese investors for U.S. dollar assets.

Despite oversimplification, these scenarios do highlight the macroeconomic variables that influence currency exchange rates. Changes in exchange rates reflect changes in:

- **Trade Balances:** If Country A consistently buys more from Country B than B buys from A, A's currency will tend to depreciate relative to B's.
- **Investment Flows:** If real expected returns on investment increase in Country A relative to expectations in Country B, A's currency will appreciate relative to B's. Therefore:
  - **Interest Rates:** If interest rates rise in Country A relative to rates in Country B, A's currency will tend to appreciate relative to B's.
  - **Inflation Rates:** If the rate of inflation in Country A rises relative to that of Country B, A's currency will tend to depreciate relative to B's.
  - **Economic Growth:** If the economic growth in Country A is expected to accelerate relative to Country B's growth rate, A's currency will tend to appreciate relative to B's.

Observation of these macroeconomic variables occasionally leads to unambiguous conclusions about the direction of exchange rates. If, for example, the economy of the United Kingdom were entering a recession, U.K. inflation is accelerating, real interest rates are declining, and the country is running a large trade deficit with the European continent, we would expect the pound to depreciate relative to the euro. Indeed, we would be very surprised if it did not. But the job of a currency forecaster is seldom that easy. More often, there is considerable uncertainty regarding all these variables, and the forecaster's best guesses as to the direction of each variable might point in different directions with respect to the sterling-euro exchange rate.

For example, consider a combination of circumstances:

1. U.S. economic growth is accelerating while Japan is sinking into a recession.
2. U.S. interest rates seem somewhat more likely to rise than to decline while Japanese interest rates are clearly headed lower.
3. Inflation in the U.S. may start creeping upward while Japan is experiencing price deflation.
4. The U.S. is running a large and increasing trade deficit with Japan.

Some of these circumstances would lead the dollar to appreciate relative to the yen; others would suggest dollar depreciation. Several of the circumstances are subject to uncertainty. So, under this combination of conditions, the dollar might appreciate, depreciate, or remain unchanged versus the yen. An exchange rate economist seeking to predict the direction of exchange rates would have to exercise judgment as to which influence will predominate. To make matters even more complicated, exchange rates, like interest rates, are influenced by government economic policy.

GOVERNMENT EXCHANGE RATE AND INTEREST RATE POLICY

On the most fundamental level, governments influence exchange rates by implementing good or bad economic policy. If the government of Country A adopts policies that lead to steady economic growth and price stability while Country B's government policies lead to boom and bust cycles and rising inflation, over time A's currency will appreciate relative to B's. Such basic economic policies should be the primary focus for forecasters and investors formulating a long-term outlook regarding currency exchange rates. Investors who fundamentally disagree with the economic policies of their own country's government should hold a substantial proportion of foreign assets and should probably *not* hedge the currency risk.

Governments seldom adopt consistently bad or consistently good economic policy. Consequently, most exchange rate analysis focuses on policies that effect shorter-term shifts in exchange rates.

Most government economic policy is aimed at managing domestic macroeconomic variables such as the Gross Domestic Product growth rate, the inflation rate, and the unemployment rate. Exchange rates are of interest only to the extent that they influence these fundamental measures of economic performance. Thus, if economic growth is slow, a government might try to stimulate an increase in exports by reducing the exchange rate. If foreign investors are fleeing a country's financial markets because the currency is depreciating, the government might try to stabilize the exchange rate. Governments also sometimes view exchange rates as economic policy objectives in and of themselves, taking a strong or stable exchange rate as a matter of national prestige or as an instrument of foreign policy.

More generally, highly volatile currency markets raise the cost of doing international business by increasing the time and resources devoted to exchange rate hedging activities. All major trading countries, therefore, have an interest in damping exchange rate fluctuations and in making sure that exchange rate changes take place in an orderly manner.

So governments may have good reasons to want to influence exchange rates. They can do so in two ways: (1) directly through intervention in the foreign exchange (forex) market, and (2) indirectly by manipulating other policy instruments. Direct intervention is possible because all governments maintain foreign exchange reserves. Usually these reserves are held by the central bank, although intervention in the forex market is usually undertaken upon direction by the country's political leadership. Thus, if the Japanese government wishes to support the yen against the U.S. dollar, the typical practice will be for the government to direct the Bank of Japan to use its dollar reserves to purchase yen through open market transactions with forex dealers.

Governments frequently intervene directly in currency markets in this way, particularly during periods of unusual exchange rate volatility. And such open market operations usually have the desired effect in the short run. That is, if the Bank of Japan starts selling its dollars and buying yen, the number of yen required to buy one dollar will likely decrease (the yen will appreciate) for two reasons. First, the additional increment of demand from the Japanese central bank could push the yen/dollar exchange rate slightly. Second, the yen might appreciate even more if market participants anticipate further BOJ open market buying of the currency. Market participants who anticipate such future central bank intervention might buy yen — and push down the exchange rate — in anticipation of being able to sell their positions at a higher price after forex intervention starts again.

The effectiveness of government intervention over longer periods of time is much less certain. Monetary authorities, particularly the U.S. Federal Reserve System, the Bank of Japan, and the European Central Bank (the "big three"), hold huge volumes of foreign currency reserves and can implement substantial open market operations for weeks on end. Even their combined resources, however, are dwarfed by the daily volume of private sector foreign exchange transactions. If macroeconomic and financial market conditions in a country militate strongly for currency depreciation, no feasible volume of foreign exchange intervention will be able to reverse the trend. Therefore, if governments wish to influence exchange rates effectively, they must do so indirectly by adjusting their key macroeconomic policy tools.

The most effective indirect tool available to policymakers for influencing exchange rates is the aggregate supply of the nation's currency — the money supply — made available. As we discuss in Chapter 4, central banks operate in domestic financial markets to expand or contract the reserves available to the country's banking system. The level of reserves, in turn, determines the aggregate volume of funds banks make available to firms and consumers in the economy. In Chapter 4 we saw how these open market operations can influence the level of short-term interest rates. Now we observe that changes in the aggregate volume of funds banks can lend will also change the supply of the country's currency available for exchange into other currencies.

Suppose the Bank of England begins selling U.K. Treasury bills on the open market, thereby reducing the level of bank reserves (the purchase price of the bills will be transferred from an account at the Bank of England). One effect of this "tightening" operation will be to raise short-term interest rates in the U.K. Now we see that the reduction in the volume of pounds sterling that U.K. banks are able to lend will also tend to increase the value of the domestic currency relative to that of other countries. Thus, the operation of monetary policy can (1) raise short-term interest rates in the domestic market; (2) increase the foreign exchange value of the country's currency; or (3) have a combination of both effects.

Indeed, the impact of monetary policy on interest and exchange rates is so closely intertwined that a central bank wishing to tighten monetary policy without increasing the exchange value of the country's currency will have to execute a combination of open market operations in domestic money markets and forex markets. Such combined open market currency operations are extremely delicate and may not be successful.

CHAPTER 7

Choosing the Best Structure for the Family Bond Portfolio

B uilding a bond portfolio is a "top-down" process. In this regard, investing in bonds is very different from investing in equities. In the stock market, the portfolio construction process begins when the investor identifies a collection of individual companies with good prospects whose stock is trading at attractive prices. At some point in the process, the investor will review this collection of prospective holdings from a portfolio point of view and decide whether the group of buy candidates is overexposed in, say, cyclical companies or insufficiently weighted in technology, but building a stock portfolio is very much a "bottom-up" process.

Fixed-income investors must also choose individual securities to buy, but, the choice of specific bonds, while very important, is much less crucial than in the equities market. There can be very substantial differences in the returns on the stocks of three different automotive companies such as Ford, Daimler-Chrysler, and Toyota, but any differences in the returns on five-year bonds of these three issuers are likely to be very small.

At the same time, while each of these corporations offers only one common stock to investors, fixed-income obligations of, say, Ford Motor Corporation may range from very short-term commercial paper to 30-year bonds. Some Ford bonds may be callable; some may not. Some may pay a fixed coupon, while others may pay a floating rate. With fixed-income investments, it may not be the identity of the specific issues that matters, but the overall characteristics of the portfolio: its duration, its convexity, its yield curve structure, and its average credit quality. That is why we characterize the building a bond portfolio as a top-down process.

We can synthesize the material introduced so far by showing how the concepts we have developed can be used to help define the right broad characteristics for a bond portfolio that will meet a family's needs. We focus first on the characteristics of portfolios of bonds all denominated in a single currency. Then we discuss the considerations involved in deciding how much international diversification is right for a family portfolio and, when fixed-income investment is denominated in other than the base currency, how much of the exchange rate risk to hedge. Chapter 13 provides material needed to take this process the next step, from the broad structural objectives for the portfolio to the selection of individual bonds.

DEFINING INVESTMENT OBJECTIVES

As in any decision making process, it is important to begin with a clear understanding of objectives. A portfolio manager's objectives can be stated broadly and vaguely or in very specific terms. The more precisely the goals are stated, the better the job the portfolio manager can do. Therefore, the best way to begin this synthesis is by discussing portfolio management objectives and how one can express them clearly.

Investors are frequently asked to state their goals. Many securities dealers go so far as to require registered representatives opening new accounts to ascertain prospective clients' portfolio objectives, and then offer only those investments that are consistent with these goals. Typically, however, the objectives listed in these exercises are stated in very vague terms. A ranking of such broad goals as "steady income," or "preservation of principal," may provide some indication as to what types of investments are patently unsuitable for a particular investor, but it provides little guidance in making decisions on the margin among the broad array of suitable alternatives.

Common Investment Objectives

Some of the terms investors use to express their objectives are:

Asset-Liability Matching

There are some circumstances, more common for institutional than for family portfolios, in which it is relatively easy to set investment objectives. If the investor knows he or she will need a certain amount of money at a certain point in time, the investment objective is, "Have X dollars on Y date." More broadly, the objective is to make sure that the assets (the investments) match the liability (the funding requirement).

Income

Income usually refers to the coupon payments on a portfolio of fixed-income investments, although the concept may also incorporate the price accretion of a bond purchased at a discount to par or the price amortization of a bond purchased at a premium. For example, the amounts of income produced by the bonds listed in Exhibit 1 might be interpreted as being the same or different, depending on the income concept used. In all cases, the bonds are purchased on January 1, 2000, at a purchase price of approximately $100,000 and a yield to maturity of 6.00% and mature on January 1, 2010. We are considering the income earned between January 1 and July 1, 2000.

Exhibit 1: Income Produced by Three Bonds with Equal Yield

Coupon	Price @ 6.00% 1/1/2000	Maturity Value	Purchase Price	Price @ 6.00% 7/1/2000	Accretion/ Amortization	Coupon Income	Total Income
5.00%	92.56	110,000	101,817	92.84	277	2,750	3,027
6.00%	100.00	100,000	100,000	100.00	0	3,000	3,000
7.00%	107.44	95,000	102,067	107.16	−277	3,325	3,048

This comparison highlights the importance of being as precise as possible in defining investment objectives. If "income" is a primary goal and the investor focuses on coupon income, then the preferred bond would be the 7.00% issue. At maturity, however, of the original $102,067 invested, only $95,000 would be left. An investor who focuses on coupon income and buys the premium bond will, in effect, choose to "eat into principal." So, focusing only on coupon income could lead to questionable decisions.

Preservation of Principal

This principal preservation objective is usually interpreted as directing that the market value of investments should not decline. Here, too, clarification is needed. Does this objective apply to each investment individually or to the portfolio as a whole? Does the directive to preserve principal mean that the investor does not want to buy bonds at a premium? Is any decrease at all objectionable, or only decreases in value greater than some predetermined amount?

Total Return

We discuss total return in Chapter 3. Total return is not fully specified as a portfolio objective unless the investor also indicates how much uncertainty or risk he or she is willing to tolerate. Otherwise, the portfolio manager would opt for the efficient portfolio with the highest expected return, which will also be the riskiest efficient portfolio.

Limiting Risk

The best way to specify a risk limit for a portfolio is to state a tolerance for loss; for example, investment objectives might specify: "I want to take no more than a 5% chance that my total return for the year will be negative." Or, "I'm willing to take a 10% chance of losing 5% or more of my investment on a mark-to-market basis over one year."[1]

It may not be pleasant to think about losing money on an investment, and no one builds a portfolio with the expectation of losses, but it is impossible to earn a real return higher than the yield on a short-maturity, inflation-indexed gov-

---

[1] The proper specification of a loss limit includes both an amount of loss (i.e., a total return of less than −X%), and a probability of realizing such a loss. Specifying a strict loss limit — for example, no chance of realizing more than a 10% loss — is a special case. Building portfolios consistent with a strict absolute loss limit requires either a a very low-risk portfolio or the use of derivatives.

ernment security without taking some risk of market value loss. Good investment decision making begins with the recognition of this fact.

Matching the Market

The popularity of indexation as an investment management tool grew out of a financial theory called the *efficient markets hypothesis*. According to this view, market prices at any time fully reflect the most accurate possible interpretation of all the information about investments available at that time. If so, the theory goes, no decision maker can outsmart the market by systematically picking investments that will perform better than others because no portfolio manager has any more or any better information than what the market as a whole has.

If this theory is correct, then efforts to pick and choose among investments are a waste of time, and the best thing for a portfolio manager to do is to buy a portfolio that is representative of all the securities available in a particular market. The success of such a strategy is measured by the degree to which the total return on the investor's portfolio matches the total return an index for the particular market. Here, too, further specificity is required because there are a range of market indexes among which to choose.

Beating the Market

Some investors believe that the efficient markets hypothesis is almost right in the sense that it is difficult to outperform a market index by a wide margin for a long period of time, but that there are occasions on which an astute portfolio manager can produce excess returns. If so, an appropriate investment objective would be some degree of outperformance of an index.

As with any directive to maximize returns, the investment objective should also specify a risk limitation. For example, an investor might say, "I want to exceed the total return on the Lehman Brothers Municipal Bond Index by as wide a margin as possible, but with no more than a 20% chance of earning one percentage point less than the total return on that index."

The Best Way to Define Objectives

None of these ways of defining investment objectives is perfect, but some of the alternatives are better than others in that the good ones provide the portfolio manager with clearer guidance as to which investments are most likely to produce the desired results. When a family is investing to meet a well-defined liability, the right investment objective is to match this liability. The precise goal is to minimize the chance that, when the obligation comes due, the value of the assets available to pay it off will fall short of the amount required. In the majority of cases, however, a family's future financial requirements will not be so clearly defined.

The primary advantage of market-based performance objectives — matching or beating a market index — is that it is easy to tell whether the goal has been achieved. This is why institutions frequently use indexation as a way of evaluating professional portfolio managers. For several reasons, though, indexed-based objectives are of limited usefulness as investment objectives for families.

For one thing, the composition of any broad market index is determined at least as much by the financing needs of the major types of obligors — governments, corporations, and so on. Therefore, the average mix of securities in a market may or may not reflect the investment needs of any families.

Second, a market portfolio will only suit the needs of a family whose objectives are the same as the goals of the "average" investor in the market. For a family that is much more or much less risk-averse than the average, the market portfolio may make little sense as a benchmark. In particular, early in a household's life cycle the family may have more tolerance for risk than the average investor in the market, while an older household may be more risk-averse. So a younger family might want to build a riskier portfolio than the market average, while the older family would want a less risky collection of holdings than the market average. The market portfolio, as reflected in a broad market index, wouldn't be appropriate for either investor.

This is not to say that a family portfolio manager should have no use at all for bond market indexes. The performance of various indexes does convey potentially useful information. For example, if the total return on the Salomon Brothers Broad Investment Grade Bond Index for a particular year is large and negative, no investor in the fixed-income markets should be particularly surprised if his or her own portfolio also produces a negative total return. Indeed, as we will see, it is difficult to apply our preferred way of stating investment objectives — risk-limited total return — without some reference to a market index.

Stating investment objectives in terms of income or protection of principal also suffers from shortcomings. Distinctions among coupon income, accretion of discount, amortization of premium, and market price change may not be particularly important, because all these items of income are interchangeable. Simple reinvestment can turn coupon income into an increase in portfolio market value, and increases in market value can turn into cash income if one sells or borrows against the appreciated assets.[2]

Defining investment risk tolerance in terms of protection of principal is subject to the same shortcomings; change in the market value of an investment portfolio is simply another component of total return. If, in a given year, the market value of an investment declines substantially, but the yield component of total return is very large, the portfolio manager can simply reinvest some of the coupon income and bring the "principal" value of the investment back to where it had been. This should be an acceptable portfolio management strategy, but it is unclear whether it is consistent with the goal of preserving principal value.

---

[2] Distinctions among various types of income can become important for tax purposes (see Chapter 11) or in illiquid markets where it might be expensive to cash in investment gains. While taxes and liquidity are important investment considerations, they are secondary considerations that should follow, not precede, a clear statement of investment objectives.

Exhibit 2: Hypothetical Monthly Portfolio Returns

Period	Total Return
1	5.4%
2	–0.7%
3	2.9%
4	6.1%
5	0.2%

Under these circumstances, the most effective way to state the investment objective is to define the goal as *maximum total return subject to a clear limit on tolerable risk*. For example, the goal might be to maximize total return but to incur no more than a 10% probability of realizing an annual total return of less than 0. All ways of stating investment goals are subject to shortcomings. Among the available alternatives, *risk-limited total return* is the least objectionable.

As an investment objective, risk-limited total return avoids the disadvantages associated with the other ways of stating goals. Total return encompasses the broadest definition of income, and avoids misleading distinctions between coupon income and price changes. Further, in contrast to market index-based objectives, each household can establish its own goals by specifying its tolerance for risk.

Risk-limited total return does have some important disadvantages as an investment objective. It is impossible to tell whether the goal has, in fact, been achieved in any single period. To see this problem, consider the series of hypothetical monthly portfolio returns in Exhibit 2. Suppose the investment objective for this portfolio is to maximize total return but to incur no more than a 10% risk of realizing a loss in any month. Now consider the first month. Is 5.4% really the highest return the investor could have earned that month while satisfying the risk limit? Or does the loss in the second month reflect a 10% probability or some higher level of risk? In both cases, it is impossible to know whether the right amount of risk is being taken or whether the realized return is the maximum that could be achieved.

This is a major problem; a performance objective is pretty useless if no one can tell whether or not it has been achieved. Yet while success or failure at achieving the goal of risk-limited maximum total return may be unverifiable in any one period, there are good ways of determining whether this objective has been achieved over a period of time. For example, suppose an investor who has targeted no more than a 10% risk of a monthly loss finds that his or her portfolio has experienced negative returns over three of the most recent 12 months. This would provide strong, but not necessarily conclusive evidence, that the portfolio manager is taking too much risk.

Bond market indexes can also prove helpful in this regard. An investor who targets a low probability of loss but who consistently realizes returns higher than the market as a whole should be concerned that too much risk is being taken. Conversely, an investor who is willing to accept a substantial degree of risk but whose portfolio consistently underperforms a market index may conclude either that not enough risk is being taken or that the portfolio is not efficient. By evaluating the portfolio frequently and by making use of information about returns on broad bond market indexes, an investor can deduce whether the portfolio is performing as it would if the investment objectives were being achieved.

Selecting a Return Horizon

So how long should a portfolio manager's investment horizon be? This general issue can be decomposed into two specific questions: (1) How frequently should the portfolio be "marked to market"? and (2) At what point should the investor decide whether the objectives have been realized?

The first question is somewhat easier to answer. Portfolios should be marked to market as frequently as is practicable, especially when markets are volatile, but in any case several times before the investor decides whether the investment objectives are being achieved. This guideline offers different specific answers to different investors. Daily, or more frequent, market valuations will be essential to an active trader aiming to earn short-term capital gains on a monthly basis. For most family investors, however, receiving information with such frequency will be a distraction. Standard practice in the securities industry is to provide investors with market valuations of their portfolios on a monthly basis, and for most families this should be sufficient. When fixed-income markets are particularly volatile, it may make sense for a family investor to request an interim market valuation.

The choice of an investment horizon — the length of time before the portfolio manager decides whether the objectives have been achieved — involves a trade-off. On the one hand, it takes time to determine whether a portfolio is achieving maximum returns while incurring no more than the stipulated level of risk. Very high returns relative to an index for one or two months may not necessarily indicate that too much risk is being taken. A sequence of two or three months during which the portfolio realizes losses, especially if broad market indexes are also experiencing losses, will not necessarily indicate that the risk of loss is greater than, say, 10%. This is why it is important to mark the portfolio to market several times before deciding whether investment goals are being met, and the more such observations the portfolio manager has, the greater the degree of confidence one can have in the conclusions.

If the portfolio is not meeting its objectives, the sooner the investor realizes this fact and modifies the investment strategy, the better. With monthly valuations, it is probably premature to draw conclusions about the performance of a portfolio with any degree of confidence in less than about one year. Yet it probably is not necessary to wait much longer than three years before deciding that the portfolio is not doing what it is supposed to do. So a reasonable investment horizon for a fixed-income portfolio that is monitored monthly would be somewhere between one and three years.

This is not to say that investors should wait at least one year before making adjustments in a portfolio. The goal of seeking maximum returns subject to a risk limit would call for more frequent portfolio shifts if the portfolio manager's expectations regarding expected returns or return variances or covariances change.

What, then, should a portfolio manager do if experience indicates that the investment objective is not being achieved? The ability to maximize total returns subject to a risk limit depends on how well the portfolio manager forms expectations about return distributions. For example, if the decision maker systematically underestimates the variance of asset returns over time, the portfolio will be riskier than the investor wants it to be, and losses will occur more frequently than anticipated. Or, a portfolio manager who systematically overestimates correlations among asset classes will not realize the benefits of diversification and will build portfolios that are more volatile than they need to be to achieve the expected returns.

In Chapter 3 we discussed three ways of forming expectations: analysis of historical data, forecasting, and inference from current market prices. None of these approaches is foolproof, and most portfolio managers develop expectations by using a varying combination of all three methods. When a portfolio consistently fails to behave as expected, the most likely reason is that the decision maker's expectations about asset returns have been off the mark, and the best remedy is for the portfolio manager to change his or her approach to forming expectations.

Two examples will illustrate the process. First, consider a portfolio manager who has been relying heavily on inference from current market prices to form expectations about the future, and who is willing to incur, say, a relatively high 25% probability of loss but who has been underperforming a broad market index for a long period of time. In such a situation, it might make sense for the portfolio manager to rely more on historical data or market forecasts to form expectations and adjust the portfolio accordingly.

The second example is more problematical. Suppose a highly risk-averse investor has been relying on economic forecasts to form expectations, has traded the portfolio very actively, and has earned a substantially higher total return than a broad market index for 10 of the last 12 months. It might be very difficult for such an investor to view this portfolio performance as a failure to achieve investment objectives. Yet it is highly unlikely that interest rate forecasts would be correct such a high percentage of the time, and the consistently higher returns provide *prima facie* evidence that too much risk is being taken. This investor would do well to rely less on forecasting ability and consider the implications of other ways of forming expectations.

Selecting the Desired Duration

Selecting the right duration for a portfolio is the most important, and usually the most difficult, decision a fixed-income portfolio manager must make. The decision does become easy if the portfolio manager is absolutely certain about the direction of bond prices; a convinced "bull" will buy the longest-duration portfolio available while the convinced "bear" will aim for the shortest duration possible, preferably overnight. Most of the time, however, most investors are uncertain about the direction of interest rates. One may believe that interest rates are somewhat more likely to rise than to fall, but opinions are seldom stronger than that.

The analytical framework presented in Chapter 4 provides guidance for decisions regarding duration in the face of the kind of uncertainty most portfolio managers face under most circumstances. The basis of the decision should be the portfolio manager's expectations regarding the distribution of future returns: expected returns, the standard deviation of the return distribution, and the correlations among the returns on different assets. For purposes of selecting a portfolio duration we need consider only expected returns and standard deviations.

To clarify the duration decision, we will limit the portfolio manager's choices to four maturity ranges of U.S. Treasury securities as listed in Exhibit 3. The exhibit lists the average yields on U.S. Treasury notes and bonds in these maturity categories as of the end of August 1997, the annualized standard deviation of monthly returns on these asset classes over the ten-year period preceding that date, the average durations of the securities in each category. The risk measure presented in this analysis is the risk of loss, i.e., the probability of realizing annual returns of less than 0. In this example, we consider three alternative estimates of expected returns: (1) a "neutral" scenario in which the yields on U.S. Treasury bonds are unchanged at the end of the one-year period, (2) a "bullish" scenario in which yields are lower by 25 basis points over the period, and (3) a "bearish" scenario in which yields rise by 25 bp over the period.

Exhibit 3: Expected Returns and Probabilities of Loss for U.S. Treasury Portfolios by Duration

Maturity Sector	1 - 3 Yrs.	3 - 7 Yrs.	7 - 10 Yrs.	10+ Yrs.
Yield 8/29/97	5.94%	6.20%	6.42%	6.66%
Return Standard Deviation	2.03%	4.33%	6.32%	8.84%
Duration	1.675	3.74	6.05	10.15
Neutral Scenario:				
Yields Unchanged				
Probability of Loss	0.17%	7.60%	15.50%	22.57%
Bullish Scenario:				
Yields Decline 25 bp				
Expected Return	6.358%	7.138%	7.933%	9.195%
Probability of Loss	0.085%	4.963%	10.488%	14.916%
Bearish Scenario:				
Yields Rise 25 bp				
Expected Return	5.520%	5.268%	4.908%	4.120%
Probability of Loss	0.322%	11.189%	21.889%	32.061%

Source: Goldman, Sachs & Co.

Exhibit 4: Probability of Loss by Portfolio Duration

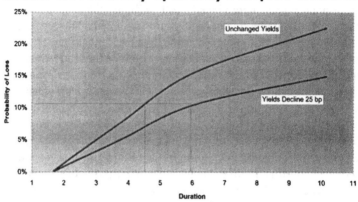

A quick look at Exhibit 3 leads to one immediate conclusion. With initial yields at these levels, a rational investor who anticipates an across-the-board 25 basis point increase in bond yields would buy bonds with the shortest durations. Under this bearish scenario, the expected returns on the riskier assets, the longer-maturity bonds, are lower than the expected returns on the less risky investments. Since the only reason to take more risk is to earn a higher expected return, there is no reason for a bearish investor to extend duration in this environment.

The neutral and bullish scenarios represented in Exhibit 3 do not lead to obvious conclusions about the right portfolio duration. In these cases, there is a trade-off between higher expected returns and higher return volatility. If the investor's investment objective is loss-limited total return, the portfolio manager should build a portfolio with the longest duration such that the probability of losing money does not exceed the specified level.

Exhibit 4 illustrates the results of this exercise.[3] The heavier lines track the relationship between portfolio duration and probability of loss under the two "problematic" interest rate scenarios. An investor who believes the "neutral" scenario and who wishes to incur no more than a 10% risk of loss would build a portfolio with a duration of about 4.4. Another investor with the same loss limit who believes the bullish scenario would opt for a portfolio duration of about 5.75.

It is important to be precise about what is being said here. Given the shape of the yield curve when the portfolio is purchased and the investor's belief that bond yields are most likely to remain unchanged, and assuming that the degree of uncertainty regarding returns will be the same as it has been over the previous ten years, a U.S. Treasury portfolio with a duration of 4.4 is the portfolio with the highest expected return that has no more than a 10% probability of realizing a return of less than 0 over a one-year period.

---

[3] For each maturity category of Treasuries, given the expected returns in the neutral and bullish scenarios and the historical standard deviations of returns, we calculate the probability that the one-year returns would be less than 0 using a standard normal distribution.

Exhibit 5: Two Hypothetical Bonds

Characteristic	Bond A	Bond B
Coupon	7.00%	5.75%
Maturity	January 1, 2010	January 1, 2002
First Call Date	January 1, 2001	Non-callable
First Call Price	100.00	Non-callable
Purchase Yield	6.00% to first call	5.75% to maturity
Purchase Price	100.957	100.000

There is no magic here. The portfolio will meet the investor's objectives only to the extent that the assumptions made in selecting the duration prove to be correct; that is, only to the extent that the investor's expectations are correct. The purpose of these tools is not to eliminate uncertainty. One purpose is to provide a systematic way to organize facts, opinions, and assumptions to produce investment conclusions. The other purpose is to avoid surprises. The investor who builds a portfolio with a 4.4-year duration should not be "surprised" at the portfolio's loss of value if, instead of staying the same, interest rates rise substantially. Nor should it be surprising that monthly losses on a 4.4-year duration portfolio occur more frequently than 10% of the time if the bond market is much more volatile than it was between 1987 and 1997.

Selecting the Desired Convexity

Callable bonds tend to perform relatively well in stable interest rate environments while non-callable bonds do better when markets are volatile. To see this phenomenon, compare the performance of two hypothetical bonds, purchased on January 1, 2000, as interest rates change. Exhibit 5 shows the characteristics of the two bonds. Bond A matures in 2010. Because its coupon is substantially higher than current market yields at the time the bond is purchased, however, the investor might safely assume that the bond will be redeemed in one year on its first call date. Bond B matures in two years, and, assuming no credit risk, it will remain outstanding to maturity.

Exhibit 6 plots the total return on the two bonds over a one-year horizon, given interest rate changes by the end of the period ranging from a decrease of 200 basis points to an increase of the same amount. The non-callable bond will produce a higher one-year total return unless interest rates are more than about 15 basis points lower by the end of the year.

Duration decisions are made on the basis of investor expectations regarding bond returns and the degree of uncertainty. Convexity decisions are based on investors' outlook with respect to volatility. An investor who expects markets to remain relatively stable over a period of time should feel comfortable enjoying the somewhat higher yields on callable bonds. A portfolio manager who expects markets to be volatile should probably build a convex portfolio, avoiding bonds that are vulnerable to being called.

Exhibit 6: Prices of Callable and Non-Callable Bonds as Yields Change

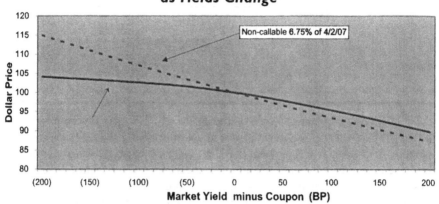

There is much more to be said on the subject of convexity of bond portfolios and the decision to buy callable or non-callable bonds. We discuss these topics in more detail and with more precise quantification in Chapter 17.

Selecting the Desired Yield Curve Structure

Portfolio managers can choose among three basic yield curve structures:

- *Bullets*: Most of the bonds in the portfolio have durations very close to the target portfolio duration
- *Barbells*: Most of the bonds in the portfolio have durations either much shorter or much longer than the target portfolio duration.
- *Ladders*: Bonds in the portfolio have a range of durations.

Three main considerations dictate the investor's choice of a portfolio yield curve structure: expectations regarding the change in the slope of the yield curve; expectations regarding market volatility; and portfolio liquidity requirements.

As with everything else involved with efficient fixed-income portfolio management, yield curve strategy involves a trade-off. Under some market conditions, barbells offer benefits over bullets, but these benefits usually come at the cost of a somewhat lower yield on the barbell. Exhibit 7 illustrates why this is so. This chart presents a curve of yields on bonds with maturities up to 30 years. A plot of yield against the duration allows us to compare the yields on bullet portfolios and equal-duration barbells. Any barbell is a linear combination of a short- and a long-maturity bond. In Exhibit 6 the straight dotted line (B) represents the yields on portfolios consisting of various combinations of 1-year and 30-year bonds. In all cases, because the duration yield line for bullet portfolios (A) is curved, the yield on a barbell will be lower than the yield on an equal-duration bullet portfolio.

Exhibit 7: Portfolio Yields by Duration

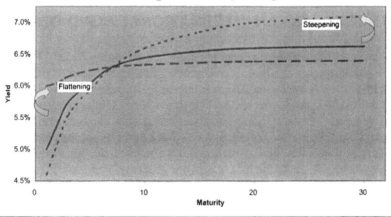

Exhibit 8: Flattening and Steepening Yield Curves

Reduced yield is the cost of a barbell. What is the benefit? One benefit is discussed in Chapter 5. The barbell portfolio is more convex than the bullet portfolio; that is, if interest rates move substantially in either direction, the total return on a barbell will be higher than that of the bullet, even though the durations of the two portfolios are the same and the yield on the former is generally lower.

The second potential benefit of a barbell is that it will do better than a bullet to the extent that the yield curve flattens over the valuation horizon. If the yield curve steepens, though, the bullet portfolio will likely produce a higher return than an equal-duration barbell.

This assertion makes common sense, as illustrated in Exhibit 8. Here are three curves with equal yields at the seven-year maturity. Suppose the solid line (A) is the initial yield curve and then over a period of one year the curve flattens and begins to look like the dashed line (B). Now compare two portfolios, (1) a single 7-year bond, and (2) a barbell of 30-year bonds and 1-year bonds with an average duration equal to that of the 7-year. In price terms, the barbell will do better. The price of the 1-year will not change at all because it matures at the end of the period. The price of the 30-year bond will increase, however, because, with the flattening, its yield is now lower. The price of the 7-year bond may change slightly even though the curve is fixed at the 7-year maturity, because at the end of the year it is a 6-year bond.

In most flattening scenarios, the barbell will outperform the bullet in price terms. The question is: Will the flattening be substantial enough so that this price outperformance compensates the investor for the lower yield on the barbell?

Just as a barbell has a tendency to perform well when the yield curve flattens substantially, bullet portfolios will do well when the curve either steepens or remains more or less unchanged. Ladder portfolios represent a compromise between bullets and barbells. Compared to a bullet portfolio, a ladder involves less yield give-up than a barbell, produces less benefit in terms of portfolio convexity, and generates less relative price performance in a flattening scenario.

STRUCTURING AN INTERNATIONAL BOND PORTFOLIO

We have said that building a bond portfolio is a top-down process. The first steps involve determining the best overall portfolio structure; selecting the individual securities is the last step. Building an international bond portfolio can be thought of as a *two-track* top-down process. The process is two-track because two types of decisions must be made. In track one, an international fixed-income investor must decide the right duration, convexity, and yield curve exposure for the portion of the portfolio invested in each national bond market. So, for example, a family with investments in both the U.S. dollar and euro bond markets might work through the considerations outlined in this chapter and decide to build a barbell portfolio with a duration of 5.0 years in the former and a bullet portfolio with a 3.5-year duration in the latter.

The second track involves currencies and exchange rate risk. International investments diversify risks in two ways. First, over any given period of time, the total return of different countries' bond markets, measured in local currency terms, can vary. Second, given any local currency performance, exchange rate fluctuations can affect returns in base currency terms. Thus, if the Japanese yen bond market turns in a large positive return in local currency terms in one year, but the dollar appreciates substantially against the yen, a U.S. dollar-based investor may experience a loss on unhedged investments in Japanese bonds.

Building an international portfolio involves two separate decisions: (1) how much to invest in each country's bond market, and (2) how much of the resulting currency risk to hedge. The first of these questions is dealt with in Chapter 13. Here we consider exchange rate hedging.

SIEGEL'S PARADOX

Exchange rate risk can enhance expected returns on a bond portfolio. A simple example illustrates why this is so. Suppose one-year bank deposits denominated in both U.S. dollars and Japanese yen pay 5.00%. Assume further that the dollar-yen exchange rate is 100 ¥/$ today and that in one year's time it will be either 80 ¥/$ or 120 ¥/$ with equal probabilities. An investor who purchases a one-year U.S. dollar deposit for $100 will have $105 at the end of the year with certainty. Alternatively, a dollar-based investor can purchase ¥10,000 today. At the end of the year, this investor will have ¥10,500 with certainty. This ¥10,500 will be worth either $131.25 (= ¥10,500 ÷ 80¥/$) or $87.50 (= ¥10,500 ÷ 120¥/$). Because these outcomes are equally probable by assumption, the expected value of the yen investment at the end of the year is $109.37 (= [$131.50 + $87.50]/2). This is higher than the certain outcome of $105. So a risk-neutral, or even fairly risk-averse, dollar-based investor would prefer the yen-denominated investment.

This conclusion may be odd in its own right, but the strangeness increases when we realize that under similar assumptions of equal percentage changes in the exchange rate the yen-based investor would prefer the dollar-denominated asset. Suppose the interest rate assumptions are the same, but this time assume that the exchange starts at 0.01 $/¥ and will be either 0.012$/¥ or 0.008$/¥ at the end of the year. The yen based investor can end the year with ¥10,500 with certainty or with either ¥8,750 (= $105 ÷ 0.0120$/¥) or ¥13,125 (= $105 ÷ 0.008$/¥). So the expected value of the dollar-based investment for the yen-based investor is ¥10,938.

Furthermore, investors are better off, the more volatile the exchange rates. Look again at the U.S. dollar-based investor, and assume now that the dollar-yen exchange rate will be either 50¥/$ or 150¥/$. Under these assumptions, the value of ¥10,500 at the end of the year will be either $210 or $70, and the expected value will be $140!

This collection of oddities is referred to as "Siegel's paradox" after the economist who first noted them.[4] Subsequent economic literature has demonstrated that Siegel's paradox is more than a mathematical curiosity; it has real significance for investors and financial markets. It would be a mistake, however, to draw too strong a conclusion from the simple example used to illustrate the general point that exchange rate volatility can enhance returns on non-base currency investments. The primary implications to take away are that foreign investments always promise higher expected returns than base currency investments, and the more volatility in exchange rates, the better. The more realistic the model used to analyze the situation, the more realistic and reasonable the results should be.

Even the most realistic analyses of international diversification reach the conclusion that adding a modest amount of unhedged foreign currency exposure

---

[4] Jeremy J. Siegel, "Risk, Interest Rates, and Forward Exchange," *Quarterly Journal of Economics*, May 1972.

to a portfolio that starts out 100% invested in the base currency increases expected returns and/or reduces expected return volatility substantially. At the same time, a realistic analysis concludes that too great an unhedged foreign currency exposure would probably lead to more volatility in base currency returns than most investors would want to tolerate.

What then is the "right" amount of unhedged currency exposure? As with everything else in the world of investments, there is no certain right answer to this question, although an article by Fischer Black does point toward a reasonable answer that has some theoretical justification.[5] Black shows that under reasonable assumptions about markets and about the average investor's tolerance for risk, investors as a group will hedge roughly 80% of their foreign currency exposure. Because the analysis that leads to this conclusion ignores such important considerations as market inefficiency, taxes, and regulatory impediments to international investing, it would be a mistake to apply this 80% number as a universal rule of sound investment policy.

In the absence of any better rule of thumb, however, it makes sense to adopt a number like 80% as reasonable compromise between too much foreign exchange rate risk in a portfolio and too little. Investors who hold international bond portfolios might start with this 80% figure and then modify it slightly in one direction or another, depending on their expectations regarding exchange rates in the near future.

For example, suppose a euro-based investor holds $5 million in U.S. dollar-denominated investments paying an average of 6.00%. The value of these investments at the end of the year will be about $5,304,500 (= $5,000,000 × $(1.03)^2$). To hedge 80% of the foreign exchange exposure, the investor might sell about $4,250,000 (0.80 × $5,304,500 = $4,243,600) one-year forward for euros. If the investor thinks that the dollar is likely to appreciate compared to the euro over the course of the year, it might make more sense to hedge only 75% of the currency exposure. If so, the forward sale might be for only $4 million. If the investor is bearish on the dollar (bullish on the euro), it might make more sense to hedge 85% of the future value of the dollar investments by selling about $4,500,000 forward.

CONCLUSION

Our aim has been to show how a family investor can make the most important decisions regarding a fixed-income portfolio: choices regarding duration, convexity, yield curve structure, and unhedged foreign exchange exposure. These decisions will be relatively easy for portfolio managers who have strong views about the direction of interest and exchange rates, the level of market volatility, and the slope of the yield curve in each national bond market. Investors without strongly held

---

[5] Fischer Black, "Equilibrium Exchange Rate Hedging," *Financial Analysts Journal*, July-August 1989.

opinions on these matters will generally want to gravitate toward the middle of the bond market, and then make modest adjustments in this middle-of-the-road portfolio to account for any feelings regarding return distributions.

A middle-of-the-road portfolio will have a duration between 4.0 and 6.0, the range of the average durations of the government bond markets in industrialized countries. When the investor perceives that rates are somewhat more likely to rise than to fall, portfolio duration might be targeted at the shorter end of this range.

A middle-of-the-road portfolio will include some callable and some non-callable bonds. To the extent that the investor expects markets to be relatively stable over the investment horizon (of about one year), a greater proportion of callable bonds will make sense. With respect to the yield curve, most of the time the portfolio should be structured as a compromise between a bullet and a ladder, with individual bond durations spread out over a narrow range around the target portfolio duration.

To the extent that the portfolio holds a large number of callable securities with market prices close to par, a bit more of a barbell structure might replace some of the convexity sacrificed to buy the callables. Also, to the extent that the investor thinks the yield curve is more likely to flatten than to steepen, a more pronounced barbell might make sense.

With regard to foreign exchange exposure, it is reasonable to view leaving 20% of non-base currency exposure unhedged as the middle-of-the-road approach. Leaving a bit more unhedged when the investor expects his or her base currency to do poorly in exchange markets would amount to a reasonable adjustment, as would hedging a bit more when the investor is bullish on the base currency.

In this way — beginning with a middle-of-the-road portfolio and making adjustments around the edges — an investor can home in on the structure that stands the best chance of meeting the family's investment objectives. Identifying the target portfolio structure is just the beginning of the process of building a portfolio. Next the portfolio manager must select real-world securities to buy in real-world markets.

Part II

CHAPTER 8

Sectors of the Bond Market: A Global Perspective

T he bond market is global in several senses. Some form of public market for negotiable debt instruments exists in almost every country of the world. Many bond portfolios include obligations of issuers in several different countries, and issuers routinely seek to borrow outside their domestic markets. As a practical matter, however, from the point of view of family investors, fixed-income investments divide themselves into two types:

- The mature bond markets, the fixed-income markets of the industrialized countries with freely convertible (or "hard") currencies.
- The emerging debt markets, the market for bonds of issuers domiciled in developing countries.

To some extent, the distinction between these two broad market segments is artificial. In the process of its economic development, a country crosses over into the mature sector. Further, there may be little difference from an investment point of view between the bonds of a strong double-B-rated Mexican corporation such as Pemex and a U.S. company with a similar credit rating. The history and the operation of the two market segments, however, are different enough to justify separate discussions.

The mature fixed-income markets include the bond and money markets of the European Union, Australia, Canada, Japan, New Zealand, Norway, Switzerland, and the United States.[1] In all these countries the central government, subnational governments, and private corporations issue negotiable debt instruments. Most issuance consists of local currency obligations of domestic governments or corporations, but there are important exceptions. For example, eurodollar bonds are U.S. dollar-denominated obligations issued outside the

---

[1] The EU countries include Austria, Belgium, Denmark, Finland, France, Germany, Greece, Ireland, Italy, Luxembourg, the Netherlands, Portugal, Spain, Sweden, and the United Kingdom.

United States, mostly in Europe, and *samurai* bonds are yen-denominated obligations of non-Japanese obligors issued in Japan. We will discuss these important exceptions later.

No one knows for certain how large the global bond market is. A reasonable estimate might be US$20 trillion. Both in terms of sheer magnitude and variety, the domestic U.S. bond market is the most important, as illustrated in Exhibit 1. It would not be unusual for an internationally diversified bond portfolio to include no U.K sterling-denominated issues or even no yen bonds, but it would be very surprising if such a portfolio included no U.S. dollar-denominated obligations.

THE EMU BOND MARKET

The Maastricht Treaty, an agreement among 11 western European countries to adopt a common currency, the euro, and to phase out their old individual currencies beginning in 1999, has created the second-largest bond market in the world. The ramifications of the European Monetary Union with respect to both the real economy and the financial markets are just beginning to work themselves out. Even before the EMU went into legal effect, 10-year French and Italian government bonds, for example, which had been very different securities in terms of price performance, had become nearly perfect substitutes. For the year 1992, the correlation between daily yield changes on benchmark 10-year French and Italian government bonds was 0.09; that is, they were nearly completely uncorrelated. By 1998, after monetary union became inevitable, the correlation was 0.95.

Exhibit I: Capitalization of Global Bond Markets by Currency

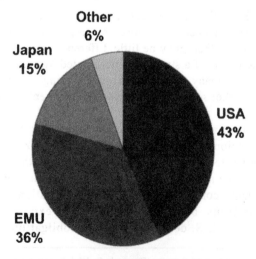

Source: Federal Reserve Board; Goldman, Sachs & Co.

Exhibit 2: Sovereign Credit Ratings of EMU Member Countries

Country	Moody's	S&P
Austria	Aaa	AAA
Belgium	Aa1	AA+
Finland	Aaa	AA
France	Aaa	AAA
Germany	Aaa	AAA
Ireland	Aaa	AA+
Italy	Aa3	AA
Luxembourg	Aaa	AAA
Netherlands	Aaa	AAA
Portugal	Aa2	AA-
Spain	Aa2	AA

Source: Bloomberg Financial Markets

The unification of 11 individual EMU domestic bond markets, each with its own peculiarities, into a single market will not take place instantaneously. Regularization of financial market practices over a fairly short period of time, however, is nearly inevitable. The political establishments of the EMU member countries — both the governing and major opposition parties — are all fully committed to making the union a success. As part of their efforts in this regard several have taken steps to conform their public debt operations to a common EMU-wide standard. Also, major securities exchanges in different European countries have merged. For these reasons, we can anticipate that within a few years a new EMU bond market will emerge with its own unique characteristics.

At this point the EMU market is evolving very rapidly. The eleven predecessor markets still retain many of their unique characteristics, but the unifying process has begun. We describe the market as it is today, but readers should be aware that our observations will likely become obsolete fairly quickly.

THE EMU GOVERNMENT BOND MARKET

It goes without saying that central government bonds offer the highest credit quality. Some EMU member countries carry credit ratings lower than triple-A (see Exhibit 2). In all cases, though, the 11 EMU member credit ratings are double-A or better.

Exhibit 3 summarizes the salient characteristics of the government bonds of the largest EMU members. Investors also need to be aware that withholding taxes may be imposed on interest income earned on government bonds.[2] Several years ago, such taxes were common among European government bond markets.

Although the government bonds of these countries are now much closer substitutes for one another than they were prior to currency unification, they will

---

[2] Withholding taxes are discussed more fully in Chapter 11.

not become indistinguishable. Investors will never become completely indifferent between holding, say, 10-year German Bundesanleihen (Bunds) or 10-year Spanish Bonos y Obligaciones del Estado (Bonos). What will become indistinguishable across countries will be the euro yield curve. It is likely that either the German or the French government bond markets or some combination of the two will emerge as the benchmark for the rest of the EMU member markets. In fact, yields on other government bonds and on euro-denominated private sector obligations are now quoted on a spread basis relative to the bund or Obligations assimilables du Trésor (OAT) yield curve. Thus, a five-year Belgian government bond might be offered for sale at a yield of 5 basis points over the five-year German or French government bond.

The shape of this euro yield curve will be influenced by all the same forces we identify in Chapter 3 as affecting yield curves in general: central bank monetary policy, expectations regarding monetary policy, inflation expectations, fiscal policy, and so on. Under the Maastricht Treaty, a single European Central Bank (ECB) oversees monetary policy. As in the world's other large currency union, the United States, inflation rates may differ slightly from region to region, but, also as in the U.S., EMU investors will likely overlook these regional differences in assessing the real (inflation-adjusted) returns on different assets.

Exhibit 3: Characteristics of Major EMU Government Bond Markets

Country	Payment Freq.	Government Issues	Coupon	Initial Maturities (Years)	Amt. Outstanding Euros, billions	% EMU Total
Germany	Annual	Bundesobligationen (BOBL)	Fixed	5	670	24%
		Bundesanleihen (Bunds)	Fixed	10		
		Bundesschatzanweisungen (Schatz)	Fixed	1–7		
France	Annual	Bons du Trésor à taux fixe et à intérêt annuel (BTAN)	Fixed	2–5	642	23
			Fixed	10, 20, 30		
		Obligations assimilables du Trésor (OAT)	Floating	10		
		Inflation-Indexed OATs				
Italy	Semiannual	Buoni Poliennali del Tesoro (BTP)	Fixed	3 - 30	586	21
		Certificati di Credito del Tesoro (CCT, BOT)	Floating	1 - 7		
Netherlands	Annual	Dutch State Loans (DSL)	Fixed	5 - 15	251	9
Spain	Annual	Letras del Tesoro	Fixed	1	251	9
		Bonos y Obligaciones del Estado (Bonos)	Fixed	3, 5, 10, 30		
Others					390	14
Total					2,791	100%

Source: Goldman, Sachs & Co.

Government bonds can play two important roles in family portfolios. First, because of their high credit quality and ready availability across a wide range of maturities, government bonds will constitute an important component of any large bond portfolio. An investor seeking to accumulate a position in seven-year euro-denominated bonds may or may not be able to find corporate issues that meet the requirement, but will be able to choose among a wide array of offerings in the EMU government bond market. Government bonds may also be the investment vehicle of choice for residents of non-EMU countries seeking to establish positions in this bond market.

Second, because of their liquidity, government bonds are the most effective trading vehicle for investors wishing to adjust the duration of their bond portfolios. Government bonds are not, however, the best vehicle for the majority of family investors who tend to hold individual bond positions for six months or more. For this investment purpose, liquidity is not a primary concern, and the additional yield offered by non-government bonds will usually enhance returns. Although the new currency union may encourage the development of a larger and more diverse euro-denominated corporate bond market, at present, investors seeking high-quality non-government fixed-income investments in the EMU market must look to bank obligations to fill their portfolios.

THE ROLE OF BANKS

Commercial banks play a particularly important role in continental European financial markets. Bank loans are the primary source of financing for corporations and local governments in Europe. The banking sector, in turn, raises funds in two ways: (1) by accepting deposits, and (2) by issuing debt instruments in the capital markets. Bank debt instruments constitute the bulk of private sector fixed-income obligations available in the European financial markets.[3]

Banks accept three different types of deposits: demand deposits (checking accounts); time deposits (savings accounts and non-negotiable CDs); and negotiable certificates of deposit (CDs). Purchasers of negotiable CDs have the right to sell these instruments to other investors before the stated maturity date. Thus, unlike demand and time deposits, CDs are a capital market instrument. Most CDs have terms to maturity of less than one year, but longer-term certificates of deposit also exist.

From an investor's point of view, deposits are the most secure obligations of commercial banks. In most industrialized countries, some bank deposits are secured both by the financial institution's assets *and* by a deposit insurance program operated and guaranteed either explicitly or implicitly by the central government.

---

[3] While bank bonds play a particularly important role in the European financial markets, much of our bank debt discussion also applies to obligations of banks in the U.S., the U.K., Japan, and other countries.

Commercial banks also raise funds by issuing a variety of fixed-income instruments that are not deposits and not protected by national deposit insurance programs.

Bank Regulation

As we saw in Chapter 4, the process by which banks transform deposits and other borrowings into loans is overseen by central banks such as the Federal Reserve System or the European Central Bank. Because banks borrow from and lend to each other so actively, unsound banks are a threat to a country's entire financial system. Banking system failures can lead to economic depression. Such systemic crises occurred repeatedly in the nineteenth century until the governments of industrialized countries stepped in and imposed standards of soundness as a precondition for receiving a banking license.

Among the standards banks must meet are a series of capital adequacy requirements. A bank is required to maintain capital at least equal to a prescribed percentage of the institution's assets. A bank's assets are the loans it has made and the securities it has purchased for its investment portfolio. The process by which different categories of loans and securities are added up to constitute a bank's total assets involves a complex formula in which loans made to and securities issued by different types of borrowers and bond issuers are assigned a variety of "risk weights." The specifics of this formula are of little interest to most family investors.

The definition of a bank's capital is also complex, but it is more relevant to family fixed-income portfolio managers than the formula for adding up assets. Regulators must ensure that some of the funds raised to finance lending and investing activities provide a bank a degree of flexibility in meeting its financial obligations. Deposits allow the bank no flexibility; banks must be prepared to meet any requests for withdrawals immediately in the case of demand deposits or exactly on schedule for time deposits or CDs. If a bank finances its lending and investments entirely by accepting deposits and then experiences losses on its loans or investments, any net withdrawals by depositors could lead to a bank failure. Similarly, if the bank finances itself partly with deposits and partly with bonds having definite maturities, the institution would risk default if it experienced losses on its loans or investments at the particular time principal payments on bonds are due. To be considered capital, a source of funds must allow the bank some leeway in meeting its obligations.

The simplest form of capital consists of the proceeds of public offerings of common stock. The bank owes no financial obligation to its stockholders; there is no maturity date on which principal is due, and bank directors can simply decide not to pay a dividend during a period of financial stress. Issuing new common stock to raise capital is costly for banking organizations; new stock issues dilute existing shareholders' interest in the institution and risk depressing the stock price.

For this reason, regulators do not require that banks meet their full regulatory capital requirement by issuing common stock. When they assess a bank's capital adequacy, regulators may also count certain types of fixed-income instruments issued by banks. Fixed-income capital securities provide the issuer with greater flexibility in meeting debt service obligations by providing fixed-income investors with less security than traditional bonds.

Senior Bank Obligations

Non-deposit fixed-income securities issued by commercial banks fall into several distinct categories.

Banks in all countries issue large volumes of senior *debentures*, traditional fixed- and floating-rate bonds issued in a variety of currencies with definite maturities. Interest and principal payments on these instruments are secured by the full financial resources of the bank. In the event of default, bondholders can force the issuer to stop doing business as usual and take whatever steps are legal and necessary to meet its obligations.[4]

Bank debentures may be denominated in the currency of the bank's home country, but large banks will generally issue such securities denominated in any major global currency, seeking out the market that offers the issuer the best deal on a currency-hedged basis. Of all of the non-deposit obligations of a commercial bank, debentures offer the most security to investors, carry the highest credit ratings, and offer the lowest yields.

One particular type of bank obligation, the *Pfandbrief*, has been unique to Germany, although German banks have begun to use this financial product in other EMU member countries. *Pfandbriefe* are obligations of commercial banks that are secured by pools of either home mortgage loans or loans to German governments. The market is huge by any measure; the DM1.3 trillion in *Pfandbriefe* outstanding by mid-year 1998 is roughly equivalent to the size of the German government bond market.

Each bank's issues of *Pfandbriefe* are collateralized by home mortgage or public sector loans on the institution's books. That is, interest and principal payments on a pool of specific home mortgages or government loans secure interest and principal payments on each specific *Pfandbrief* issue. The sufficiency of collateral is monitored by an independent trustee. Thus *Pfandbrief*-holders have a claim on both a pool of high-quality collateral *and* on the general financial resources of the issuing bank. Because of the collateralization and because the German banks that issue *Pfandbriefe* tend to be of strong credit quality in their own right, these securities are rated triple-A.

Typical maturities for *Pfandbriefe* range from two to 10 years. The securities always pay a fixed-annual coupon. Yields on *Pfandbriefe* tend to be only

---

[4] Bondholders have the right, under a court's supervision, to seize control of an industrial corporation that fails to meet its obligations under a bond indenture. The same is not true in the case of a commercial bank that defaults on debentures. Any post-default resolution of a bank's affairs will take place under the supervision of regulators, whose primary responsibilities are to protect depositors and to maintain the viability of the country's financial system. As with other corporate obligations, however, bank bondholders can prevent a defaulting issuer from continuing with normal business operations.

slightly higher than yields on German government bonds. For example, as of late 1998 the yield on the benchmark five-year German government bond was 4.20%; that of a typical five-year *Pfandbriefe* was 4.69%.[5] The largest issues of jumbo *Pfandbriefe* are also very nearly as liquid as German government bonds.

Bank Capital Securities

Because neither debentures nor *Pfandbriefe* provide the issuing bank with any flexibility regarding the timing or amount of scheduled payments, these securities are not considered capital instruments by regulators. The hallmark of a fixed-income bank capital security is that the bondholders *not* be able to force the issuer to cease normal operations. To put it differently, the security provisions accorded holders of bank capital instruments are weaker than those of debenture holders, and this is reflected in lower credit ratings on these securities and higher yields.

Several years ago, regulators in most countries began to count perpetual obligations, bonds with no final maturity, as a form of regulatory capital. In response, banks seeking to improve their regulatory capital ratios — a precondition for expanding their businesses — issued large volumes of *perpetual floating-rate notes* (FRNs). These notes generally pay quarterly coupons equal to LIBOR plus a spread.[6] As the name implies, the securities have no final maturity, although the issuing bank retains the right to redeem the instruments at some point after issuance. Most of the perpetual FRNs currently outstanding could be called at this point if the issuing bank chooses. Many of these notes are still outstanding, and they constitute a substantial proportion of the bank bonds outstanding in Europe. Most of the outstanding securities in this category, even those issued by European and Japanese banks, are denominated in U.S. dollars.

Initially investors anticipated that because these notes paid floating rates their prices would remain close to par. This turned out not to be the case. To illustrate what happened, suppose a bank with a strong Aa1/AA+ credit rating issued a perpetual floating-rate note paying a coupon reset semiannually at LIBOR + 12.5 basis points at par. Suppose that subsequently the bank's financial condition deteriorates, and its credit rating is reduced to A3/A- so that investors will no longer accept perpetual notes of this bank at a floating yield of LIBOR + 12.5 bp, but, instead, will demand LIBOR + 50 bp. If so, the price of this perpetual FRN will decline to about 94.00.

Such price decreases were frequent as the world's banking system suffered through the financial crises of the late 1970s and 1980s. Investors, stung by such unanticipated losses, withdrew from the market for these securities and the consequent shortage of buyers reduced the liquidity of the perpetual FRN market. Illiquidity further tainted the securities, because, with a perpetual security, the investor's only out is a bid from another buyer. Since these events, perpetual

---

[5] According to Bloomberg Financial Markets.

[6] The London Interbank Offered Rate (LIBOR) is the most commonly used index for short-term interest rates.

FRNs have tended to trade in an illiquid world of their own. The securities are plentiful, and the market occasionally offers opportunities to family investors who can hold portfolio positions for a long period of time and who are seeking investments with minimal interest rate risk but moderate credit risk.

The unpopularity of perpetual FRNs with investors led banks and regulators to develop alternative fixed-income capital securities, and two new structures appeared during the 1990s: *capital notes,* and *step-up perpetuals.*

Capital notes are fixed- or floating-rate notes with definite initial maturities of at least ten years. Two features distinguish these securities from traditional debentures. First, the interests of the owners of capital notes are subordinated to those of depositors and debenture holders. In the event that the bank is ever unable to meet all its financial obligations and is liquidated, depositors will be paid first, holders of senior debentures will be paid second, and holders of capital notes will receive whatever, if anything, is left. Capital noteholders would, however, be paid in full before any remaining funds are distributed to holders of the bank's preferred or common stock.

Second, the bank issuing capital notes retains the right to suspend cash coupon payments for periods of up to five years. During any such period, interest due on the notes will continue to accrue, however, and interest due on the instruments need not be paid in full until the final maturity date.

Regulators consider the proceeds received by banks from capital note issues to be capital because suspension of cash coupon payments provides the institution with flexibility in meeting its financial obligations during periods of financial stress.

The most recent innovation in the field of bank capital securities is the development of step-up perpetual FRNs. The original perpetual FRNs paid a coupon set at a constant spread over LIBOR forever. Investors do not like the lack of liquidity inherent in an instrument likely to remain outstanding indefinitely. The newer variety of perpetuals reflects an attempt to address this objection. The newer FRNs pay a floating coupon set at a modest spread to LIBOR for a predetermined period of years, after which time the coupon will step up to a much higher level.

For example, in March 1998 Sumitomo Bank issued a step-up perpetual FRN with a coupon initially set at Japanese yen LIBOR + 90 bp. Under the terms of the offering, the coupon will step up to LIBOR + 240 bp in 2008. At that time and thereafter, Sumitomo Bank will have the right to redeem the securities at par. The idea behind this structure is that, when the coupon steps up, the bank will have a strong incentive to redeem these notes and replace them with another, less expensive, source of equity capital. Of course this structure presupposes that in March 2003 Sumitomo Bank will consider Japanese yen LIBOR + 240 bp to be very high, and the instrument will be redeemed. If fixed-income capital instruments of Japanese banks are offering higher yields than yen LIBOR + 240 bp, the bank will decide to leave the notes outstanding. If so, the investor will, in effect, own a traditional perpetual floating-rate note paying what would, under these conditions, be a below-market coupon.

Clearly, bank obligations, which account for a substantial proportion of the non-government bonds available in the European markets, come in a number of different types. Some of these instruments are highly secure and liquid; a few, in fact, may in effect be guaranteed by central governments of industrialized countries. Others offer the investor much less security and very limited liquidity. Bank securities have an important role to play in family fixed-income portfolios. Even perpetual FRNs offer yields that are high enough to compensate for the risks and illiquidity associated with these securities, but investors who participate in this sector should understand the differences among alternative bank bond investments.

Exhibit 4 illustrates the variety of fixed-income securities issued by commercial banks by listing the outstanding obligations of Banque Paribas, a French institution. The securities include only the direct obligations of the Paribas home office; the numerous notes and bonds issued by Paribas branches outside France are omitted. The credit ratings on this one institution's obligations range from A2 to Baa1. Structures included both fixed- and floating-rate obligations and notes paying annual, semiannual, and quarterly coupons. The obligations are denominated in a variety of currencies with no particular bias toward the French franc.

Exhibit 4: Outstanding Obligations of Banque Paribas as of September 1, 1998

Coupon	Maturity	Composite Credit Rating	Payment Frequency	Call Provision	Currency
Floating	2002	A2	Quarterly	NCL	U.S. Dollar
Floating	2005	A3	Semiannual	NCL	U.S. Dollar
0%	2008	A2	Annual	NCL	Deutschemark
Floating	2012	A2	Semi-annual	Callable	Deutschemark
Floating	Perpetual	BBB1	Quarterly	Callable	U.S. Dollar
Floating	Perpetual	NR	Quarterly	Callable	U.S. Dollar
1.60%	2001	A2	Semiannual	Callable	Japanese Yen
3.90%	2001	A2	Annual	NCL	Deutschemark
5.75%	2007	A2	Annual	NCL	ECU
5.75%	2007	A2	Annual	NCL	French Franc
6.00%	1998	A2	Annual	NCL	French Franc
6.88%	2009	A3	Semiannual	NCL	U.S. Dollar
Floating	2010	A2	Annual	Callable	Austrian Schilling
Structured Note	2000	NR	Annual	NCL	Luxembourg Franc
8.00%	2004	Subordinated	Annual	NCL	Luxembourg Franc
8.13%	2002	Sr. Unsecured	Annual	NCL	Luxembourg Franc
8.35%	2007	A3	Semiannual	NCL	U.S. Dollar
9.13%	2000	NR	Annual	NCL	Luxembourg Franc
9.50%	1999	A2	Annual	NCL	French Franc
Variable	2009	A2	Annual	NCL	Italian Lira
Variable	2007	A2	Annual	NCL	Italian Lira

Source: Bloomberg Financial Markets

Exhibit 5: Makeup of the Japanese Bond Market

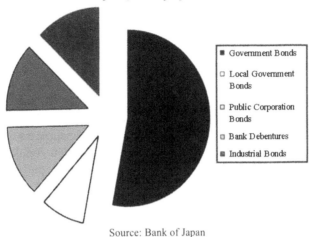

Source: Bank of Japan

THE JAPANESE YEN BOND MARKET

The Japanese yen bond market is the third-largest in the world after the United States and the European Monetary Union. This is not surprising, given the size of the Japanese economy and the Japanese government's policy of running substantial budget deficits. The Japanese bond market also offers a wider variety of types of obligations than the EMU market, although fewer than the U.S. market (see Exhibit 5). Central government obligations account for about 53% of the domestic Japanese bond market. Bank debentures account for only about 13% of the total, in contrast to the EMU, where bank obligations constitute the bulk of the non-government bonds in the market. In Japan obligations of public (government-owned) and non-financial corporations each also account for about 13% of the total. Local government bonds account for the remaining 9%.[7]

Despite the market's huge size and the variety of types of bonds available, the Japanese bond market has not been attractive to family investors. Personal investments of residents account for 20% of total holdings of Japanese common stocks but only 5% of domestic bonds. Non-Japanese investors play an even smaller role in this fixed-income market. Foreigner holdings account for about 12% of Japanese stocks and 4% of bonds, and the vast bulk of the latter are in institutional hands.

Several characteristics of the Japanese bond market account for the relatively minor role played by family investors. For non-Japanese, although purchasing Japanese government bonds is a relatively straightforward transaction during Tokyo business hours, the time zone difference is an important consideration; there are no overlapping normal business hours between Tokyo and New York

---

[7] Numbers total 101% due to rounding.

and very few between Tokyo and London. More important, however, both for Japanese and foreign investors, have been the extremely low yields offered by Japanese fixed-income securities. By late 1998 short-term bond yields had fallen below 0.50% and long-term yields below 2.00%. Under these conditions, direct, unhedged investments in Japanese bonds have not been attractive.

To be sure, purchasing Japanese fixed-income securities and hedging the cash flows into currencies of countries where interest rates are higher generally produces investments with competitive yields (see Chapter 6). Including currency-hedged Japanese bonds in a diversified international fixed-income portfolio can make a great deal of sense; the very insularity of the Japanese market enhances the benefit of such investments in terms of risk diversification. Yet diversification for its own sake is not particularly compelling for most family portfolio managers; to be worthwhile, foreign fixed-income investments must offer a reasonable likelihood of outperforming the household's home market on a total return basis.

As Japanese bond yields declined between 1989 and 1997, that market produced superlative total returns, as illustrated in Exhibit 6. The vast majority of portfolio managers, individual and institutional, who failed to participate in the Japanese market during the 1990s missed an outstanding opportunity. By the end of the '90s yields in Japan had fallen to such low levels that few investors believed they could decline any farther. With little prospect of further price appreciation in the Japanese bond market, most family investors are inclined to look toward more promising fixed-income sectors for diversifying investments.

OTHER NATIONAL MARKETS

The world's other mature bond markets — Canada, Australia, New Zealand, Norway, Sweden, Switzerland, and the U.K. — are much smaller than those of the "big three" individually and, indeed, collectively. Nevertheless, these markets do play an important role in many families' fixed-income portfolios. For one thing, individual investors feel most comfortable with bonds of their own countries. Thus, even though Australian government bonds amount to less than 0.6% of the global government bond market, these securities constitute a substantial proportion of the typical Australian family's fixed-income holdings.

Exhibit 6: Total US Dollar Returns of Hedged Investments in Five Government Bond Markets, 1990–1997

Country	Return
Germany	76%
France	86%
U.S.	95%
U.K	98%
Japan	119%

Source: Goldman, Sachs & Co.

In addition, several of these markets play a much larger role in non-residents' portfolios than one might expect looking just at their size. In fact, non-resident individual investments in these markets collectively probably exceed foreign households' participation in the much larger Japanese market. The reasons for non-residents' participation in each of these markets differ. For example, because of geographic proximity, Canadian bonds offer U.S. investors a relatively comfortable entrée into international fixed-income investments. The structure of the Canadian bond market and its operational conventions are also familiar to U.S. investors. As in the U.S. market, domestic Canadian issues include federal government obligations, provincial and municipal bonds, and corporates. And as in the U.S., Canadian bonds pay semiannual coupons and are issued with a wide range of maturities and structural features.

Because of geographic proximity, familiarity, and economic linkages, Australian and New Zealand issues are a natural foreign investment for wealthy families in east and southeast Asia. From time to time, European and North American families have also invested in Australian or New Zealand bonds, despite the time zone inconvenience, because yields in these markets have been much higher than yields available elsewhere in the industrialized world.

Swedish bonds are a particularly common holding in international bond portfolios both because the market is larger than the size of the Swedish economy would lead one to expect and because the Swedish government has made an effort to induce non-resident participation in its domestic bond market.

Finally, because the U.K. and Switzerland play a major role as financial centers, international investors naturally gravitate to these bond markets. Even though the local bond market is relatively small, it would not be surprising, for example, to find a Saudi Arabian family with substantial assets in Switzerland holding a proportion of Swiss domestic bond issues. The Swiss bond market has been dominated by corporate issuers, both Swiss and foreign.

Similarly, sterling-denominated bonds get more attention from international investors than the size of the U.K. economy would warrant. In the U.K. the government bond market, the "gilt" market, plays the predominant role, although there are also active domestic British corporate and mortgage-backed securities markets.

OFFSHORE BOND MARKETS

Most securities denominated in any country's currency are offered by issuers within that country and purchased by the country's residents. This is not always the case, however. The oldest and largest exception is the eurodollar bond market. Eurodollar bonds are securities denominated in U.S. dollars that are issued in Europe. The issuers may or may not be U.S. entities. The purchasers are generally, but not exclusively, non-residents of the United States. Typical transactions in this market would involve the sale of five-year, U.S. dollar-denominated bonds by the Ford Motor Corporation or Sumitomo Bank through the London offices of a syndicate of underwriters. The syndicate might consist of a combination of North American, Japanese, and European headquartered firms. The initial purchasers of the offerings might be a combination of European insurance companies, the asset management arms of several Swiss banks, and a number of European families. Eventually some of the securities might wind up in the portfolios of U.S. residents, both institutional and individual.

The impetus for the development of the eurodollar market, which began in the late 1960s, came from two directions. First, in the early post-World War II years, the U.S. ran substantial trade deficits with western Europe. This left European institutions and individuals holding U.S. dollars and looking for ways to put the funds to work in investments. One alternative might have been to use the funds to purchase U.S. securities within the United States, but at the time the tax treatment of investments held by foreigners in the U.S. discouraged this alternative. In particular, taxes were withheld on the investment income of foreigners on securities purchased in the United States. Laws passed around the same time began requiring registration and reporting of all investment holdings, which created a demand for unregistered, or "bearer," dollar-denominated securities outside the United States. Second, the process of issuing corporate securities within the United States under the jurisdiction of the Securities and Exchange Commission (SEC) was heavily regulated, and thus cumbersome and expensive for issuers. U.S. corporations began to look for ways to streamline the process of borrowing dollars on the capital markets.

Thus the Eurodollar market was a response to the demand of non-U.S. investors for dollar-denominated investments issued outside the jurisdiction of U.S. tax authorities and the desire of issuers for access to U.S. dollar-denominated financing unimpeded by U.S. securities regulation. What developed is a highly flexible, innovative bond market.

The offshore bond markets have outgrown these roots. Issuance is no longer confined to U.S. dollar-denominated securities. There are now euro-sterling, euro-drachma, and euro-euro issues. Nor is issuance confined to U.S. entities; all major global borrowers, including several U.S. government agencies, have issued bonds in the euro markets.

"Offshore" markets are not confined to Europe. Non-U.S. obligors, for example, frequently issue bonds in the United States. The purpose here is to enable companies like Toyota or ABN-Amro Bank to diversify their sources of funding to include the U.S. investor base and to provide American investors with a broader array of corporate credits. Non-U.S. issuers who do tap the U.S. market must comply with the full array of SEC regulations, including registration and financial reporting requirements. Bonds of non-U.S. issuers sold in the United States are referred to as *Yankee bonds*. An analogous market exists in Japan, where the securities are referred to as *Samurai bonds*.

Although the offshore markets do not fall under the direct supervision of any country's tax or regulatory authorities, this does not mean that "anything goes" in the eurobond sector. Issuers are constrained by general anti-fraud legislation; the fact that obligations are issued "offshore" will not immunize a corporation against civil liability to investors who purchased bonds on the basis of intentionally misleading information provided by the issuer. The issuer of eurobonds, however, is not required to prove to the SEC or some other regulatory body *before issuance* that the disclosure statement accompanying the securities issue is complete and accurate. Likewise, investors will not necessarily escape home country taxation of interest income simply because the bonds are bearer securities purchased outside the taxing jurisdiction. If a tax auditor discovers unreported income on eurobonds that is subject to taxation, the investor will have no escape. Issuers of eurobonds, however, are not required *proactively* to report the identity of owners to any authorities.

The offshore markets in general, and the euromarket in particular, are attractive investment venues for many wealthy families for two broad reasons. The first is the absence of tax reporting. In this regard, we must distinguish between tax evasion and tax avoidance. The former, failing to fulfill a legal requirement to report income to home country tax authorities and thereby evading taxes that are legally due, represents criminal behavior. No doubt some family investors purchase eurobonds for this illegitimate reason. Managing one's financial affairs, however, so that income earned will *not be subject* to taxation — tax avoidance — is a legal and legitimate economic activity. Municipal bond purchases by U.S. taxpayers represent a form of tax avoidance. For residents of some countries, moving assets offshore has a similar effect.

The tax treatment of assets held outside a taxing jurisdiction varies from country to country. In many cases, although taxes are due if home country authorities become aware of investment income earned, in general there is no enforceable legal requirement that taxpayers report income on assets held outside the home country. To deprive tax authorities of an independent source of information about bond holdings, many international families prefer to avail themselves of Swiss bank secrecy laws and to purchase bearer bonds in offshore markets.

The second reason many investors find the eurobond market attractive is the wide variety of bond issues available in this sector; an international family can meet all its fixed-income investment needs in the euro-bond market. In terms of credit quality, eurobond issues range from European central governments such as Germany and Spain down to speculative-grade corporate bonds. Both floating- and fixed-rate bonds are common. Eurobonds with maturities longer than 10 years are relatively uncommon, but this is more reflective of European investors' preferences; if buyers wanted 30-year eurobonds, issuers would gladly offer them. Almost all eurobonds are non-callable, but, again, this appears to reflect investor preferences.

Given these attractive features, it is not surprising that many non-U.S. families have bond portfolios of almost all eurobonds. U.S. residents may not participate in eurobond new issues; a dealer offering these securities to a U.S. resident would violate the registration requirements of the Securities and Exchange Act of 1933. At most times this restriction is irrelevant for U.S. investors; most of the issuers in the eurodollar market also offer bonds within the United States, and comparable bonds generally offer the same yield in the two markets. On occasion, though, investors may be able to buy a eurobond offering a slightly higher yield than a comparable U.S.-registered security.

U.S. residents are not completely precluded from taking advantage of such opportunities when they arise. The registration requirements administered by the SEC do not apply to secondary market transactions. The SEC considers sales and purchases that take place more than 90 days after securities are initially issued secondary trades. Thus, U.S. investors may purchase eurobonds about three months after the bonds first come to market.

EMERGING DEBT MARKETS

Issuers in the emerging debt markets include national governments, government agencies, and corporations domiciled in Latin America, Eastern Europe, the Middle East, East and Southeast Asia, South Africa, and Russia. Obligations issued and traded in this market fall into three categories: "Brady bonds," other hard-currency issues, and local currency issues.

All three types of emerging debt obligations share some general characteristics. Most important, emerging market bonds are riskier than most other fixed-income instruments. Broadly speaking, the risks associated with this sector of the market are the same as those affecting all fixed-income investments: default risk and market interest rate risk. In this particular market, however, these risks combine in ways that produce much more volatile returns than other fixed-income sectors and, indeed, more volatility than the returns of the equity market.

Most emerging debt issuers carry speculative-grade credit ratings below Baa3/BBB–. These low credit ratings reflect the underdeveloped condition of local economies. Specifically, the economies of many emerging market borrowers are highly dependent on single commodities or industries. If the price of the commodity declines sharply or if the key industry is affected by a global slowdown, the country's government might be force to choose between maintaining a minimally acceptable standard of living for its people and meeting debt service obligations. Most emerging market governments, when faced with such choices, have opted to default or, to put it more politely, to reschedule debt service obligations. Thus investors who have lent to emerging market borrowers have on occasion experienced substantial credit losses — realizing only a few cents on the dollar of loans — when economic conditions have turned adverse for borrowers.

Exhibit 7: 1997 Monthly Total Returns for Five Asset Classes

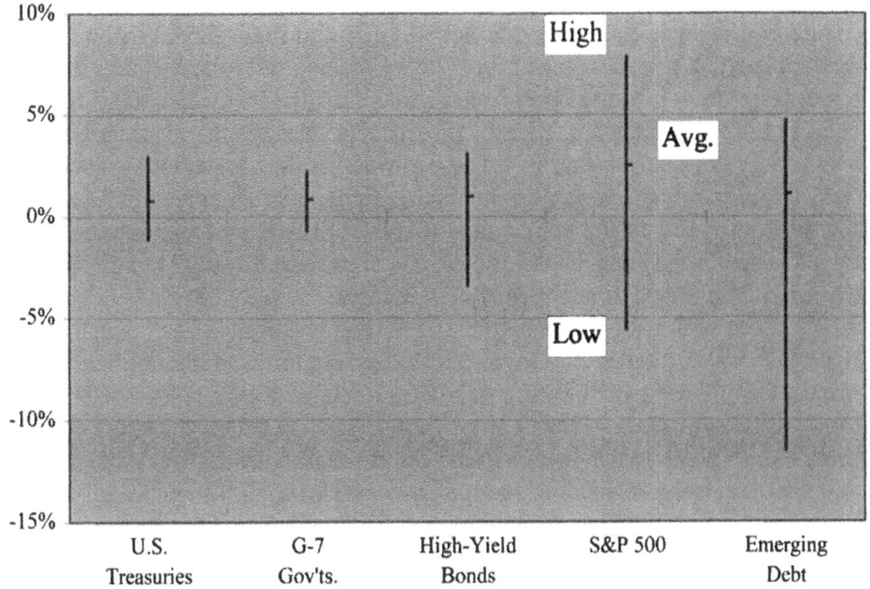

Source: Goldman, Sachs & Co.; J.P. Morgan

Interest rate volatility in the emerging debt markets is also accentuated. To illustrate this volatility, Exhibit 7 summarizes monthly U.S. dollar total returns for 1997 in five markets: U.S. Treasury bonds, G-7 government bonds (on a currency-hedged basis), high-yield bonds, S&P 500 common stocks, and emerging market bonds. Over the course of the year, emerging market bonds performed well by producing a total return greater than that of any of the other fixed-income sectors. The market is also, by far, the most volatile of the five.

Several characteristics of the emerging debt market other than its low average credit quality account for this volatility. The sector is attractive to a relatively small number of short-term performance-oriented investors. Short-term flows of funds into or out of the emerging debt market can be a substantial proportion of the roughly US$200 billion outstanding. In a relatively small market dominated by a small number of investors, slight shifts in sentiment can lead to huge shifts in prices.

BRADY BONDS

Emerging debt is not new. "Developing" countries began issuing bonds in the nineteenth century; at that time the United States was one of the emerging debt markets, and many a European investor was left holding worthless U.S. railroad or municipal paper in the wake of one of the repeated financial crises of the 1800s.

Emerging market debt in its current form began to develop in the late 1980s. In the decades prior to that period, most emerging market borrowers — sovereigns, agencies, and corporations — borrowed funds directly from commercial banks. The financial turmoil of the 1970s and 1980s left emerging market borrowers unable to meet their obligations in full and forced many sovereign debtors to renegotiate the terms of these loans. The volume of such borrowing was so large and the shortfall in the borrowers' ability to pay was so substantial that G-7 governments were called upon to intervene in the renegotiations. Part of the solution involved the conversion of some of the bank loans into marketable bonds. These new fixed-income securities are called "Brady" bonds after then-Secretary of the U.S. Treasury Nicholas Brady.

The structures of Brady bonds reflect their origins. One objective of the Brady plan was to attract new investors, beyond the commercial banks, to the market for emerging debt. In the wake of the financial crises of the 1980s, investors were skeptical about the ability of these issuers to meet debt service obligations. One way to place a floor under the market value of Brady bonds was to collateralize some of the debt service payments with highly secure investments. In particular, principal payments on many Brady bonds are secured by zero-coupon U.S. Treasury obligations held in escrow by a third party. Further, some interest payments are secured by funds held in escrow and invested in high-quality corporate obligations. Typically interest payments due over a period of between 12 and 18 months will be collateralized in this way. Even if an issuer fails to make any further debt service payments, the market value of collateralized Brady bonds should not fall below the sum of the market values of the collateral.

Not all Brady bonds are collateralized this way, so investors should be sure of the exact nature of the security for any particular instrument they buy. There are four main varieties of Brady bonds, and their characteristics are summarized in Exhibit 8.

The Brady bond program was successful in several respects. First, it alleviated the immediate financial pressure on several of the largest developing countries, freeing resources to devote to economic growth. Second, as a prerequisite for participation in the Brady program, developing countries were required to implement financial reforms under the supervision of the International Monetary Fund and the World Bank. These reforms have borne fruit in terms of greater financial stability and enhanced investor confidence.

Other Hard-Currency Issues

By creating a variety of liquid instruments with limited risk, the Brady Bond program succeeded in attracting new, non-bank investors into the emerging debt markets. These include insurance companies, pension funds, smaller individual investors through emerging debt mutual funds, and wealthy families. As the demand side of the market grew, the supply of securities also expanded beyond the original Brady bond structure.

Exhibit 8: Varieties of Brady Bonds

Type	Typical Maturity	Typical Coupon	Collateral
Par Bonds	25- – 30-year bullet	Below market rates	• Principal secured by U.S. Treasury zeroes. • 12-18 months interest secured by double-A-rated securities.
Front-Loaded Interest Reduction Bonds ('FLIRBs')	15- – 17-year bullet	Fixed coupon steps up over five to seven years. Then the coupon converts to a floating rate over LIBOR.	• No principal collateral. • Interest collateralized only during the step-up period.
Discount Bonds	30-year bullet	LIBOR + $^{13}\!/_{16}$	• Principal secured by U.S. Treasury zeros. • 12-18 months interest secured by double-A-rated securities.
New Money and Debt Conversion Bonds (DCBs)	15- – 18-year amortizing	LIBOR + $^{7}\!/_{8}$	None.

Source: Goldman, Sachs & Co.

After the completion of the initial Brady program restructuring of outstanding bank debt, several of the largest emerging market issuers began tapping the capital markets directly for new funds with offerings of fixed- and floating-rate debt across a range of maturities denominated in industrialized countries' ("hard") currencies. These newer issues, mostly issued in the eurobond market, are not collateralized. Most of the non-Brady emerging market issues are U.S. dollar securities, but a large minority are denominated in other hard currencies. Corporations domiciled in developing countries have also begun issuing hard-currency bonds through international capital markets.

The emerging corporate debt market is characterized by considerable variety in terms of maturity, coupon structure, currency, and issuer industry. The credit quality of emerging market corporate issuers also varies over a wide range, but Moody's and Standard & Poors will not assign a higher rating to a corporate issuer than its home country rating. Thus, in 1998 an Argentine corporation would not be assigned a credit rating higher than Ba3/BB–, the sovereign rating of Argentina.

Local Currency Bonds

International investors can purchase bonds denominated in the local currencies of several emerging markets. The most common type of local currency fixed-income security, and the variety most attractive to international investors, is short-term obligations of the central government. The governments of both Mexico and Brazil, for example, offer Treasury bills with a variety of short-term maturities on a regular basis. Local currency securities expose investors to two varieties of risk: credit risk and exchange rate risk. The reality of the credit risk involved in short-term local currency obligations of central governments was brought home clearly to investors in 1998 when the Russian government, in effect, defaulted on its ruble-denominated treasury bills.

In Chapter 6 we discussed exchange rates among hard currencies and how fluctuations in these rates affect international investments. International investors who purchase emerging market local currency notes and bonds also face exchange rate risk. While we assume that one currency can always be exchanged for another at the then-current market price, history has taught us that this assumption may not always hold true with respect to developing countries' currencies. Emerging debt market investors face the additional risk that the local government may limit or suspend the convertibility of its local currency, leaving the investor with an essentially useless investment. Chapter 6 also assumes that investors can reduce or eliminate currency risk by executing forward foreign exchange transactions. Forward foreign exchange markets do exist for a number of emerging market currencies, but these markets are much less liquid than those for hard currencies. Thus the technique of buying foreign currency-denominated bonds and hedging the exchange-rate risk may not be practical for emerging market local currency bonds.

EMERGING DEBT IN FAMILY PORTFOLIOS

As with most other types of bonds, emerging debt can play different roles in different families' fixed-income portfolios. For wealthy residents of developing countries, emerging debt may constitute the bulk of the family's bond holdings. Just as a New Zealand family might be expected to hold a large proportion of New Zealand bonds and make its initial foray into international investing by buying Australian paper, a Brazilian family would be likely to invest heavily in both real- and U.S. dollar-denominated issues of their national government and local companies, and to diversify initially perhaps into Argentine bonds. To be sure, the incentive to move funds abroad by investing in foreign issues may be particularly strong for residents of countries with volatile economies and political systems. Thus, a Brazilian family might tend to hold a greater proportion of foreign bonds than an Australian family. "Home market bias," though, affects residents of all countries.

Emerging debt plays a very different role for residents of industrialized countries. While returns on emerging market bonds been much more volatile than other asset classes, returns have also been relatively uncorrelated with the performance of other markets. Thus, emerging debt should be viewed as a separate asset class, distinct from the mature bond markets on the one hand and the equity markets on the other. A family's decision to invest in emerging markets should turn on the same considerations that influence the choice of other asset classes — traditional fixed-income, large-capitalization stocks, small-capitalization stocks, emerging market equities, commodities, and real estate — to include in the portfolio. In the case of emerging markets, the issue is whether, in a family's view, the higher expected returns offered by these securities and their low correlation with other assets' returns are worth the substantially higher volatility of the markets.

In general, investors seeking to construct portfolios that offer relatively high returns by incurring relatively high risk will want to include emerging market bonds in their asset mix. Investors seeking to build lower-risk portfolios with lower expected returns will avoid this asset class. Holdings of mature market bonds belong in almost all families' portfolios. Emerging market bonds belong in relatively few.

CHAPTER 9

Sectors of the Bond Market: A Domestic U.S. Perspective

The U.S. bond market is as old as the Republic itself. In fact, much of the impetus for the adoption of the Constitution of the United States came from the pressure of dealing with the negotiable debt instruments issued by the Continental Congress to finance the Revolutionary War. In terms of size and complexity, though, the bond market of the year 2000 is really the creation of the last 20 years. The rapid growth of the U.S. bond market after 1980 is depicted in Exhibit 1.

Exhibit 1: U.S. Credit Market Debt Outstanding

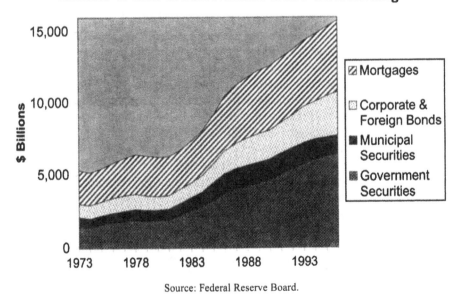

Source: Federal Reserve Board.

While the growth of U.S. Treasury debt accelerated at unprecedented peacetime levels after 1980, we also witnessed the creation of huge markets encompassing entirely new types of negotiable fixed-income securities. In 1977 the mortgage-backed securities market was just getting started, while asset-backed securities had not yet been invented. The corporate bond market of 1970 was a relatively conservative venue dedicated, for the most part, to the leisurely processing of issues for highly rated electric utilities. By the late 1990s, the Securities and Exchange Commission's deregulation of the process of corporate bond issuance had transformed that market into a highly liquid and intensely active fixed-income sector. At the same time, more aggressive techniques of corporate finance had created a $200 billion per year market for non-investment-grade (high yield or "junk") bonds.

Thus, the U.S. fixed-income market as we know it now is a relatively new institution, and its evolution continues to be very rapid. This dynamism means that material in texts on fixed-income markets written just a few years ago can be out-of-date. The same is true for some of the material in this book in a few years.

GOVERNMENT BOND MARKETS

Three types of government entities in the United States issue negotiable debt instruments to the public: the United States Treasury, federal government agencies or government sponsored enterprises (GSEs), and state governments and their instrumentalities.

The Treasury Bond Market

The U.S. Department of the Treasury issues bonds for two purposes: (1) to raise funds to finance any annual operating deficit of the Federal government, (i.e., to pay the federal government's bills for goods and services to the extent that tax revenues are insufficient to do so), and (2) to cover principal payments that come due on debt issued to finance past deficits (i.e., to roll over maturing debt).

Treasury securities are considered to be of the highest credit quality of any U.S. dollar-denominated debt obligations. The "full faith and credit" of the United States is pledged to meet debt service payments on these securities. Further, Congress has the power to create currency to make these debt service payments. The value of such currency might fluctuate relative to other currencies or to any given commodity (such as gold), but there can be no doubt that an investor who holds a $1,000 U.S. Treasury note maturing on May 15, 2002, will receive 1,000 U.S. dollars plus interest in legal tender from the Treasury on that date.

Varieties of Treasury Securities

The U.S. Treasury issues four types of negotiable direct obligations: Treasury bills, Treasury notes, Treasury bonds, and Treasury inflation protection securities.[1] Bills mature within one year of their date of issuance. Typically, the Treasury auctions three- and six-month bills weekly and one-year bills at less frequent intervals. Bills do not pay coupons, but are issued at a discount price as zero-coupon securities. Treasury notes have maturities between two and ten years of their date of issuance and pay semiannual coupons. Treasury Bonds, like notes, pay semiannual coupons, but they have initial maturities longer than ten years. The Treasury has not retained the right to call bonds issued after 1984, but before that time bonds were issued that can be redeemed five years before their maturity date. Many callable Treasury bonds remain outstanding.

In 1997, the Treasury began issuing Treasury inflation protection securities (TIPS). The principal value of these securities changes over the life of the instrument to maintain a constant purchasing power as measured by the Consumer Price Index for all urban consumers (CPI_u). The Treasury Department has announced its intention to continue issuing TIPS as a part of its overall debt management program.

The current maturity structure of negotiable Treasury debt is illustrated in Exhibit 2. This structure has been relatively stable over time.

Exhibit 2: Effective Maturity of Outstanding U.S. Treasury Notes and Bonds

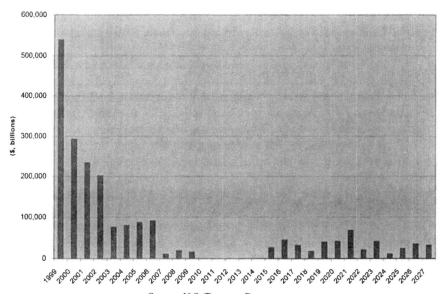

Source: U.S. Treasury Department.

[1] The Treasury also issues two types of non-negotiable securities. U.S. savings bonds are sold in small denominations. These securities can be redeemed early at the cost of some accrued interest income, but cannot be transferred to third parties. State and local government series (SLGS) are issued directly to municipalities for use in defeasance escrows.

The Liquidity of the Treasury Market

Treasury securities offer the lowest yields of any taxable bonds of comparable maturity in the U.S. domestic market. The only bonds that offer consistently lower nominal yields than Treasuries are tax-exempt municipal bonds. Several characteristics of Treasuries help explain their special status in this regard. First, as noted, the credit quality of Treasury obligations is, by definition, unsurpassed.

Second, the market for Treasury securities is the most liquid and the most efficient fixed-income market in the world. Specifically, the bid-asked spread for even the least actively traded Treasury notes or bonds is seldom wider than three or four 32^{nds} of 1%. That is, assuming unchanged interest rate levels and no significant passage of time, an investor who purchases a 10-year Treasury note at a dollar price of $102^{12}/_{32}$ can expect to sell the same security at a price of $102^{10}/_{32}$. The differential tends to be wider in most other fixed-income markets.

Further, the market for Treasury securities is highly flexible. Treasury notes and bonds can be "stripped" and "reconstituted"; that is dealers can separate the various coupon payments from the principal payment on any given security and sell the components separately. And a dealer who owns all the components of a stripped bond or note can recombine them into a single security. In addition, it is relatively easy and inexpensive for investors to borrow funds to purchase Treasury securities by using the bond or the note itself as collateral for the loan. A variety of regulatory and tax law impediments make it difficult to finance the purchase of other fixed-income securities as efficiently. Similarly, it is relatively easy to sell a Treasury bond or note short in order to create a position whose value will rise if interest rates increase.

Low-cost financing for Treasury positions and the ready ability to short the Treasury market are also the prerequisites for a deep and active market in Treasury-based derivative contracts. Financial futures contracts for 3-month and 2-, 5-, 10-, and 30-year Treasury securities trade actively, as do options on these futures contracts and over-the-counter options on specific Treasury notes and bonds.

For these reasons, Treasury notes and bonds are the preferred trading vehicle for market participants who want to speculate on the direction of interest rates or to hedge the market value of bond portfolios. Active trading also means that yields and prices for Treasury securities tend to be more volatile than those of other types of bonds over interest rate cycles. Because Treasury notes and bonds trade so actively, prices of these securities tend to rally more quickly and by more than those of comparable-duration corporate or municipal bonds when interest rates are declining and to sell off by more when rates start to rise.

Finally, interest on U.S. Treasury obligations is exempt from state income taxes.

Value Within the Treasury Market

At any particular time, different Treasury securities will offer different yields. The primary determinant of the yield on any given bill, note, or bond will be the instrument's duration; in the typical upward-sloping yield curve environment, longer-duration bonds will offer higher yields. And the term "duration," rather than "maturity," in the previous sentence is used intentionally.

Consider two Treasury notes, one maturing on January 15, 2008, and one on February 15 of the same year. Suppose the coupon on the shorter bond is 4.00%, that on the latter is 8.00%, and that the yield on both bonds is approximately 5.00%. Even if the yield curve were upward sloping, we would not be surprised to find that the yield on the shorter-maturity bond is higher than that on the longer because the duration of the 4.00% bond is substantially greater than that of the 8.00% (8.11 versus 7.28). In fact, the Treasury note market is so efficient that if the yield curve were upward sloping and if a professional government bond trader were to notice that the yield on the 1/15/2008 maturity is lower than that of the 2/15/2008 maturity, the trader would sell the former short and go long the latter to "arbitrage" this misvaluation.

Besides duration, three other bond characteristics influence the yield on individual Treasury bonds: call features, liquidity, and technical market conditions. The effect of call features on bond yield is treated in Chapter 17. With regard to liquidity; all Treasury securities are liquid but some are more liquid than others. In general, larger Treasury issues and newer issues are more liquid than older, smaller offerings. Further, certain Treasury securities, typically the most recently issued 2-, 3-, 5-, 10-, and 30-year issues are treated as benchmark securities. They may also be referred to as "on-the-run" Treasuries, while older issues are said to be "off-the-run." Yields on other fixed-income instruments, including corporate bonds, mortgage- and asset-backed securities, and other instruments are quoted as a spread over these benchmarks. Thus a corporate trader might quote a 9-year industrial bond as yielding 57 basis points over the yield on the 10-year on-the-run Treasury note. The benchmarks are also the most actively traded, and the bid-asked spread on these bonds might translate into a half a basis point in yield compared with about 2 basis points for the least actively traded Treasuries.

Several technical market conditions can influence the yield on particular Treasuries. For example, bond traders and investors also frequently sell Treasury securities short, particularly the benchmarks. That is, either to offset (or hedge) a long position in some other bond or simply to create a trading position that will benefit if interest rates rise, a trader might sell the on-the-run five-year Treasury note for delivery in two weeks without actually owning the security. Benchmark five-year notes are so actively traded that, when it comes time to deliver the security, buying the required amount is usually easy. It sometimes happens that short positions in a particular Treasury obligation grow so large that "short-covering" demand bids up the price of the bond or note, pushing the yield below levels consistent with the security's duration and liquidity. When this happens traders say that the note or bond is trading "on special."

The Role of Treasuries in a Family Portfolio

U.S. Treasury securities can play several roles in family fixed-income portfolios. Some investors like having a position in Treasuries because of their superlative credit quality. Further, investors seeking non-callable bonds with very long maturities have few choices other than Treasuries. The most attractive feature of these instruments from a family portfolio manager's point of view, however, should be their liquidity. Investors who wish to fine-tune their portfolio's duration over the course of interest rate cycles should hold some proportion of Treasury bills, notes, or bonds. Because of the narrow bid-asked spread in this market, and ignoring tax considerations, managing a Treasury position will be the least costly way to adjust portfolio duration.

U.S. Government Agency and Government Sponsored Enterprise Securities

At various times since the 1930s, the Congress of the United States has created government agencies and has chartered government-sponsored enterprises (GSEs) authorized to issue negotiable debt instruments. Some of these agencies and GSEs were created to deal with a specific problem and, while they still may have debt outstanding, are no longer active as issuers in the market.

Two agencies — the Financing Corporation (FICO) and the Resolution Funding Corporation (Refcorp) — were created as part of the effort in the late 1980s to resolve a widespread solvency crisis in the savings and loan or thrift industry. Debt service of these agencies is paid either out of dedicated streams of federal government revenues or through direct congressional appropriation. Both FICO and Refcorp have completed their borrowing programs, so while their bonds remain outstanding, no new ones are being issued.

Several agencies and GSEs are active issuers.

The Federal Home Loan Bank System

The FHLB was created to act, in essence, as the central bank for the savings and loan industry. The agency borrows funds by issuing notes and bonds in the capital markets and lends the proceeds to thrift institutions that are members (and owners) of the system. All the loans are secured by very high-quality collateral. Interest and principal payments on the loans to members generate more than enough revenue to meet interest and principal due on the system's debt obligations.

The Farm Credit System

The FCS raises funds in the capital markets to make loans to financial institutions, which, in turn, lend money to the agricultural and fisheries industries. Again, loans to financial institutions are collateralized by very high-quality assets, and system revenues are more than adequate to meet debt service on FCS obligations.

The Federal National Mortgage Association (Fannie Mae) and the Federal Home Loan Mortgage Corporation (Freddie Mac)

These two GSEs were chartered by Congress to pursue a public purpose: encouragement of home ownership by enhancing the efficiency of the market for mortgages. Both are also, however, for-profit public companies owned by institutional and individual stockholders. Along with other financial operations, these GSEs issue bonds and notes in the capital markets and use the proceeds to purchase single- and multi-family home mortgages from financial institutions. Payments on these mortgages provide revenues that are more than sufficient to meet interest and principal payments on Fannie Mae and Freddie Mac outstanding debt obligations.

The Tennessee Valley Authority

The TVA is the oldest of the federal agencies. It was created in the 1930s to develop the economy of the Tennessee River valley by building dams and electric power plants. The Authority was and is authorized to issue negotiable debt securities to finance its capital programs. The wholesaling of electric power provides the revenues for operations and debt service.

Student Loan Marketing Association

Sallie Mae is similar to Fannie Mae and Freddie Mac in that all three are government-chartered, stockholder-owned, for-profit corporations pursuing both profits and public policy purposes. As its name implies, Sallie Mae's public purpose is to make loans more readily available to college and university students by issuing debt instruments and using the proceeds to purchase student loans from financial institutions. As with Fannie Mae and Freddie Mac, loan payments by borrowers provide more than enough revenues to Sallie Mae to cover debt service on the GSE's obligations.

The notes and bonds issued by government agencies and GSEs, unlike Treasury securities, are not backed by the full faith and credit of the United States. All the currently active issuers produce revenues from their operations, and the expectation is that these revenues will be sufficient to meet all debt service payments on agency obligations. These revenue-producing agencies currently operate ongoing borrowing programs to finance their operations.

Absent the guarantee enjoyed by holders of Treasury securities that Congress will "print money" if necessary to meet interest and principal payments, agency securities are of slightly lower credit quality than Treasuries. For that reason, and also because the bid-asked spread in the agency market is slightly wider on average than for Treasuries, agency securities yield slightly more than otherwise comparable Treasury bills, notes, and bonds.

Agency paper, however, is considered the second-best credit in the U.S. financial markets for three reasons. First, Congress has authorized at least some explicit financial support for each of these agencies, usually in the form of a line of credit with the U.S. Treasury. Second, because each of the agencies enjoys substantial political support, Congress would very likely bail out a troubled agency if the authorized credit lines prove insufficient. Finally, the impact on global financial markets of a default by any of these agencies would be so devastating that Congress would probably be forced to go to any lengths, including printing money to avoid such an eventuality.

Value Within the Agency Market

The primary advantage Treasury securities offer over agency and GSE obligations is liquidity. Investors who plan to adjust portfolio duration more often than, say, twice a year might want to hold some Treasury bills, notes, or bonds to assure that these shifts will not be too expensive in terms of bid-asked spread. Agency and GSE securities offer two advantages over Treasuries: slightly higher yield, and a greater range of bond structures. The agency and GSE issuers have been particularly innovative in offering securities with structures that investors may want, such as callable notes or securities with returns indexed to the performance of other markets.

The most important determinants of the yield on any given agency or GSE security are duration, structure, perceived credit quality, and liquidity. Under normal circumstances, when the yield curve is upward sloping, the longer the duration of an agency and GSE instrument, the higher its yield. The upward slope of the agency yield curve is usually more pronounced (or its inversion less pronounced) than that of the Treasury curve. To put it differently, the yield spread offered by agency securities over Treasury instruments with comparable maturity and structure widens as duration increases. We will see that the corporate bond market also exhibits this tendency.

Differences in the structure of two bonds issued by the same agency or GSE will also have a substantial influence on their relative yields. For example, if we compare two bonds of the same agency with identical coupons, one callable and the other not, even if both are priced at discounts to par, we will find that the yield on the callable bond is higher than that of the non-callable.

All U.S. government agencies are considered excellent credits, although investors make distinctions among the various issuers. Such distinctions were more pronounced in the late 1980s, when crises in the thrift industry and the agricultural economy clouded some of the agencies' long-term financial prospects. At that time, yields on, for example, Farm Credit System obligations were somewhat elevated over other agencies' securities. When Congress effectively resolved these crises in a way that enhanced the financial security of agency bondholders, investor confidence in these credits was restored across the board. By the late 1990s, yield differentials among different agency issuers for comparable maturities and structures had become very small.

The final source of differences in yields on different agency bonds is differences in liquidity. All else held equal, agency bonds with simple (non-callable) structures that were originally issued as part of a very large offering will generally carry a slightly lower yield than smaller, highly structured issues. Early in 1998, Fannie Mae and Freddie Mac began an effort to take advantage of this liquidity premium by offering a series of large, simple benchmark issues with a range of standard maturities.

Municipal Bonds

The most compelling feature of municipal bonds for investors, and the reason these securities play such a large role in the portfolios of U.S. families, is that interest income on most bonds issued by state and local governments is, for the most part, exempt from federal income taxation. Because of this favorable tax treatment, municipal bonds usually yield less than Treasury bonds of comparable maturities. Further, interest on municipal bonds issued within most states is exempt from that state's income taxes.

The tax treatment of municipal bonds is far from straightforward; for example, interest on some bonds may be exempt for some taxpayers but not for others. The salient details are treated more fully in Chapter 12. In this chapter we describe the bonds simply as securities without reference to their tax treatment.

All securities in this sector of the fixed-income market are called "municipal" bonds, but not all of them are issued by municipalities. State general governments, local general governments, and special-purpose agencies of state and local governments are all authorized to issue negotiable debt instruments. These issuers tap the municipal market for two purposes: to raise funds for capital investment projects, and to refinance outstanding high-coupon debt. Unlike the federal government, state and local governments seldom issue bonds to cover operating deficits.

Certain state and local government agencies are authorized to issue bonds on behalf of certain private sector institutions such as not-for-profit hospitals, colleges, and universities and — under limited circumstances — for-profit corporations. One special class of state and local agencies issues tax-exempt bonds and uses the proceeds to purchase mortgages for low-income first-time home buyers.

Aside from tax exemption, four unique characteristics distinguish the municipal market from other global and domestic fixed-income sectors: heterogeneity, bond insurance, long maturities, and advance refunding.

Heterogeneity

Because there are so many state and local governments in the United States, there are a host of individual borrowers in the municipal market. The exact number is uncertain, but it probably approaches 100,000. A brief description of the types of issuers in the municipal market will illustrate the variety of types of issuers.

The broadest breakdown is between general obligations (GOs) and revenue bonds. The former are issued by general state and local governments and are backed by the full faith and credit of the issuer. In many states, a majority or supermajority vote of the electorate (e.g., a two-thirds majority) is required to authorize issuance of GO bonds. Revenue bonds may be issued by general governments or by special-purpose government agencies. These bonds are not secured by the full faith and credit of the issuer but are backed by a specific stream of revenues and usually by a debt service reserve fund. Common types of revenue bonds are listed in Exhibit 3.

When a municipality borrows funds in this market, it seldom issues a bond with a single maturity. Instead, tradition or state law usually require that the financing be structured as "serial bonds," with a proportion of the principal amount maturing each year. The typical structure is illustrated in Exhibit 4, which depicts the cover page of the official statement for a typical municipal bond issue.

Because of the large number of issuers and because each municipality will issue separate bonds with 20 or so different maturities each time it enters the market, the number of different municipal bonds outstanding at any one time exceeds two million. In any financial market this degree of heterogeneity inevitably leads to illiquidity. Bid-asked spreads on bonds of a few very large issuers (e.g., the City of New York, the State of California) may be relatively small, but traders who make markets in bonds of the many smaller municipalities will generally demand extra compensation in terms of a wider bid-asked spread.

Insurance

Because many issuers in this market are relatively unknown and because small retail investors in the tax-exempt bond market are assured by a "triple A" credit rating, third-party bond insurers have come to play a major role in this sector. These are special-purpose insurance companies that guarantee the timely payment of principal and interest on financial instruments. Because the companies maintain top-grade credit ratings, the bonds they insure are automatically rated triple-A. These companies play a small role in several fixed-income markets, but in the municipal market they have come to play a major role. More than 50% of the new bonds offered in 1998 came to market with bond insurance.

Exhibit 3: Common Types of Municipal Revenue Bonds

Type of Bond	Source of Funds for Debt Service
Special Tax Obligations	A dedicated stream of specific tax revenues, e.g., a portion of a local sales tax.
Water and Sewer Revenue Bonds	Fees paid by residents for water supply and/or sewer services.
Electric Revenue Bonds	Net revenues of a municipal-owned electric utility (e.g., the Los Angeles Department of Water and Power).
Toll Road Revenue Bonds	Tolls.
Hospital Revenue Bonds	Net operating revenues of a hospital.
Pollution Control Revenue Bonds	Lease payments by a corporation on pollution control facilities financed by tax-exempt bonds.
Mortgage Revenue Bonds	Payments by homeowners on mortgages purchased with bond proceeds.

Exhibit 4: The Cover Page of an Official Statement for a Municipal Bond Issue

NEW ISSUE-BOOK ENTRY ONLY

RATINGS: Moody's: Aa2
Standard & Poor's: AA
Fitch IBCA: AA
(See "Ratings" herein)

In the opinion of Co-Bond Counsel, under existing statutes and court decisions, interest on the Bonds is excludable from gross income for federal income tax purposes pursuant to Section 103 of the Internal Revenue Code of 1986, as amended (the "Code"), and under existing statutes interest on the Bonds is not treated as an item of tax preference in calculating alternative minimum taxable income for purposes of the alternative minimum tax imposed under the Code with respect to individuals and corporations; such interest, however, is included in the adjusted current earnings of certain corporations for purposes of calculating the alternative minimum tax imposed on such corporations. See "Tax Exemption" herein for a description of certain other provisions of law which may affect the federal tax treatment of interest on the Bonds. In the further opinion of Co-Bond Counsel, under the existing laws of Tennessee, the Bonds and the income therefrom shall be free from all Tennessee state, county and municipal taxes except for inheritance, transfer and estate taxes and except to the extent such interest may be included within the measure of corporate privilege taxes imposed pursuant to the laws of the State of Tennessee.

OFFICIAL STATEMENT
RELATING TO THE ISSUANCE OF
CITY OF MEMPHIS, TENNESSEE
$70,000,000
General Improvement Bonds, Series 1999A

DATED: April 1, 1999

DUE: October 1, as shown below

The $70,000,000 General Improvement Bonds, Series 1999A (the "Bonds") are issuable in fully registered form without coupons. The Bonds will be registered in the name of Cede & Co., as nominee of The Depository Trust Company, New York, New York ("DTC"). DTC will act as securities depository of the Bonds. So long as Cede & Co. is the registered owner of the Bonds, as the nominee for DTC, principal and interest shall be payable to Cede & Co., as nominee for DTC, which will, in turn, remit such principal and interest to the DTC participants for subsequent disbursements to the beneficial owners of the Bonds. Individual purchases of the Bonds will be made in book entry form only, in denominations of $5,000 or multiples thereof. Beneficial owners of the Bonds will not receive physical delivery of bond certificates. (See "The Bonds—Book-Entry System" herein). Interest on the Bonds is payable at the rates specified below on April 1 and October 1, commencing October 1, 1999. Interest on the Bonds will be calculated on the basis of a 30-day month and a 360-day year.

The Bonds are subject to optional redemption prior to maturity as more fully described herein.

The Bonds are being issued to fund various capital improvements in the City. The Bonds will be direct obligations of the City for which its full faith and credit are pledged and are payable from taxes levied on all taxable property in the City subject to taxation by the City without limitation as to rate or amount.

MATURITY SCHEDULE

Maturity October 1	Principal Amount	Interest Rate	Price/Yield To Maturity	Maturity October 1	Principal Amount	Interest Rate	Price/Yield To Maturity
2001	$2,440,000	5.00%	3.54%	2010	$3,520,000	4.375%	4.45%
2002	2,530,000	4.00	3.66	2011	3,685,000	4.50	4.55
2003	2,625,000	4.00	3.68	2012	3,865,000	4.50	4.65
2004	2,730,000	4.00	3.80	2013	4,055,000	4.625	4.75
2005	2,840,000	5.00	3.93	2014	4,255,000	4.625	4.80
2006	2,960,000	5.00	4.03	2015	4,475,000	5.00	4.88*
2007	3,085,000	4.00	4.13	2016	4,705,000	4.75	4.93
2008	3,220,000	4.125	4.20	2017	4,950,000	4.75	4.98
2009	3,365,000	4.25	4.30				

5.00% $10,695,000 Term Bond due October 1, 2019 at a price of 100%

The Bonds will be offered when, as and if issued and subject to the receipt of the approving legal opinions of Hawkins, Delafield & Wood, New York, New York and Charles E. Carpenter, A Professional Corporation, Memphis, Tennessee, Co-Bond Counsel. It is anticipated that the Bonds will be delivered on or about May 5, 1999 in New York, New York.

This Official Statement is dated April 7, 1999

---

* Priced to 10-01-09 par call

Although issuer defaults are extremely rare in the municipal market, investors can indeed take comfort in the additional layer of credit protection provided by these companies. And insured municipals will inevitably play an important role in the bond portfolio of a U.S. taxpayer. The primary benefit of insurance may not be the credit enhancement *per se* but the fact that, because traders need less information about insured issues than they do for uninsured issues, insured bonds tend to trade with more liquidity; i.e., with a narrower bid-asked spread.

Long Maturities

In most of the world's fixed-income markets, bonds with maturities greater than 20 years are relatively rare. Some corporate issuers, particularly public utilities, will occasionally offer 30-year bonds. And the U.S. Treasury was an active issuer of very long-term obligations in the 1980s and early 1990s. But even the Treasury Department has taken steps to reduce the average maturity of its outstanding debt. Because state and local governments, however, often use the proceeds of bond issues to finance the construction of very long-lived capital assets such as highways, sewer systems, or public buildings, it makes sense for these issuers to offer bonds with maturities of 30 years or more. Although many municipal bonds have final maturities 20 or 30 years after they are issued, few bonds issued in the last 20 years have remained outstanding that long.

Some longer-term municipals are issued without call features, but typically municipal bonds are callable by the issuer 10 years after the securities are initially offered. Issuers tend to exercise this right after interest rates have declined so that high-coupon debt can be replaced with bonds carrying lower interest rates. Since bond yields have been declining on average over the past 20 years, issuers have repeatedly taken the opportunity to reduce debt service costs by exercising their option to call high-coupon debt.

Advance Refunding

Corporations and government agencies also issue callable bonds and will refund outstanding issues for the same reasons municipalities do. Corporations and agencies, however, usually wait until the bond's first call date before deciding to exercise their option to redeem the bond before maturity. Municipalities have another choice. Instead of waiting until the call date, a municipality might issue refunding bonds early. The proceeds of the new "advance refunding" issue are then used to purchase a portfolio of U.S. Treasury securities. The idea is that the interest and principal payments on the Treasury portfolio will be sufficient to make all scheduled interest payments on the outstanding high-coupon bond until its call date and then allow redemption of the bond at the issue's call price. The issuer deposits the Treasuries with the trustee for the old high-coupon bonds with instructions that the cash flows from the portfolio be used to make all required payments on the old bonds. The trustee is further instructed to redeem the old bonds on the first possible call date. At this point, the issuer no longer has any obligation with respect to the old, or refunded, bonds. The security for the refunded issue is no longer the municipality's ability to meet its debt service obligations, but rather the interest and principal payments on the Treasury portfolio.

Such municipal bonds are referred to as prefunded bonds, as pre-res, or as escrowed bonds. In most cases pre-res will be rated triple-A and the bondholder can be confident that the securities will be redeemed on the first call date.[2]

Corporations and government agencies could enter into similar transactions. But because corporate and agency bonds yield more than Treasuries, this kind of advance refunding would be costly to the issuer of taxable bonds. Although municipals yield less than Treasuries, an issuer that executes an advance refunding is not permitted under tax law to profit from this spread. Advance refunding escrows must be invested in specially issued Treasury securities with a yield that is tied to that of the new refunding issue, but the municipality will not lose money on the difference between the refunding bond yield and the yield on the escrow investments.

Prefunded municipals are sometimes referred to as "tax-exempt Treasury notes." This is not precisely true, but it is not too much of a distortion.[3]

Determinants of a Municipal Bond's Yield

As with Treasury and agency securities, the primary determinant of the yield on any given municipal bond is the security's duration; yield increases with duration. This relationship between yield and maturity or duration is particularly pronounced in the municipal bond market. The yield curve for tax-exempt municipal bonds is invariably much steeper than the yield curves for Treasury or corporate securities, and, unlike for the Treasuries, the municipal yield curve has never been inverted.

Again, as with agency securities, the yield on a municipal bond will also be influenced by the security's structure — its coupon, call provisions, and sinking funds — and by market perceptions of its credit quality. Differences in credit quality in the municipal market are, however, substantially greater than in the agency and GSE sector, and these credit-related yield differences can be substantial.

While interest on most municipal bonds is fully tax-exempt, there are differences in tax treatments of bonds in this market sector. At the extreme, interest on some municipal bonds is fully taxable. "Taxable municipals" are issued to finance projects that do not qualify for tax-exemption under the federal tax code. Other differences in tax treatment that affect bond yields are discussed more fully in Chapter 11.

---

[2] Changing the bond's rating to triple-A after a refunding requires a payment by the issuer. Not all issuers make it a routine practice to apply for the new rating.

[3] One lingering question abut pre-res is what would happen to the Treasuries held in escrow in the event of a bankruptcy of an issuer with prefunded bonds outstanding. Because such events have been extremely rare, there is not enough case law for us to make a firm conclusion in this regard.

PRIVATE SECTOR FIXED-INCOME SECURITIES

Corporate Bonds

Corporate bonds are negotiable debt instruments issued by for-profit business enterprises. Not all issuers in this market are corporations — partnerships and privately owned firms also issue securities that are usually called "corporate bonds" or "corporates." Although not as heterogeneous as municipal bonds, corporates are available in a wide range of varieties. In fact, one of the best ways to understand how the corporate bond market works is to consider the ways in which market participants categorize securities in this sector; the particular way any given corporate bond is categorized goes a long way toward telling a trader or investor what yield spread that bond should offer over a comparable-maturity Treasury security.

The categorization scheme most commonly used to characterize corporate bonds has three dimensions: credit rating, registration status, and industry.

Credit Rating

The corporate bond market is divided into two broad sectors with regard to credit rating, namely, investment grade and non-investment-grade. The latter category is also frequently referred to as the high-yield or "junk bond" sector. Bonds rated Aaa, Aa, A, and Baa by Moody's Investors Service or AAA, AA, A, or BBB by Standard & Poor's are considered investment-grade. Bonds rated Ba, B, C, and D by Moody's or BB, B, C, and D by S&P are labeled non-investment-grade or speculative grade.

The categorization into two separate sectors of the corporate bond market reflects the fact that relatively few institutional investors actively invest in both sectors simultaneously. Some institutions are restricted from investing in the speculative-grade bond market either by law or regulation or by internal investment policy. In fact, some investment advisors are required to sell any bond that is downgraded from investment-grade to junk status. Other investors, such as high-yield bond mutual funds, buy few investment-grade bonds. Family portfolio managers are free to invest in either sector, but most securities dealers apply different suitability standards to investment grade as opposed to high-yield bond purchases.

Registration

Any security offered to the general public in the United States must be registered with the Securities and Exchange Commission (SEC). Bonds and other securities that have not gone through the registration process may also be sold, but in such cases the SEC imposes restrictions on who may buy these instruments. Eurodollar securities issued outside the jurisdiction of the SEC, for example, can be sold to investors within the U.S. once the bonds become "seasoned."

Unregistered bonds issued within the United States may be sold only to large institutions or to "accredited investors" pursuant to a private placement. The

SEC has established standards related to net worth and level of sophistication as to who may qualify as an accredited investor. Regulators have also established procedures for executing a private placement, requiring, most notably, that the seller obtain an "investor letter" from the buyer. The contents of this letter vary from situation to situation, but it will always attest to the fact that the investor is aware of the risks involved in purchasing private placements in general and the specific security in particular.

Well-to-do family investors can usually qualify as "accredited investors," and thus may gain access to privately placed corporate bonds.[4] A third method of distributing unregistered securities, mostly corporate bonds, effectively precludes participation by most family investors. In 1991, the SEC issued Rule 144a allowing sales of unregistered securities to "Qualified Institutional Buyers (QIBs)." A QIB is an *institution* holding or managing at least $100 million in securities (other than cash equivalents). A few very large family portfolios held through a special-purpose corporation or trust may qualify as QIBs, but most family investors are effectively foreclosed from participation in this market, both in initial offerings and in the secondary market.

Industry

Corporate bonds are broken down further by the issuer's industrial classification. As Exhibit 5 indicates, not all these categories are what we ordinarily think of as industries. The classification is relevant, however, because participants in the corporate bond market consider all the issuers in the particular category as a group. Thus, a portfolio manager may speak of increasing exposure to the "utility sector" or of substituting "sovereigns" for "multilaterals" within in the "Yankee sector."

Exhibit 5: Categories of Corporate Bonds by Issuer Industry

Industry	Examples
Industrials	Manufacturers
	Retailers
	Airlines
	Conglomerates
	Entertainment
Utilities	Electric Utilities
	Telephone Companies
Financials	Commercial Banks
	Thrift Institutions
	Securities Firms
	Insurance Companies
Yankees	Foreign or international entities issuing in the U.S. corporate market, including:
	• Sovereign governments
	• Corporations
	• Multilateral agencies (e.g., the World Bank)

---

[4] Municipal bonds may also be issued as private placements as may other types of fixed-income securities.

Value within the Corporate Bond Market

The yield on any given corporate bond will depend on many of the same characteristics that affect yields on Treasuries, agencies, and municipals. As always, duration will be the single most important determinant in most cases. Structural characteristics — such as call features, sinking funds, coupon — will play a role. And, of course, the credit quality of the specific issuer will be very important. In this sector, more than in the others, however, bond rating, registration, and industry also play a primary role. Two bonds with nearly identical durations, structures, and credit ratings may trade at very different yields if one is, say, a registered financial and the other a 144a Yankee corporate. Likewise, bonds of two issuers in the same industrial category with very similar durations, credit structures, and fundamental credit quality may offer radically different yields if one is rated BBB– and the other BB+.

The Role of Corporate Bonds in a Family Portfolio

Income on most U.S. families' investments is subject to taxation, and for these portfolios corporates are likely to represent a smaller component than municipals.

Nevertheless, corporate bonds do play important roles in many family portfolios. First, non-U.S. residents derive no benefit from purchasing municipal bonds, which are exempt only from U.S. income taxation. Families outside the U.S. seeking to diversify their fixed-income portfolios into the U.S. market should and do have substantial holdings of corporate bonds, either registered and issued in the United States or initially offered in the Eurodollar market. Second, U.S. family investments do include some funds that are not subject to taxation or that are taxable but do not benefit from holding municipal bonds. The most common examples are family charitable foundations or the charitable remainder unit trusts. Corporates can play an important role in such portfolios.

Finally, at times high-yield corporate bonds can play a role as a unique asset class even in portfolios that are subject to taxation. These investments are subject to substantially greater credit risk than investment-grade corporates or government bonds, but, as usual, greater risk may be associated with higher expected returns, even after tax, than what is offered by bonds with higher credit ratings. Particularly when the high-yield sector of the corporate bond market has, for one reason or another, been subject to disruption, portfolios including junk bonds may be on the efficient frontier.

Mortgage-Backed Securities

The classification of mortgage-backed securities (MBS) as private sector instruments is somewhat problematical. The obligors who make most of the payments that secure MBS — households making monthly home mortgage payments on single-family residences or landlords making payments on mortgages for multi-family rental or commercial properties — are, indeed, members of the private sector. In many ways, however, the MBS sector is a creation of the federal government. It could not operate as it does now without the historical and ongoing public sector involvement.

Whole Loans to Mortgage Passthroughs

Most mortgage-backed securities available in the market today are created by three government sponsored enterprises: Fannie Mae, Freddie Mac, and the Government National Mortgage Association (Ginnie Mae).[5] These three institutions purchase single- and multi-family home mortgages from "mortgage originators," mostly savings and loan institutions or commercial banks. The homeowner who took out the mortgage is generally unaware of the transaction because, in most cases, the originator will continue to service the loan. Once they have purchased the mortgages, Ginnie Mae, Fannie Mae, and Freddie Mac may choose to hold the loans as investments on their own balance sheet, financing the purchase by issuing the kinds of debt instruments described as agency or GSE securities. More often Ginnie, Fannie, and Freddie choose to package pools of mortgage loans into a class of MBS called "passthroughs."

Owners of these passthroughs receive a pro rata share of the monthly cash flows — interest, scheduled principal payments, and prepayments — paid by the homeowners in the pool. Payment of principal and interest on these securities is guaranteed by Ginnie Mae, Fannie Mae, or Freddie Mac, as the case may be. The Ginnie Mae guarantee reflects the full faith and credit of the United States. Passthroughs created by the two GSEs are referred to as "conventional" mortgage passthroughs to distinguish them from Ginnie Maes. The passthroughs are then sold, as negotiable fixed-income instruments, to other investors.

Somewhat surprisingly, often the investors who purchase passthroughs are the same savings and loans and banks that originated the mortgages in the first place. A financial institution that sells individual home mortgages (called whole loans) to, say, Fannie Mae and then purchases Fannie Mae passthroughs benefits from the combination of transactions in two ways. First, the passthrough is a better credit than a collection of whole loans both because of the added diversification provided by a large pool of mortgages and because of the GSE guarantee. Second, agency passthroughs are more generic and therefore more liquid than collections of whole loans. In fact, enhancing the liquidity of the market for home mortgages — and thereby indirectly reducing the cost of financing a house — is one of the primary objectives Congress had in mind when it created Ginnie Mae, Fannie Mae, and Freddie Mac.

Ginnie Mae purchases only whole loans that are guaranteed by the FHA or DVA. Fannie Mae and Freddie Mac confine their purchases to mortgages

---

[5] Ginnie Mae is an agency of the federal government that operates under the auspices of the Department of Housing and Urban Development (HUD). Ginnie Mae confines its mortgage purchase and passthrough creation activities to home mortgages guaranteed by either the Federal Housing Administration (FHA) or the Department of Veterans Affairs (DVA). Thus, unlike Fannie Mae and Freddie Mac passthroughs, Ginnie Maes are secured by the full faith and credit of the United States.

below a specific size that meet certain credit standards. In 1999, for example, Fannie and Freddie limited their purchases to mortgages of $240,000 or less. Whole loans that do not conform to the requirements of Ginnie Mae, Fannie Mae, or Freddie Mac — "jumbo" mortgages that are too large for Fannie and Freddie, for example — may also find their way into pools, but passthroughs created with non-conforming mortgages, referred to as "private passthroughs," do not carry the guarantee of a government agency or GSE.

Prepayment Uncertainty and Its Consequences

Mortgage passthroughs are problematic securities for many investors because the timing of the cash flows is subject to so much uncertainty. While a fixed-rate home mortgage has a predetermined schedule of interest and principal payments, the homeowner retains the right to prepay the mortgage earlier than the scheduled final payment date. Homeowners prepay their mortgages if they sell their houses. More and more frequently in recent years, homeowners have prepaid outstanding mortgages as interest rates have declined by refinancing at lower interest rates. Such prepayments are passed through to the owners of mortgage passthroughs into which the individual mortgages have been pooled.

Unanticipated prepayments work against the interest of investors. Prepayments tend to increase when interest rates are low, and when this occurs passthrough-holders are forced to reinvest principal that has been returned early at lower interest rates. Some investors can tolerate this risk; others cannot. In particular, financial institutions, such as banks and thrift institutions, that borrow money to purchase investments like mortgages can get into trouble if the passthroughs they own prepay either sooner or later than anticipated.

Consider first an institution that has borrowed funds at a rate that will fluctuate over time depending on the general level of interest rates and uses the loan proceeds to purchase fixed-rate mortgage passthroughs. If interest rates rise, the cost of borrowing will increase, but the yield on the investments will remain the same, and the institution will either earn less income than it anticipated or, in the extreme, lose money. Suppose instead that the institution borrows funds for a term at a fixed rate and, again, uses the proceeds to purchase passthroughs. In this case, the institution will get into trouble if interest rates decline. The loan will remain outstanding at a fixed interest cost, but the passthroughs purchased with the borrowed funds will likely be redeemed early because of prepayments. The institution will then have to reinvest the prepayment proceeds at a lower yield, which may or may not exceed the interest cost of the fixed-rate borrowing.

These scenarios are not just theoretical. In fact, it is situations very much like this that created the "thrift crisis" of the late 1980s in the United States. Other developments contributed to the problem, but, to a substantial degree, the failure of large numbers of savings and loans — institutions required by law to invest heavily in whole loans and passthroughs — can be traced to the sharp rise of interest rates after 1979 and their continual decline beginning in 1982.

Prepayment uncertainty is not as devastating to all investors as it can be to financial institutions, such as savings and loans, which borrow funds to buy mortgages. Mutual funds, insurance companies, and individuals might be disadvantaged to some extent if prepayments are either much faster or much slower than anticipated, but these investors will not go broke because of the performance of their mortgage portfolios.

Passthroughs to CMOs

The distinction between investors for whom prepayment uncertainty is a big problem and those who can cope with it more easily sets the stage for the next step in the of evolution in the mortgage-backed securities market: the development of collateralized mortgage obligations (CMOs).

CMOs are securities issued by Real Estate Mortgage Investment Conduits (REMICs), special-purpose entities created by financial institutions that purchase passthroughs and repackage the cash flows paid by the underlying whole loans into a series of different "tranches." As scheduled interest and principal payments and prepayments on the passthroughs are received, these cash flows are directed to different tranches of CMOs according to rules established when the REMIC is created. CMOs are designed to *reallocate* the prepayment uncertainty among the investors in the REMIC.

In the simplest CMO structure, one tranche will be designated the first to be redeemed when prepayments are received. Once this "A-tranche" CMO is fully redeemed, additional prepayments will all be directed to redeem the "B-tranche" CMO of the REMIC, and so on. CMOs subject to this simple payment rule are referred to as sequential-pay CMOs. Investors who purchase the A-tranche will be subject to less uncertainty regarding the timing of their cash flows than a holder of a passthrough would be. The A-tranche holder may not be completely certain about when this CMO will be fully paid off, but the security is unlikely to be outstanding for more than a few years. The holders of the later tranches, however, may be subject to greater uncertainty about when they will receive the expected cash flows than they would be if they owned the underlying passthroughs.

The earlier tranches of sequential-pay REMICs have substantially lower yields than the later tranches for two reasons. First, given the typical upward slope of the yield curve, securities with shorter expected average lives, like the early tranches, will offer lower yields. Second, investors who buy the later tranches demand higher yields as compensation for the greater uncertainty they accept. Thus, the development of REMICs enables both types of buyers to participate in the market for MBS. Investors, like financial institutions, that need greater certainty, can buy the earlier tranches. Those who can live with cash flow uncertainty can find securities, that will compensate them for the risks they are able to bear.

The evolution of REMICs did not stop with the development of the sequential-pay structure. The next step, the development of the planned amortization class (PAC) tranche, reduced uncertainty even further for some investors, while increasing it even more for others. As its name implies, a PAC CMO is issued with a stated schedule of interest and principal payments. As cash flows are received on the underlying passthroughs, every effort is made to make sure that the scheduled payments on the PAC tranches are made as anticipated, and that the PACs are redeemed no sooner and no later than scheduled. If prepayments come in somewhat faster or slower than what is assumed when the REMIC was structured, the timing of cash flows directed to the PAC tranches will be unaffected. Instead, other tranches of the REMIC, referred to as "PAC support tranches," will bear the impact. In fact, cash flows on a PAC CMO will be paid according to the predetermined schedule *unless* prepayments on the passthroughs come in at extremely high or extremely low rates.

A full description of any PAC security includes information about its "bands," the prepayment rates below or above which principal redemption payments will be received by the investors sooner or later than the planned amortization schedule. In most cases, these bands will be very wide; that is, circumstances would have to be very unusual for the bands to be broken and the anticipated schedule missed.

PAC CMOs are subject to even less uncertainty than the early tranches of sequential-pay CMOs, and, accordingly, a PAC CMO will offer a lower yield than an otherwise comparable sequential-pay CMO with the same expected average life. Likewise, a PAC support tranche will be subject to greater uncertainty than the later tranches of a sequential-pay structure. Thus, a support tranche will generally offer even higher yields than a sequential-pay CMO with the same expected average life.

Exhibit 6 presents a general schematic of the transformation of individual home mortgages into passthroughs and then into CMOs. The potential variations on this general structure seem limitless. In general, each REMIC created by a financial institution will offer a different combination of these basic structures. In addition, the cash flows paid on mortgage passthroughs can be repackaged in other ways. For example, dealers can strip passthroughs in much the same way as U.S. Treasury bonds are stripped into interest-only (IO) and principal-only (PO) strips.

Adjustable-Rate Mortgages

Many homeowners elect to finance their purchases with adjustable-rate mortgages (ARMs) rather than fixed-rate loans. ARMs are usually structured with a low "teaser" rate for the first year followed by a mortgage with an interest rate that changes, usually once a year, depending on an interest rate index. The most common such indexes are U.S. Treasury bill yields, although many others are used. The interest rate charged on ARMs does not, however, float freely. Most such mortgages specify the maximum amount by which the rate charged on the principal balance may increase in any one year (the annual cap) and the maximum rate that may be charged in any year over the life of the loan (the lifetime cap). As with fixed-rate whole loans, pools of ARMs are also assembled into passthroughs. Investors comparing these investments with other floating-rate securities need to take into account the impact of annual and lifetime caps on portfolio performance.

Exhibit 6: Schematic Structure of a CMO

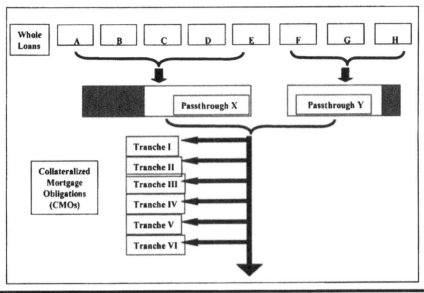

Other common structures for mortgage whole loans include balloon mortgages, which provide for a fixed rate of interest for a period of years, usually five or seven. After this period, the principal amount of the loan either comes due in full (a balloon payment), or the loan converts to a predetermined ARM structure.

Prepayments on both ARMs and balloon mortgages are common because these securities have shorter maturities than a 30-year mortgage passthrough, uncertainty regarding the prepayment rate has somewhat less of an impact on investors. Therefore, passthroughs created with ARM or balloon whole loans are seldom restructured into CMOs through REMICs.

Explaining MBS Yields

As with all other fixed-income securities, the yield on any given MBS — passthrough, CMO, IO, or PO — depends on the security's duration, its credit quality, and its structure. For most MBS, credit quality is not an issue; payments on the vast majority of passthroughs are guaranteed by GSEs or are rated triple-A for other reasons. There are some exceptions to this general rule, though. For example, commercial mortgage-backed securities (CMBS) represent pools of mortgages on office buildings, industrial properties, shopping centers, and so on. These securities are not guaranteed by government instrumentalities, and some of them carry triple-B or lower ratings, depending on the quality of the underlying properties and on the structure of the commercial mortgage passthrough. Because of their credit quality and because of their structure, CMBS should probably be thought of as more like corporate bonds than single-family mortgage-backed securities.

Also, not all passthroughs or CMOs are created by government agencies. Pools of jumbo or otherwise non-conforming single-family whole loans are packaged into MBS, and some of these securities carry ratings below triple-A. Evaluation of these credits requires detailed data about the credit quality of the loans in the underlying pool along with information about any additional layers of credit protection built into the passthrough or CMO structure itself. Evaluating private passthroughs requires an understanding of both complex credit analysis and prepayment analysis.

Yields on mortgage-backed securities usually increase as the particular passthrough or CMO's expected average life increases. This can be seen most clearly in the case of PAC CMOs with wide bands. The payment schedule on these securities is subject to very little uncertainty, and there is a clear relationship between expected average maturity and yield among the PAC tranches of a given REMIC structure.

Structure, broadly defined, is, however, by far the most important determinant of the yield of any given mortgage-backed security. The problem for the investor with any MBS, even a PAC bond with the broadest possible bands, is uncertainty regarding the duration of the investment. Indeed, because the timing of the cash flows of a MBS is highly uncertain, simply defining the appropriate yield concept is difficult. The most useful way of defining yield for these securities is as the internal rate of return of the cash flows at an assumed prepayment rate. A quotation of a "cash flow yield" on a MBS and has no meaning, unless the assumed prepayment rate is also quoted. The problem is to determine the most appropriate prepayment rate to use in estimating the yield of any given MBS.

As with a callable bond, the redemption date of a mortgage passthrough or CMO will depend on the level of interest rates. With a callable bond, if rates are lower than the coupon when the call date arrives, the bond will very likely be redeemed. With an MBS, if rates fall below the weighted average coupon (WAC) on the underlying whole loans, prepayments will speed up, and the average life of the security will shorten. If rates drop to levels much lower than the pool's WAC, the average life of even some of the PAC CMOs backed by the pool might be shortened.

The yield on any given mortgage-backed security — defined as the cash flow yield at a given prepayment rate — will depend crucially on investors' expectations about what the prepayment rate will be and on the degree of uncertainty regarding the prepayment rate. The higher the expected prepayment rate, the shorter the expected average life, and, if the yield curve is upward sloping, the lower the cash flow yield will likely be. The greater the uncertainty about prepayments, expected prepayment rates held constant, the higher the cash flow yield should be.

Estimating prepayment rates and prepayment sensitivities of passthroughs and CMOs with varying characteristics is one of the most complex undertakings in the field of fixed-income analysis. Major Wall Street firms compete with one another to develop computer models designed to estimate how prepayments will vary depending on the level of interest rates, the weighted average underlying mortgage rate (weighted average coupon) of a pool, the vintage of the pool (how long ago most of the mortgages were originated), the geographic location of the homes financed by mortgages in the pool, and the ways in which interest rates have varied since the underlying mortgages were originated.

A complete discussion of how these models work and what they imply regarding the valuation of MBS is well beyond the subject matter of this book. Some of the analytical issues involved in developing these models are touched on in Chapter 16.

MBS in the Family Portfolio

Family fixed-income portfolio managers should approach the MBS market with caution. To be sure, many securities in this market can make a great deal of sense for some family portfolios. Investors seeking a somewhat higher yield than what is offered by U.S. Treasury securities who are willing to accept a modest level of risk regarding the timing of cash flows may want to consider *some* PAC CMOs and, possibly, *some* sequential-pay CMOs. The emphasis is on "some." Just because a CMO is labeled a PAC bond or a short-maturity sequential-pay instrument does not mean that its cash flow pattern will be predictable. A CMO originally issued a few years ago as a PAC bond, for example, may be backed by very high-coupon mortgages. Prepayments on those mortgages may already have exceeded the upper level of the PAC CMO's bands, and the security may be prepaying very quickly. Purchasing such a bond at a substantial premium to par could be a big mistake.

If it is important to do business with major well-known dealers when purchasing any fixed-income investment, it is especially so with MBS. CMOs with extremely volatile cash flow patterns have been sold to individual investors because the dealer was able to quote a very high cash flow yield. If a potential buyer isn't sophisticated enough to ask the dealer what prepayment assumption is used to calculate that yield, much less to ascertain whether the assumption is reasonable given the characteristics of the mortgages underlying the particular MBS, the offering may seem like a good deal for an investor. It may be, but it probably isn't.

ASSET-BACKED SECURITIES

The mortgage-backed securities market serves as the model for another market in which obligations of large numbers of consumers are pooled and packaged into securities. The asset-backed securities (ABS) market developed in the late 1980s and has grown rapidly in terms of both the volume of instruments outstanding and the types of consumer receivables that have been securitized. Securities backed by credit card receivables constitute the largest class of securities in this market, but pools of automobile loans, home equity loans, mobile home loans, student loans, and other assets are also common.

The typical ABS has a relatively short average life; final stated maturities seldom exceed seven years, and most are much shorter. Prepayments of ABS are possible. Because prepayments on these types of consumer loans tend to be less sensitive to interest rates than mortgage prepayments, early redemption is less of a problem in this market than it is in the MBS sector.

Most ABS are rated triple-A, although lower-rated tranches of asset-backed offerings are also common. Unlike most MBS, asset-backed securities, with the exception of some pools of student loans, are not guaranteed by any government agency or GSE. Security for ABS investors comes from several sources. First, the underlying assets tend to be of excellent average credit quality. The vast majority of credit card holders make all their payments on a timely basis.

Second, an offering of asset-backed securities usually incorporates some credit support in the form of a debt service reserve fund or a subordinated tranche of ABS. If the pool of loans experiences an unanticipated level of defaults, funds in the reserve would be drawn down to meet scheduled debt service payments. Alternatively, if funds are insufficient to meet scheduled debt services payments on all tranches of ABS backed by a given pool of assets, periodic payments would be reduced on a subordinated tranche of securities by enough so that no payments would be missed on the senior tranches.

Moody's, S&P, and other rating agencies have developed detailed criteria, based on the historical quality of the assets in the pool and the structural features of the offering, for assignment of credit ratings to asset-backed securities. Issuers of ABS — usually the financial institutions, such as commercial banks, that sponsor the credit cards or make the automobile loans — structure their offerings so that the bulk of the ABS secured by each pool of assets will be assigned a top-quality credit rating.

Investing in the ABS market is not subject to as many potential pitfalls as buying mortgage-backed securities. Family portfolios of taxable fixed-income investments should probably include some ABS from time to time, but restricted to the more highly rated tranches.

CHAPTER 10

Credits and Credit Analysis

T he credit quality of a bond is a measure of the issuer's ability and willingness to pay the promised cash flows on time. The credit quality of bonds is
of interest to investors for two reasons. In the extreme, an issuer may be
unable or unwilling to meet debt service obligations; that is, the issuer may
default on the bond. An actual default on bonds an investor holds can be devastating, in that it can lead to large negative returns on the investment. Defaults on
bond issues are extremely rare.

A less devastating but much more common occurrence is a deterioration
of issuer credit quality short of default. Changes in market perceptions of an
issuer's ability to meet debt service obligations can have a huge effect on the market value of bonds, even while actual default by the issuer remains highly
unlikely. Such changes in market perception take place all the time. If the issuer
in question never defaults, then an investor who holds the bond will receive all of
the scheduled cash flows. As we will see, however, the deterioration in market
perceptions of the issuer's credit will have a definite adverse affect on the performance of the investor's bond portfolio.

Traditional credit analysis focuses on the probability of default. Any borrower can default; even a national government with power to print money can
default by refusing to honor its obligations as, most recently, the Russian government did in 1998. For some issuers, though, this probability is extremely small,
and the bonds of these issuers are assigned the highest credit rating of "triple-A."
At the opposite extreme, the issuer may have already failed to meet an interest or
principal payment on an outstanding bond — have already defaulted — and the
bonds of such borrowers will be assigned to the lowest rating category of "D." In
this traditional view, rating categories, as they decline from triple-A down to D
reflect increasing probabilities of default.

Until the 1980s this view of credit quality as measuring the probability of
an either-or event was adequate. The development of the high-yield or "junk" sector of the corporate bond market then challenged credit analysts to take a more

nuanced view of credit quality. The complication is that bonds don't simply disappear after an event of default. Instead, the rights of the bondholders change.

Before the default, bondholders have few rights enforceable against the issuer other than to receive scheduled debt service payments. Subsequent to a default, bondholders can, with the approval of a court of law, proceed legally against the issuer in a number of ways. Acting through the bond trustee, bondholders can force the issuer to change its management practices, to liquidate assets, or even to liquidate the entire enterprise and to distribute the proceeds of the sale of assets to the bondholders. Issuers that have defaulted or are about to default may have recourse to bankruptcy laws and bankruptcy courts to forestall immediate action by bondholders. The courts, however, are required to recognize an array of bondholders' rights against an issuer that has failed to meet its obligations under an indenture.

As a practical matter, this means that in most cases bondholders can recover a considerable proportion of their investment even after an issuer has defaulted. The value of such post-default recoveries may not equal the par amount of the bonds that were outstanding when the issuer defaulted, and payment of recoveries may be delayed for many months or even years. The potential for investment recovery subsequent to a default differs across issuers. Bonds of an issuer likely to provide greater recovery potential should be viewed as a better credit than those offering minimal recovery potential, even if the probability of default is the same for both.

Distinctions with respect to recovery began to assume importance when investors began buying large volumes of sub-investment-grade bonds on which default was a real possibility. Making these distinctions in credit analysis requires a broader definition of credit quality. Under this broader view, the credit quality of a bond is proportional to the ratio of (1) the present value of the expected cash flows to be paid on the bond to (2) the present value of the contract cash flows, both discounted at the "riskless" interest rate for the appropriate maturity. For a U.S. Treasury security, the value of this ratio is 1.00; as there is no likelihood that the Treasury will fail to meet all its debt service obligations, the expected value of the cash flows is the same as the contract cash flows. At the opposite extreme, for an issuer that has defaulted, has no cash to make additional debt service payments, and owns no assets with any material market value, the ratio would be 0.00; the present value of the expected cash flow is zero.

Unfortunately, between these extreme cases, providing a precise estimate of the credit quality ratio becomes extremely difficult. Credit ratings are thus expressed as letter grades, as ordinal, qualitative assessments, rather than as precise numerical estimates of a credit ratio. The credit rating is intended to provide a coherent way of organizing information about credit quality; precise estimates of a bond's numerical "credit ratio," as defined above, are not attainable.

Fixed-income credit analysis is an advanced and highly specialized professional discipline. Managers of family fixed-income portfolios should not expect to perform their own credit analysis, especially since rating agencies and bond dealers maintain highly skilled staffs of analysts and provide credit information to investors at no charge. (The issuer pays for the credit rating.) Our discussion, which outlines the main determinants of credit quality, is meant to enable the reader to be an informed consumer, not a producer, of quality credit analysis.

THE DETERMINANTS OF CREDIT QUALITY

The facts and circumstances that enable an analyst to evaluate the credit quality of a bond issue fall into three categories:

1. The economic and financial condition of the borrower.
2. The provisions of the bond indenture.
3. The issuer's willingness to pay.

Economic and Financial Condition of the Borrower

In order to make debt service payments, issuers require, first and foremost, sufficient income or net revenues. A corporate borrower needs sufficient free cash flow, net earnings after paying production expenses, to pay interest and principal when due. For non-government issuers, the most common measure of this free cash flow is "earnings before interest, taxes, and depreciation" or "EBITD." For as long as EBITD exceeds debt service requirements, the issuer can meet its obligations. Credit analysts who specialize in corporate bonds attempt to synthesize information about broad economic trends, developments in the issuer's industry, and facts about the issuer itself into intermediate- and long-term estimates of EBITD. If it looks like EBITD will be insufficient at some point in the future, the likelihood of eventual default increases, and the present value of the expected cash flows decreases.

The ability of a government or government agency to service debt obligations depends on the entity's ability to raise sufficient revenues. Receipts must be sufficient to cover governmental operating expenses with enough left over to pay interest and principal on outstanding bonds. In the case of general governments, tax revenues and intergovernmental grants constitute the predominant source of revenues for both operations and debt service, and, tax rates held constant, the level of tax collections is driven by national or regional economic conditions. For a state government in the U.S., the primary driver of credit quality will be the condition of the regional economy as measured, most broadly, by gross state product.

In the case of foreign currency-denominated national government debt — euro-denominated Brazilian government bonds, for example — credit analysts will also focus on the ability of the issuer to convert local tax revenues into euros. Thus, analysis of sovereign credit quality turns on such variables as the country's foreign exchange reserves and its balance of payments, in addition to the condition of the domestic macroeconomy.

Government enterprises, such as government-owned utilities or wastewater treatment plants, derive revenues for debt service by selling their products to or levying fees on local residents. Like taxes, enterprise revenues depend on local and national economic conditions. Analysis of enterprise issuers also bears some resemblance to corporate credit analysis. The enterprise's ability to collect revenues depends on consumer demand for the service that the enterprise provides and the ability of management to operate the facilities efficiently.

Revenue for interest and principal payments on asset-backed securities, including mortgage-backed securities, comes from payments by individual homeowners, credit card holders, and so on. The credit quality of ABS or MBS is enhanced by structural features (discussed below) and, in some cases, by government agency guarantees. The credit quality of many asset pools is also dependent on the ability of individual obligors to make timely payments on their home mortgages, automobile loans, revolving credit lines, and so on. Individual households' ability to meet their obligations, in turn, depends on general macroeconomic conditions.

In the case of MBS, the ability to pay may also depend on specific conditions in the housing sector of the economy. If housing prices drop sharply, even while general economic conditions are good, homeowners who move may have difficulty paying off their mortgages with the proceeds of the sale. Credit analysts who specialize in the ABS and MBS markets keep a sharp eye on macroeconomic conditions in general and on the conditions of regional housing markets and published statistics on credit card and mortgage delinquencies and defaults in particular.

The Provisions of the Bond Indenture

The indenture is the legal contract between a bondholder and the issuer. The provisions of these contracts fall into two broad categories, the first of which is "covenants." Covenants set forth the issuer's obligations to the bondholder. The most obvious of these is the obligation to make scheduled interest and principal payments. If the issuer has many sources of revenues, the indenture might specify which particular revenue streams will be available to pay debt service. For example, an issuer that has offered many individual issues of asset-backed securities might specify that debt service for a particular issue will be secured by collections on one particular pool of assets and no others. Covenants also specify the circumstances under which the issuer may call bonds before maturity and the procedures to be used in the event of a call. Failure by the issuer to perform as specified in the covenants is an "event of default under the indenture." The second category of indenture provisions specifies the bondholders' rights *vis-à-vis* the issuer and other creditors subsequent to an event of default.

Corporate and sovereign bond indentures typically include relatively few specific covenants. Municipal bond issues, particularly revenue bond issues, typically include many more such provisions. In addition to a pledge to pay interest and principal on schedule, municipal bond covenants may include provisions requiring the issuer to levy taxes or charge fees high enough so that revenues will exceed operating costs and debt service requirements by a specified margin. For example, a turnpike authority might pledge to set tolls high enough so that total revenues will exceed operating expenses and debt service obligations by 20%.

Other covenants may limit the issuer's ability to issue additional bonds. Corporate bond covenants might include provisions that require certain actions on the part of the issuer in the event of a change in corporate control. Thus, a highly rated corporation might pledge to redeem its bonds early in the event that the company is acquired by a lower-rated purchaser.

Indentures for ABS and MBS describe the way in which cash flows received on the underlying consumer obligations will be allocated among securityholders. In the case of ABS, the covenants may limit the degree to which new assets may be added to the pool.

Subsequent to an event of default, the bondholders may, under the supervision of a court, obtain title to the issuer's assets. The processes by which bondholders may seize the assets of a defaulted issuer are much clearer in the private sector than for sovereign or municipal bonds. Public sector bankruptcies are extremely rare, so there is little precedent for what would happen if bondholders tried to seize a government's assets. Further, it isn't clear that a court would transfer ownership of public property from a government to bondholders.

There is considerably more precedent for private sector defaults and liquidations. Bond indentures specify the rights of bondholders under these circumstances. When the bond is a "debenture," a general obligation of a corporate issuer, all the issuer's assets are fair game for bondholders after a default. Corporate general obligations are also referred to as "unsecured debt." By contrast, "secured" lenders' right of seizure and liquidation is limited to certain specified assets. Examples of the latter include "first mortgage bonds" issued by investor-owned utilities. Subsequent to a default on a first mortgage, bondholders might be able to attach, for example, only a specific power plant owned by the utility. If so, other assets of the issuer, such as transmission facilities, would not be subject to seizure by first mortgage holders. Covenants may also limit bondholders' rights of seizure of the assets of specified subsidiaries of an issuer. In the event of a default by the General Motors Acceptance Corporation, for example, bondholders might have no right to seize the assets of the General Motors Corporation.

Companies frequently issue several classes of debt, whose holders rank differently in the event of default. If the company's assets were liquidated, proceeds of the sale would be paid first to holders of "senior" obligations of (or liens on) the issuer. Only after senior lien bondholders had been paid in full would funds be transferred to holders of "junior lien" or "subordinated" bonds. Further, prior to a default, if sufficient funds are not available to meet debt service on all of an issuer's obligations, interest and principal payments due to senior bondholders would be paid first, and investors holding subordinated bonds would receive whatever was left. Under these circumstances, the subordinated bonds would be in default, while the senior obligations would not be. If this happened, the right of subordinated bondholders to seize company assets that are pledged in the first instance to senior bondholders might be limited.

Exhibit 1: Post-Default Recoveries per Dollar of Face Value by Seniority and Nature of Security

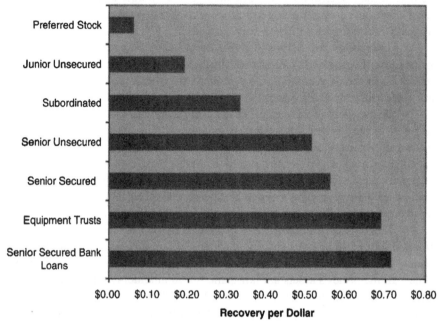

Source: Moody's Investors Service.

A corporation's or municipality's particular combination of senior and subordinated debt, along with its common equity and any preferred stock, is referred to as its "capital structure." Early in 1998, Moody's Investors Service released a study of corporate bond defaults between 1920 and 1997.[1] It examines the relationship between a defaulted bond's rank in the issuer's capital structure and the bondholder's post-default recovery rate. As illustrated in Exhibit 1, senior bondholders recovered substantially more than junior lien holders.

For these reasons, subordinated bonds are of lower credit quality than senior obligations of the same issuer, and this is usually reflected in a difference in the bonds' credit ratings. If a company's senior bonds are rated AA+, for example, "senior subordinated" bonds might be rated AA−, and "junior subordinated" of the same issuer might be assigned an A+ rating. More generally, the provisions of a bond indenture influence credit quality. The stronger the covenants — requiring substantial excess debt service coverage, protecting bondholders from the adverse effects of a "change of control," and limiting the issuer's ability to sell additional bonds secured by the same revenues — the higher the rating on the issuer's bonds.

---

[1] Moody's Investor's Service, Historical Default Rates of Corporate Bond Issuers, 1920-1998 (January 1999).

Issuer's Willingness to Pay

The vast majority of public- and private sector bond issuers are willing to endure considerable economic pain to avoid defaulting on debt obligations. Meeting obligations is not only an ethical and legal imperative, but also makes good financial sense. Most economic entities must borrow on a regular basis to finance capital investments or to meet seasonal cash flow needs. Subsequent to a default, even if an entity were to manage to emerge from bankruptcy as a going concern, borrowing costs for the issuer will inevitably be substantially higher than they would have been otherwise. Public and private issuers' willingness to pay debt service has been called into question often enough, however, so that investors do need to take this possibility into account.

In the public sector, the main risk in this regard is political. One example of a politically driven unwillingness to pay occurred in Orange County, California, in 1995. The County, a wealthy suburban jurisdiction, had experienced severe market value losses in its investment portfolio. Its ability to meet its outstanding financial obligations was jeopardized, and it filed for bankruptcy protection. A modest sales tax increase would have raised enough revenue to remedy the shortfall and to meet all obligations in a timely manner. The voters rejected the tax increase proposal, though, which delayed the resolution of the problem for as long as one year at some cost to creditors.

In the private sector, changes in issuers' willingness to pay is referred to as "event risk." On occasion, corporations that had once been careful to maintain investment-grade credit ratings will change their business strategy in a way that increases the risk of default. For example, an AA-rated corporation, knowing full well that the move will reduce its credit rating to BB–, may decide to issue large volumes of debt to finance the acquisition of other companies in volatile industries. Such a shift in strategy can be interpreted as a reduced commitment to paying debt service on bonds that had been outstanding before the change. Alternatively, an issuer with a long-standing investment-grade rating might be acquired by a corporation with, say, a B+ rating. The acquired firm's ratings will drop with its acqusition. A few corporate bond indentures include provisions designed to protect bondholders against such events, but this is relatively uncommon.

In either case, a full assessment of an issuer's credit will incorporate an analysis of the issuer's willingness to endure economic pain or forgo business opportunities to meet debt service payments and of any developments that might jeopardize this commitment.

WHY CREDIT QUALITY MATTERS

The credit quality of individual bonds in an investor's portfolio and the weighted average credit quality of the portfolio as a whole are important for two reasons. First, actual default on any of the bonds the investor holds would be a very bad thing. Even if the investor eventually recovered 100% of the principal amount of defaulted bonds through a post-default recovery, the process of resolving a bankruptcy will usually take time. As time passes, the investor will not usually receive coupon income, and until their fate is decided, the bonds will probably be highly illiquid.

Historically defaults have tended to peak during periods of economic distress. In Moody's statistical study of corporate default rates between 1920 and 1997, not surprisingly, the peak year is 1929, when 9.2% of corporate issuers defaulted. In recent years defaults have been much less common, particularly among investment-grade issuers. Even among speculative-grade issuers with Moody's ratings of Ba1 or lower, average default rates averaged only 3.38% between 1970 and 1997.

Actual defaults can affect investor returns, but the main influence on investors' returns is the impact of credit improvement and deterioration on bond prices. Suppose an investor purchases at par a non-callable 10-year, Aa/AA-rated corporate bond yielding 50 bp over 10-year Treasury notes or approximately 6.00% as of early Spring 1998. Then assume that immediately after the purchase an event occurs that impairs the issuer's ability to meet debt service payments and drives the bond's ratings to Ba-/BB-. As of early 1998 10-year bonds with that rating were yielding 250 bp over 10-year Treasuries or about 8.00%. Under these assumptions, the price of the bonds would fall from approximately par to about 86.40. In other words, the downgrade would lead to a 13.6% decrease in the market value of the bond. If nothing else happens, the investor's total return for the year — price change plus coupon income — will also be negative to the tune of – 7.6%. Of course if the bond does not default — and even double-B-rated bonds seldom do — the investor can hold the downgraded bond to maturity and not experience any loss of the cash flows he or she contracted to receive from the issuer.

Nevertheless, owning a double-B-rated bond rather than a double-A issue puts the investor at greater risk of default without receiving a yield the market says is adequate compensation for that incremental risk. To put it differently, if the investor had been willing to take double-B-level credit risk, he or she could have earned 8.00% on a high-yield bond. But the initial decision to buy a double-A-rated bond suggests that this investor wants more than 200 bp additional yield as compensation for taking this much additional credit risk. After the downgrade, the investor will be taking double-B credit risk but earning only the 6.00% coupon.

Changes in credit quality can also benefit a portfolio. Suppose now that the investor purchases a non-callable 10-year double-B-rated bond at par to yield 8.00%. Then assume that the rating agencies upgrade the issuer's credit to Baa3/BBB-. As noted in a previous chapter, the market for sub-investment-grade bonds is much thinner than the market for investment-grade securities, even bonds that qualify only marginally as investment-grade. An upgrade from junk to investment-grade status might lead to a 100-basis point decline in the security's market yield spread over comparable Treasuries. It might be reasonable, therefore, to expect that the market yield on the bond would decrease from 8.00% to 7.00% with the price rising from par to 107.11, and the investor's total return for the year of the upgrade — the percentage price change plus the 8.5% coupon — would be 15.11%.

Credit quality is important to investors because it identifies both downside risks and upside opportunities.

MEASURING CREDIT QUALITY

Credit Ratings

On a theoretical level, credit quality is a quantitative concept: the probability of default, or the credit quality ratio. As a practical matter, it is not possible to arrive at meaningful numerical estimates of these statistics for individual bond issues. Therefore, the actual practice of credit analysis is a qualitative process involving judgments about the *relative* credit quality of different issues. The official definitions of rating categories published by the bond rating services (Moody's, Standard & Poor's, Fitch, IBCA, Duff & Phelps) reflect the qualitative, subjective, and relative nature of credit ratings. These definitions are similar across all the agencies; Standard & Poor's are described in Exhibit 2. Letter grade ratings may also be accompanied by an indication of whether the agency believes the credit is gradually improving or deteriorating, or whether the next rerating of the issuer's bonds is likely to be upward or downward.

In most cases, the agencies assign credit ratings to individual issues at the request of the issuer shortly before the bonds are brought to market. The issuer generally pays the rating agency's fee. To analyze the credit, the rating agency will review the issuer's financial statements, interview management, inspect facilities, and evaluate the economic environment in which the borrower operates. Large and frequent issuers are subject to much more intense and continuous scrutiny. Communication between the chief financial officer of a large leveraged corporation or municipality and the agency analyst assigned to that credit will be frequent and highly detailed.

Credit ratings apply to all bonds with the same priority of payment within the issuer's capital structure. For example, an A3/A- rating might apply to a new issue of senior subordinated debt of a corporation and to all other senior subordinated obligations of the same issuer. Occasionally a rating agency will assign a rating to a bond issue even though the issuer has not applied or paid for the rating.

The agencies regularly update credit ratings, even if no new offering is on the calendar, if there is a material change in the issuer's condition. Sometimes this rerating process takes place in two stages. First the rating agency announces that it is reconsidering the issuer's credit by placing the rating "on review" (Moody's) or on "credit watch" (S&P). In making this announcement, the agency will usually also indicate whether it is considering an upgrade or a downgrade. Once it completes the credit review, the agency will announce a new rating and take the issuer off credit watch or the equivalent.

Exhibit 2: Standard & Poor's Corporate Bond Ratings Definitions

AAA: An obligation rated AAA has the highest rating assigned by Standard & Poor's. The obligor's capacity to meet its financial commitment on the obligation is extremely strong.

AA: An obligation rated AA differs from the highest-rated obligations only in small degree. The obligor's capacity to meet its financial commitment on the obligation is very strong.

A: An obligation rated A is somewhat more susceptible to the adverse effects of changes in circumstances and economic conditions than obligations in higher-rated categories. However, the obligor's capacity to meet its financial commitment on the obligation is still strong.

BBB: An obligation rated BBB exhibits adequate protection parameters. However, adverse economic conditions or changing circumstances are more likely to lead to a weakened capacity of the obligor to meet its financial commitment on the obligation.

Obligations rated BB, B, CCC, CC, and C are regarded as having significant speculative characteristics. BB indicates the least degree of speculation and C the highest. While such obligations will likely have some quality and protective characteristics, these may be outweighed by large uncertainties or major exposures to adverse conditions.

BB: An obligation rated BB is less vulnerable to nonpayment than other speculative issues. However, it faces major ongoing uncertainties or exposure to adverse business, financial, or economic conditions which could lead to the obligor's inadequate capacity to meet its financial commitment on the obligation.

B: An obligation rated B is more vulnerable to nonpayment than obligations rated BB, but the obligor currently has the capacity to meet its financial commitment on the obligation. Adverse business, financial, or economic conditions will likely impair the obligor's capacity or willingness to meet its financial commitment on the obligation.

CCC: An obligation rated CCC is currently vulnerable to nonpayment, and is dependent upon favorable business, financial, and economic conditions for the obligor to meet its financial commitment on the obligation. In the event of adverse business, financial, or economic conditions, the obligor is not likely to have the capacity to meet its financial commitment on the obligation.

CC: An obligation rate CC is currently highly vulnerable to nonpayment.

C: The C rating may be used to cover a situation where a bankruptcy petition has been filed or similar action has been taken, but payments on this obligation are being continued.

D: The D rating, unlike other ratings, is not prospective; rather, it is used only where a default has actually occurred – and not where a default is only expected.

Source: Standard & Poor's Website: http//www.standardandpoors.com/ratings/corporates/index/htm

Exhibit 3: Average One-Year Default Rates by Rating

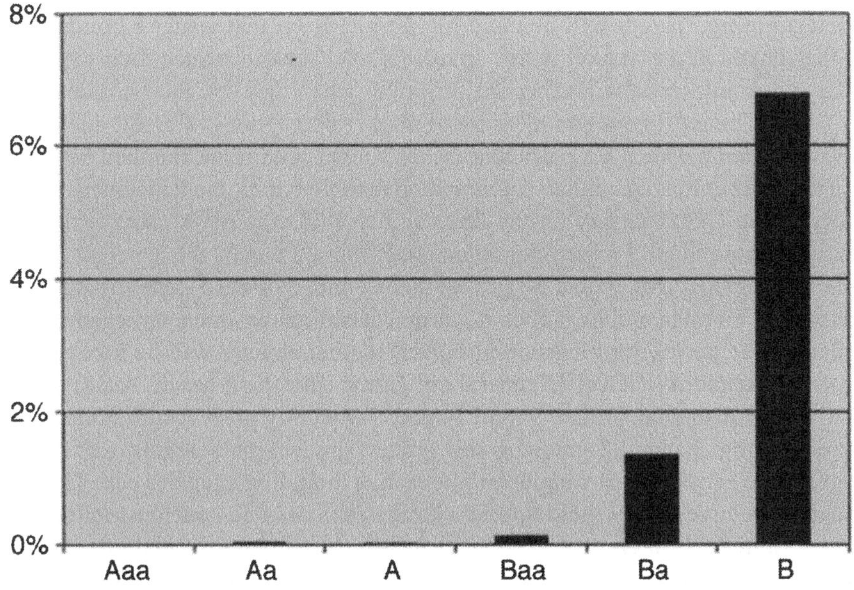

Source: Moody's Investor's Service, *Historical Default Rates of Corporate Bond Issuers, 1920-1998* (January 1999).

A common cliché in the fixed-income markets is that actions by rating agencies tend to follow, rather than lead, market developments. In some sense, this is true; not all events that affect credits can be foreseen, and individual market makers can react more quickly to dramatic developments than organizations can. Just because the agencies have failed to predict some dramatic credit-related events, however, does not necessarily mean that credit ratings are useless as indicators of default probabilities or quality ratios. In fact, the incidence of default increases quite dramatically as credit rating decreases.

Exhibit 3 illustrates this relationship. It presents some of the results of a study conducted by Moody's that calculates the proportion of bonds with various credit ratings that defaulted each year from 1970 through 1997. The statistical analysis provides strong evidence than lower-rated bonds are substantially more likely to default than investment-grade issues.

Credit Spreads

The important predictive role of credit ratings notwithstanding, family portfolio managers should not rely solely on rating agency announcements to signal that the credit quality of bonds is changing. Investors, particularly those holding sub-investment-grade bonds, should also pay careful attention to market perceptions of individual credits and classes of credits. The collective perception of market participants regarding credit quality is reflected most clearly in relative bond yields. If market participants begin to believe that an issuer's credit quality is deteriorating, buyers will demand higher yields on that issuer's bonds than on other bonds in the market, while investors who seek to reduce their exposure to the worsening credit will accept lower prices when they sell their holdings.

The most common measure of market perceptions of credit quality is the *yield spread* between the particular issuer's bonds and some standard benchmark. In the market for U.S. dollar-denominated taxable bonds, the benchmark will usually be the U.S. Treasury on-the-run security with maturity closest to that of the bond being quoted. For yen-denominated corporate bonds, the benchmark will be the closest-maturity Japanese government bond. For euro-denominated bonds, yields on German and/or French government obligations have emerged as benchmarks. For tax-exempt municipal bonds, the benchmark will be a comparable-maturity triple-A-rated state general obligation (the "high-grade" scale).

Substantial shifts in credit spreads frequently precede and seldom follow credit rating changes. Sometimes this reflects the fact that markets can react more quickly to breaking news about an issuer than the rating agencies can. The "information" conveyed by yield spread changes can also be spurious; markets may react to news in ways that are inappropriate. Such cases validate the agencies' deliberate effort to assign ratings that will stand through the course of the business cycle.

To illustrate two edges of the credit spread sword, we will look at two case studies of yield spread changes. The first involves the yield spread of New York City general obligations over high-grade tax-exempt bonds. New York City endured a well-publicized financial crisis during the late 1970s when some scheduled debt service payments were delayed for a short time. By 1983, the City had regained a low investment-rade rating, and since then market and rating agency perceptions of New York City's credit have been influenced by standard analytical considerations: the level of economic activity, management capability, current and projected debt service obligations, and so on. Since the City's credit is subject to considerable scrutiny and since economic conditions in the region have been volatile, there have been eight rating changes by either Moody's or Standard & Poor's since 1983. At the same time, the credit spread for New York City general obligations has fluctuated with considerable volatility over a wide range. Sometimes rating changes have anticipated spread moves; more often, the market has adjusted to developing conditions more rapidly than the agencies.

Exhibit 4 tracks the yield spread for 10-year New York City GOs over triple-A-rated state GOs and notes the two most recent occasions on which one or the other of the agencies has changed the City's credit ratings. No significant shift in the spread preceded the upgrade by Moody's early in 1998. The downgrade by S&P was announced in the middle of a period in which the yield spread was increasing, indicating that the market was worried about the City's credit before one of the agencies validated the concern.

Exhibit 4: Yield Spread: 10-Year New York City General Obligations over 10-Year Triple-A-Rated State General Obligations

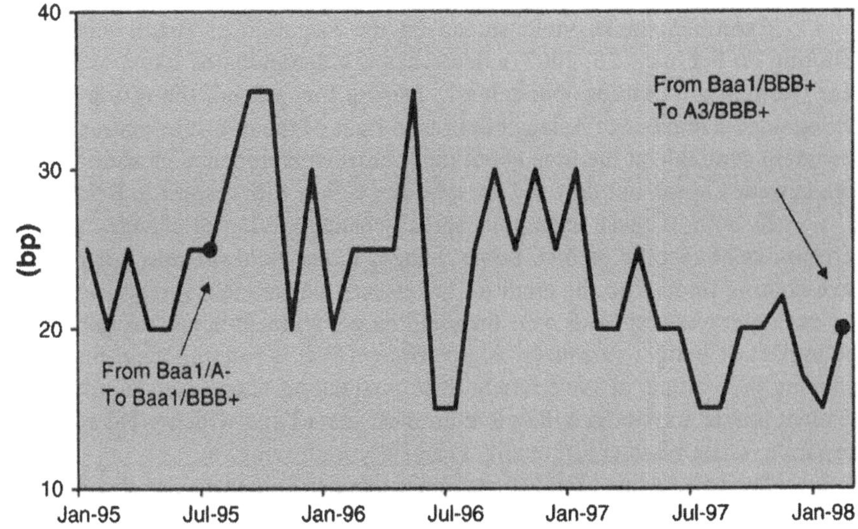

Source: Goldman, Sachs & Co.

The second example focuses on the impact of the Asian financial crisis of late 1997 on yields on Brazilian government bonds. In October and November of 1997, investors who had been aggressively buying bonds issued by governments and corporations in southeast and east Asia began to be concerned about the level of these countries' short-term foreign currency borrowing (mostly U.S. dollars). If commercial bank lenders refused to roll over these short-term borrowings when they came due, a rush by borrowers to convert local currencies into U.S. dollars to meet debt service obligations might force a sharp drop in exchange rates. If foreign currencies became much more expensive for Asian borrowers, they might not be able to pay off the loans that were coming due, leading to widespread defaults. These concerns spread rapidly from one country to another, reducing the prices of local currencies and widening spreads on the foreign currency bonds of Asian issuers.

To some extent, the concerns about Asia's finances were justified. Heavy short-term borrowing of funds used to finance consumption or uneconomical capital investments was probably much too common in several of the affected countries. Then concerns about emerging markets in one part of the world spilled over to developing economies in other regions. The Asian contagion led to a sharp widening of yield spreads for foreign currency bonds of Latin American issuers such as the Republic of Brazil.

The Brazilian credit story is a complex one. As it happened, the country faced a period of heightened uncertainty late in 1997 as the government was trying to implement an austere fiscal program one year before general elections. Further, while the situation was nowhere near as troublesome as in Asia, many

Brazilian borrowers did make use of short-term foreign currency borrowings that had to be rolled over. None of these concerns, however, was pronounced enough to justify the dramatic widening of yield spreads on Brazilian bonds.

Exhibit 5 tracks yield spread on the Republic of Brazil 8.00% issue maturing on February 26, 2007, a deutschemark-denominated issue, over the 10-year German government benchmark. During this period, the rating agencies downgraded a number of Asian countries in light of the new information that was becoming available at the time about those borrowers' reliance on short-term foreign currency credi, but they did not take any action with respect to Brazil.

In both of these examples, spread changes reflected changes in market perceptions of specific credits. Some changes in the yield spreads, however, may have nothing to do with the credit of the issuers whose yield spread is widening. For example, wider spreads over the yield on government bonds may also reflect the impact of budget surpluses. A government that is running a surplus will be reducing the volume of government debt outstanding. Decreased supply of government bonds may reduce the yield on these issues and widen yield spreads on corporate issues when credit quality is actually improving.

The bottom line of this discussion is that portfolio managers should not rely on a single source of information. Market yield spreads frequently move sharply when the rating agencies are taking no action. Sometimes this means that the market is anticipating the agencies' eventual response to real credit changes. Frequently, the market is over-reacting. It is important to know what the market is saying, but it is equally important to apply independent judgment to this information.

Exhibit 5: Yield Spread: Brazil 8.00% of 2/26/07 over 10-Year German Government Benchmark

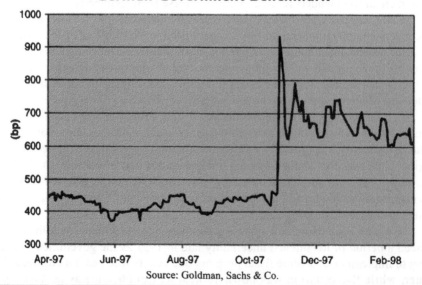

Source: Goldman, Sachs & Co.

MANAGING PORTFOLIO CREDIT QUALITY:
AVOIDING TWO BIG MISTAKES

Family investors commonly make two major mistakes in managing the credit quality of their portfolios. Some conservative investors decide to avoid credit risk entirely by buying only home currency-denominated bonds fully guaranteed by a central government. Such a policy might make sense if the investor has a policy avoiding all risks to principal. To be consistent with such a policy, the investor's entire investment portfolio would have to consist entirely of risk-free investments; i.e., short-term home currency-denominated government securities.

Suppose the investor's portfolio includes common stocks and government bonds with durations greater than one year. Such a portfolio is incurring some risks, presumably in order to earn an enhanced return. But there isn't anything about credit risk that makes assuming it inherently worse than interest rate risk or stock price risk.

A slightly less extreme, but only slightly less mistaken, version of the same "conservative" strategy is to establish a firm policy of not buying bonds rated, say, Aa3 or lower. The logic behind such absolute investment rules is also questionable. The investor is, in effect, saying that there is no yield differential between bonds rated A1 and those rated Aa3 that would make the former more worth buying than the latter.

This is not to say that there aren't circumstances in which it makes sense for portfolio managers to improve the average credit quality of their portfolios. Investors who moved their bond portfolios into all triple-A credits just before the onset of the great depression in 1929 would have been very happy they had done so by the end of the next decade. In general, it makes sense to sell weaker credits and buy stronger credits whenever it looks like the economy is likely to sink into recession. It also might make sense to upgrade when credit spreads are unusually tight and when the compensation for taking credit risk is lower than it had been. But a policy of avoiding all credit exposure while willingly taking other risks is patently inconsistent.

In fact, historical experience tells us that it makes good economic sense to hold a diversified portfolio of lower-rated credits. The Moody's study we have cited also includes an estimate of average one-year credit losses realized on diversified portfolios of bonds in a range of rating categories from B to Aaa. The authors of the Moody's report combine information about average default rates by rating category and data on post-default recoveries to arrive at their estimates of annual losses.

In Exhibit 6, we subtract these one-year loss estimates from indicative yields as of early 1998 on U.S. dollar-denominated corporate bonds of various credit qualities. The result is an estimate of net yield after expected credit losses. The statistics indicate that as of early 1998 moving down in credit quality from U.S. Treasuries to Ba-rated bonds produces increases in expected net yields. Historical loss experience on B-rated bonds was severe enough and nominal yield differentials between B and higher-rated bonds were narrow enough at that time so that it did not appear advantageous to buy the average B-rated bonds.

These statistics are suggestive. They are not definitive. They suggest that trading down in credit can be useful in the sense that investors could expect to earn more on lower-rated bonds, except for the very lowest category. The results do not mean that it only or it always makes sense to hold bonds rated Ba. Nor can we conclude that it never makes sense to own any B-rated bonds. Given the historical experience since 1970, investors can expect to do better *on average* with the lower-rated credits.

The second big mistake family investors make is at the other extreme of the risk spectrum. It is dangerous to concentrate a portfolio's credit risk in a small number of issues. The statistics presented in Exhibit 6 indicate that *on average* credit losses on portfolios rated Ba or better are small relative to the yield pickup offered by lower-rated bonds. These average losses reflect a very large number of issues on which investors realize no credit losses, however, and a very small number on which losses may be substantial.

There are two ways to avoid losses that exceed the average for a rating category. One way is to diversify. An investor who owns a portfolio that includes small positions in all the bonds in a rating category will, by definition, experience the average performance of that category.

The second way to avoid losses, and to perform even better than the averages suggest, is to pick the lower-rated bonds that have a lower default probability or a higher expected post-default recovery rate than the average for the rating category. In other words, the investor might avoid realizing average losses by buying bonds that are, literally, under-rated by Moody's and S&P.

Neither of these approaches is entirely satisfactory. As a practical matter, it is impossible for an investor to own a bond portfolio that reflects the market as a whole. Not all bonds are available at all times. And, in any case, a portfolio including a very large number of very small positions would be disadvantageous in other respects. The idea of picking the "right" credits is a good one. Building a bond portfolio does require some selectivity, but investors should not expect to be able to do better credit analysis than the rating agencies on average over any period of time.

Exhibit 6: Loss Rates and Net Yields on Bonds by Credit Rating

Credit	Loss Rate (%)	Avg. Yield (%)	Net Yield (%)	Yield Pickup vs.					
				Treas.	Aaa	Aa	A	Baa	Ba
Treas.	0.00	5.76	5.76						
Aaa	0.00	6.21	6.21	0.45%					
Aa	0.02	6.28	6.26	0.50	0.05%				
A	0.00	6.47	6.47	0.71	0.26	0.21%			
Baa	0.06	6.79	6.73	0.97	0.52	0.47	0.26%		
Ba	0.70	7.52	6.82	1.06	0.61	0.56	0.35	0.09%	
B	3.57	8.98	5.41	−0.35	−0.80	−0.85	−1.06	−1.32	−1.41%

Sources: Moody's Investors Service; Goldman, Sachs & Co.

Fortunately these approaches are not mutually exclusive. Portfolio managers should do their best to select the best *available* bonds within any given credit rating. At the same time, investors should aim to build diversified portfolios. There is no "right" answer regarding how many different credits are required to make a portfolio diversified. Certainly the number of different positions should be larger for lower-rated credits than for triple-A-rated securities. A reasonable rule of thumb might be that positions in credits rated below A3/A- should not constitute more than 5% of an investor's portfolio, while no single speculative-grade investment should account for more than 5%. Investors should also monitor potential industrial concentrations in their bond portfolios. It would be worrisome, for example, if 25% of a bond portfolio with an average rating of Baa2/BBB were concentrated in, say, the retailing industry. These rules of thumb can be violated for short periods of time as the investor builds the portfolio or if unusual opportunities arise, but diversification should be the norm.

MONITORING PORTFOLIO CREDIT QUALITY

Portfolio managers need information about credits in order to select bonds for purchase and to decide which bonds, if any, to sell. Most large institutional investors do their own credit evaluations. Mutual funds and insurance companies employ large staffs of credit analysts to conduct original research on issuers and bond structures. Few family portfolio managers will have the time, the inclination, or the need to dig deeply into the credit quality of individual bonds. Instead, family investors will generally be consumers of credit analysis undertaken by others. Fortunately, there are a number of independent sources of information on many corporate and municipal credits.

Portfolios consisting entirely of bonds rated A, provided there are no high concentrations of holdings, do not require frequent credit review. Investors should be aware of any change in the credit rating of the bonds that they own and should make sure that some mechanism is in place to provide such information. Beyond that, a semiannual or quarterly review of portfolio credit quality using the most recent rating agency reports should be sufficient.

Portfolios with substantial volumes of bonds rated Baa1/BBB+ or lower require more intensive credit monitoring. In this case, too, investors will want to know about any official actions by rating agencies. Portfolio managers will want to tap into other sources of information on lower-rated credits. In the case of corporate bonds, published research by investment dealers will be the most readily available source of information beyond the rating agencies. Wall Street firms that make active markets in high-yield and emerging market bonds publish credit research on these issues. Also, to the extent that corporate issuers of junk bonds also have common stock outstanding, fixed-income investors can gain insights from analysis prepared by equity analysts.

Wall Street research does not cover all issuers of high-yield bonds, so before purchasing a bond rated below A3/A-, investors should ascertain what information about the issuer will be available on an ongoing basis. Before buying any sub-investment-grade bond, family portfolio managers without the capacity to do their own original credit analysis will certainly want to make sure that there will be at least two independent sources of ongoing credit information about the issuer.

CHAPTER 11

Operation of the
Public Bond Markets

I remember a few years ago, shortly after moving to a new town, collecting a cartload of fresh fruits and vegetables at a supermarket and then finding a place at the end of a long checkout line. When I finally got to the cashier and had unloaded all my items on the counter, I was informed that all the items had first to be weighed and priced in the produce department. In this case, the cost of not knowing the market convention was some wasted time and the embarrassment of reloading my items while making others wait. For an investor building and managing a large bond portfolio, the cost of misunderstanding bond market conventions can be much higher. The purpose of this chapter is to outline the operating conventions of the major sectors of the global bond markets.

THREE WAYS OF ORGANIZING FINANCIAL MARKETS

All the securities markets around the world fall into three broad categories: private markets, exchange markets, and dealer markets. In private markets, as the name implies, securities are traded through direct negotiation between buyers and sellers. Third-party intermediaries may facilitate these negotiations as paid agents for one party or the other, but the intermediary never actually takes possession of the securities. Private markets tend to work best for unique or particularly complex investments.

In dealer and exchange markets, buyers and sellers do not negotiate with one another directly. In both cases, sellers sell to and buyers buy from financial institutions, and the intermediary actually takes ownership title to the securities. These intermediaries may be either brokers or dealers.

A broker will invariably match up individual buyers and sellers of the same securities position and then "cross" the trade for the instrument. No transaction will take place until the broker has identified both the buyer and the seller. So, although the broker actually owns the security for a short period of time, in these transactions the intermediary is never at risk with respect to changes in the security's price and, in the case of bond transactions, never earns any accrued interest. The advantage that a brokered transaction provides over direct negotiation between buyer and seller is anonymity. The broker's compensation is usually a small fee.

Dealers differ from brokers in that they will "make markets" in securities. That is, a dealer is willing to purchase a security from a seller without necessarily having identified a buyer. Dealers may also "go short" securities by selling to a buyer without necessarily having identified a willing seller. Thus, a dealer is willing to be at risk with respect to changes in securities' prices and to carry stocks or bonds in inventory for a period of time.

Exchange Markets

Brokers or dealers may agree to conduct all transactions at an agreed-upon place at scheduled times, to announce all buy and sell orders for listed securities publicly, and to execute all purchases and sales at publicly disclosed prices. The place may be a physical space, such as the corner of Broad and Wall Streets in the City of New York, or, increasingly often, it may be an address in cyberspace. This "place" is referred to as an exchange, and the securities that are traded in this way are referred to as exchange-traded investments. Common stocks are the most familiar exchange-traded securities. Most futures contracts are traded on exchanges.

On the exchange, one or more market makers for each listed security continually posts prices at which the dealer is willing to buy and sell a specified block size of a stock or bond: bid and offer (or ask) prices, respectively. Investors seeking either to buy or sell a stock will contact a member of the exchange where the security is traded, and the member will execute the order on the appropriate side of the market. Exchange members attempt to post prices at which buy and sell orders are in balance. Exchanges work best for securities that are traded actively enough on a daily basis so that market makers have sufficient information about order flows to enable them to quote a two-sided market for a large number of securities with a narrow bid-asked spread without creating a large imbalance of orders.

Dealer Markets

In a dealer market, there is no central meeting place, no agreement among dealers regarding public posting of orders, and no disclosure requirement with respect to transaction prices. Investors seeking to purchase or sell securities will approach dealers active in a particular market. The dealer may fill a buy order for a specific security in several ways.

First, it may act as a broker by locating a willing third-party seller of the instrument in question in the desired quantity. If the dealer happens to hold the particular security in inventory in the right amount, the dealer may sell that inventory position. Or a dealer may "go short" a security it does not already own by agreeing to deliver it on the settlement date. In the last case the dealer will seek to "cover" the short position before settlement. If the customer wishes to sell a security, the dealer may use this order to cover an outstanding short position, or may happen to find a matching buyer immediately, or may "go long" the instrument by taking it into inventory.

Because dealers are willing to be at risk with respect to the market value of the securities in which they trade by carrying long or short positions, most sales and purchases in a dealer market are referred to as "principal" transactions because the intermediary acts as a principal and not as an agent. In markets organized in this way, dealers may quote two-sided markets for certain actively traded securities, but not necessarily for all or most of the instruments they are willing to buy or sell.

Dealer markets work best for investments that are not particularly unusual or complex but that do not trade frequently. Relatively infrequent trading reduces the chances that the intermediary will be able to find matching buy and sell orders simultaneously, and this precludes the development of an efficient exchange. At the same time, the generic nature of the securities in question allows dealers to go long or short the instruments with a high degree of confidence in their ability to offset these positions at market prices within a reasonably short period of time.

Most bond markets are dealer markets. Some bonds are listed on exchanges, but even for these securities most transactions take place off the exchange by means of principal transactions executed through dealers, and the bid-asked spreads for blocks of more than about $100,000 are generally narrower in the dealer market than on the exchange. Other fixed-income instruments are issued and traded through private transactions, but these account for a relatively small proportion of all fixed-income activity.

THE PRIMARY MARKET

Sales of securities by issuers to initial investors are referred to as "primary" market transactions. Sales of outstanding securities from one investor to another are "secondary" market transactions. The conventions of the primary and secondary markets differ in important respects.

Dealers as Underwriters in Syndicates

Almost all public new issues (i.e., not private placements) come to market through a dealer transaction. That is, even if the security will eventually be traded on an exchange, the issuer will initially sell the securities to a dealer, and the dealer will distribute the bonds or stocks to initial investors. When it acts in this capacity, a dealer will purchase the security from the issuer and then sell the bonds to investors; a dealer acting as the initial purchaser of a new issue is thus referred to as an "underwriter," and the process of initial distribution is referred to as an "underwriting." When they execute secondary market transactions, either on an exchange or in a dealer market, dealers usually act on their own.

In the primary bond market, underwriters frequently constitute themselves as a team of firms referred to as an "underwriting syndicate." In most cases, a syndicate will purchase securities from an issuer as a group and sell the bonds to investors as a group. Underwriting profits or losses — the difference between the price paid to the issuer and the prices paid by the initial investors — are divided among the members of the team according to a prearranged set of syndicate rules.

The difference between the price paid to the issuer for the securities and the prices paid to the syndicate members by the initial purchasers has two components. A part of this differential — the "underwriting spread" or "takedown" — is agreed to by the issuer as compensation to the syndicate for the underwriting service. The second component, which may decrease the syndicate's total profit, reflects changes in the market price between the time the securities are purchased from the issuer and the time they are sold to investors. Such subsequent price changes are usually negative, since if the market is rallying, investors will snap up the securities from the syndicate at the initial offering price. If prices are declining at the time of the offering, investors may hang back in hope of getting a better price on bonds left in the syndicate's hands.

Not all primary market activity is conducted by syndicates. Dealer firms participate separately, and not as members of a syndicate, in initial sales of bonds and notes by the U.S. Treasury Department. Also, occasionally, corporate or municipal bond issues will be purchased and distributed by a single firm acting alone as an underwriter. Finally, some issuers have begun selling bonds directly to investors over the internet.

Methods of Sale

There are four methods by which issuers price and sell initial offerings of bonds: auctions, advertised or competitive sale, negotiated transactions, and medium-term note offerings.

Auctions

In an auction, the issuer announces the volume of bonds to be sold and the sale date and time. Before the deadline, auction participants submit bids. Each bid consists of a yield and a par amount. A participant may submit more than one bid. For example, a firm participating in an auction of five-year Treasury notes might submit one bid for $50 million par amount at a yield of 6.250% and an additional bid for $100 million at a yield of 6.255%.

The manager of the auction assembles all the bids, and determines the lowest yield so that par amounts bid at that yield or lower add up to the total being offered.[1] This yield may be referred as the "stop-out" yield or the "winning" yield. The coupon may be announced either before or after bids are submitted. Participants who submit bids at lower yields than the stop-out will receive the

---

[1] The buyer at most auctions outside the bond market is the bidder willing to pay the highest price. In the case of bond auctions, the winner bids the lowest yield.

par amount they bid. Those who submit a yield exactly equal to the stop-out will usually receive a pro rata proportion of the par amount they bid.

In a standard auction, each buyer pays a price for the bonds or notes, given their coupon, that produces the yield that he or she actually bids. In a "dutch auction," all bidders pay the same price, the price that produces the winning yield.

Auctions work best for straightforward, widely understood obligations of issuers that offer new securities with some regularity. The prime example of such securities is central government bonds of major industrialized countries. It is not surprising, therefore, that most G-7 finance ministries, including the U.S. Treasury Department, offer their securities through some form of auction mechanism. Some short-term municipal securities are also sold through auctions.

Advertised or Competitive Sale

Advertised or "competitive" sale is seldom used outside the U.S. tax-exempt bond market; and some municipalities are required by law to use this technique. Occasionally a regulated public utility will also use this method if it is required to do so. In an advertised sale, the issuer will announce the par amount and maturities of bonds to be sold and the deadline for submission of bids. Dealers form syndicates to bid on the bonds, and one of the underwriters takes responsibility for submitting the joint bid as "book runner."

Traditionally, all bids in a competitive bond sale have been submitted on an all-or-none basis. That is, one and only one of the bidding syndicates would be awarded all the bonds. This is still standard operating procedure for most advertised sales, although recently some issuers, especially those who have offered their bonds for competitive sale on the internet, have awarded individual maturities or parts of maturities separately. Thus, the competitive sale process may be becoming more like the auction process.

The bids consist of a coupon and net purchase price paid to the issuer for each maturity of bonds being offered. If only one maturity is being offered, the determination of the winning bid is relatively easy; it is the combination of coupon and net purchase price that produces the lowest yield to maturity. If, as is usually the case with municipals, the issue consists of multiple maturities offered as serial bonds, the winning bid is the one that produces the lowest internal rate of return on all the cash flows to be received and paid by the issuer. The issuer or its agent receives all the bids, validates the calculations, and shortly thereafter awards all the bonds to the syndicate that bid the lowest internal rate of return.

Negotiated Transactions

Negotiated transactions are the most common method by which issuers sell new bonds. In this case, the issuer selects an underwriting syndicate before announcing a bond offering. The syndicate may include a single dealer firm, but more often the issuer will appoint a lead or senior manager and several comanagers.

The issuer may also identify a number of dealer firms to serve in a selling group. A selling group is able to offer securities to its customers, but will not participate in the division of profits or losses under the rules agreed to at the time the syndicate was formed.

Once the syndicate is in place, the issuer and underwriters will work together to decide on the size, maturity, structure, and timing of the planned bond issue. The syndicate and its legal counsel will also usually work with the issuer and its counsel to prepare offering documents that are consistent with market standards and regulatory disclosure requirements. Once the offering is announced and preliminary offering documents have been made available to investors, the syndicate will solicit orders, provide market information to the issuer, and, possibly, restructure the offering in light of investor reactions. Finally, the syndicate will commit to underwrite the bonds at a specific price.

In most cases, a few days will pass between the announcement of a bond offering and the actual pricing. This period could last longer if investors are unfamiliar with the issuer or if the structure of the offering is innovative or particularly complex. For some subinvestment-grade initial offerings, underwriters organize a multi-week, multi-city "road show" to introduce the new credit to investors. Well-known issuers with underwriting syndicates in place may announce, market, and price a simply structured new issue all within a few hours.

Medium-Term Note Offerings

A method of sale that combines some of the attributes of both advertised and negotiated offerings has become more important in recent years. The medium-term note (MTN) market developed in the 1980s after the Securities Exchange and Commission changed its regulations regarding new issues. Previously, each individual offering of securities had to be registered with the SEC. For most issuers, the registration process is routine, but it does take time.

Many new issues still come to market after completing a full registration process, but frequent issuers may now make use of what is called "shelf registration." That is, the SEC now allows well-known companies to register once for a large amount of issuance, but then bring the securities to market over time in smaller quantities without revisiting the regulator each time.

Issuers that make use of shelf registration will usually appoint a group of underwriters to serve as MTN dealers. When the company decides that it wants to issue securities, the corporate treasury office will notify the members of this group. The members of the dealer group will then compete to provide the corporation with the best all-in cost of funds available in the market that day. The company then selects the dealer to underwrite that particular "tranche" of MTNs.

Pricing New Issues: Contrasts Among Market Sectors

The process used to price negotiated new issues differs for the U.S. corporate and government agency markets on the one hand and the municipal bond market on the other. The processes used to price non-government new issues in Europe and Asia fall somewhere between the U.S. corporate and municipal "syndicate" practices.

Corporate Bonds

In the corporate market, a new issue is introduced to the market with an announcement from the issuer and the syndicate. The announcement indicates the approximate dollar amount to be borrowed, the security's maturity, and the latest date on which the issue will be priced. After the announcement and the distribution of prospectuses to potential buyers, "official price talk" will begin. These conversations will be about the yield spread on these bonds relative to the U.S. Treasury benchmark security with maturity closest to that of a bond issue.

For example, the price talk on a March 1998 new issue of $200 million XYZ, Inc., debentures maturing in 2008 might begin at 80 basis points over the yield on the U.S. Treasury 5.50% note of February 2008, the 10-year benchmark security. Investors would be notified of the new offering and the official price talk by their salesperson at a syndicate member firm. During this marketing period investors are given the opportunity to "circle" the bonds; that is, the investor commits to buy a specific amount of the securities, provided that the yield spread at the final pricing is not narrower than the price talk. During the marketing period the syndicate may adjust the price talk in light of information it receives; once the bulk of the offering is "circled" at a spread that is acceptable to the issuer, the underwriters will end the marketing period. If an offering is committed to in this way sooner rather than later in the marketing process, the syndicate might price the deal before the announced date.

On the pricing date for the issue, the syndicate, in consultation with the issuer, determines the new issue's coupon and its dollar price. If the marketing process is successful from the issuer's point of view — that is, if there is more than enough demand for the issue at "80 over" so that there is room to "tighten" the offering while retaining a sufficient volume of orders — the coupon and dollar price will produce a yield that is, say, 78 bp over the yield on the Treasury benchmark at the time of pricing.

So, for example, if the yield on the Treasury 5.50% of February 2008 is 7.417% at the time of pricing, the yield on the new XYZ issue should be 8.197% (= 7.417% + 0.78%). Thus, the issuer might set the coupon at 8.125%, to give it a "round number" and, if so, the syndicate would price the issue for sale to investors at 99.515 to yield 8.197% to maturity. If the issuer and the syndicate had negotiated, say, a ⅜ underwriters' discount (underwriting spread or takedown), the net price received by the issuer would be 99.140 (= 99.515 − 0.375) and the all-in cost of financing for the issuer, expressed as yield, would be 8.868%. The value of this underwriting spread on this $200 million issue would be $750,000.

This process usually produces a volume of "circled" bonds that approximately equals the amount being offered. If the offering is oversubscribed — that is, if the volume of circled bonds exceeds the amount being offered by a substantial margin

— the lead manager of the syndicate allocates securities among investors. Allocation decisions are subjective. Investors who circled their bonds earlier in the marketing process or who are better customers of the lead manager may get better treatment. Allocations cannot, however, be completely arbitrary, because investors who feel ill-treated can and do embarrass the lead manager by complaining to the issuer.

If instead the book of orders is not filled by the final pricing date at yield spreads that the dealers consider appropriate, the syndicate will underwrite the unsold portion of the offering and attempt to distribute the securities over a short period of time. Even though syndicate members will usually hedge the interest rate exposure involved in being long bonds (by selling U.S. Treasury notes or futures short), the underwriters will remain at risk because they may eventually be forced to sell the securities at wider yield spreads.

For example, suppose the XYZ bonds are not all sold at the original dollar price of 99.515, and $100 million of bonds are retained by the syndicate. Assume further that there is no change in Treasury note yields. The syndicate meets market resistance when it tries to distribute the bonds at a spread of 78 bp of the 10-year Treasury and is unable to sell the remaining securities at a spread of less than 85 bp. With an unchanged Treasury market, this would translate into a dollar price of 99.046. Under these circumstances, the syndicate would lose 0.469% of par (= 99.515 − 99.046) on $100 million in bonds or $469,000. The syndicate's profit on the $100 million sold at the original price would be $375,000, so the net loss on the underwriting would be $94,000. Investors who had purchased $100 million at the original price would also realize a loss of market value equal to $94,000.

Municipals

Practices in the municipal market differ from these corporate conventions for several reasons. First, in the tax-exempt sector there is no standard, actively traded benchmark comparable to the U.S. Treasury yield curve.[2] Second, while corporate bond issues almost invariably consist of a single maturity, municipal new issues typically include bonds with as many as 20 different maturities. These differences make it more difficult for dealers to communicate with potential buyers during the marketing period for a bond issue; instead of being able to talk about the yield spread over Treasuries, a single number that will be invariant with respect to general interest rate levels, municipal underwriters must talk about many different numbers, all of which change whenever the market moves.

As in the corporate market, the municipal pricing process begins with the announcement of the offering. At the outset of the marketing period, in addition to announcing the approximate pricing date and total dollar amount, the issuer and

---

[2] The so-called high-grade curve, an estimate of yields on triple-A-rated state general obligations is emerging as a benchmark in the municipal market. Because these interest rates reflect only a guess about where hypothetical bonds might trade, the high-grade scale is of limited usefulness as a guide to new issue pricing.

syndicate also indicate the approximate maturity structure of the various serial and term bonds in the issue. Salespeople at the syndicate member firms discuss the issue with investors, solicit indications of general interest, and attempt to ascertain how potential buyers view the bonds of this particular issuer relative to other municipalities whose bonds are trading actively. For example, a salesperson might ascertain that the manager of a large mutual fund believes that 20-year bonds of a new Massachusetts Water Resources Authority (MWRA) issue with a 5.00% coupon would be fairly valued at a yield between 5 and 10 basis points less than the yield of an outstanding 20-year 5.00% Massachusetts Turnpike Authority bond. If the latter recently traded at a yield of 5.26% to maturity, the client's opinion will be useful to the underwriters; absent a major shift in interest rates, the syndicate might begin by offering MWRA 5.00%s at a yield between 5.16% and 5.21%.

At the end of the marketing period, the syndicate managers commence an "order period" by distributing a preliminary pricing wire to the members of the syndicate. This message sets the dollar amount, coupons, dollar prices and yields, and call provisions of each maturity of bonds being offered. The prices and yields reflect information gathered from investors during the marketing period. Syndicate members' salespeople will then solicit investor orders for the various maturities.

Because it is more difficult to pin down potential investors in the tax-exempt market, municipal underwriters tend to be surprised more often than their corporate counterparts by deals that are heavily over- or undersubscribed at the preliminary pricing. Consequently, *repricing*, after the release of the preliminary pricing wire, is much more common in the municipal market than in the corporate sector. If the offering as a whole is heavily oversubscribed at the preliminary pricing, the syndicate managers might lower the yields on all maturities across the board. Investors who entered orders at the higher yields then have the option of accepting the lower price or dropping all or a portion of their order. Likewise, if the preliminary pricing elicited too few orders, the offering may be "cheapened." Investors who entered orders at the lower preliminary yield will, of course, be confirmed their bonds at the new, higher yields, and new orders will generally be forthcoming.

Offerings are usually repriced only once. If, after repricing, the issue is still oversubscribed, the lead manager allocates bonds among investors, as in the corporate market. If the deal remains undersubscribed even after repricing, the syndicate will underwrite the issue at the final pricing and remain at risk until the bonds are sold.

Family Investors in the Primary Market

In the case of G-7 central government securities — such as U.S. Treasuries, Japanese government bonds — investors can be indifferent between buying in the new issue or secondary markets. These sectors of the bond market are so efficient that there should be little difference in yield between two Treasury securities with identical coupons maturing on the same date if one had been issued the day before the trade and the other had been issued twenty years previously.

In the corporate and municipal markets, the main advantage of buying bonds in the primary market is price transparency. In exchange markets, all prices are posted publicly. In dealer markets, like most fixed-income sectors, prices of primary market transactions are public, but the prices in the secondary market need not be publicized and generally are not. In the secondary market, therefore, buyers may have reason to wonder whether another investor who purchases the same security at the same time might pay a lower price. Later we will discuss some of the ways family portfolio managers can alleviate this doubt by validating the pricing of secondary market transactions. At this point, though, it is sufficient to make two observations regarding primary markets.

First, the initial price at which primary market syndicates sell bonds to initial investors must be publicized. Second, it is illegal to sell bonds to investors at anything other than the publicly announced prices until the syndicate manager announces that the securities are "free to trade." Thus, purchases in the primary market are not subject to the same potential uncertainty as those made in the secondary market.

Whatever the theoretical advantages of primary market purchases, as a practical matter it is generally difficult for family portfolio managers to participate in the primary market in an effective way. Effective participation in the primary market requires more or less constant availability during business hours when deals are being priced. In the municipal market, investors need to respond to preliminary pricing, repricing, and final pricing by either confirming their orders or dropping out. In the corporate sector, deals may be announced and priced within a few hours. This is not a problem for institutional investors who are always at their trading desks and can rely on backup personnel when they are on vacation. But family portfolio managers may often be unavailable when decisions have to be made.

Furthermore, both institutional and individual investors who enter orders for new issues have no guarantee that they will be allocated the entire amount they wanted. It is possible to be limited to, say, only 20% of an order after spending a great deal of time evaluating a particular new issue. Or, an investor can wind up with a very small allocation that amounts to an odd lot in the bond market. Too many small positions can reduce a bond portfolio's liquidity.

Family investors do have some opportunities to participate in the primary market. In fact, some corporate and emerging market bond issues issued in Europe are specifically designed to appeal to individual investors. In the municipal bond market, some issuers go out of their way to require syndicate procedures to assure "retail" participation. For example, some municipalities require that if a transaction is oversubscribed, all *bona fide* orders from individual investors will be filled before any institutional orders. In other cases, the marketing period for retail investors begins a day or so before the institutional marketing period to give dealers an opportunity to convey information about the offering to large numbers of retail investors. Such retail order periods are usually accompanied by some special priority on bona fide retail orders in the allocation of oversubscribed bonds.

Family portfolio managers should be prepared to participate in the primary market when offerings are structured to accommodate purchases by individual investors. Unless and until these retail-friendly syndicate practices become much more widespread, however, most families will continue to buy most of their bonds in the secondary market.

THE SECONDARY MARKET

For investors who are most accustomed to buying and selling the common stocks of companies with large market capitalization, the most unusual characteristic of the bond market is that not all bonds are available at all times. An investor who decides to buy shares of, say, IBM can purchase essentially unlimited quantities at any time during exchange trading hours. Very large buy or sell orders might affect the market price, and substantial transactions might require the services of a dealer firm with block trading capabilities, but stock trading volume is such that timely execution of any order is always possible.

The same is not true of individual bonds. An investor seeking to buy, for example, $5 million worth of IBM 6.50%s of January 15, 2028, might or might not be able to execute the transaction on any given business day.

Finding Bonds

An investor seeking to buy particular IBM bonds would contact one or more bond dealers. If one or more of these dealers happens to be making active markets in this particular bond, completing the purchase is then relatively easy. Suppose dealers are quoting an active market in blocks of $1 million IBM 6.50%s of '28, bidding the bond at 97.500 and offering at 97.875. Even if none of the dealers the investor calls happens to hold the IBM 6.50%s, it could still be easy to execute the buy transaction, if other bond dealers are making a 97.500/97.875 market. The dealer-to-dealer market is very active, and it would ordinarily not be difficult for the investor's direct contact to locate the bonds "in the street."

If no dealers happen to hold this particular bond, the only way to obtain the securities is to induce another investor to sell $5 million of the IBM 6.50%s of '28. The dealer "working the inquiry" contacts investors who hold these bonds and solicits indications of selling interest. If the buyer is lucky, one or more investors might want to reduce their exposure to the IBM credit and therefore be willing sellers at 97.500. More likely, investors will decide that these bonds are more valuable than they thought they were from the fact that someone is seeking to buy them and decide not to offer the securities at less than, say, 98.250.

The IBM 6.50%s of '28 are about as liquid as corporate bonds get. The issuer is very well-known, and the original issue size was $700 million. A $5 million order for these securities is unlikely to affect the market, and the purchase price is likely to be closer to 97.875 than to 98.250. The outcome is not so certain if the investor is seeking bonds of a less well-known issuer from a smaller-sized offering or with unique structural characteristics. In general, it is usually easier to buy bonds that were recently issued in large amounts by well-known issuers.

Bonds become available in the secondary market in several ways. Usually the most actively traded bonds — the ones with the narrowest bid-asked spreads — tend to be recent new issues that have been freed to trade. Investors who participate in the primary market may be allocated more or fewer bonds than they anticipated, and trading in new bonds may be active for a period of weeks or months as investors adjust their holdings. In addition, some institutional investors operate as active traders aiming to take advantage of anticipated changes in interest rates or perceptions of individual credits. Although these active traders don't usually quote two-sided markets for specific bonds, they may be more willing to sell positions at only a slight premium to the offered side price in the dealer market. Thus, in the IBM example, an active trading investor might be willing to sell at 98.000, only ⅛ above the dealer offering price, rather than waiting for 98.250.

Other bonds become available when investors who are not usually active traders decide to sell parts of their portfolio. Sales occur when investors need to raise cash or make some strategic shift in the composition of the portfolio. Unsolicited sell orders thus provide the market with bonds that are less actively traded on a day-to-day basis. The bid-asked spreads on these securities may be somewhat wider than for the actively traded issues.

The final source of bonds for secondary market transactions is "solicited sell orders." A dealer, working on behalf of investors seeking to buy a specific bond or type of bond that are not actively traded, contacts investors known to hold such securities to inquire about their willingness to sell. This can be an expensive way to acquire securities, and an investor should have a very good reason for seeking bonds that are not actively traded.

Liquidity

The transaction cost to investors of acquiring fixed-income portfolios is the total of the bid-asked spreads on the bonds they buy. In most cases, investors buy bonds on the offered side of the market, and they sell on the bid side. Prudent practice is to evaluate a portfolio at its liquidation value, the amount of cash the investor could realize if the portfolio had to be sold in a short period of time. So, if an investor acquires a portfolio at an aggregate purchase price of $10 million, and if the portfolio consists of bond positions with an average bid-ask spread of ⅜%, the market value of the portfolio immediately after purchase would be $9,962,500 (= $10,000,000 − $37,500). This lower figure should appear on the account statement received from the portfolio custodian.

The more liquid a security, the narrower the bid-asked spread. Liquidity differs across fixed-income market sectors and across securities within each market. Central government bond markets in general and the U.S. Treasury market in particular are the most liquid. Within the U.S. Treasury market, the benchmark or "on-the-run" securities — usually the most recently issued bond or note of a given maturity — are somewhat more liquid than other bonds with very similar maturities. The typical bid-asked spread of $\frac{2}{32}$ (0.0625%) for an on-the-run U.S. Treasury note can be taken as a reasonable lower bound on this differential.

In the European and government bond markets, bid-asked spreads are of similar magnitude. Prices in these markets are generally quoted in decimal form (rather than 32^{nds}), and bid-asked spreads in the larger markets are generally about 0.05% of par. In Japan, where the benchmark effect is particularly strong, the bid-asked spread on the on-the-run security can be as narrow as 0.01% of par. A bid-asked spread of $\frac{2}{32}$ (0.0625%) on a 10-year 6.00% bond initially trading at par translates into a yield difference of 0.84 basis points (0.0084%).

The U.S. mortgage-backed securities, U.S. government agency, and Pfandbrief market is also highly liquid. The bid-asked spread on standard mortgage trades rivals that on off-the-run Treasury securities. For inactively traded Treasury securities — coupons stripped from Treasury bonds issued several years ago in relatively small size, for example — the bid-asked spread might be two or three times as wide as for a benchmark issue.

In the corporate and municipal bond markets, bid-asked spreads are wider on average and more variable across individual issues. In the corporate market, these actively traded bonds are usually recently issued bonds of well-known companies with simple structures. In the municipal market, recently issued long-term (20+ years) triple-A-rated insured bonds are the most liquid. For the most actively traded investment-grade bonds in these sectors, bid-asked spreads might amount to only $\frac{1}{8}$% or even less.

Many bonds are only slightly less liquid. For example, non-callable older bonds — those issued several years before the trade date — of well-known issuers will be almost as liquid as recent issues, with bid-ask spreads of, say, $\frac{3}{8}$% or so. Callable bonds of well-known issuers that are trading above their redemption prices might be less liquid, trading with bid-asked spreads in the 0.50% to 1.00% range.

At the extreme end of the spectrum are bonds with subinvestment-grade credit ratings and unusual structures issued by less well-known entities. For these bonds, bid-asked spreads may be 2% or 3% of par, or even greater. Or there may be no bid or no offering for a particular bond. Immediately after release of very good news about an issuer, none of a bond's holders may be willing to sell until the impact of the development on the security's price becomes clearer; thus, "no offering." Likewise, immediately after the release of very bad news, there may be "no bid."

All else held equal, liquidity is a good thing for bond investors. At the same time, the decision as to which of two bonds to buy — a relatively liquid or a relatively illiquid issue — should turn on a cost-benefit analysis. Yields on relatively illiquid bonds are usually somewhat higher than liquid bond yields. The additional yield compensates the investor for the added investment cost of a wide bid-asked spread. This tendency is seen in Exhibit 1 which lists the yields on U.S. Treasury securities with maturities of approximately five years.

Exhibit 1: Yields on Comparable U.S. Treasury Securities

Coupon	Maturity	Yield (May 4, 1998)
5.50%	2/28/2003	5.630%
5.50	3/31/2003	5.646
5.75*	4/30/2003	5.630
10.75	5/15/2003	5.694
11.125	8/15/2003	5.712

* Benchmark

Source: Goldman, Sachs & Co.

The size of a bond transaction can also affect the bid-asked spread. Very large orders for specific bonds or narrowly defined types of bonds can push up the price. For example, blocks of $1 million IBM 6.50%s of '28 are bid by dealers at 98.875 and offered at 99.125, and an investor who wants to buy $100 million of these bonds might have to pay 99.50 or even more. The potential impact of large orders will not generally be a problem for family portfolio managers, although investors seeking to purchase over the course of a week, say, $20 million in, for example, double-A-rated Virginia tax-exempt municipal bonds with maturities between 2008 and 2009 could push the price of such securities up.

Small block size also affects liquidity, and this can be a problem for family portfolio managers. A $10,000 position would be considered an odd lot in the municipal bond market, and an investor who purchases such a block for 98.500 and then immediately wants to sell the bonds might find that the best bid is for 97.000. A 1.5% bid-asked spread for such a position does not necessarily reflect gouging. The difference in dollar costs is only $150, which may barely cover the dealer's back-office cost of processing.

The minimum efficient block size varies from market to market. In the U.S. municipal bond and eurodollar markets, where retail investors play a major role, efficient block sizes tend to be smaller. In these markets, blocks of as little as $100,000 will get competitive bids, although investors who can build diversified portfolios with position sizes of at least $250,000 should probably gravitate toward the larger size. In more institutional markets such as the U.S. corporate and mortgage markets, efficient block sizes start closer to $1 million.

Family Investors in the Secondary Bond Market

As a practical matter, most families' bond portfolio transactions will take place in the secondary market. The key to successful participation in this market is price validation. Validating the price at which a common stock, or other exchange-traded security, is bought or sold is not a problem. Public posting of all purchase and sale prices makes it very obvious whether the investor traded closer to the highest or the lowest prices realized at the time of the trade. In a dealer market, there is no such public posting. For bonds characterized by wide bid-asked spreads, even very active institutional traders may be uncertain about how close a purchase price is to the dealer offered side of the market.

Bond buyers are not, however, completely uninformed when it comes to validating pricing, particularly with respect to relatively liquid bonds. First, when they buy or sell any large block of bonds, investors should attempt to ascertain how comparable issues are priced in the market. For example, closing prices for U.S. Treasury and agency securities reported in daily newspapers can provide some guide as to whether a particular purchase or sale is "on the market." It is unlikely that actual trades will take place at the exact levels quoted in the *Wall Street Journal*, because markets can move between the time of a transaction and the official close of the market. Furthermore, transactions of different sizes can carry different bid-asked spreads. Nevertheless, any substantial discrepancy between a transaction price and the official closing price, particularly if bond price movements are subdued over the day, should be questioned.

New issue pricing is also a useful reference point for secondary market transactions. If comparable bonds are priced on the same day as the investor's purchase or sale, any difference between the yields should be understandable. For example, suppose an investor buys a 10-year double-A-rated corporate bond at a yield of 6.12% and that on the same day a different Aa-rated company issues 10-year bonds at a yield of 6.25%. There should be a good reason for the difference in yields such as, for example, that the new issuer is on credit watch for a downgrade.

More generally, investors seeking to build bond portfolios should consider several offerings of different bonds, and investors seeking to sell bonds should ascertain which of their current holdings will attract the most aggressive bids. Many investors opt to do business with more than one bond dealer in order to be able to compare offerings and bids. Few family portfolio managers will want to do business with more than two or three dealers because of the time required to establish and relationships with registered representatives of dealer firms.

Gathering information about comparable pricing is useful, and routinely spot-checking transaction prices is prudent, but the trading desk of a major bond dealer will always have more and better information about the market value of a bond than any portfolio manager. Even for institutional investors, information gathering can never substitute completely for a relationship of trust between the portfolio manager and the dealer representative.

In a dealer market it is especially important to do business with a large, well-known, and reputable firm. But reputation alone is not enough. Registered representatives of dealers should be asked to justify bond pricing and to provide evidence, usually in the form of price or yield levels for comparable transactions. Investors should be wary if such information is provided grudgingly and if explanations of bond pricing are often confusing.

Transaction Costs and
Professional Portfolio Management

There are ways investors can reassure themselves that the prices they pay for bonds are not radically different from the offered side of the dealer market, and pricing may become more transparent as internet-based bond trading develops, but secondary market bond pricing will never be as transparent as exchange or new issue pricing. Thus, there will always be some lingering doubt even for the largest and most active investors as to whether they are paying the same price an institution would for any given bond. There is no doubt that a $5,000 investor for a family portfolio will pay a higher price per bond than a $1 million institutional purchase, if only because the per-bond back-office processing cost is higher for a smaller transaction. Private investors who enter larger, but relatively infrequent, orders should also expect to pay slightly more for bonds than active institutions that buy and sell hundreds of millions of dollars worth of bonds each week; as in many other markets, active traders get quantity discounts on transaction costs. If the market for active institutional traders on a particular bond is 98.500 bid/ 98.875 offered, a substantial private investor who pays par for the bond would have a right to feel ill-used, however.

Some substantial family investors seek to avoid the risk of paying substantially more than institutions by turning portfolio management over to investment advisors working for a flat fee. As with any other business matter, the decision to hire professional investment managers involves costs and benefits. Aspects of the costs and benefits of professional management are discussed throughout this volume.

Access to "institutional pricing," however, is probably not one of the chief benefits investment advisors offer. First of all, not all institutions manage to buy bonds on the offered side of the dealer market. Further, even if institutions always buy on the offered side, typical management fees are high relative to incremental bid-asked spreads on bonds. To see this, we can compare the basis point value of the incremental bid-asked spread a substantial family investor might pay relative to the offered side of the dealer market with the fees investment advisors typically charge. Family portfolio managers should feel confident about detecting egregious markups above the offered side, but may not be able to pick up, say, a half-point increment to an institutional bid-asked spread. A half-point on a 10-year bond translates into between 6 and 7 basis points of yield. This is much smaller than the management fee most investment advisors charge.

Many family investors may decide that the full array of investment advisory services justifies the fees involved. In and of itself, though, institutional pricing of bond purchases is a relatively small proportion of the benefit of professional management.

CHAPTER 12

Taxes and the Fixed-Income Portfolio

Taxation of investment income produces two problems for investors. Most important, the tax bill reduces the portfolio income the investor gets to spend or reinvest. Second, because it is apparently impossible for governments to design systems to tax investment income that are unbiased across alternative investments, investors must consider a wide range of tax questions when building their portfolios. Taxes affect the full panoply of investment decisions ranging from the broadest asset allocation issues down to very specific decisions like whether to enter into a transaction on December 31 or January 2.

We do not intend to provide comprehensive guidance regarding fixed-income investment decisions under different tax systems. There are too many different tax systems in the world, each of them quite complicated in its own right, and there are too many different tax situations in which individual investors can find themselves. Further, tax systems change frequently. Good advice published in one year could be downright harmful if taken a year later. Making the right specific decisions about portfolio construction and transaction timing requires the assistance of professional, home country, or international tax advisors.

Instead, the goal here is to show the way taxes affect family fixed-income portfolio management, which we do by examining the general impact of two very different tax regimes: the United States and Germany. It makes sense to select these two countries as examples because they are large, and because they impose very different tax systems on investment income. We conclude with a brief discussion of international taxation as it affects the management of family fixed-income portfolios.

KEY CHARACTERISTICS OF TAX SYSTEMS

Most industrialized countries tax investment returns in some way. Likewise, most jurisdictions treat interest and dividends as a component of "ordinary income" and tax it at the same rate as wages, salaries, rents, royalties, and so on. However,

195

each country's tax code calculates taxable investment income slightly differently, and the differences matter a great deal. Among the key characteristics of a tax system with respect to its treatment of income on fixed-income investments are:

1. Whether investment income is taxed at all.
2. How interest income is defined.
3. Whether or not capital gains are taxed.
4. Whether short-term gains are treated differently from long-term gains, and, if so, what the difference is and what the required holding period is for long-term gains treatment.
5. The extent to which losses can be carried forward (or backward) between tax periods.
6. Whether different types of investment returns are taxed as they accrue or only upon receipt of cash.
7. Whether and to what degree various types of investment expenses — interest expense on borrowed investment funds, management fees, hedging costs — offset investment income for tax purposes.
8. Whether there are any specific tax-advantaged investments or tax shelters.
9. How gains and losses on derivatives transactions (e.g., futures, forwards, options) are treated under various circumstances.
10. Whether taxes are withheld from interest payments.

A few taxing jurisdictions exempt all capital gains from taxation (Hong Kong and most Swiss cantons are examples). Somewhat more common are tax systems that exempt long-term capital gains (on assets held for more than some specified period), but levy a tax on short-term or speculative gains. For example, in Germany, capital gains realized on the sale of assets held for more than 12 months are completely exempt from taxation. More common still are systems that tax all gains, but impose different rates on such returns depending on the length of the investor's holding period (e.g., the United States). At the other end of the spectrum, some countries tax a broad range of capital gains at a uniform rate (e.g., the United Kingdom).[1] In most places gains are taxed upon realization, i.e., when an asset is sold at a price above its amortized purchase price.

The way capital gains are taxed has a profound influence on how investors manage their portfolios. First, preferential taxation of capital gains relative to dividend or interest income gives investors an incentive to select assets expected to generate a good proportion of their total return through price appreciation rather than cash income. For this reason, we should expect investors in countries that don't tax capital gains or tax them at low rates to have a relatively large proportion of their portfolios in stocks as opposed to bonds. We would also expect that a cut in capital gains tax rates would, over time, lead to a portfolio reallocation from bonds to stocks.

---

[1] The U.K. has a single tax rate on capital gains, but allows an exemption up to a maximum amount, as well as indexation for inflation, which acts to reduce the effective tax rate.

Second, if investors perceive capital gains taxes as high, they will think long and hard before selling an asset whose value has increased substantially since it was acquired. For example, an investor who holds a large position in a stock with a very low tax basis — the amount that is subtracted from the proceeds realized upon sale to calculate the taxable gain — may prefer to borrow against the market value of the stock to fund consumption expenditures or other investments rather than sell shares and realize a gain. Indeed, a large part of what top-echelon tax advisors do is help investors accomplish their financial goals without actually selling low-basis stock positions.

Third, if the tax code specifies preferential tax treatment of gains on assets held longer than a specified period of time, there will be a strong incentive to hold securities for at least that long. Only a dramatic change in the outlook for interest rates should induce a German investor, for example, to sell a bond at a gain within 12 months of the purchase date. Likewise, in the United States, where gains on assets held for longer than one year qualify for preferential tax rates, investors will be loathe to sell securities at a gain before that time, absent an offsetting short-term capital loss that has been or can be realized on some other investment.

This points to the fourth implication of capital gains taxation for portfolio management. Just as investors sitting on large amounts of unrealized capital gains will be reluctant to sell their securities, these same investors should be eager to realize losses on other investments whenever possible. Losing money on an investment on a mark-to-market basis is never a good thing. The pain of owning an "underwater" investment can be mitigated, however, if realization of that loss allows the investor to sell investments with low tax bases without paying capital gains taxes.

THE MULTIPLE U.S. TAX SYSTEMS

The political charge that the U.S. tax system is incredibly complex is justified. For a U.S. taxpayer, building a tax-efficient investment portfolio can be a daunting task.[2]

For one thing, the U.S. federal government, in effect, imposes two different tax systems on individual taxpayers. Many taxpayers are required to calculate their federal tax liability in two different ways: under the "standard calculation" and under the alternative minimum tax ("AMT"). A portfolio that is efficient under one tax system may be highly inefficient under the other. To make matters worse, taxpayers may not know with certainty which tax system they will be subject to until after the tax year is over, and their tax deductions are behind them.

Moreover, most U.S. states levy income taxes (or other taxes on investments) of their own. The rules governing Federal and state tax calculations are similar, but not identical, and investors need to take both systems into account when building an investment portfolio.

---

[2] Again, this is in no way a complete guide to the Internal Revenue Code. U.S. taxpayers should consult their own tax advisors regarding the specific tax treatment of specific investments and circumstances.

The Standard Calculation

Under the standard calculation, the taxpayer begins with *adjusted gross income* and reduces this figure by the amount of allowable deductions. The difference is *taxable income*, and the taxpayer's liability is the product of taxable income and the appropriate tax rate. The tax rates are listed in tables and reflect income levels — rates are graduated so that those with higher taxable incomes pay higher tax rates — and marital status.

Interest, dividends, rents, and royalties are treated as part of adjusted gross income. Different proportions of realized capital gains are included, depending on how long the assets have been held. Thus, for a taxpayer in the top 39.6% bracket, the effective rate of taxation on net gains realized on assets held for less than one year is 39.6%; for assets held more than 12 months, the effective rate is 20%.

The tax code imposes limits on the extent to which capital losses can be used to offset ordinary income. Allowable deductions include interest paid on residential mortgages, medical expenses above a certain percentage of income, certain state and local taxes paid, and charitable contributions. Interest paid on funds borrowed to finance certain investments can be deducted from investment income in calculating taxable income. Other investment expenses, such as management fees and some, but not all, hedging costs may not be deducted unless they exceed 2% of the taxpayer's income.

The Alternative Minimum Tax (AMT)

Under the AMT calculation, taxpayers begin with their standard calculation taxable income and then add back some, but not all, of the deductions that are allowed under the standard calculation. The sum is AMT taxable income, and the taxpayer's liability is the product of AMT income and a flat 28%. The taxpayer must pay either the result of the standard calculation or the AMT, whichever is larger.

Under the AMT, the tax rate imposed on interest, dividends, and short-term capital gains is 28%. Gains realized on the sale of assets held for more than 12 months are, as under the standard calculation, taxed at an effective rate of 20%. All investment expenses that may be deducted under the standard calculation may also be deducted under the AMT.

Tax-Advantaged Investments

Before the passage of the 1986 Tax Act, the U.S. Internal Revenue Code included a wide range of provisions that allowed investors to "shelter" taxable income. The passage of that law eliminated most of the ways investors could reduce the taxes paid on their investment assets. Indeed, the 1986 law went so far as to eliminate the difference in tax rates imposed on long-term capital gains, on the one hand, and ordinary income or short-term gains, on the other. The preferential treatment of long-term capital gains has been reintroduced gradually since 1986. Beyond this preference, municipal bonds remain the only major tax-advantaged investment available to U.S. taxpayers.

Interest on most municipal bonds is exempt from federal income taxation under both the standard calculation and the AMT, although interest on approximately 15% of municipal bonds outstanding is fully taxable under the AMT. An even smaller proportion of municipal bonds pay interest that is taxable under both federal systems. Interest on these "taxable municipals" may or may not be exempt from state income taxation.

What is "Interest Income" Under the U.S. Tax Code?

The most important influence of a tax system on fixed-income investments is the way the law defines taxable interest income. The yield differential between tax-exempt municipal bonds and taxable bonds is the most striking example of this impact in the U.S. market. Because interest income on most municipal bonds is exempt from taxation under the U.S. tax code, taxpayers will buy municipal bonds paying much lower yields than comparable taxable securities.

Consider two bonds, an A1/A+ 10-year corporate bond yielding 7.00% to maturity and a 10-year, A1/A+ rated municipal bond priced to yield 5.00%. For a non-taxpayer there would be no question as to which security to buy: the one offering the much higher yield. For a taxpayer the question is not so simple. If the taxpayer is in the 39.6% bracket and pays no state income taxes, the after-tax yield on the corporate is 4.23% (= 7% × [100% − 39.6%]), lower than the after-tax yield on the municipal bond at 5.00%. On an after-tax basis, the municipal clearly dominates. A taxpayer in the 15% tax bracket would make the opposite decision. At this lower tax rate, the after-tax yield on the corporate is 5.95%, 95 basis points higher than the after-tax yield on the municipal.

More generally, taxpayers will prefer the municipal bond if:

Tax Rate > 1 − (Municipal Yield ÷ Taxable Bond Yield)

In this example, the municipal will be more attractive than the corporate for tax-payers facing a tax rate above 29% (= 100% − [(5.00%/7.00%) × 100%]).

Discount and Premium: Taxable Bonds

A second way the tax code's definition of interest income influences bond valuation is through the treatment of returns on bonds purchased at either a discount or premium to par. For taxable bonds, the U.S. tax code treats interest income in a way that is consistent with basic fixed-income mathematics. For example, taxable income on a (non-municipal) bond purchased at a discount is defined to include both cash coupon payments and the accretion of the discount. Taxpayers have the option of calculating this accretion based on two methods: the straight line method or the constant-yield (or "scientific") method.

Suppose that on July 1, 2000, an investor purchases $1 million face amount of a bond maturing on July 1, 2010, with a 4.00% coupon priced at 85.123 to yield 6.00%. Each full year the investment will pay $40,000 in coupon income. Over 10 years the value of the bond will accrete to par at an average, or straight-line rate, of $14,878 per year. Taxpayers who opt to calculate accretion of discount using the straight-line method would report $54,720 for each full tax year. Alternatively, the investor could choose to accrete the discount so that the yield to maturity computed at the accreted price is always the purchase yield of 6.00%.

When the bond is purchased on July 1, 2000, the purchase price is $851,225. Now the price of a bond with a 4.00% coupon, a 6.00% yield, and a June 1, 2010, maturity purchased on December 31, 2000, would be 85.676. The accreted dollar value of the investment using the constant-yield method would be $856,762, and the taxpayer would have accrued taxable income of $5,537 (= $856,762 – $851,225). Over the same 6-month period, coupon income will be $20,000, so total taxable income on this security for the year 2000 will be $25,537.

Exhibit 1 demonstrates the effect of the different methods. The total tax bill over the life of the investment is equal for the two methods of calculating accretion; it equals 39.6% of the sum of total accretion and all coupon income. The straight-line method produces higher tax payments than the constant-yield calculation in the earlier years and relatively lower payments in the later years, meaning that the constant-yield method produces a lower present value of tax payments.

This shows why the constant-yield or scientific calculation is economically superior to the straight-line method from the taxpayer's point of view. The straight-line method is much simpler computationally, however, so taxpayers who own relatively small amounts of short-maturity bonds might reasonably decide to adopt it. For taxpayers who hold substantial portfolios of fixed-income securities, the more complex method will probably be worth the trouble.

Exhibit 1: Taxable Cash Flow Calculations on a $1 Million Par Value 10-Year Bond Purchased at a Discount

Tax Year	Coupon Income	Constant Yield			Straight Line		
		Accretion	Income	Taxes*	Accretion	Income	Taxes*
2000	$20,000	5,537	25,537	10,113	7,439	27,439	10,866
2001	40,000	11,577	51,577	20,424	14,877	54,877	21,731
2002	40,000	12,282	52,282	20,704	14,877	54,877	21,731
2003	40,000	13,030	53,030	21,000	14,877	54,877	21,731
2004	40,000	13,823	53,823	21,314	14,877	54,877	21,731
2005	40,000	14,665	54,665	21,647	14,877	54,877	21,731
2006	40,000	15,558	55,558	22,001	14,877	54,877	21,731
2007	40,000	16,506	56,506	22,376	14,877	54,877	21,731
2008	40,000	17,511	57,511	22,774	14,877	54,877	21,731
2009	40,000	18,577	58,577	23,197	14,877	54,877	21,731
2010	20,000	9,709	29,709	11,765	7,439	27,439	10,866
Total		14,8775	548,775	217,315	148,775	548,775	217,315
Present Value				154,224			155,419

* Assumes a 39.6% tax rate.

Taxable bonds purchased at a premium to par are treated in an analogous way consistent with bond mathematics. Investors may offset taxable income with premium amortization. Taxpayers are required to amortize the premium purchase price of a taxable bond on a constant-yield basis.

Discount and Premium: Municipal Bonds

A bond will trade at a discount if its coupon is below its market yield. This may occur for one or a combination of two reasons. If a bond is initially issued at a price of par, and interest rates subsequently rise, the bond's price will fall. The difference between such a bond's market price and par is referred to as a "market discount." But not all bonds are initially offered to the public at par. For example, an issuer seeking to raise $100 million might decide not to issue $100 million face amount of 6.00% bonds at par but instead to offer bonds with a face value of $108 million with 5.00% coupons priced at 92.674 to yield 6.00%. This transaction would also generate $100 million in net proceeds. Such a security is referred to as an *original issue discount* (OID) bond. If interest rates rise subsequent to the sale of an OID bond, the security's market price will fall below its initial offering price, say, to 89.50. If so, the discount to par will reflect a combination of market discount and OID. Issuers may also offer original issue premium bonds to investors.

The distinction between an OID and a market discount is irrelevant for most purposes relating to taxable bonds, but the difference is very important for tax-exempt municipal bonds. For taxable bonds, accretion of both OID and market discount is treated as taxable interest income. For municipals, accretion of OID is tax-exempt, but accretion of most market discount is treated as taxable income. Specifically, if a municipal bond is purchased at a price that represents more of a discount to its accreted offering price than 0.25% per full year remaining to maturity, that discount is treated as ordinary income, with taxes due annually or when the bond is sold or redeemed, at the taxpayer's option.

Suppose an investor purchases at a price of 95.00 $1 million face amount of 10-year bonds that were originally issued at par. Suppose further that the investor holds the bond to maturity. When the bonds are redeemed at par, the investor will realize $50,000 of ordinary income. The income is treated as ordinary income because the bond was purchased at a dollar price of 95, a price below 97.5 and thus at a discount of more than 0.25% per full year to the 10-year maturity. At the ordinary income tax rate of 39.6%, the tax bill due at maturity will be $19,800, and the net (after-tax) redemption proceeds will be $980,200, not $1 million. This will reduce the after-tax yield to maturity of the investment. If the bond had been purchased at a price of 98.00 — representing a discount of less than 0.25% per full year to maturity — the $20,000 realized when the bond matured would be treated as a long-term capital gain. Not only would this gain be taxed at a lower rate under current U.S. tax law, but the investor might also be able to offset the gain with a long-term capital loss that may have been realized elsewhere in the investment portfolio.

Exhibit 2: Market Prices of Two Hypothetical Tax-Exempt Bonds

	Bond A	Bond B
Issue Date	6/1/00	9/5/98
Settlement	6/1/00	6/1/00
Coupon	4.50%	4.50%
Maturity	6/1/10	6/1/10
Initial Yield	5.50%	4.50%
Initial Price	92.386	100.000
Market Price*	92.386	90.110

* Assumes 39.6% tax rate.

This treatment of market discount bonds leads to some pricing oddities in the municipal market, where two bonds with the same coupon and maturity can trade at very different prices, depending on whether the security is an original issue discount bond or a market discount bond. Consider the two bonds represented in Exhibit 2. Why are the market prices of the two bonds so different?

If the prices were the same, but the buyer of Bond B had a tax liability due when the bond matured or was sold, while the buyer of Bond A did not, then the after-tax return on Bond A would be higher than that of Bond B. At the same price, therefore, no one would want to buy Bond B. In fact, 90.110 is the dollar price that produces an *after-tax* yield to maturity on Bond B of 5.50%, equalizing the after-tax yields on the two investments. This is not necessarily to say that the price of Bond B *will* be 90.110 if that of Bond A is 92.386. In fact, investors might demand a higher after-tax yield — and a price lower than 90.110 — as compensation for the fact that market discount bonds may exhibit greater volatility and less liquidity than bonds trading close to par.

The tax treatment of bonds purchased at a premium also differs for municipals and taxable bonds. Specifically, the tax code does not allow taxpayers to deduct amortization of premium purchase prices on tax-exempt municipal bonds from taxable income. Nor may taxpayers realize a capital loss when a tax-exempt bond purchased at a premium is redeemed at par.

THE GERMAN TAX SYSTEM

The income tax system of the German Federal Republic as it affects fixed-income investments is much simpler than that of the United States. For one thing, there is no large class of tax-exempt bonds comparable to U.S. municipals. Second, gains on investments held for less than 12 months are taxed as ordinary income, while for longer holding periods gains are fully tax-exempt.

The contrast between the tax treatments of long-term capital gains and ordinary income, which includes interest income, in Germany is particularly stark. In the U.S., the difference between the long-term capital gains tax rate and the highest ordinary income tax rate is 19.6 percentage points (20% vs. 39.6%). In

Germany, the difference is 56% (0% vs. 56%). It is therefore somewhat surprising that German family investors hold such a high proportion of their financial assets in the bond market. There may be historical reasons for this anomalous behavior, and it is not surprising that, as their domestic financial markets become more flexible, German families have begun to shift their portfolios into the equity markets.

One way the German tax system does distort investment decisions is through a definition of interest income that is not consistent with bond mathematics. The German tax code defines interest income as coupon payments plus the accretion of most original issue discount. This definition is interesting for what it leaves out. First, accretion of market discount, unlike original-issue discount, is not treated as taxable income. Second, no allowance is made for the amortization of premium purchase prices. Finally, the system treats the accretion of very small original issue discounts as tax-exempt. These distinctions are important to top-bracket German taxpayers because, when a component of return is defined as interest income, it is taxed at a 56% rate.

The impact of these rules on the after-tax yields on various bonds is striking. Exhibit 3 depicts the cash flows and after-tax yields on a variety of bonds with different structure and tax status, all priced to produce the same before-tax yield. The after-tax cash flow calculations assume that discount is accreted on a straight-line basis. Coupon income and accretion of original issue discount is taxed at 56%, while accretion of market discount is exempt from taxation.

Although the German *Finanzamt* treats OID as interest income, the taxation actually takes place at redemption of the bond (or upon sale). The German tax law is essentially unbiased between par bonds and OIDs. The code is, however, strongly biased in favor of market discount bonds and against bonds purchased at a premium. Thus, under German tax law, a rallying bond market, which turns most outstanding bonds into premium-priced securities, effectively increases the tax on newly acquired fixed-income investments. By contrast, a bear bond market leaves outstanding bonds priced at a discount and creates a class of tax-advantaged investments for German taxpayers.

INTERNATIONAL TAXATION

Discussion of international taxation can become very complicated very quickly. The taxation of income earned by non-residents in each country is governed by a combination of the tax laws of the country in which the income is earned, the country in which the investor resides, and the provisions of any tax treaty between the two countries. Families with substantial financial interests in more than one country will require the services of international tax experts to manage their multiple obligations and to make sure the family does not pay more in total than is legally required. Private investors considering even relatively modest allocations to foreign bond markets need to be aware of certain basic potential international tax ramifications, if only to know what mistakes might be made.

204 Taxes and the Fixed-Income Portfolio

Exhibit 3: Before- and After-Tax Income on Bonds Purchased for DM1 Million with Different Coupons and Tax Statuses for German Taxpayers

Bond	Par Bond		Original Issue Discount		Market Discount		Premium	
Coupon	5.50%		3.00%		3.00%		8.00%	
Maturity	6/1/10		6/1/10		6/1/10		6/1/10	
Before-tax Yield	5.50%		5.50%		5.50%		5.50%	
Purchase Price	100.000		81.156		81.156		118.844	
Cash Flows	Before Tax	After Tax	Before Tax	After Tax	Before Tax	After Tax	Before Tax	After Tax
6/1/00	(1,000,000)	(1,000,000)	(1,000,000)	(1,000,000)	(1,000,000)	(1,000,000)	(1,000,000)	(1,000,000)
6/1/01	55,000	24,200	36,966	16,265	36,966	16,265	67,315	29,619
6/1/02	55,000	24,200	36,966	16,265	36,966	16,265	67,315	29,619
6/1/03	55,000	24,200	36,966	16,265	36,966	16,265	67,315	29,619
6/1/04	55,000	24,200	36,966	16,265	36,966	16,265	67,315	29,619
6/1/05	55,000	24,200	36,966	16,265	36,966	16,265	67,315	29,619
6/1/06	55,000	24,200	36,966	16,265	36,966	16,265	67,315	29,619
6/1/07	55,000	24,200	36,966	16,265	36,966	16,265	67,315	29,619
6/1/08	55,000	24,200	36,966	16,265	36,966	16,265	67,315	29,619
6/1/09	55,000	24,200	36,966	16,265	36,966	16,265	67,315	29,619
6/1/10	1,055,000	1,024,200	1,269,162	(1,569)	1,269,162	1,248,461	908,754	871,057
IRR	5.50%	2.20%	5.50%	2.19%	5.50%	3.46%	5.50%	1.19%

For example, private investors need to be aware that most countries' tax codes include provisions for *withholding* as taxes a proportion of interest and dividend income payments to non-resident investors. The rules regarding withholding are quite complex and vary between each pair of countries (country of taxpayer's residence and country of bond issuance). Taxes withheld by a foreign country may be taken as a credit against the investor's home country taxes. Certain types of investments by residents of certain countries may be exempt from withholding on a jurisdiction-by-jurisdiction basis. Investors may be able to reclaim withheld coupon income by application to the taxing authority. Even where recovery is allowed, however, the formal act of applying for repayment of taxes withheld may trigger adverse tax consequences in the investor's home country. At the very least, claims for foreign tax credits or applications for waiver or recovery of withholding require additional paperwork and some degree of inconvenience.

Investors considering investing in a country new to them or in a new type of investment in a country where they have already invested (e.g., buying bonds in a country where one already owns stocks) should be sure to ask about the tax ramifications. None of these considerations should deter investors from adding foreign bonds to their portfolios. Considerable progress has been made in recent years to simplify international taxation of investment income, and any remaining complexities become routine after the first few transactions.

CONCLUSION

It is worth reiterating that this chapter is not intended to serve as a tax guide. Only a few of the potentially relevant provisions of a few tax systems are discussed. Our purpose is simply to illustrate two important tax-driven investment considerations. First, elements of any tax code — even some of its subtlest and most abstruse provisions — can exert a profound influence on the "right" investment decision. Examples are the application of the alternative minimum tax in the U.S. and the anomalies of the German definition of interest income, and there are many more.

Second, management of a taxpayer's investment portfolio is *not* a "one size fits all" exercise. Investments that make perfect sense for one taxpaying family at one time may be highly tax-inefficient for another family at the same time. And investments that are very attractive on an after-tax basis for any given family at a given in time may make no sense at all for the same family at a different time.

The most basic lesson of this chapter should be that communication between family portfolio managers and family tax advisors should be detailed and continuous.

CHAPTER 13

Managing a
Cash Bond Portfolio

A t the conclusion of Part I of this book we synthesized the basic elements of bond math and interest rate dynamics to provide a framework for selecting target portfolio duration and maturity structure. This chapter provides a synthesis of the material presented in Part II. The aim is to express what we know about the various global bond sectors, the principles of credit analysis, and the investment implications of various tax systems in terms of concrete guidance about how to build and manage a family portfolio by buying and selling specific blocks of individual bonds.

SELECTING MARKET SECTORS

Once the portfolio manager has identified a target duration and maturity structure (bullet, barbell, or ladder), the next step is to select two or three broad bond market sectors in which to invest. Chapters 8 and 9 described all the major bond market sectors of the world. A chief investment officer at a large institution should probably expect to develop some level of expertise in all of these sectors. It makes sense for a family portfolio manager, however, to focus on a much smaller number of sectors, both because of the limited time available for developing usable market knowledge and because the benefits of diversification can diminish rapidly as the number of different markets increases beyond two or three.

More precisely, it makes sense for family portfolio managers to identify a single bond market sector as their primary fixed-income investment arena, and then to identify at least one and, at most, three, "principal alternative sectors." The primary sector should meet most of the family's fixed-income investment needs, and many private portfolio managers are satisfied with investing in a single market. However, as we saw in Chapters 8 and 9, each individual market is subject to its own unique sector risks, and the benefits of diversification are substantial enough that it is worthwhile spending the time and effort required to develop a working familiarity with at least one additional type of bond.

Identifying the Primary Sector

The choice of a primary fixed-income sector may seem obvious in some cases. For example, municipal bonds may appear to be the clear choice for investments subject to U.S. income taxation. Not all U.S. taxpayers, though, necessarily benefit from choosing municipals over other types of bonds. U.S. families that derive all their income from investments may find that if they hold only municipal bonds their taxable income will be so low that their marginal tax rate is below 28%. At a 15% tax rate, corporate bonds usually yield more after tax than tax-exempt municipals. The answer for these investors is to buy enough taxable bonds to get their taxable income up to the point where municipals start to make sense. So, even in the most "obvious" cases, it is worth going through the exercise of considering the pros and cons of the full array of fixed-income alternatives before identifying the primary sector.

The following is a full list of the considerations that influence the evaluation of candidate primary fixed-income sectors.

First, *the primary sector of involvement should be consistent with a family's fundamental investment objectives*. For example, neither speculative-grade corporate nor emerging market bonds would make sense as a primary sector for an investor seeking to build a relatively low-volatility portfolio. Similarly, while occasional investments in Japanese government bonds (JGBs) might make sense for a family aiming for the high-return/high-volatility end of the efficient portfolio frontier, such a family would probably be ill-served by JGBs as its primary fixed-income investment vehicle.

In this regard, it probably also makes sense for the primary sector to be denominated in the family's base investment currency: either its home market currency or the currency in which investment returns are measured. Although investment in one or more foreign bond markets provides considerable diversification benefits, some degree of "home currency bias" makes sense for family investors.

To put this discussion differently, while we don't recommend confining fixed-income investments to a single sector, the primary sector should be the single sector the family would choose if required to pick only one.

Second, *information about the primary market in general and about individual issues within the market should be readily available to the portfolio manager.* Like the first criterion, this consideration argues in favor of some home market bias for family portfolio managers. It may also make sense for families to limit exposure to sectors that make excessive demands on the portfolio managers' time or strain most non-professionals' analytical capabilities. Management of a speculative-grade corporate bond portfolio requires careful attention to business developments in a large number of different companies, while investors who hold large volumes of mortgage-backed securities must study prepayment models and monitor prepayment trends closely. Successful management of government, government agency, investment-grade corporate, or emerging market bond portfolios requires either much less detailed information or information about a much smaller universe of issuers.

This is not to say that families should avoid high-yield bonds or mortgage-backed securities. The point is rather that government, investment-grade corporate, or emerging market bonds are probably more appropriate as the core holding in a family's fixed-income portfolio because these markets are easier to follow.

Third, *the investor's primary market should make sense from the point of view of tax treatment and regulatory suitability.* As long as tax-exempt bonds yield substantially more than comparable taxable bonds after tax, the tax-exempt market should be the primary investment sector for a taxpayer. Application of this principle in practice can be complicated. As of the 1998 tax year, for a top-bracket, standard-calculation U.S. taxpayer paying a 39.6% marginal federal rate and a 0% state tax rate, municipals should be the primary investment vehicles as long as yields on these securities exceed 60.4% of yields on comparable-quality corporates. For U.S. taxpayers paying the 28% federal alternative minimum tax rate and, say, an effective 7% state rate on the margin, municipals will make sense only to the extent that they yield more than 72% of state tax-exempt U.S. government agency securities or more than 65% (= 100% − [28% + 7%]) of corporate bonds.

For similar reasons, investors who hold offshore investment funds that are beyond the reach of home country tax authorities will want to avoid investments subject to ownership registration and/or withholding requirements on coupon income. Many of these investors select the eurocurrency market — where securities are issued outside any country's regulatory purview and frequently in bearer form — as their primary fixed-income sector.

Investors must also consider potential regulatory impediments to participation in a candidate primary market. For example, during the early 1990s many high-yield corporate bond issues came to the U.S. market in fully registered form. By 1998, however, most new issues in this sector were being distributed pursuant to Rule 144a, effectively precluding participation in new issues by individual U.S. residents, although purchases in the secondary market remain possible. While the high-yield market *may* have made sense as a primary fixed-income investment vehicle for a small number of U.S. families in the early 1990s, this choice became less viable by the end of the decade. There are no such impediments to participation by families in the investment-grade corporate or municipal bond markets.

Finally, *a family's primary bond market sector should offer an adequate degree of liquidity and diversification potential.* This criterion argues against adopting as the primary sector a relatively small or narrowly defined market that might appear to suit the family's needs most precisely. For example, we recommend some home market bias in the selection of a primary fixed-income sector, and even investors in countries with relatively small or undeveloped bond markets might prefer to invest at home. If the local market includes only a limited range of issuers or maturities, though, it may make sense for investors to look elsewhere. Thus risk-tolerant investors in, say, Venezuela, might be better off defining their primary fixed-income market as Latin American emerging market debt rather than confining the bulk of their purchases to their home market.

Similarly, for any given credit quality and maturity, investors in high-tax U.S. states will usually earn the highest after-tax yields if they buy "double tax-exempt" in-state municipal bonds. Confining investments to the in-state market may be feasible for residents of large states such as California or New York, but residents of smaller high-tax states may not find sufficient liquidity and diversification in their home state markets. They may be better off defining their primary market as "all municipal bonds" rather than as, say, "Minnesota state tax-exempt municipal bonds.[1]"

Selecting Principal Alternative Sectors

Many of the same considerations that influence the selection of a primary sector also enter into the choice of a family's principal alternative sectors, but, perhaps, with somewhat less force. The performance characteristics of an alternative sector should not be inconsistent with the family's fundamental investment objectives, although precise consistency with investment objectives is not essential in this case. For example, if the family is seeking to build a low-volatility portfolio, speculative-grade corporate bonds would not make sense as a primary sector, but modest exposure to this market might make sense. Similarly, occasional forays into the U.S. Treasury bond market as a vehicle for speculating on changes in interest rates might be appropriate for a family willing to accept higher risk. Investment in alternative markets should not be tax-*in*efficient, but it should not be necessary to earn the same after-tax yields for the same level of risk as in the primary sector. Finally, an investor's tolerance for illiquid positions or for concentrated credit risk may be greater with respect to alternative investments that constitute a relatively small proportion of the fixed-income portfolio.

The requirements for a good principal alternative sector are different from those applied to a primary market. First, because the purpose of alternative sectors is to provide diversification, a market will be a good alternative to the extent that its returns are *not* highly correlated with those of the primary investment venue. For this reason foreign bond markets are a good place to look for alternative investments. U.S. taxpayers are fortunate in this regard, because the correlation between returns on municipal bonds and on other U.S. dollar fixed income sectors has been relatively low, so alternative investments in Treasuries, agencies, or corporate bonds provide almost as much diversification as would positions in the non-dollar bond markets.

Second, the diversification provided by an alternative market can create the opportunity to add modest investments offering higher expected returns with higher volatility without increasing overall portfolio risk. Thus, it is reasonable to

---

[1] This includes obligations of Minnesota municipal issuers as well as bonds issued by public entities in Puerto Rico. Interest on the obligations of the latter and of the U.S. Virgin Islands, Guam, and the Mariana Islands is exempt from state taxes in all 50 states.

seek alternatives among the riskier and less liquid bond market sectors such as longer-duration, more highly structured, and lower-credit quality sectors.

How Much of Each?

There is no uniformly right answer as to how much of a portfolio should be dedicated to the family's primary market and how much to the principal alternative sectors. The answer is somewhat easier for U.S. taxpayers than for other types of investors. The tax advantage of municipal bonds is so great that it will cost a U.S. investor a great deal to forgo buying tax-exempts for any significant portion of the portfolio. This is especially so for residents of high-tax states. Therefore, it probably does not make sense for these investors to devote more than 25% of their total fixed-income asset allocation to anything other than the municipal market. At the same time, anything less than about 10% would probably not provide meaningful diversification.

Because diversification is the most expensive for U.S. taxpayers who can benefit from municipals, the 10%-25% recommended for these investors probably constitutes a lower bound for allocation to one or more alternative sectors. Once an allocation to a particular sector exceeds 50% of the fixed-income portfolio, it becomes the holder's primary investment vehicle. The best allocation within this relatively broad 10%-50% range will depend on a variety of facts and circumstances. For example, if the investor is only willing to devote the time and effort necessary for involvement in a single alternative sector, the secondary allocation should be closer to 15% than 50%. A portfolio manager willing to be involved in two or three principal secondary markets may go as high as a 50% aggregate allocation to alternatives, or even more, possibly.

SELECTING INDIVIDUAL BONDS

Suppose the portfolio manager has decided on a target portfolio duration and yield curve structure and has identified the primary and principal alternative bond market sectors. The next step, and the final step in the portfolio construction process, is to fill the portfolio with specific individual bonds.

In a few, perfectly liquid, homogeneous sectors characterized by very high credit quality, this process can be accomplished quickly and easily. For example, an investor seeking to build a $20 million U.S. Treasury portfolio with a five-year duration in a barbell including two- and 10-year bonds should be able to accomplish the task in a few minutes at publicly quoted prices. The same would be true of the European government and mortgage-backed securities markets.

In the high-grade corporate bond, high-yield, municipal, and emerging debt markets, constructing the portfolio may take somewhat longer; at the extreme, it might take an investor several months to assemble a satisfactory portfolio. The process can be prolonged for two reasons. First, an acceptable portfolio of less-than-perfect credits requires some degree of diversification. Second, bonds of the right issuers with the right maturities and the right structure may not be readily available in dealer inventories when the investor is seeking to put funds to work.

Yield, Diversification, and Liquidity

Construction of a portfolio of corporate, municipal, or emerging market bonds with specified duration and maturity structure turns on trade-offs among three values: yield, diversification, and liquidity. In general, the higher the average credit quality of a bond portfolio, the lower the average portfolio yield. The risk involved in buying bonds with lower credit ratings can be mitigated by diversifying holdings across a large number of issuers in an array of different industrial sectors and economic regions. Yet because the bid-asked spread tends to be wider proportionately for very small blocks, to the extent that credit risk diversification reduces the average size of individual bond positions within the portfolio, increased transaction costs can eat up some of the yield benefit of lower average credit quality.

As with so many other trade-offs in economic affairs, resolving the yield-diversification-liquidity conundrum will be easier to the extent that the investor holds a very large portfolio. A family that can afford to purchase 30 different bond positions of $2 million each may feel comfortable with an average credit quality in, say, the A3/A– range. An investor with $5 million to invest who can, therefore, afford only 10 different positions of $500,000 might want to confine purchases to bonds rated Aa2/AA or better. For both portfolios, increasing yield comes at the cost of increased risk of credit loss. Because the investor holding the larger portfolio can achieve greater credit diversification without sacrificing liquidity, the wealthier family should be able to achieve better investment results on average.

The Sources of Credit Risk Diversification

The number of credits is important, but diversification is not provided solely by the number of different issuers represented in the portfolio. A portfolio that includes 50 different issuers would not necessarily be diversified if 49 of those issuers account for a total of only 5% of the market value of the portfolio. Even equal-sized holdings of 50 different issuers' bonds would not represent a diversified portfolio if all 50 were, for example, rural school districts in Louisiana all dependent for their economic well-being on the price of sugar cane. Nor would a portfolio be well-diversified if all the issuers represented were in closely related industries; a portfolio including only airline, hotel real estate investment trusts, cruise line, and gaming industry bonds would not be diversified because the performance of all these industries is highly correlated. A combination of oil company and airline bonds produces more diversification because one industry tends to do well when the price of petroleum is high, and the other does better when it is low.

This discussion suggests a number of portfolio concentrations that need to be considered when evaluating the diversification of a bond portfolio. These are:

- *Single issuer concentration:* The proportion of the portfolio accounted for by each of the issuers.

- *Industrial concentration:* The proportion of the portfolio accounted for by issuers involved in a single industry.
- *Geographic concentration:* The proportion of the portfolio accounted for by issuers located in or dependent upon a single economic region.
- *Economic risk concentration:* The proportion of the portfolio affected in the same way by specific economic variables such as the condition of the macroeconomy and the prices of individual commodities.

There are no hard-and-fast rules as to how much any particular degree of concentration is too high. If the U.S. Treasury as an issuer of bonds accounts for 50% of a portfolio, that probably isn't a problem. It would, however, be problematic if a single double-B rated issuer were to account for 15%. A 30% concentration of risk in a single non-cyclical industry — supermarket chains, for example — might not be as troublesome as the same percentage holdings in a volatile industry such as brokerage firms. The point here is not to define a fixed rule, but to identify characteristics of bond holdings and groups of bond holdings that should be considered when building or managing a fixed-income portfolio.

In the absence of hard-and-fast diversification standards, a few rules of thumb may provide guidance. For example, if an individual, investment-grade issuer rated single-A or lower accounts for more than 5% of an investor's total portfolio, there should be a good reason. One good reason might be a particularly positive outlook for the economic prospects of the company or municipality and anticipation of an upgrade. But such a concentration should be subject to careful scrutiny before purchase and frequent reevaluation thereafter.

In a U.S. corporate bond portfolio, holdings exceeding 20% in a single industry should be subject to scrutiny. Such industrial concentration might be appropriate if the outlook for the industry is positive or if the industry is non-cyclical, but a 20% industry concentration should not be considered normal.

Likewise, in a municipal bond portfolio, more than a 30% concentration of *uninsured* bond holdings in a single state or economic region should have some specific justification. Special tax treatment of in-state bonds might justify such a concentration, but the investor should be aware of the concentration risk and should be prepared to purchase secondary market or portfolio bond credit insurance if a regional economic recession begins to appear likely.

THE PORTFOLIO CONSTRUCTION PROCESS

A U.S. Example

The portfolio manager will begin the process of assembling a bond portfolio with some ideal structure in mind. The manager might, for example, want to build a $20 million portfolio with the characteristics listed in Exhibit 1. With these objectives in mind, the investor will begin purchasing securities. Selecting the first few bonds will be relatively easy. Suppose, for example, a dealer is offering $1 million

Ford Motor Credit Corporation (A/A1) 7.20%s of 6/15/07 at a spread of 79 bp to the 10-year U.S. Treasury or at a yield of 6.23% and a dollar price of 106.611. At this price, these bonds have a duration of 6.646, very close to the target duration. This bond is nearly a perfect candidate for this target portfolio structure.

Suppose that the next bond to come along is $1 million IBM (A1/A+) 7.50% of 6/15/13 offered at 77 bp over the 10-year at a yield of 6.21% and a dollar price of 112.474. At 9.3 years, the duration of this security is greater than the target and a little bit long to be consistent with the goal of building a "bullet" portfolio where most of the bonds have individual durations close to the 6.5 year target. Given the investor's objectives, this bond is marginal. Now suppose the dealer's representative makes a convincing case that IBM is an improving credit and that the spread of 77 bp over the 10-year Treasury represents good value. The investor offered such a bond and such a pitch might reasonably decide to buy, considering that the process of building the portfolio has just begun and that there will be ample opportunities to compensate for the suboptimal structural features of this security as more bonds are accumulated.

Assume that this process continues for several more purchases, including several agency bonds, until the portfolio is as depicted in Exhibit 2.[2] At this point, when the investor has purchased a bit more than 60% of the total portfolio, it is a good time to consider the characteristics of the portfolio as it stands now in order to decide what kinds of bonds to buy, and what types to avoid, as the process continues. The weighted average credit quality of the portfolio is approximately A1/A+, slightly lower than the target Aa3/AA−. Therefore, unless the investor now decides to modify the average credit quality target, additional purchases should be rated higher than Aa3/AA−. Also, the investor has acquired $4 million par amount of bonds issued by commercial banks. This will account for 20% of the total $20 million portfolio, and the investor should avoid purchasing any more bank securities. The portfolio holds $4 million par amount of government agency securities, and, given the goal of a 25% allocation to the sector, should acquire $1 million more.

Exhibit 1: Hypothetical Portfolio Structural Objectives

Characteristic	Objective
Duration/Average Maturity	6.5/2006-2007
Maturity Structure:	Bullet
Sector	Primary Sector: Corporate Bonds ((75%)
	Principal Alternative: U.S. Agencies (25%)
Credit Quality	Average at least Aa3/AA−
	All Investment-Grade
Maximum Concentration	Single Corporate Credit = 5% of Par
	Single Industry = 20%
	Single Economic Risk Factor = 20%

[2] The investment process described here assumes that the portfolio manager will be able to keep track of duration and other portfolio characteristics. Family portfolio managers can either invest in their own systems for calculating these statistics or can rely on information and analysis provided by the dealer who holds the portfolio in custody.

The most problematic characteristic of the portfolio at this point is its exposure to interest rate changes. The objective was to build a portfolio with an average maturity in the 2006 to 2007 range and a duration of 6.5. The average maturity of the portfolio at this point is mid-year 2009. That this is somewhat longer than the target average maturity is attributable largely to the purchase of the NB Capital Trust securities maturing in 2027. Because this bond has such a high coupon (8.25%), however, it is likely that the security will be redeemed close to the first call date in 2007. Given this likelihood, it makes more sense to evaluate this portfolio with respect to its duration rather than its average maturity.

In Exhibit 2 are two alternative calculations of weighted average portfolio duration. Duration I is the "duration to worst"; that is, the duration to maturity or the first call date, whichever produces a lower yield to the investor. Because both the callable bonds in the portfolio are trading above their call prices, this calculation provides the duration to call in all cases. Duration I is somewhat shorter than the target duration of 6.5, suggesting that the investor has room to add longer-duration and/or longer-maturity bonds while acquiring the final $8 million in par amount.

Duration II is a more subjective measure.[3] It is duration to call for any bond that is highly likely to be redeemed on the first call date and duration to maturity for any bonds that are non-callable or that are trading below or very close to their call price. Thus, in this calculation duration of the 8.25%s of 2027 is to the call date because this bond is very likely to be called, while the duration of the Home Loan Bank bonds is the duration to maturity. By this measure, the duration of the portfolio is slightly shorter than the 6.5 target.

The duration analysis of the portfolio leads to two conclusions about what additional bonds to buy. There is not a lot of room to buy bonds with durations much shorter or much longer than the target; that is, the investor should seek bonds with durations very close to 6.5. Second, given the duration uncertainty introduced by the relatively large position in the callable Home Loan Bank bonds, the investor should probably avoid buying additional callable bonds trading very close to their redemption prices.

The investor's choices will be much more limited when acquiring the final $8 million bonds for the portfolio than they are for the first $12 million. The manager will probably have to pass on many more attractive offerings. And acquiring the last few bonds will probably take longer than it took to buy the first few. Indeed, if it takes an inordinately long period of time to fill in the final purchases so that the portfolio's characteristics exactly match the objectives, the investor may want to consider relaxing some of the constraints on the portfolio structure. The investor might, for example, temporarily increase the single-industry limitation to, say, 30% and buy a few more bank obligations. Unless the investor is very lucky or is confining investments to government bond markets, the final purchases in a portfolio will almost always involve some minor compromise of investment objectives.

---

[3] Chapter 17 presents a more sophisticated methodology for measuring the duration of callable bonds. The parallel calculations presented here will suffice for most family portfolio management purposes.

Exhibit 2: Interim Phase of Portfolio Construction

Issuer	Rating	Par Amount	Coupon	Maturity	First Call Date	First Call Price	Purchase Price	Market Value	Duration I	Duration II
Ford Motor Credit	A1/A	1,000,000	7.20%	6/15/07	NCL	NCL	106.611	1,066,110	6.2	6.2
IBM	A1/A+	1,000,000	7.50%	3/1/08	NCL	NCL	112.474	1,124,740	9.3	9.3
Kroger	Baa3/NR	1,000,000	6.38%	3/1/08	NCL	NCL	99.600	996,000	7.2	7.2
Citicorp	A1/A	1,000,000	6.38%	1/15/06	NCL	NCL	101.650	1,016,500	6.1	6.1
Chase Manhattan Corp.	A1/A–	1,000,000	6.25%	11/15/08	NCL	NCL	100.658	1,006,580	6.0	6.0
NB Capital Trust (Nationsbank)	A1/A–	1,000,000	8.25%	4/15/27	4/15/07	103.85	112.410	1,124,100	6.4	6.4
Fleet Financial	A3/BBB+	1,000,000	7.13%	4/15/06	NCL	NCL	105.728	1,057,280	6.0	6.0
Fannie Mae	Aaa/AAA	2,000,000	5.75%	2/15/08	NCL	NCL	99.703	1,994,060	7.3	7.3
CNA Financial	A–/A3	1,000,000	6.75%	11/15/06	NCL	NCL	102.575	1,025,750	6.4	6.4
Federal Home Loan Bank Board	Aaa/AAA	2,000,000	6.37%	1/30/08	1/30/01	100.00	100.090	2,001,800	2.4	7.1
Total/Average	A1/A+	12,000,000	6.70%	6/6/09				12,412,920	6.1	6.4

Imagine now that the portfolio accumulation process has continued and that the completed portfolio is as described in Exhibit 3. The process illustrated here has been quite successful. The upper and lower bounds of portfolio duration bracket the target tightly, and the average credit quality is right on target. The only compromise has been to purchase $1.25 million of McDonalds Corp. medium-term notes, amounting to 6.25% of the portfolio's par value, which exceeds the single-issuer concentration limit of 5%. The portfolio manager may have justified the exception because these bonds are undervalued at a yield of 6.04% and because McDonalds is a strong and improving credit. The purchase of New Zealand government bonds might look like an exception in a portfolio confined to the corporate and government agency markets, but "yankee sovereign" issues — U.S. dollar obligations of foreign governments issued in the United States — are usually considered part of the corporate bond market.

An International Example

The process of building an international bond portfolio is very similar. The only substantial difference is that an international portfolio will, in general, require some currency hedging. To illustrate, suppose a euro-based investor wants to put €20 million to work in the investment-grade fixed-income markets. The investor has decided to build a portfolio with the structural characteristics listed in Exhibit 4.

As in the U.S. example, the investor begins purchasing individual bonds to fill in this target structure and finds that some parts of the portfolio are easier to accumulate than others. Specifically, it will be relatively easy to fill in the Scandinavian and Greek sectors of the portfolio because government bond markets are highly liquid. Buying euro-denominated corporate bonds may be a bit more of a challenge, because that market is still in early stages of development. Suppose, then, that the accumulation process has gone on for a few days, and at this stage the portfolio is as described in Exhibit 5.

At this point the manager has assembled a bit more than half of the portfolio. The process of accumulating the Scandinavian and Greek positions is complete. Nearly two-thirds of the U.S. dollar position is in place, but only about one-third of the EMU holdings have been acquired. The durations of holdings are within target in the European markets, but the U.S. holding is short of its target duration range. To complete the process, the investor will have to buy a substantial volume of euro- (or predecessor currency) denominated bonds and will have to seek out U.S. dollar-denominated paper that is a bit longer than the current holdings.

As in the U.S. market, buying the last few bonds, especially in the euro-denominated corporate market, will probably take longer than purchasing the first few issues. Suppose, though, that the investor completes the process and assembles the portfolio illustrated in Exhibit 6. At this point, the process of building a single-country bond portfolio would be complete. In the case of an international portfolio, however, the manager still has some work to do.

Exhibit 3: Completed Portfolio

Issuer	Rating	Par Amount	Coupon	Maturity	First Call Date	First Call Price	Cost	Duration I	Duration II
Cash		129,570					129,570	0	0
Ford Motor Credit	A1/A	1,000,000	7.20%	6/15/07	NCL	NCL	1,066,110	6.8	6.8
IBM	A1/A+	1,000,000	7.50%	3/1/08	NCL	NCL	1,124,740	7.1	7.1
Kroger	Baa3/NR	1,000,000	6.38%	3/1/08	NCL	NCL	996,000	7.2	7.2
Citicorp	A1/A	1,000,000	6.38%	1/15/06	NCL	NCL	1,016,500	6.0	6.0
Chase Manhattan Corp.	A1/A–	1,000,000	6.25%	11/15/08	NCL	NCL	1,006,580	7.8	7.8
NB Capital Trust (Nationsbank)	A1/A–	1,000,000	8.25%	4/15/27	4/15/07	103.85	1,124,100	6.4	6.4
Fleet Financial	A3/BBB+	1,000,000	7.13%	4/15/06	NCL	NCL	1,057,280	6.1	6.1
Fannie Mae	Aaa/AAA	2,000,000	5.75%	2/15/08	NCL	NCL	1,994,060	7.4	7.4
CNA Financial	A–/A3	1,000,000	6.75%	11/15/06	NCL	NCL	1,025,750	6.5	6.5
Federal Home Loan Bank Board	Aaa/AAA	2,000,000	6.37%	1/30/08	1/30/01	100.00	2,001,800	2.4	7.2
Pacific Bell Telephone	A1/AA–	750,000	5.88%	2/15/06	NCL	NCL	738,944	6.1	6.1
Southwestern Bell Telephone	Aa3/AA	1,000,000	6.63%	7/15/07	NCL	NCL	1,039,890	6.8	6.8
McDonalds Corp.	Aa2/AA	1,250,000	6.50%	8/1/07	NCL	NCL	1,290,038	6.9	6.9
Fannie Mae	Aaa/AAA	1,000,000	5.75%	2/15/08	NCL	NCL	1,000,000	7.4	7.4
New Zealand Government	Aa1/AA+	1,000,000	8.88%	12/15/06	NCL	NCL	1,276,090	6.5	6.5
AT&T Corp.	Aa3/AA	1,000,000	7.75%	3/1/07	NCL	NCL	1,110,280	6.5	6.5
Abbott Labs	Aa1/AAA	1,000,000	6.00%	3/15/08	NCL	NCL	1,002,268	7.4	7.4
Total/Weighted Average	Aa3/AA–	19,000,000					20,000,000	6.4	6.8

Exhibit 4: Hypothetical International Portfolio Structural Objectives

Market	Allocation	Target Duration	Target Maturity Structure	Types of Issuer	Currency Hedge (%)
EMU	50%	4.0 – 5.0	Bullet	Government, Corporate	N.A.
Sweden or Denmark	15%	4.0 – 5.0	Bullet	Government	0%
Greece	5%	3.0 – 4.0	Bullet	Government	0%
U.S. Dollar	30%	4.0 – 5.0	Bullet	Corporate, Agency	80%

Exhibit 5: Interim Phase of International Portfolio Construction

Sector	Issuer	Par Amount	Curr.	EUR Equivalent	% Final Portfolio	Rating	Cpn	Maturity	Price	Market Value	Duration
EMU	Repsol	1,500,000	EUR	€1,500,000	7.50%	A2/A–	3.75%	2/23/04	96.700	€1,450,500	3.62
	Allied Domecq	1,500,000	EUR	1,500,000	7.50%	A2/A	4.75%	12/14/05	98.250	1,473,750	5.05
	Ford	1,500,000	EUR	1,500,000	7.50%	A1/A	3.75%	7/12/04	96.400	1,446,000	3.99
Total/Wtd. Avg.				4,500,000	22.50%					4,370,250	4.22
Scan.	Sweden	12,500,000	SEK	1,434,309	7.17%	Aa1/AAA	5.00%	1/15/04	100.250	1,437,894	3.42
	Denmark	11,500,000	DKK	1,546,322	7.73%	Aaa/AAA	5.00%	8/15/05	101.250	1,565,651	4.73
Total/Wtd. Avg.				2,980,631	14.90%					3,003,546	4.10
Greece	Greece	325,000,000	GRD	1,000,770	5.00%	A3/A–	6.60%	1/15/04	100.500	1,005,774	3.25
Total/Wtd. Avg.				1,000,770	5.00%					1,005,774	3.25
U.S.$	NTT	1,500,000	USD	1,428,571	7.14%	Aa1/AA+	6.00%	3/24/04	98.700	1,410,000	3.62
	G.E. Capital Corp.	1,300,000	USD	1,238,095	6.19%	Aaa/AAA	6.13%	12/30/02	101.000	1,250,476	2.71
	FNMA(5NC2)	1,000,000	USD	952,381	4.76%	Aaa/AAA	5.88%	4/23/04	97.700	930,476	3.70
Total/Wtd. Avg.				3,619,048	18.10%					3,590,952	3.32
Total				12,100,449						11,970,522	

Exhibit 6: Completed International Portfolio

Sector	Issuer	Par Amount	Curr.	EUR Equivalent	% Final Portfolio	Rating	Cpn	Maturity	Price	Market Value (Euros)	Duration
EMU	Repsol	1,500,000	EUR	€1,500,000	7.50%	A2/A–	3.75%	2/23/04	96.700	€1,450,500	3.62
	Allied Domecq	1,500,000	EUR	1,500,000	7.50%	A2/A	4.75%	12/14/05	98.250	1,473,750	5.05
	Ford	1,500,000	EUR	1,500,000	7.50%	A1/A	3.75%	7/12/04	96.400	1,446,000	3.99
	Hypotheken Bank in Essen, Pfandbrief	1,500,000	EUR	1,500,000	7.50%	Aaa/AAA	3.500%	3/17/04	96.600	1,449,000	3.71
	Cades	1,500,000	EUR	1,500,000	7.50%	Aaa/AAA	3.375%	7/12/04	96.200	1,443,000	4.03
	Kredit fuer Wiederaufbau	1,500,000	EUR	1,500,000	7.50%	Aaa/AAA	3.500%	7/15/04	96.650	1,449,750	4.03
	Japan Financial Corp (Gov't Guaranteed)	1,400,000	EUR	1,400,000	7.00%	Aa1/AAA	3.625%	3/9/04	96.200	1,346,800	3.67
Total/Wd. Avg.				10,400,000	52.00%					10,058,800	4.02
Scan.	Sweden	12,500,000	SEK	1,434,309	7.17%	Aa1/AAA	5.00%	1/15/04	100.250	1,437,894	3.42
	Denmark	11,500,000	DKK	1,546,322	7.73%	Aaa/AAA	5.00%	8/15/05	101.250	1,565,651	4.73
Total/Wd. Avg.				2,980,631	14.90%					3,003,546	4.10
Greece	Greece	325,000,000	GRD	1,000,770	5.00%	A3/A–	6.60%	1/15/04	100.500	1,005,774	3.25
Total/Wd. Avg.				1,000,770	5.00%					1,005,774	3.25
U.S.$	NTT	1,500,000	USD	1,428,571	7.14%	Aa1/AA+	6.00%	3/24/04	98.700	1,410,000	3.62
	G.E. Capital Corp.	1,300,000	USD	1,238,095	6.19%	Aaa/AAA	6.13%	12/30/02	101.000	1,250,476	2.71
	FNMA(5NC2)	1,000,000	USD	952,381	4.76%	Aaa/AAA	5.88%	4/23/04	97.700	930,476	3.70
	Hutchison Whampoa	1,500,000	USD	1,428,571	7.14%	A3/A	6.950%	8/1/07	97.750	1,396,429	5.62
	FHLMC(10NC3)	1,000,000	USD	952,381	4.76%	Aaa/AAA	6.450%	4/29/09	96.800	921,905	6.80
Total/Wd. Avg.				6,000,000	18.10%					5,909,286	4.41
Total				20,381,401						19,977,405	

In this example, the investor has decided to accept exchange rate risk within Europe, but to hedge 80% of the U.S. dollar exposure. The first step in currency hedging is to decide the appropriate term for the hedge. Markets for currency forwards are highly efficient, especially when the two currencies involved are the euro and the U.S. dollar for transactions extending out a year or more. Nevertheless, there is some transaction cost involved in forward contracts. Rolling hedges frequently will multiply these costs. This would argue for putting a relatively long-term currency hedge in place by selling dollars forward for euros, say, one year forward. However, any modification of the portfolio during the 12-month period might require reversing all or part of the forward exchange contract, and this too would involve some transaction cost.

The right term for the hedge balances these two considerations. Investors who do not expect to manage their portfolios actively might opt for longer-term currency forward contracts. Those who expect to rebalance frequently should probably limit their hedges to contracts extending three months forward or less.

In this example we will assume that the investor has opted for a six-month forward sale. To illustrate the process, we assume that the spot exchange rate is 1.050$/€ and the forward rate is 1.070$/€. The market value of the dollar-denominated investments is $6,204,750, and the average yield on these investments is 6.57%. So, at the end of six months under unchanged market conditions, the value of the U.S. dollar investments will be about $6,408,576 (= $6,204,750 × [1 + (6.57%/2)]), and 80% of this figure is $5,126,869. The investor might reasonably decide to round this figure down to $5 million and sell this amount of dollars six months forward for €4,672,897 (= $5,000,000/1.070). This hedging transaction completes the international portfolio construction process.[4]

MANAGING THE PORTFOLIO

The noisy debate among financial advisors regarding buy-and-hold investment strategies versus active management will probably never end. The issue will never be resolved because neither side has the right answer for all investors under all circumstances. Not even the most dedicated advocate of the buy-and-hold strategy would argue that a U.S. taxpayer who has realized large volumes of capital gains in a tax year should pass up the opportunity to realize losses on bonds if interest rates rise substantially during the same year. And not even the most rabid active manager would argue that a family should shift the duration of its core fixed-income portfolio substantially in response to the latest release of each new economic statistic. In fact, a reasonable resolution to this debate is relatively straightforward.

---

[4] The investor might also choose to put hedges in place as U.S. dollar securities are accumulated rather than waiting until the entire portfolio is purchased. If so, the final transaction would be whatever forward sale of dollars is required so that the total forward sale is $5 million.

Family portfolios require two types of management: maintenance management and restructuring management. A third type of activity, opportunistic management, is optional. The goal of maintenance management is to make sure that characteristics of the portfolio continue to match a set of unchanging structural objectives over time. Restructuring management is the response to a change in the structural objectives. Opportunistic fixed-income management is the response of families who devote a portion of their overall investment portfolio to more aggressive strategies. Most of the opportunities such investors find will be in the equities sector, but some may occasionally be found in the fixed-income markets. Some varieties of such opportunistic fixed-income investment strategies are discussed in Chapters 14, 18, and 19.

Maintenance Management

The characteristics of a bond portfolio will inevitably change over time. At the very least, the duration of the portfolio will drift down as weeks and months go by. Duration will also change as interest rate levels change. Issuer credit quality is always in flux, and may require some adjustment to keep average and minimum credit quality on target.

To illustrate some of these effects, let's return to the hypothetical U.S. corporate/agency portfolio. With the passage of one year's time and no change in interest rates, the duration of the portfolio would be between 5.77 and 6.28. Thus the passage of time brings the portfolio duration — even on the assumption that most of the callable bonds would remain outstanding to maturity — below the target level of 6.5. More realistically, assume also that one year after the portfolio is assembled interest rates have fallen by 75 basis points. As Exhibit 7 indicates, under these assumptions the duration of the portfolio would be between 5.83 and 6.33.

A rally in bond prices slightly lengthens duration because the majority of the bonds in the portfolio are convex; that is, falling rates have the effect of increasing their durations. Even so, the duration extension effect is not strong enough to offset the full impact of one year's aging, and, unless the investor has changed the structural objectives, the portfolio is too short. The shortening effect is accentuated by the fact that it is less likely than one year earlier that the callable bonds will remain outstanding to maturity; that is, the effective duration of this portfolio is now probably closer to 5.83 than to 6.33.

On the assumption that the investor still wants a bullet maturity structure, maintenance management will involve selling some of the shortest securities and buying bonds with durations slightly longer than 6.5 years. For example, the transactions listed in Exhibit 8 would bring portfolio duration up to 6.51 years. The assumption of a 0.5% bid-asked spread underlies the hypothetical proceeds and purchase prices. Portfolios consisting entirely of very long-maturity, non-callable bonds require relatively little maintenance management aimed at keeping duration constant. In duration terms, shorter-maturity bonds age more quickly than long-maturity bonds, as illustrated in Exhibit 9.

Exhibit 7: Hypothetical Portfolio After One Year and a 75 bp Decrease in Yields

Issuer	Rating	Par Amount	Coupon	Maturity	First Call Date	First Call Price	Market Price	Duration I	Duration II
Cash		129,570						0	0
Ford Motor Credit	A1/A	1,000,000	7.200%	6/15/07	NCL	NCL	111.021	6.3	6.3
IBM	A1/A+	1,000,000	7.500%	3/1/08	NCL	NCL	117.078	6.6	6.6
Kroger	Baa3/NR	1,000,000	6.375%	3/1/08	NCL	NCL	104.714	6.7	6.7
Citicorp	A1/A	1,000,000	6.375%	1/15/06	NCL	NCL	105.621	5.4	5.4
Chase Manhattan Corp.	A1/A–	1,000,000	6.250%	11/15/08	NCL	NCL	106.105	7.3	7.3
NB Capital Trust (Nationsbank)	A1/A–	1,000,000	8.250%	4/15/27	4/15/07	103.85	113.124	6.4	6.4
Fleet Financial	A3/BBB+	1,000,000	7.125%	4/15/06	NCL	NCL	109.499	5.5	5.5
Fannie Mae	Aaa/AAA	2,000,000	5.750%	2/15/08	NCL	NCL	104.929	6.9	6.9
CNA Financial	A–/A3	1,000,000	6.750%	11/15/06	NCL	NCL	106.896	6.0	6.0
Federal Home Loan Bank Board	Aaa/AAA	2,000,000	6.370%	1/30/08	1/30/01	100.00	101.157	1.5	6.6
Pacific Bell Telephone	A1/AA–	750,000	5.875%	2/15/06	NCL	NCL	102.802	5.5	5.5
Southwestern Bell Telephone	Aa3/AA	1,000,000	6.625%	7/15/07	NCL	NCL	108.632	6.3	6.3
McDonalds Corp.	Aa2/AA	1,250,000	6.500%	8/1/07	NCL	NCL	107.917	6.4	6.4
Fannie Mae	Aaa/AAA	1,000,000	5.750%	2/15/08	NCL	NCL	105.220	6.9	6.9
New Zealand Government	Aa1/AA+	1,000,000	8.750%	12/15/06	NCL	NCL	130.416	5.9	5.9
AT&T Corp.	Aa3/AA	1,000,000	7.750%	3/1/07	NCL	NCL	115.003	6.0	6.0
Abbott Labs	Aa1/AAA	1,000,000	6.000%	3/15/08	NCL	NCL	105.428	6.9	6.9
Total/Weighted Average	Aa3/AA–	19,000,000						5.83	6.33

Exhibit 8: Maintenance Management Transactions to Extend Duration

Bond	Proceeds/Cost
Sell	
Fleet Financial, 7.125%, 4/15/06	$1,089,513.67
Federal Home Loan Bank Board, 6.37%, 1/30/08, Callable 1/30/01 @ 100	$2,013,029.28
Citicorp, 6.375%, 1/15/06	$1,050,928.62
Total	$4,153,471.57
Buy	
BankBoston NA, 6.375%, 3/25/08	$1,049,487.14
First Union Corp., 6.00%, 10/30/08	$1,030,237.67
Federal Home Loan Bank Board, 6.413%, 5/27/08	$2,095,876.35
Total	$4,175,601.15
Difference (Net Cash Requirement)	$22,129.59

Exhibit 9: Impact of One-Year's Aging on 6.00% Par Bond Duration by Maturity

Maturity	Duration	Maturity	Duration
30 Years	14.25	5 Years	4.39
29 Years	14.07	4 Years	3.61
Difference	0.18	Difference	0.78
% Diff.	1.2%	% Diff.	17.7%

Credit quality management is even more important for long-duration portfolios. Credit quality maintenance may be required when credits in the portfolio deteriorate or improve. The implications of deterioration are more obvious. If one of the credits in the portfolio is downgraded below Baa3/BBB– it will no longer meet this hypothetical portfolio's investment-grade rating requirement. At this point, the portfolio manager may decide either to replace the bond or to modify the portfolio parameters; in either case, some management decision is required. Also, if enough of the credits are downgraded so that the average rating of the portfolio falls below Aa3/AA– standard, some swaps out of lower-rated into higher-rated issues may be necessary.

A large number of upgrades also requires some decision on the part of the manager. All else held equal, a higher-rated portfolio is better than a lower-rated one. This hypothetical investor's willingness to hold a portfolio of less-than-perfect credits reflects, though, some inclination to take credit risk in exchange for higher bond yields. This investor could reasonably decide that the average credit quality of this portfolio had become too high, and might sell some of the higher-rated or upgraded credits and buy somewhat lower-rated investment-grade bonds offering higher yields.

There is no single right answer about how often a portfolio should go into the shop for maintenance management. It depends on the characteristics of the portfolio and the precision with which the manager wants to satisfy the objectives. We have seen that the duration of a portfolio will drift downward more quickly, the shorter the average maturity of the bonds. Thus, a portfolio holding mostly three-year notes will require more management to keep its duration from shortening too much than will a portfolio of mostly 20-year bonds. Likewise, triple-B-rated corporations or municipalities tend to be subject to more vicissitudes than triple-A-rated issuers or U.S. government agencies. Thus, portfolios with poorer average credit quality will require relatively more maintenance.

The level of transaction costs should also affect the frequency of maintenance. Investors in relatively illiquid markets or investors who hold relatively small-sized bond positions should probably not build portfolios that require a great deal of maintenance.

Finally, a portfolio manager's tolerance for deviations from the stated portfolio objectives will influence how much maintenance is needed. A manager who insists on actual portfolio duration falling within 0.2 of the target will need to do more maintenance than an investor who is satisfied with being within eight months of the optimal number. Investors who have more of a tolerance for deviation from stated objectives should recognize this fact and, when they do undertake maintenance management, should build portfolios with durations slightly longer than what they might consider ideal so that it will take more time for duration to shorten to the point when action is called for.

Restructuring Management

As the name implies, maintenance is aimed at maintaining a portfolio structure that reflects the manager's investment objectives and market views. Restructuring is instead a response to changes in the manager's fundamental objectives or investment views. Suppose, for example, that the investor holding our hypothetical portfolio decides to move to a higher-risk, higher-return point on the efficient frontier. Such a change would probably involve reducing the size of the investment-grade bond portfolio and shifting assets into the stock market. It might also involve a downgrade of the target average credit quality and, perhaps, also a purchase of subinvestment-grade bonds in the high-yield or emerging debt markets. Accordingly, at the very least, the investor would want to sell some of the agency and strong double-A bonds in the portfolio listed in Exhibit 3 (e.g., government of New Zealand, Abbott Labs) to raise funds for the shift into equities. Another choice is to sell some of the weaker double-As and stronger single-As and use the proceeds to buy high-yield bonds.

Portfolio restructuring might also reflect a change in interest rate expectations. The current structure, with its 6.5 duration and bullet shape, reflects a moderately optimistic view about the direction of bond prices and the expectation that the yield curve will not flatten. If expectations indicate rather that rates are more likely to rise and the yield curve to flatten, the investors would want to shorten portfolio duration and shift to a more barbell-like structure. Such a shift would require substantial trading because the current holdings fall into such a narrow range of maturities. The process would involve selling the longest-duration bonds listed in Exhibit 3 first (Chase Manhattan, Abbot Labs, Fannie Mae) and using the proceeds to buy a barbell consisting of mostly short-maturity notes and very long-duration bonds. Initially the purchases should consist mostly of short-duration assets because one of the aims of the restructuring would be to reduce weighted average portfolio duration.

Reasonable investors can and do disagree about how much restructuring management is the right amount. To be sure, basic investment objectives should change very gradually over the investor's personal life cycle and in response to major shifts in economic or life circumstances (e.g., sale of a business, retirement, marriage, divorce, death). Thus, too frequent shifts in fundamental investment objectives — very aggressive one month, very defensive the next, and then back again — are probably symptomatic of a financial neurosis. It is harder to dismiss relatively infrequent restructuring activity that reflects changes in the portfolio manager's views about market conditions and directions. And investors with a taste for trading may wish to change their portfolio durations relatively frequently in response to surprising economic statistics around the world. Other very active managers might consider shifting assets among fixed-income sectors as yield spreads vary.

Most family portfolio managers will consider restructuring transactions only when long-term views change in a substantial way. In our hypothetical example, a variety of evidence accumulated over a period of several weeks might lead the manager to conclude that the economy is growing too quickly, that interest rates are likely to begin rising, and that, therefore, the 6.5 duration is no longer appropriate. The response would be to set a new, shorter portfolio duration target and then to sell long-duration bonds and replace these with shorter-duration notes or, in the extreme, money market instruments until the portfolio is at the new target. Each investor will reach a different conclusion about how much such restructuring management may be needed.

Radical shifts in portfolio structure in response to ephemeral evidence are probably inappropriate for most families. At the same time, it makes little sense to ignore strong evidence that the premises underlying one's current investment strategy are wrong.

MANAGEMENT AND TAXES

How much maintenance, restructuring, or opportunistic management a family should expect to do depends crucially on the tax treatment of capital gains and losses. Our discussion of management to this point applies to places and situations where taxation is not an issue, such as countries where there is no capital gains taxation or tax-exempt funds such as family foundations. If, as in Germany, there is a minimum holding period after which capital gains become tax-exempt, there would have to be a very good reason to execute transactions more frequently than every 12 months. In building their portfolios, investors should realize that maintenance more frequently than once a year in Germany could be very expensive if bond prices rally in the meantime. Accordingly, investors should, for example, target a duration for their purchases that is roughly six months longer than their ideal target. That way the portfolio's duration will be right on target on average over each one-year period, and the investor will be able to avoid the risk of paying taxes on realized gains.

In jurisdictions that tax capital gains, holding-period considerations can also be important. In the U.S. and many other countries, the tax treatment of long-term capital gains is much more favorable than that of short-term trading profits. In these places, investors should have a very good reason for realizing a gain on the sale of a security held for too short a time to qualify for long-term tax treatment. Further, because taxes are levied on net gains, after deducting capital losses, investors in these countries should actively seek opportunities to realize losses. Once losses are realized, they can be used to offset gains that have been or may be realized on other investments.

Consider a U.S. investor who has realized a large long-term capital gain through, for example, the sale of a company. Suppose further that this investor holds a position in a 5.00% 20-year, Aaa/AAA-rated bond with a face value of $1 million that was purchased at par more than 12 months previously. This investment is paying $50,000 per year. Assume, however, that interest rates on the bid side of the market have risen so that the bond's yield is now 5.286% and its bid price is now 96.50. A sale of this position produces a loss of $35,000 that can be used to offset part of the long-term capital gain realized on the sale of the company. The offset will reduce the investor's capital gains tax bill by 20% of $35,000 or by $7,000. If the investor devotes this tax savings, along with proceeds of the sale of the 5.00% 20-year bond, to the purchase of a new municipal bond at an offered-side market yield of 5.236%, the annual income produced on the investment will be $50,894 (= 5.236% × [$965,000 + $7,000]). So the combination of transactions — the realization of a loss to offset a gain and the investment of the sale proceeds plus the tax savings in a new municipal bond — has increased the investor's return.

Loss realization requires some degree of care. In the U.S. and elsewhere, tax authorities may disallow "losses" incurred on "wash sales," when an investor sells a security at a loss and then immediately buys exactly the same or a very similar investment. In most fixed-income markets, however, there are enough alternative investments that are different enough to avoid wash sale rules but similar enough to serve roughly the same role in an investment portfolio.[5] In fact, tax

---

[5] This is a useful point at which to reiterate the *caveat* that this book is not intended to provide tax advice. Investors considering selling securities at a loss and reinvesting the sale proceeds should consult their own tax advisors about the potential applicability of wash sale rules.

swapping of this type is one of the most common fixed-income management transactions that family portfolio managers engage in. Family investors should keep their eyes open for such opportunities, which will occur whenever interest rates rise substantially.

One final portfolio management ramification of taxation is unique to the United States. Interest income on municipal bonds is tax-exempt, but profits realized on the sale of bonds are taxed in the same way as any other capital gain. An investor who sells a municipal bond at a gain is essentially converting tax-exempt income, which would be received over time, into taxable capital gains.

For example, consider $1 million of a 5.00% 10-year tax-exempt municipal bond purchased at par. This investment will pay $50,000 per year tax-free. Suppose that by the end of the first year after purchase yields on this bond have declined to 4.50% on the bid side. At that point, the market price of the investor's bond will be 103.669. Suppose also that there is another nine-year bond in the market of similar credit quality yielding 4.85% on the offered side of the market and that the investor wants to sell the original investment and buy the more attractive bond. Without capital gains taxes, the investor could sell the bond for $1,036,690, buy the "cheaper" bond, and lock in annual tax-free income of $50,279.47. This trade might may sense. If the investor has to pay a 20% tax rate on the $36,690 gain on the trade, there would be only $1,029,352 to reinvest in the bond yielding 4.85% and only $49,923.57 of tax-free income after the bond swap.

The difference in the tax treatment of interest income and capital gains means that managing U.S. municipal portfolios after a bond market rally, either for maintenance purposes or to restructure, can be expensive for U.S. taxpayers. This has three implications. First, the cost of realizing gains should reinforce the message that taxpayers should take every opportunity to realize capital losses. The rules regarding loss carryforwards mean that investors should realize losses even if they are uncertain about whether there will be gains in the portfolio. Second, U.S. taxpayers should build portfolios that will require relatively little maintenance management. This consideration, taken by itself, suggests that U.S. taxpayers should hold bonds with somewhat longer maturities — which age more slowly in duration terms — than they would buy solely on the basis of their expectations regarding interest rates. Also, since weaker credits may tend to be more volatile, taxpayers should probably target somewhat higher average credit qualities for their municipal bond portfolios than they would otherwise. Finally, frequent restructuring management is even less appropriate for U.S. taxpayers than for family portfolio managers in general.

MANAGEMENT AND TRANSACTION COSTS

The relative level of transaction costs in the investor's primary and principal alternative sectors will also influence the frequency of maintenance and restructuring management. Likewise, the degree to which an investor wishes to manage the portfolio actively should influence the selection of market sectors. Investors who select relatively illiquid sectors, such as small state municipal bonds, callable U.S. government agency notes, or speculative-grade corporates, as their primary fixed-income sectors should probably not build portfolios that will require frequent maintenance management. Thus, an investor building a portfolio of, for example, Ohio municipal bonds, should target a somewhat longer average duration than might be chosen otherwise. The shorter a portfolio's duration, the more frequently maintenance is required, and it will be relatively expensive in this case.

Investors who anticipate engaging in frequent portfolio restructuring should account for this expectation when selecting their investment sectors. Government bond markets will serve these investors best either as a primary investment sector or as a principal alternative sector. If the latter, the primary sector could be relatively illiquid and would not be restructured frequently. Instead, the investor could adjust the duration of the overall fixed-income portfolio by taking positions in the government bond market.

Part III

CHAPTER 14

Leverage and Short Sales in the Fixed-Income Markets

o far we have presented general material that should be of interest to most bond investors. With this chapter, we begin to focus on topics that will be of interest only to those who expect to manage their fixed-income portfolios actively, with the aim of achieving fixed-income investment goals in the most efficient way possible — albeit not necessarily the simplest or the most straightforward way. Our subject in this chapter is the whys and wherefores of borrowing money to buy bonds and selling bonds one does not own to create short positions.

Active managers of equity portfolios are familiar with both these investment techniques. Brokerage firms routinely accommodate investors seeking to buy stocks "on margin." If the margin requirement is 50%, an investor who wishes to purchase 1,000 shares of a stock trading at $30 would be required to deliver $15,000 in cash to the securities dealer. The dealer will lend the investor the remaining $15,000 and charge a short-term interest rate on the loan. If the price of the stock declines to $25, the investor will have lost $5,000 out of the initial $15,000 and will be required to post half of that amount as additional margin. Specifically, a 50% margin requirement, based on the lower stock price, would be $12,500, but the value of the investor's cash deposit will be only $10,000 so the investor will get a "margin call" for an additional $2,500.

An investor who expects a stock's price to fall can create a short position by borrowing stock from a dealer, and selling the borrowed stock. In this case, the investor will have to deposit part of the sale proceeds with the dealer who executes the transaction to secure the eventual purchase of the security to cover the short position. Such funds earn a short-term interest rate for the investor.

Relatively few family portfolio managers engage in leveraged purchases or short sales. Those who do so are much more likely to enter into such transactions in the stock market than in the fixed-income sector. Both types of transactions are entered into with the aim of benefiting from or avoiding losses on substantial changes in security prices. Stock prices are more volatile than bond prices, so it isn't surprising that most leveraged purchases and short sales take place in the equity market. Furthermore, tax laws effectively preclude selling municipal bonds short or buying tax-exempt bonds with borrowed funds. This limits the use of these investment techniques in the fixed-income market because municipals account for the bulk of most U.S. families' fixed-income holdings and because margin purchases and short sales are more common in the U.S. market than elsewhere. Nevertheless, the bond market does accommodate leveraged purchases and short sales of taxable fixed-income securities, and such transactions can be very useful in a variety of ways to family portfolio managers who understand the potential risks and benefits.

THE USES OF LEVERAGE

Leverage in the fixed-income market — buying bonds with borrowed funds or borrowing funds against a pledge of fixed-income securities as collateral — can be used to accomplish four different investment goals:

1. To borrow funds, for whatever purpose, at the lowest available interest rate.
2. To enhance profit from anticipated increases in bond prices.
3. To earn a positive "carry."
4. To adjust portfolio characteristics without trading bonds or adding new cash.

Using Fixed Income Securities to Collateralize Efficient Borrowing

Loans collateralized by government or government agency securities typically carry the lowest interest cost available to borrowers in financial markets. Rates on such loans are typically just a few basis points higher or lower than other broad market short-term interest rates such as LIBOR, and much lower than rates charged on margin loans or unsecured borrowings. For this reason, investors who own government or agency securities outright who wish to borrow funds on a short-term basis for whatever purpose will frequently find that borrowing against their fixed-income portfolios through a repurchase agreement is the lowest-cost way of raising funds.

The advisability of such borrowing must be compared to the option of simply selling some investments. If borrowing makes sense, however, then leveraging government or agency bonds that one owns will probably make the most sense.

Leverage and Speculation

Leverage can provide an efficient way to speculate on an increase in the price of a security. Investors who anticipate a drop in bond yields in the near future can take several courses to act on this expectation. The simplest is to extend the duration of their fixed-income portfolios by selling some of their shorter-maturity bonds and buying longer-term and/or lower-coupon instruments. Leverage can play a role in this process.

A bullish investor may not own a bond portfolio or may not wish to radically alter an existing portfolio merely to take advantage of what might be a temporary drop in interest rates. In such cases, investors can use leverage to speculate on short-term shifts in interest rates.

An example will illustrate how leverage can magnify returns on *correct* interest rate expectations. Suppose an investor expects yields on 30-year U.S. Treasury bonds to decline soon and wishes to take advantage of the move. Suppose further that this investor can purchase these bonds using 10:1 leverage and that $1 million in cash is available for such "opportunistic" investments so that the investor can purchase $10 million in long bonds.[1] Now suppose that yields on 30-year U.S. Treasury bonds decline by 25 basis points instantaneously, and that the investor liquidates the position after this rally. If this happens, the price of the Treasuries will increase to 103.976, and the value of the investor's long position will increase to $10,397,606.

The investor will have purchased the bonds on the offered side of the Treasury market and will be selling on the bid side. If we assume a 2/32 of a point bid-asked spread (0.0625%), this will reduce the net proceeds by $6,250. So net sale proceeds will be $10,391,356 (= $10,397,606 – $6,250), and the return on the initial investment will be 39.1% (= [$10,391,356 – $10,000,000]/$1,000,000) over a two-week period.

So leveraged speculative positions can produce substantial returns *if the investor's expectations are borne out.* By the same token, such positions are extremely risky. In this example, the investor may be using all of its borrowing capacity to purchase the long position so that *any* increase in interest rates will lead to a margin call and demand for more collateral. Further, a 70-basis point rise in rates would wipe out the investor's initial cash position.

Because of the degree of risk involved, very few family investors use leverage to speculate on the direction of interest rates. Those who do are advised to monitor these positions very frequently, checking bond market conditions several times a day, and to adopt — and stick to — precise profitability objectives and strict loss limits.

"Carry" and Its "Cost"

Our leverage example is unrealistic in that it assumes that the change in interest rates take place instantaneously. If the leveraged position is carried for some time, a complete analysis of its profitability must account for two additional elements

---

[1] To simplify matters further, we also assume that the bonds are purchased on an interest payment date so that the invoice price of the purchase is also $10 million. The leveraged purchase of bonds trading with accrued interest would require borrowing a proportion of the full price of the securities, which complicates the calculations but does not alter the economics of the illustration.

of return: the interest paid and/or accrued on the bond position, and the interest paid on the borrowing used to finance the purchase. The net interest earned or paid on the leveraged bond investment is referred to as the "carry" or the "cost of carry" on the position.

To illustrate the impact of carry, we can modify the example by assuming that the interest rate change in question does not take place instantaneously but rather over a 6-month period. We also assume that the investor will pay 4.00% per year in interest on the $9 million borrowed portion of the $10 million aggregate purchase price. Over the 6-month period, the interest paid or accrued on the bond investment will equal $250,000 (= $10,000,000 × 5.00%/2) while the interest paid on the loan will be $180,000 (= $9,000,000 × 4.00%/2), so the carry on the leveraged position will be $70,000. If at the end of the 6-month period the yield on the bond has fallen from 5.00% to 4.75%, the flat price will be 103.946, and the market value of the position will be $10,394,551.[2]

Under these assumptions, the total return on the transaction will include a price change of $394,551 plus the carry on the transaction of $70,000, less the transaction cost of $6,250 or a total return of $458,301 or 45.8% on the initial investment of $1 million. This represents a higher percentage return than in the case of the instantaneous interest rate changes, but, of course, a speculator is more interested in the price action than in the carry and would rather see expectations borne out immediately than have to keep the $1 million tied up for six months.

Carry as an End in Itself

The carry on a leveraged position has a wide range of other implications for bond portfolio management and fixed-income analysis as will become apparent as we progress through Part III. At this point, we merely illustrate how "positive carry" can be something of an end in and of itself for leveraged investments in fixed-income.

Suppose an investor can purchase a 3-year 6% U.S. Treasury note at par at a yield of 6%, and finance up to 90% of the purchase price at an interest cost of 3%. In other words, we hypothesize an "efficient" borrower in an environment in which the yield curve is steep. This investor could, for example, use $1 million in cash to purchase a portfolio of $10 million Treasury notes. On an annual basis, assuming no change in borrowing cost or bond yields, the leveraged "long" position would pay $600,000 (= 6.00% × $10 million) in interest income. The borrowing cost would be $270,000 (= 3.00% × $9 million). The net interest income, or carry, on the position will be $330,000, or, expressed as a percentage of the cash put up for the transaction, 33%.

The Risks of Carry Trades

Returns this high are almost invariably compensating investors for substantial risk, and leveraged bond investments are no exception to this generalization. The

---

[2] This reflects a slightly different price change from the previous example because now the bond is a 29.5-year security, not a 30-year.

first risk is that the borrowing rate might increase. In fact, if the borrowing rate increases by 300 basis points, the leveraged position will produce no more in net interest income than a simple purchase of $1 million in Treasury notes on an unleveraged basis. As we saw in Chapter 4, a steeply upward-sloping yield curve may reflect the general expectation among bond market participants that interest rates are likely to rise over time. Such market expectations may be right or wrong, but an investor who establishes a leveraged long position in the expectation of earning a large positive carry is, in effect, taking a "contrarian" position against the prevailing market view. This particular risk need not necessarily trouble a leveraged investor; the investor can simply "unwind" the leveraged position by selling the bonds to repay the loan.

The second risk — the chance that the price of the purchased bonds may decline — is more worrisome. To see why this is so, note first that the investor in this example has put up $1 million in cash to purchase $10 million in securities, thereby using its entire leverage capacity. Therefore, any loss of market value on the Treasury notes will immediately trigger a call for additional collateral. This in and of itself may not be a problem if the investor has other unpledged, "marginable" securities held in custody by the bond dealer that can be used to provide additional collateral. If the leveraged investment accounts for a substantial proportion of the investor's total portfolio of liquid, "marginable" securities, though, calls for additional collateral could force liquidation of the leveraged bonds at a loss.

Furthermore, because leverage will magnify the effect of bond price changes, there is a good chance that changes in bond prices could more than offset the benefit of a large positive carry, leading to a *negative* total return on the position. In this example the investor will be netting $330,000 in positive carry over the course of a year. This amounts to 3.3% of the total long bond position. A decrease in the price of the bonds from 100.00 to 96.70 (= 100.00 − 3.30) would offset the net interest income, and any greater price decline would leave the investor with less money at the end of the year than at the beginning.

One year after the purchase of a 6.00% 3-year bond at par, the price of the (2-year) security would be 96.70 if its market yield were 7.88%. Therefore, the leveraged transaction in this example will produce a total return of 0% if yields on 2-year bonds rise to 7.88% by the end of the year. If the yield on 2-year notes at the beginning of the year had been slightly lower than the 3-year yield at that time, say, at 5.88%, then the break-even yield increase would be 200 basis points. Any greater increase will result in a negative total return.

A yield change of this magnitude may seem very large. Yet year-end versus year-end yield changes on 2-year U.S. Treasury notes exceeded 200 basis points five times during the period from 1981 through 1998.

Borrowing at a low short-term interest rate and investing in higher-yielding, longer-term, fixed-rate bonds in order to earn a positive carry is an investment strategy that frequently looks very attractive. A great many investors, both institutional and private, have made a great deal of money since the early 1980s by doing just this. Leveraged carry trades can make sense in aggressively managed family fixed-income portfolios. But investors who consider such strategies should realize that a great many investors, both institutional and private, have also lost a lot of money on such positions. Indeed, a large segment of the financial services industry was destroyed by depending on this strategy.

Leveraged carry positions were the essential business of thrift institutions — savings and loans and savings banks — in the U.S. These institutions raised funds by taking deposits that could be withdrawn at any time and, thus, paid variable interest rates. The money amassed in this way was used to purchase fixed-rate home mortgage loans with contractual average maturities of 12 years or so. When interest rates increased sharply after 1979, the thrifts' cost of borrowing rose while the market value of their assets, the fixed-rate mortgages, declined. After struggling for nearly a decade to recover, many of the nation's thrift institutions were forced out of business, leaving the U.S. taxpayer with a substantial liability to the insured depositors.

The experience of the thrift industry and our explanations of leverage should provide two clear warnings for family portfolio managers who make use of this investment tool. First, leveraged positions must be watched carefully. Any leveraged position should be marked to market and reconsidered frequently: weekly if markets are stable, daily or more frequently if markets are volatile. Second, bonds purchased on a leveraged basis should be highly liquid securities that can be sold quickly and easily as soon as the position no longer makes sense.

Adjusting Portfolio Duration through Leverage

To see how leverage can be used to change portfolio characteristics, consider a German taxpayer who holds a euro-denominated bond portfolio with a market value of €10.5 million and a weighted average duration of 3.5. Suppose the investor wishes to extend this portfolio duration to 5.0, and believes that bonds with maturities of about seven years offer the most value along the euro yield curve. Assume also that the portfolio was purchased three months ago at an aggregate price of €10 million so that there is an unrealized short-term capital gain of €500,000 on the portfolio. To simplify matters, assume that all the bonds in the portfolio are identical with respect to coupon (3.75%), maturity (11/15/03 for a 1/1/00 settlement), and market price (100.50). If 7-year euro-denominated bonds yield 4.00%, these securities will have a duration of 6.0. Lengthening the duration of a portfolio from 3.5 to 5.0 by swapping into bonds with durations of 6.0 would require the sale of 60% of the existing portfolio. That is:

$$5.0 = (0.40 \times 3.5) + (0.60 \times 6.0)$$

In this case the transaction would generate €300,000 in short-term capital gains, which would be taxed at 56% for a German taxpayer. Executing the duration extension transaction in this way would cost this investor €168,000 in income taxes.

In this situation, investors can choose among several alternative courses of action, each offering a different combination of advantages and risks. First, they could execute the transaction as described, and incur the substantial tax cost.

A second alternative is to postpone execution of the duration extension transactions for nine months, at which point any gains would be treated as long-term under German tax law and would be exempt from taxation. This option might make sense if the duration extension is intended as a long-term strategic shift rather than an attempt to profit from an anticipated near-term market move.

A third way to achieve the duration extension without realizing such large gains would be to buy longer-term bonds instead of 7-year paper. For example, if the investor purchases 30-year 4.50% bonds at par, with a duration of 16.3, the transactions required to achieve a portfolio duration of 5.0 involve selling only 12% of the portfolio, realization of only €60,000 in short-term capital gains, and a tax bill of €33,600. This approach would make sense if the investor has only a mild preference for 7-year bonds. A fourth class of alternatives — the use of fixed-income derivative instruments such as forward purchases, financial futures, or options — is discussed in Chapter 18.

A final way to achieve the portfolio management objective is to use leverage. Suppose the investor is in a position to borrow up to 75% of the market value of a bond investment. In this case, the investor can purchase up to €42 million (= €10.5 million [1 − 0.75]) in bonds based on the value of the initial portfolio. The investor can use some of this potential purchasing power to buy enough 7-year bonds to raise the portfolio duration to 5.0.

To calculate how many 7-year bonds to buy, it is useful to look at the interest rate exposure of this portfolio in a slightly different way. Specifically, we will use the value of "oh one" ("V01"): the amount by which the portfolio's market value changes if interest rates change by one basis point (0.01%). This number will be related to the portfolio's duration. As of January 1, 2000, the V01 of a portfolio consisting of €10 million par amount of 3.75% coupon bonds maturing on 11/15/03 would be €3,243.99; the market value of the portfolio changes by that amount for each 1 basis point change in yields. Our aim is to raise this figure to about €5,000 through a leveraged purchase of 4.00% bonds maturing in 2007. So we want to add a position in 7-year bonds with a V01 of €1,756.01 (= €5,000 − €3,243.99).

Now for each 1 basis point of yield change, the price of a 4.00% 7-year bond initially priced at par would change by 0.06 points. So the par amount of 7-year bonds that has a V01 of €1,756.01 would be €2,925,681 (= €1,756.01/ 0.06%). The total market value of the portfolio will now be €13.4 million: 3-year bonds with a market value of €10.5 million and 7-year bonds with a market value of about €2.9 million. The 7-year position will be purchased with borrowed funds. The interest rate sensitivity is the same as that of the €10.5 million portfolio of 60% 7-year bonds and 40% 3-year bonds. The leveraged transaction involves no realization of short-term gains. The leverage can be viewed as a more-or-less permanent feature of the portfolio or as a temporary expedient for a 9-month period until the short-term gains on the initial portfolio turn into long-term gains.

Each of these ways of extending portfolio duration is associated with different advantages and disadvantages. On the positive side, the use of leverage allows the investor to adjust duration quickly and concentrate the purchases in the maturity sector that looks most attractive, all the while avoiding realization of short-term capital gains.

One important disadvantage is that an investor who holds a leveraged investment may be required to deliver additional cash to the dealer. In our discussion of leveraged equity positions, we note that if the price of the stock declines the investor is subject to a margin call and is required to deposit additional cash or sell some of the stock at a loss. The same thing can happen in the case of a leveraged bond investment.

In this particular example, the equivalent of a margin call would be unlikely. On the presumption that the €10 million par value of 3-year bonds — the investor's collateral — is held in custody by the dealer providing the financing for the purchase of the €2.9 million of 7-year bonds, at a leverage ratio of 4:1 the investor could finance bonds worth as much as €42.0 million. As it is, the leveraged position consists of €2.9 million, so mark-to-market losses would have to be huge before a margin call became likely. If the investor were making greater use of leverage, or if a higher proportion of collateral is required for the particular type of bond or for the particular investor, calls for additional collateral would be much more likely.

The leveraged €13.4 million portfolio's market value will be as sensitive to interest rate changes as a €10.5 million portfolio consisting of 60% 2007 bonds and 40% 2003 bonds. The total return on these two portfolios will not necessarily be identical. Although the market value fluctuations of the two portfolios are nearly identical, the periodic income component of the two returns will be different because of the carry on the leveraged position. The exact interest rate charged on the borrowed €2.9 million will depend on the particular mechanism used to execute the leveraged purchase (margin loan, repurchase agreement); in general, however, the periodic charge will be reset frequently and, consequently, will reflect the levels of short-term interest rates. The investor will be receiving coupon income on the full €13.4 million portfolio and paying an interest charge on the €2.9 million.

If the yield on the €2.9 million of 7-year bonds just happens to be the same as the borrowing cost on the loan of €2.9 million, the periodic income on the leveraged portfolio will be the same as that on the initial portfolio of 2003 bonds. In most cases, though, these two interest rates will differ.

The leveraged portfolio is designed to have the same exposure to changes in the yield on euro-denominated bonds as the portfolio consisting of 60% 2007 bonds and 40% 2003 bonds. For any given change in bond yields, the total return on the two portfolios will differ, depending on the average level of borrowing costs during the term of the leveraged position. Exhibit 1 illustrates this by comparing the price changes on the long positions and the total returns for the two portfolios.

Exhibit 1: Price Changes and Total Returns on Leveraged and Unleveraged Portfolios with Weighted Average Durations of 5.0

		Bond Yield Change				
		−2.00%	−1.00%	0	1.00%	2.00%
		Unleveraged Portfolio				
	Price Change, Percent	8.91%	4.30%	−0.05%	−4.15%	−8.03%
	Total Return, Percent	12.81%	8.20%	3.85%	−0.25%	−4.13%
		Leveraged Portfolio				
Borrowing Cost	Price Change, Percent	8.67%	4.17%	−0.12%	−4.22%	−8.13%
1%		13.29%	8.79%	4.50%	0.40%	−3.51%
2%		13.00%	8.50%	4.21%	0.11%	−3.80%
3%		12.71%	8.21%	3.92%	−0.18%	−4.09%
4%		12.42%	7.92%	3.63%	−0.47%	−4.38%
5%	Total Return, Percent	12.13%	7.63%	3.34%	−0.76%	−4.67%
6%		11.84%	7.34%	3.05%	−1.05%	−4.96%
7%		11.55%	7.05%	2.76%	−1.34%	−5.25%
8%		11.26%	6.76%	2.47%	−1.63%	−5.54%
9%		10.97%	6.47%	2.18%	−1.92%	−5.83%
10%		10.68%	6.18%	1.89%	−2.21%	−6.12%

First compare the two rows marked "Price Change, Percent." They are not exactly the same, but they are quite close. The 1-year total return — price change plus periodic income — of the unleveraged portfolio is unaffected by the borrowing cost; it simply doesn't enter into the equation. But because the owner of the leveraged portfolio is paying a borrowing cost, the level of this interest rate does affect the total return of the leveraged portfolio. The carry on the leveraged position adds to (reduces) the total return if the borrowing cost is below (above) the yield on the 2007 bond.

For both portfolios, however, the primary determinant of how well the portfolio performs is the change in bond yields; borrowing cost exerts a much smaller effect. The relative importance of these two influences on total return reflects, in part, that not that much money is being borrowed and also that, with interest rate changes as large as 100 bp, price change will have a much greater impact on total return than periodic income.

THE MECHANICS OF LEVERAGE: REVERSE REPURCHASE AGREEMENTS

Reverse repurchase agreements or *reverse repos* are the principal mechanism by which investors purchase bonds on a leveraged basis. Not all bond purchases can be financed through the use of reverse repo transactions. Not all countries have active repo markets, and in the U.S. bonds subject to the registration requirements of the Securities and Exchange Act of 1933 do not qualify for repo financing. As a practical matter, most repurchase agreements involve government bonds, government agency bonds, or mortgage-backed securities.

A reverse repurchase agreement is a contract between an investor and a securities dealer whereby the former borrows money from the latter using fixed-income securities as collateral.[3] An investor who wishes to finance a bond position through a reverse repurchase agreement will buy the bond in the market and then immediately sell the bond to the dealer while simultaneously agreeing to *repurchase* the same security from the dealer at an agreed-upon price on an agreed-upon date in the future. The investor who contracts to repurchase the bond in the future at a preset price will be at risk with respect to any change in the price of the security over the term of the agreement. The price at which the investor agrees to repurchase the bond will equal the original price at which the dealer bought the security from the investor plus a borrowing cost calculated at the reverse repurchase agreement interest rate (reverse repo rate) appropriate for term of the agreement.

Repurchase transactions take place pursuant to a Master Repurchase Agreement governing all the specific repo transactions entered into by the investor and a securities dealer. Dealers will specify collateral requirements for repurchase agreements with individual investors. For example, one investor might be required to post 20% collateral for purchases of U.S. Treasury securities with maturities of greater than 10 years, while another more creditworthy investor might need only 10% collateral. Collateral requirements will also vary with the maturity and credit quality of the securities in question. For any given investor, more collateral might be required for repurchase agreements involving longer-maturity and/or lower-quality bonds than for short-term high-grade instruments.

By means of a reverse repurchase agreement an investor can in effect borrow the funds required to hold a security for the term of the agreement. Upon repurchase the full market value of the investor's position will reflect the interest accrued over the term of the repo and the market price of the bonds. So the total return on the investor's position will depend on the combination of the cost of carry and the change in the market price of the bond in exactly the same way as it would in any leveraged purchase of the same security.

A further elaboration of the example of the leveraged purchase of $10 million U.S. Treasury bonds will help clarify how a reverse repurchase agreement works. We again assume that the initial market price of these 5.00% 30-year bonds is par and that the purchase takes place on an interest payment date so that the invoice price of the purchase is $10 million. The investor can leverage the purchase at ratio of 10:1, so the investor initially purchases $10 million of Treasury bonds

---

[3] Investors and dealers enter into both *repurchase agreements* and *reverse repurchase* agreements. By convention, transactions that allow investors to buy bonds on leverage are referred to as "reverse repurchase agreements." Investors can use repurchase agreements to create short positions in fixed-income securities. For the time being, we focus on reverse repos. Later in the chapter we discuss repurchase agreements or repos.

and then immediately enters into a reverse repurchase agreement for $9 million. We assume that the annualized interest rate on the borrowing, the repo rate, for a two-week term reverse repurchase agreement is 4.00%.

At the end of the two-week period under the terms of the reverse repo agreement, the investor will be required to repurchase the $9 million bonds at a price of $9,013,808.22. In practice, this repurchase will be financed by liquidating the entire position. As in the example, we assume that the flat offered-side price of the repurchased bonds is $10,376,000. Over the two-week period, $19,178.08 in interest will have accrued on the bonds. Finally, we assume again that the investor incurs a bid-asked spread of $6,250 on the sale of the bonds.

At the end of the two weeks, the investor will have:

$10,396,695.07	flat market value of bonds
+$19,178.08	accrued interest
−$6,250.00	bid-asked spread
−$9,013,808.22	repurchase price
= $1,395,814.94	

This result is exactly the same as the outcome of the example given earlier: a 39.5% return over a two-week period. The downside risk is identical as well. If the market price of the long position declines, the investor will be called upon to provide additional capital, and a 70 basis point increase in 30-year bond yields will wipe out the investor's cash position.

The interest rate charged on funds borrowed through reverse repurchase agreements is referred to as the reverse repo rate. These tend to be among the lowest interest rates available to borrowers in the financial markets.

Like other interest rates, repo rates vary depending on the term of the agreement. Most of the time the yield curve is upward-sloping, and the rate charged on a term repo extending over several weeks will be higher than the rate on overnight repurchase agreements. Most repo agreements expire within one month, and one-day (or overnight) repos are the most common. Arrangements can be made for longer-term agreements, but the repo rate for these transactions may be a bit higher.

Investors who use reverse repurchase agreements to create positive carry or speculative positions must frequently decide whether to lock in a term repo rate for a relatively long period of time or allow the agreement to roll on a daily or weekly basis. An investor who expects to hold a leveraged bond investment for a relatively long period of time and who opts to roll repo financing relatively frequently incurs the risk that short-term interest rates may rise while the leveraged long position is open. Longer-term agreements can eliminate this risk, but usually at the cost of both a somewhat higher repo rate and some degree of inconvenience if the position is unwound before the repo agreement expires.

Repo rates also vary depending on the specific security financed through the transaction; the lowest rates are charged when U.S. Treasury securities or other global government bonds are used as collateral. Rates charged on agency or

MBS repo are generally somewhat higher. It also frequently happens that the repo rate on a particular government security is much lower than rates for general government collateral; this specific security is said to be "on special." (We explain these circumstances later.)

SHORT SALES AND THEIR USES

Sale of a security an investor does not own creates a *short position*. The market value of a *long position* rises as the price of the investment increases; the market value of a short position goes up as the price of the security declines. Short sales of fixed-income are even less common in family portfolios than leveraged bond purchases, although creating a short position can be the most effective and prudent way of accomplishing a wide range of investment goals. As with leveraged long positions, a short position can be used either to adjust portfolio duration without realizing capital gains on the sale of bonds or to establish speculative trading positions.

Short Sales as a Portfolio Management Tool

To see how short sales can be used to manage portfolio duration, consider a U.S. resident for whom it is difficult to find bonds that are exempt from state income taxation. Suppose that six months previously, at great effort, this investor was able to accumulate a $12 million portfolio of in-state (double tax-exempt) 7- and 8-year municipal bonds with weighted average duration of 6.5, coupon of 4.50%, and average purchase price of 100.00. Now assume that interest rates fall over the 6-month period so that the market value of the portfolio is now $12.8 million and the investor has an $800,000 unrealized, short-term capital gain. Suppose also that the investor has now become more bearish on bond prices and would like to reduce portfolio duration to about 4.0.

One way to do this would be to sell 39.5% of the portfolio and invest the sale proceeds in very short-term (zero-duration) instruments or in a money market fund. Doing so would create two problems. First, on the assumption that capital gains are distributed uniformly across all the portfolio positions, the sale of $4.74 million par amount of bonds involves the realization of $316,000 in capital gains. If the investor faces a combined federal and state tax rate on short-term capital gains of 44%, the tax bill on $316,000 in realized short-term gains would be $139,040.

The second problem with selling $4.74 million of the bonds in this portfolio is that it might be difficult to replace these securities when and if the investor may wish to lengthen portfolio duration. By assumption, the portfolio consists of bonds that are exempt from state taxes in a state where good-quality municipal bonds are hard to find. There are several such states — Ohio, Minnesota, and Oregon, to name a few — and well-constructed portfolios of bonds that are double tax-exempt in these jurisdictions should not be liquidated without considerable thought. Similarly, an investor might own a carefully selected portfolio of corporate bonds that are all likely to improve in credit quality. Selling these attractive securities might not be the best way to reduce portfolio duration if alternative methods are available.

For both these reasons, this bearish investor should be interested in ways of reducing portfolio duration without actually selling bonds from the portfolio. There are several ways of accomplishing this objective; we discuss some of them in the ensuing chapters. The approach highlighted here — which is the paradigm of all the ways of shortening duration without selling bonds — is to sell bonds short. In this case, the practical problem to solve is how many of which bonds to sell.

Structuring a Short Sale: A First Approximation

We have hypothesized a municipal bond portfolio. For reasons that will become apparent, it is not practical for investors to short tax-exempt bonds. Instead, we show how the investor can shorten the duration of a municipal bond portfolio by shorting U.S. Treasury securities. As the discussion progresses, it should be clear that shorting government bonds to reduce the duration of a municipal or corporate bond portfolio introduces new risks that must be recognized and evaluated. As a practical matter, it is not advisable for anyone other than a full-time professional bond trader to short any fixed-income security except an actively traded government bond.

With a $12.8 million market value and a modified duration of 6.5, the dollar price value of 1 basis point of the existing portfolio is approximately $8,320 (= $12,800,000 × 6.5%/100). We wish to reduce this figure to $5,120 (= $12,800,000 × 4.0%/100). As noted, we could accomplish this by selling about a quarter of the bonds and reinvesting in money market instruments. The alternative is to sell short a block of U.S. Treasury securities with a DV01 of $3,200 (= $8,320 − $5,120).

This can be accomplished through a wide variety of short sales, depending on which particular U.S. Treasury bond or note is used. To give just two examples: $4.1 million 10-year 5% bonds priced at par would have a DV01 of $3,370 as would $2.1 million 5.25% 30-year bonds priced at par. Shortening either position would achieve the objective of reducing portfolio duration. The choice among such alternatives turns on two broad considerations.

First, as a general matter, the smaller the absolute size of the transaction, the lower the transaction cost. Bid-asked spreads in the Treasury market tend to be slightly wider, the longer the maturity of the bond in question. Nevertheless, the total bid-asked spread "paid" on $2.1 million of 30-year Treasury bonds is likely to be less than that on $4.1 million 10-year securities.

Second, the maturity of the short position should reflect the maturity structure of the long portfolio unless the investor wishes to express a view regarding changes in the slope of the yield curve. If taken to the extreme, the first consideration — that transactions with smaller absolute size are better than larger trades — would lead to shorting 30-year Treasury bonds in all cases. Yet, a position that is long 7- and 8-year bonds and short 30-year bonds reflects a very specific expectation regarding changes in the slope of the yield curve. Such a structure would make sense for an investor holding the strong view that yields on 30-year bonds are likely to rise relative to yields on 7- and 8-year paper. Unless the investor has such pronounced expectations, the most sensible thing is to short the liquid Treasury securities with maturity closest to that of the long position.

In this example, these two considerations might lead to the decision to short $4.1 million 10-year Treasury notes. Let us assume that the investor does decide to sell $4.1 million 10-year Treasury notes. As Exhibit 2 indicates, if yields on the municipal bonds and the Treasury notes change by the same number of basis points, adding the short position will have almost exactly the same effect on portfolio price performance as selling 39% of the municipals and investing in cash equivalents.

This is but a first approximation of how to achieve this portfolio management objective through the short sale of Treasury notes. To refine the analysis and to understand the impact of these management techniques on total return, we need to consider two additional aspects of short positions: (1) basis risk, and (2) the cost of carrying a short position.

BASIS RISK

Basis risk is the risk that yields on different fixed-income instruments do not move in tandem. We have seen that a particular short position in U.S. Treasury notes could have the same effect on the price performance of a municipal bond portfolio as replacing a portion of the municipal bonds with cash, *if yields on the municipals and Treasury notes change by the same number of basis points.* We can calculate the right amount of Treasuries to sell short according to the duration of the notes and the target duration for the portfolio; Exhibit 2 reflects a mathematical fact. There is no reason, though, to expect that yields on 10-year Treasury notes and on 7-year municipal bonds will shift by the same number of basis points as financial market conditions change. In fact, there is considerable evidence to the contrary.

Exhibit 2: Market Value Changes on Two Position Structures Assuming Equal Basis Point Changes in Bond Yields ($)

| | Change in Position Market Value | |
Change in Bond Yield	61.5% Municipal Bonds 39.5% Money Markets	100% Municipal Bonds (41%) Treasury Notes
−2.00%	1,127,292	1,129,081
−1.50%	828,729	832,375
−1.00%	541,640	545,512
−0.50%	265,550	268,160
0.00%	—	(0)
0.50%	(255,445)	(259,279)
1.00%	(501,204)	(509,977)
1.50%	(737,674)	(752,385)
2.00%	(965,237)	(986,783)

Exhibit 3: Weekly Yield Changes on 10-Year U.S. Treasuries and 7-Year Municipals

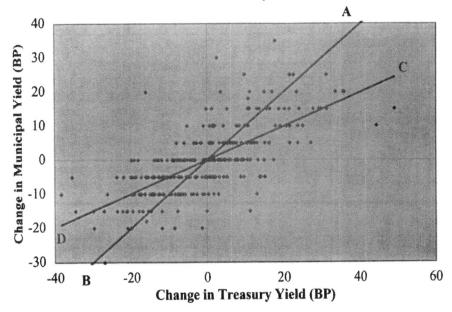

Exhibit 3 illustrates the historical relationship between one-week yield changes on 10-year Treasuries and 7-year municipals between 1993 and 1998. If yields on these two types of bonds always moved by the same number of basis points, all the observations of weekly yield changes in the two markets would fall along line AB. As the exhibit indicates, the observations are scattered, with a substantial random component. Line AB does not even represent the "average" relationship between yield changes on municipals and Treasuries. That average is represented by line CD; on average a 10 basis point change in Treasury note yields has been associated with a 5 basis point change in 7-year municipal bond yields. Further, as the randomness in Exhibit 3 indicates, there is no guarantee that the average relationship between yield changes will be realized over any given period. There have been weeks, represented by points in the upper left-hand quadrant, for example, when yields on Treasuries fell while yields on municipal bonds increased.

Basis risk can wreak havoc with the price performance of a portfolio incorporating long positions in one market and short positions in another. This possibility is illustrated in Exhibit 4. Again we wish to reduce the effective duration of a municipal portfolio from 6.5 years to 4.0 years without selling any of the tax-exempt bonds. Again, the plan is to short 10-year Treasury notes. This time however, we recognize that yields on Treasury notes and municipal bonds seldom move by the same number of basis points over any given time.

Exhibit 4: Change in Position Market Value by Relative Municipal and Treasury Yield Changes

Portfolio	Change in Municipal Yield, % Change in Treasury Yield	Treasury Yield Change			
		–2%	–1%	1%	2%
61.5% Municipal Bonds 39.5% Money Markets	N.A.	541,640	265,550	(255,445)	(501,204)
100% Municipal Bonds (20.5%) Treasury Notes	50%	528,759	264,186	(262,864)	(523,611)
	120%	1,883,394	897,649	(818,050)	(1,564,126)
	100%	1,481,038	713,114	(662,471)	(1,278,137)
	80%	1,091,145	531,439	(504,477)	(983,259)
	60%	713,294	352,577	(344,025)	(679,190)
	40%	347,084	176,480	(181,074)	(365,616)
	20%	(7,874)	3,103	(15,582)	(42,214)
	0%	(351,957)	(167,602)	152,494	291,354
	–20%	(685,525)	(335,678)	323,199	635,437

We know from analysis of the data illustrated in Exhibit 4 that the average relationship between yield changes in the two markets is 5 basis points in the municipal market for every 10 bp for Treasuries. Therefore, we will short fewer Treasuries in this case than in the equal basis point example. Specifically, since selling $4.1 million 10-year Treasury Notes was appropriate in the equal basis point illustration, in this example we will short $2.05 million Treasuries (= 0.5 × $4.1).

Exhibit 4 indicates that a short Treasury note position does provide an excellent hedge for a municipal bond portfolio — i.e., it has the effect of reducing the interest rate exposure of the investment from a duration of 6.5 to a duration of 4.0 — but *only if yields in the two markets move in the ratio anticipated when the short position was established.* If the expectations regarding relative yield changes are not borne out, the impact on portfolio market value can be substantial. Remember that the purpose of shorting Treasuries in the first place is to reduce the impact of rising interest rates on the portfolio. If yields on municipal bonds do rise, but Treasury note yields decline, the market value loss would be greater than if the portfolio's duration hadn't been reduced at all.

One natural response to this illustration of basis risk might be to ask why the investor would not simply short municipal bonds rather than Treasuries. Surely this would reduce basis risk. This is a sensible question. There can be basis risk within a particular market — the yield on one corporate bond may rise or fall relative to the yield on another corporate, for example — but such intrasector basis risk is usually relatively modest.

The alternative of shorting a municipal or corporate bond is impractical for two reasons. The first of these relates to municipal bonds in particular. The fact that interest on these securities is tax-exempt complicates short sales of municipals so much that, as a practical matter, such transactions are impossible.

Second, potential liquidity pressures make shorting anything other than government bonds and certain mortgage-backed securities very risky. An investor who shorts a security must eventually buy that particular stock or bond back to cover the sale. This leaves the investor exposed to a "short squeeze"; holders of the security in question can pressure short-sellers by withholding securities from the market, reducing the available supply of lendable bonds, and forcing up the price. Such squeezes can be successful only if a small number of investors hold a large proportion of the particular security's outstanding volume, or its "float." Therefore, the risk of a short squeeze is greater, the smaller the float. Thus, investors should feel much more comfortable shorting particular Treasury notes or bonds, with typical par amounts outstanding in excess of $10 billion, rather than municipal or corporate bonds, where securities with floats of more than $1 billion are extremely rare.

Basis risk is like any other risk involved in managing a fixed-income portfolio. In this illustration, the portfolio manager must evaluate the trade-off between, on the one hand, paying $139,000 more in taxes and giving up some bonds that are difficult to acquire versus accepting the basis risk involved in shorting Treasury notes against a municipal bond portfolio on the other. The decision will depend on all the facts and circumstances involved at the time the decision is made.

One important relationship to consider in this particular example is the ratio of yields on municipals to yields on Treasuries. Note in Exhibit 4 that the adverse outcomes occur if municipal yields rise relative to Treasury yields; that is, if municipal yields rise by more or fall by less than Treasury yields. This is less likely to happen to the extent that municipal yields are already high relative to Treasury yields.

Exhibit 5 plots the historical relationship between yields on 7-year municipals and 10-year Treasuries from 1993 through 1998. Investors might have felt less comfortable shorting Treasuries to reduce the duration of a municipal bond portfolio in the spring of 1996, when municipal yields were low relative to Treasuries, than in early 1997 when they were high. Such historical statistics provide useful information, but basing decisions on whether yields in one sector are historically high or low relative to another sector does not eliminate basis risk. The fact that the municipal/Treasury yield ratio is historically high at one time is no guarantee that it won't get higher.

"BASIS TRADES" AND RELATIVE VALUE

For an investor seeking only to reduce the duration of a bond portfolio by shorting government bonds, basis risk is a disadvantage. But basis risk can also be viewed as an investment opportunity. The profit potential inherent in *relative* yield movements across different sectors of the bond market can, in and of itself, be a reason for selling bonds short.

Exhibit 5: Yield Ratio, 7-Year Municipals over 10-Year Treasuries

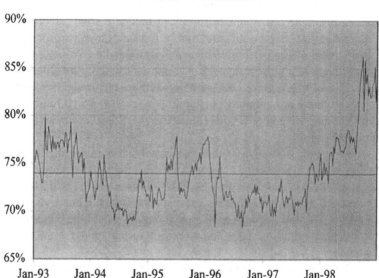

For example, suppose the economy of a country is in recession so that interest rates are relatively low and investment-grade corporate yield spreads are wide. Wide corporate spreads might reflect the market's expectation that the recession will impair the credit quality of businesses. Now suppose an investor concludes that the country's economy is likely to snap back quickly, leading to both an improvement in perceptions of credit quality *and* an increase in bond yields. Under these circumstances, the investor might want to benefit from a tightening of corporate bond spreads but would not want simply to be long corporate bonds in a rising interest rate environment. The way to benefit from these expectations would be to buy a portfolio of corporate bonds while selling short a duration-matched position in government bonds.

Applications of this investment technique — creating matched long and short positions in different securities — need not be confined to expressing views on macroeconomic trends. Investors, including some sophisticated family portfolio managers, can use this method to express views regarding the shape of the yield curve or differences in the values of closely related securities. For example, an investor who expects the yield curve to flatten but is not sure whether this flattening will be associated with an increase or a decrease in average bond yields could express this view by buying, say, 10-year bonds while shorting a duration-matched amount of 2-year government obligations.

\   The general idea behind such combinations of long and short positions is relatively straightforward; one buys the security whose yield is expected to decline *relative* to the yield on some other security and sells the latter short. In practice, structuring such transactions requires a degree of expertise. Family portfolio managers seeking to maximize the total return on their fixed-income portfolios should be willing to consider such long/short positions, but to implement these positions they should work closely with competent, experienced advisors.

REPURCHASE AGREEMENTS AND THE CARRY ON SHORT POSITIONS

One of the considerations that will influence the expert analysis of any investment position involving the sale of a bond the investor does not own is the cost of carrying a short position. Standard settlement of a trade in U.S. Treasury securities is one day after the trade date. Unless special arrangements are made, an investor who sells a Treasury bond and does not deliver the specific security the next day is required to pay a substantial penalty for this failure. Therefore, investors who wish to sell government bonds they do not own must borrow the bond, usually from the dealer who executes the short sale. Just as reverse repurchase agreements play a role in creating leveraged long positions, repurchase agreements (or repos) are used to create short positions.

Under a *reverse* repo agreement, an investor agrees to repurchase a security sold to a dealer at a specified price on a specified date in the future. The repurchase price reflects the reverse repo rate, in effect the cost of borrowing funds to finance the purchase of the security in question. Thus a reverse repo agreement creates a leveraged long position in a particular security. If the price of the security is higher at the expiration than it was when the transaction was entered into — assuming no positive or negative carry — the investor will benefit; if the price is lower the investor will lose money on the reverse repo.

Under a repurchase agreement the investor buys a bond from a dealer and agrees to resell the security to the dealer at a specified price on a specified date in the future. An investor who wishes to short the security will then immediately sell the bond into the market and deliver on the normal settlement schedule. The proceeds of this sale will be used to pay the dealer for the bond under the repurchase agreement. When the repurchase agreement expires, the investor will buy the bond in the market at the current price and deliver the security to the repo counterparty at the agreed-upon price. If the market price of the security is lower than the repo price, the investor will have made money on the short sale. If the market price is higher than the repo price, the investor will lose money.

Under a reverse repo agreement, the investor is, in effect, borrowing money from the dealer at the repo rate. Under a repo, the investor is, in effect, lending the money to the dealer by purchasing a bond for cash and agreeing to resell it to the dealer at a specified price in the future. The specified resale (repurchase) price will be higher than the original purchase price, reflecting the interest paid by the dealer on the "loan" of the funds used to purchase the bond.

These transactions require no cash outlay by the investor. The funds used to purchase the bond from the dealer under the repo would be raised by selling the bonds in the market. In practice, however, dealers require investors entering into such agreements to put up some cash to secure their performance under the repo. As with reverse repurchase agreements, the cash requirement for a repo will depend on the credit standing of the particular investor and the nature of the securities.

The cost of carrying a leveraged long position is the yield on the bond in question less the interest rate (the reverse repo rate) paid to the dealer on the borrowed funds. Not surprisingly, the cost of carrying a short position is the exact opposite of this equation. The cost of carry on a short position created through a repurchase agreement is equal to the interest rate paid by the dealer on the investor's loan of funds (the repo rate) less the interest on the bond in question. The investor will be out the interest when he or she buys the bond in the market to cover the short position. If the market yield on the bond in question is unchanged over the term of the agreement, the invoice price at expiration will be higher than the initial sale price by the additional accrued coupon plus accretion of discount or amortization of premium.

The repo rate for a given security is usually a few basis points lower than the reverse repo rate for the same security; investment dealers charge a higher interest rate on money they lend through reverse repos than they are willing to pay on funds they borrow through repos. Occasionally, if many investors wish to borrow a particular Treasury security to sell it short, repo rates on that bond can be driven to extremely low levels. If an investor wishes to borrow a certain bond, unless the dealer happens to have the particular security in inventory, some investor holding the bond must be induced to sell the security for a matching term through a repurchase agreement. A very low reverse repo rate — i.e., a very attractive borrowing cost — may induce investors who own the security that happens to be in demand to leverage their positions. By the same token, a very low rate paid on repos increases the cost of carrying a short position, thereby discouraging investors seeking to borrow the particular bond.

We noted earlier that investors sometimes establish leveraged long positions in the bond market with the intention of earning the carry on the position. Opportunities for investors to make money on such carry trades through repurchase agreements would be very unusual, because bond yields are usually much higher than repo rates. Most times the investor will earn a positive carry on a reverse repurchase agreement, while the carry on a repo will be negative.

The cost of carry must be taken into account in computing the projected return on any investment involving a short position. To illustrate this point (and as a summary) we analyze a trade involving long and short positions in different U.S. Treasury securities. Both positions are leveraged, and we assume that the dealer executing the transactions will allow the investor to put up 10% of the market value of the larger side of the position. We assume that the investor expects the yield curve to steepen substantially over a 6-month horizon and therefore wishes to buy 3-year Treasuries and to sell 30-year Treasuries short. To simplify matters, we assume that transactions are entered into at prices equal to par on February 15, 2000, and closed on August 15, 2000; because both dates are interest payment dates for Treasuries and because the purchases are at par, there is no premium, discount, or accrued interest to account for in the illustration.

Exhibit 6 lays out the assumptions. The difference between the par (and market) values of the two positions reflects the differences in the bonds' durations; the ratio of $1.8 million to $10 million is approximately the same as the ratio of 2.78 to 15.45. With this hedge ratio, small changes in the general level of interest rates — i.e., parallel shifts in the yield curve — should have no effect on the market value of the combined long and short positions. The market value of the position will change, however, if the slope of the U.S. Treasury yield curve changes between 3- and 30-year maturities. Exhibit 7 reflects this fact by presenting the total returns on the combined long/short position over a 1-year horizon, given a range of year-end interest rate levels and yield curve slopes.

Exhibit 7 illustrates several general points about this specific trade and about combinations of long and short positions in general. First, the combination of transactions does what the investor intends it to; it produces a substantial profit if the yield curve does steepen. As a percentage of the initial cash investment of $1 million, 50 basis points of steepening with long bond yields unchanged will produce a return of 14.4% over a 1-year horizon. A portion of this return — $23,000 or 2.3% — derives from the positive carry on the transaction. Carry is positive despite the fact that the 30-year bond is assumed to be trading somewhat "special" in the repo market, as reflected in the relatively low repo rate the investor is receiving on the short position.

The position is designed to have a net duration close to zero so that changes in the general level of interest rates will have no effect on the market value of the position. Being long $10 million 4.50% 3-year notes and short $1.8 million 30-year bonds achieves this goal, but only as long as any changes in the level of interest rates are relatively small. If interest rates change by 100 basis points, the $10 million/$1.8 million position becomes somewhat "bearish"; that is, the market value of the position will rise if the general level of interest rates increases.

Exhibit 6: Assumptions Underlying a Hypothetical Long/Short U.S. Treasury Position

	3-Year	30-Year
Maturity	2/15/03	2/15/30
Coupon	4.50%	5.00%
Price	100.00	100.00
Modified Duration	2.78	15.45
Par Amount	$10,000,000	($1,800,000)
Repo/Reverse Repo Rate	4.00%	3.00%
Six-Month Cost of Carry	45,000	(18,000)

Exhibit 7: One-Year Horizon Returns on a Hypothetical Long/Short U.S. Treasury Position by Year-End Interest Rate Level and Yield Curve Slope (US$)

Change in 30-Yr. Over 3-Yr. Yield Spread (BP)	Change in 30-Year Yield (BP)				
	(100)	(10)	0	10	100
−100	(283,105)	(208,791)	(203,629)	(199,024)	(180,167)
−50	(165,268)	(93,977)	(89,146)	(84,869)	(68,926)
0	(45,712)	22,504	27,000	30,942	43,923
50	75,593	140,682	144,836	148,438	158,407
100	198,679	260,586	264,393	267,648	274,552

To see why this happens, recall that the duration of bonds is not constant as interest rate levels change. Specifically, if interest rates decline by 100 basis points, the duration of the 3-year bond will increase slightly from 2.78 to 2.79 years while the duration of the 30-year bond will increase much more substantially, from 15.45 to 16.60 years. Likewise, if interest rates rise by 100 basis points, the duration of the 3-year will decline by much less than that of the 30-year. Because of these duration changes, the initial hedge ratio of $10/$1.8 will match the duration of long and short positions only if interest rates remain close to their initial levels. After any substantial shift in the general level of rates, the values of the two sides of the transactions should be adjusted.

As a practical matter, this tendency of the durations of different bonds to change at different rates as bond yields shift means that combinations of long and short positions must be monitored very closely in volatile interest rate environments. Portfolio managers who enter into such transactions should define some level of interest rate shift — e.g., 25 basis points — and recalculate the durations of both sides of the transaction whenever bond yields change by that much. Frequently, interest rate shifts will require adjustments to the size of one or the other side of the "matched" long and short positions. Family portfolio managers who create such "hedged" positions should do so only with the assistance of a bond market professional who has appropriate expertise.

CHAPTER 15

More About the Yield Curve

C hapter 4 of this book describes the yield curve — the relationship between bond yield and bond maturity — and touches on several theories of what determines the shape of this curve. We've had occasion to make use of this concept in every subsequent chapter. Clearly, even a rudimentary understanding of fixed-income securities and markets requires some insight into the yield curve, what determines its shape, and how it changes over time. It should not be surprising, therefore, that more sophisticated bond portfolio management presupposes a deeper understanding of the yield curve and its implications.

In this chapter we show that the yield curve we observe at any time provides large amounts of useful information about the bond market. We can learn how to "decode" the curve, and how portfolio managers can use the market data embedded in the yield curve to make informed investment decisions.

BENCHMARK CURVES AND FITTED CURVES

There are many yield curves. They differ by currency and issuer. Curves can be plotted using yield versus maturity or yield versus duration. For any given issuer or currency, there are different yield curves for coupon-paying and zero-coupon bonds. Curves may be observed directly and reflect actual yields on real bonds in the market, or may be estimated (or "fitted") and represent yields on the average obligation of the issuer for a specific maturity. In the latter case, no real bond of the issuer may lie precisely on the yield curve. Frequently, the yield curve for a particular issuer can't be observed or fitted directly — there may be too few bonds outstanding — but must be deduced from a bit of information about this issuer's bonds and a lot of data about other, comparable obligors.

When a bond market participant speaks of *the yield curve* in general, the reference is to the curve connecting the yields on the most actively traded — the on-the-run — central government bonds denominated in a particular currency. Thus, the JGB yield curve represents yields on the most actively traded Japanese

255

government bonds, the Euro yield curve represents yields on actively traded German or French government bonds; and the U.S. yield curve reflects benchmark Treasury bill, note, and bond yields.

Defining the yield curve in this ways has two shortcomings. First, benchmark bonds tend to be more liquid than other nearly identical bonds with slightly different coupons and slightly longer or shorter maturities. Greater liquidity usually translates into slightly lower yields. The benchmark yield curve may thus not be a good representation of the real relationship between yield and maturity across the government market as a whole. Second, using only on-the-run bonds to define the yield curve leaves us looking for a way to fill in yields for maturities between benchmark maturity dates.

There are several ways of dealing with each of these problems. Most active bond dealers estimate a "fitted" yield curve for the major bond markets. It is not necessary here to go through all the methodological issues involved in estimating a fitted curve; suffice it to say that the process uses information about the market yields on all traded government bonds to estimate the yield on a hypothetical security priced at par for each maturity.

Exhibits 1 and 2 illustrate the yield curve for the EMU government bond market for April 19, 1999. Exhibit 1 lists the benchmark bonds for each maturity, and Exhibit 2 indicates how the yields on the benchmarks compare with the fitted euro government yield curve estimated by Goldman, Sachs & Co. for the same date. The situation on that day is typical in that the benchmark yields tend to be lower than the fitted yields, and the fitted yield curve fills in all the blanks between benchmark maturities along a smooth curve.

Exhibit 1: Benchmark European Monetary Union Government Bonds, April 19, 1999

Benchmark	Issuer	Coupon	Maturity	Price 4/19/99	Yield 4/19/99
3 Mo.	Germany	0.00%	7/18/99	99.396	2.501%
6 Mo.	Germany	0.00%	10/16/99	98.785	2.499%
1 Yr.	Germany	4.00%	3/17/00	101.200	2.631%
2 Yr.	Germany	3.00%	3/16/01	100.470	2.741%
3 Yr.	France	5.50%	10/12/01	106.200	2.863%
4 Yr.	Germany	4.50%	2/18/03	104.970	3.101%
5 Yr.	France	3.50%	7/12/04	101.060	3.274%
6 Yr.	France	6.75%	10/25/04	117.110	3.299%
7 Yr.	France	7.25%	4/25/06	122.840	3.517%
8 Yr.	France	6.50%	10/25/06	118.520	3.634%
9 Yr.	Germany	5.25%	1/4/08	110.210	3.845%
10 Yr.	Germany	4.00%	7/4/09	101.100	3.866%
15 Yr.	Germany	6.00%	6/20/16	118.560	4.432%
20 Yr.	France	8.50%	10/25/19	150.020	4.658%
30 Yr.	Germany	4.75%	7/4/28	98.110	4.871%

Source: Bloomberg.

Exhibit 2: Benchmark Yields and the Fitted Euro Yield Curve
April 19, 1999

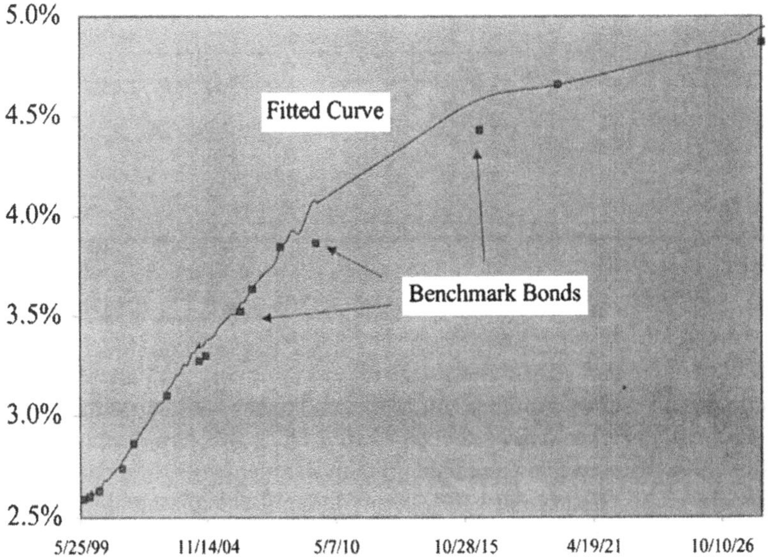

Source: Goldman, Sachs & Co.

Standard practice in the bond market is to assume that any mention of the yield curve without further specification refers to the benchmark curve. Thus, a trader who says that the 2-year to 10-year spread in the EMU market is 112.5 basis points is speaking of the benchmark bonds. Or if a corporate bond in the U.S. is priced to yield 78 basis points over "the 10-year," the reference is to the most recently issued 10-year U.S. Treasury note.

For most analytical purposes, however, the fitted curve is the right tool to use. We follow the market's practice and indicate explicitly when we are referring to the fitted curve. Family portfolio managers should be aware of this distinction because yield spreads over the "government curve" are the standard measure of the relative value of government agency and corporate bonds and mortgage-backed securities.

If a corporate bond that typically yields between 75 and 85 bp over the 10-year Treasury benchmark is offered at a spread of "95 over," it might appear that the corporate is very attractively priced. This could be so, but it may also be the case that the yield on the benchmark 10-year Treasury is unusually low compared to other government bonds; that is, the liquidity premium that benefits the benchmark Treasury might be unusually high. If so, agencies and even off-the-run Treasuries are relatively attractive, and there may be nothing particularly special about the corporate offered at 95 over.

Whenever a bond is represented as being unusually attractive relative to "the curve," it is important to find out which curve is meant and to ascertain the offered bond's value relative to both benchmark and fitted curves.

Exhibit 3: Using Zero-Coupon Yields to Calculate Coupon Bond Yields

Maturity	Zero-Coupon Yield A	Two-Year Bond Cash Flow B	Discounted Cash Flow C
7/1/2000	4.50%	$ 30	$ 29.35
1/1/2001	5.00%	$ 30	$ 28.57
7/1/2001	5.25%	$ 30	$ 27.78
1/1/2002	5.50%	$1,030	$ 925.41
Total			$1,011.11

COUPON CURVES AND SPOT RATE CURVES

Both the benchmark curve and the fitted curve report yields and maturities on coupon-paying bonds. Another important variety of yield curve is the zero-coupon curve, also referred to as the *spot rate curve*. The zero-coupon curve represents interest rates used to discount single individual cash flows received (or paid) at specific points in the future. The zero-coupon yield curve and the coupon-paying yield curve are directly related; that is, for any given coupon-paying yield curve, there is one and only one consistent zero-coupon curve and vice versa.

Exhibit 3 presents an example of how zero-coupon yields can be used to calculate the yield on a coupon-paying bond. Suppose we observe yields on zero-coupon U.S. Treasury bonds maturing at 6-month intervals as listed in Column A of Exhibit 3. Now consider a $1,000 2-year bond paying a 6.00% semiannual coupon. This bond will produce the cash flows listed in Column B. If we discount these cash flows to the present using the zero-coupon yields in Column A, the results are the numbers in Column C. The sum of these numbers must equal the price of the 2-year bond.

If the price of the 2-year 6.00% bond is more than 101.111, then, if we assume perfectly efficient markets, investors seeking 2-year Treasuries would simply buy zero-coupon bonds with maturity dates on the coupon payment date, and get the same cash flows for a lower price. If the price of the 2-year bond is less than 101.111, then investors would buy the bond and sell all the cash flows separately as zero-coupon issues and make a riskless "arbitrage" profit. Arbitrageurs would buy and sell until increased supply brought the price of zeros down enough to bring the zero- and the coupon bond prices into synch.

The yield on a 2-year bond with a 6.00% coupon priced at 101.111 is 5.41%. So the yield on a 2-year coupon-paying bond that is consistent with the zero-coupon yields in Exhibit 3 is 5.41%. This process can be extrapolated all the way out the yield curve; if we know the spot rate curve, we can calculate the associated yield curve for coupon bonds with the same maturities.

The process also works the other way. If we know the yields on a coupon-paying bond, we can calculate the consistent yield on zeros. For example, let's start with the information in Exhibit 4. Here we have the yield on one zero-coupon security, a 6-month note, and a series of yields of coupon-paying bonds, all priced at par and maturing at 6-month intervals out to two years. Our aim is to find the yields on zero-coupon bonds that are consistent with the information we have.

Now consider the 1-year 4.00% bond priced at par with a face value of $1,000, and imagine that this bond consists of two separate zero-coupon securities, one with a face value of $20.00 representing the coupon payment received at the end of six months, and another with a face value of $1,020.00 incorporating the second coupon payment and the principal payment at maturity. Since this combination of securities provides exactly the same cash flows as the 4.00% bond priced at par, the market value of the pair of zero-coupon bonds must also be par or $1,000. Since we know yield on a 6-month zero-coupon bond (3.50%), we know the market value of the initial $20.00 payment; it is $19.66 (= $20.00/1.0175). Therefore, the market value of the second zero-coupon bond paying $1,020.00 at the end of the year must be $1,000.34 (= $1,020.00 – $19.66).

We can calculate the yield on a 1-year zero-coupon bond by solving for Y in the equation:

$$\$1,000.34 = \$1,020/(1 + Y)$$

The solution here is that $Y = 4.05\%$, which is the yield on a 1-year zero-coupon bond that is consistent with (1) a 4.00% yield on a 1-year coupon-paying bond and (2) a 3.50% yield on a 6-month zero.

These calculations allow us to fill in one of the blanks in Exhibit 4 to produce Exhibit 5. This information allows us to take the next step and calculate the 18-month spot rate. In this case, we imagine that the $1,000 par bond with a 4.50% coupon consists of three separate zero-coupon securities: one maturing in six months with a face value of $22.50, another $22.50 bond maturing in one year, and a final zero-coupon bond maturing in 18 months with a face value of $1,022.50. Since we know the yields on 6-month and 1-year zeros, we also know the market values of the first and the second cash flows ($22.12 and $21.63, respectively), so simple subtraction allows us to calculate the market value of the 18-month zero ($978.76).

If we know the market value, the face amount, and the maturity, we can calculate the discount rate (or yield) that equates the two (4.566%). This gives us the yield on an 18-month zero. The result is illustrated in Exhibit 6.

Exhibit 4: Hypothetical Yields on Coupon and Spot Yield Curves: Six Months to Two Years

Maturity	Coupon A	Coupon Bond Yield B	Zero Coupon Yield C
6 Months	0.00%	3.50%	3.50%
12 Months	4.00%	4.00%	?
18 Months	4.50%	4.50%	?
24 Months	4.75%	4.75%	?

Exhibit 5: Hypothetical Yields on Coupon and Spot Yield Curves: Six Months to Two Years

Maturity	Coupon A	Coupon Bond Yield B	Zero Coupon Yield C
6 Months	0.00%	3.50%	3.50%
12 Months	4.00%	4.00%	4.05%
18 Months	4.50%	4.50%	?
24 Months	4.75%	4.75%	?

Exhibit 6: Hypothetical Yields on Coupon and Spot Yield Curves: Six Months to Two Years

Maturity	Coupon A	Coupon Bond Yield B	Zero Coupon Yield C
6 Months	0.00%	3.50%	3.50%
12 Months	4.00%	4.00%	4.05%
18 Months	4.50%	4.50%	4.57%
24 Months	4.75%	4.75%	4.83%

The process, referred to as the *bootstrap* method for calculating an implied zero-coupon yield curve, can by extrapolated all the way out to the maturity of the longest-term bonds. Spot yields calculated on the basis of a yield curve for coupon-paying bonds are referred to as "implied" or "fair" zero-coupon curves. Actual market yields on zero coupon bonds may or may not be the same as these "implied" or "fair" yields.

Exhibit 7 presents four complete yield curves for late April 1999: fitted coupon curves and implied spot curves for U.S. Treasuries and for French and German government bonds in the EMU. A comparison of these two pairs of curves illustrates an important aspect of the relationship between coupon and spot rate curves.

Notice three things about these curves. First, in both markets the zero-coupon curve never falls below the coupon curve. Second, the spread between each market's two curves is generally narrower for shorter than for longer maturities. Finally, the yield differential between the zero and the coupon curve tends to be wider in the EMU market, where the yield curve is relatively steep, than in the U.S. This relationship is clearer in Exhibit 8, which plots yield spreads between coupon bonds and zeros in basis points. These three characteristics of Exhibits 7 and 8 highlight important facts about spot and coupon yield curves.

First, if the coupon yield curve slopes upward, the zero-coupon curve will lie above the coupon curve. An upward-sloping yield curve reflects the fact that investors demand higher yields on longer-duration bonds. Since a zero-coupon bond has a longer duration than a coupon-paying bond with the same maturity (see Chapter 6), the yield on a zero must be higher than the yield on an equal-maturity coupon bond. Further, to the extent that the yield curve slopes upward across all maturities, this yield differential should be greater, the longer the maturity of the two bonds.

Exhibit 7: U.S. Treasury and EMU Government Fitted Coupon and Spot Yield Curves – Late April 1999

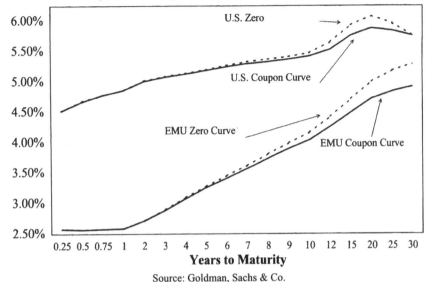

Source: Goldman, Sachs & Co.

Exhibit 8: Spot Rate over Fitted Coupon Yield Spread for U.S. Treasuries and EMU Governments – Late April 1999

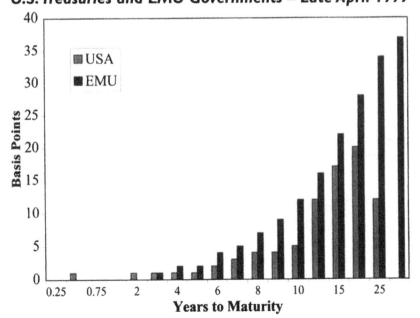

Source: Goldman, Sachs & Co.

The modified duration of a 2-year zero-coupon bond yielding 5.00% is 1.95, while the duration of a 2-year par bond with a 5.00% coupon is 1.88, a 4% difference. The differential for 30-year zeros and coupon bonds is 47% (29.3 versus 15.5, again for bonds yielding 5.00%). Since the duration differential is greater for the longer bonds, the yield differential will also, in general, be greater, as long as the yield curve slopes upward along its full range.

Finally, the differential between zeros and coupon-paying bonds will be greater, the steeper the curve. The slope of a yield curve indicates how much more yield investors demand for increments of duration. The steeper the curve, the greater the increment. So the yield differential between zero-coupon and coupon-paying bonds of any given maturity will be wider, the greater the positive slope of the curve up to that maturity.

Yield curves do not always slope upward; they are occasionally flat or inverted. A flat yield curve indicates that all cash flows in all bonds are discounted at the same rate. That is, if the curve is flat, investors are, on average, indifferent between long- and short-duration bonds. Under these circumstances, zero-coupon cash flows will be discounted at the same interest rate as everything else, so the yield on zeros will be the same as the yield on a coupon-paying bond of the same maturity (and of every other maturity).

When investors as a group believe that interest rates are headed downward, yields on longer duration bonds will be *lower* than on shorter-term securities; that is, the yield curve will slope downward. Because zero-coupon bonds have longer durations than coupon-paying bonds of the same maturity, under these circumstances the spot curve will lie *below* the coupon curve, as illustrated in Exhibit 9.

Yield curves usually slope upward, although there will be flat or inverted segments of a generally upward-sloping curve. This is seen most clearly in the case of the yield curve for U.S. Treasuries illustrated in Exhibit 7; the curve's slope is generally positive for maturities of about 20 years or less, while the segment from 20 to 30 years is inverted. When the curve's slope varies, so will the yield differential between zeros and coupon bonds. In the case of the U.S. curve for late April 1999, the zero spread over coupon bonds widens as maturity increases as long as the curve is upward-sloping, but at the point where the fitted curve inverts the spread begins to narrow.

THE USES OF ZERO-COUPON BONDS AND IMPLIED SPOT RATE CURVES

On the most basic level, our analysis should highlight the fact that, in theory, coupon-paying and zero-coupon bonds are interchangeable in a portfolio. That is, an investor intending to construct a portfolio with specific investment characteristics — cash flow patterns, duration, convexity, credit quality — could, in principle, assemble a collection of either coupon bonds, zeros, or a combination of the two.

Exhibit 9: An Inverted Yield Curve and its Implied Spot Rate Curve

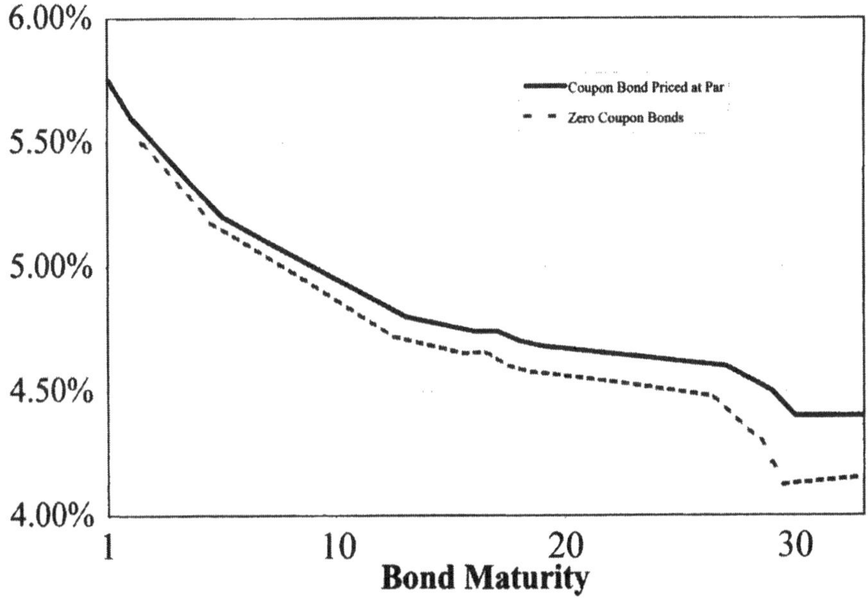

This does not mean, however, that portfolios consisting entirely of zero-coupon bonds are typical. As a practical matter, coupon-paying bonds are much more common than zero-coupon bonds. Furthermore, many families rely on the income from their fixed-income portfolios to pay living expenses, and coupon bonds provide a convenient package of cash flows to meet this common investment objective.

The theoretical equivalence of coupon bonds and portfolios of zeros does mean that zero-coupon securities should be considered just like any other candidate for inclusion in a portfolio. Before buying any bond an investor must decide whether the particular security moves the portfolio toward the target level of duration, convexity, and credit quality. At any given time, a zero-coupon bond could easily provide the best way for an investor to achieve any given portfolio management objective. When that is the case, the zero is the best bond to buy. So, while a portfolio consisting entirely of zeros would be unusual, it would also be surprising to find a large, well-managed bond portfolio that never included any zero-coupon bonds.

In fact, there are a number of specific circumstances in which adding zero-coupon bonds to a portfolio can make a great deal of sense. First, zeros offer a riskless way of matching a well-defined future liability. Suppose, for example, an investor will be required to make a $1 million payment five years in the future — perhaps to cover a charity pledge or to fund a private equity investment — and wishes to set aside the minimum amount of money required to meet this obligation. Suppose further that the yield curve is flat so that 5-year zeros and coupon obligations of the U.S. Treasury both yield 4.00%.

If the investor buys a 5-year zero with a face amount of $1 million, it will cost $820,348.30 to cover the obligation and there will be no chance, short of a default by the government, of missing the target. If the investor were to invest the same amount in a coupon-paying bond, the amount of money available at the end of five years would depend on the rate of interest earned on the nine semiannual interest payments received before the bond's maturity date. If all the coupons can be reinvested at 4.00%, the investor will have $1 million available when needed. If the average reinvestment rate turns out to be 3.00%, though, only $995,627.13 might be available when the bond matures. To eliminate this uncertainty, the investor could assume that periodic coupons would earn no interest. If so, then the investor would be required to set aside $833,333.33, or $12,985.03 more than would be required to buy a zero-coupon bond that would solve the problem. So, the zero-coupon bond provides the lowest-cost way of guaranteeing that this future liability will be met.

Second, zero-coupon bonds can provide the most efficient way of extending the duration of an existing bond portfolio. To see this, imagine that an investor holds a €10 million portfolio consisting entirely of 3-year EMU government bonds with coupons of 3.50% and duration of 2.8. Suppose that the investor wishes to increase the duration of this portfolio to 5.0. One way to do so is to sell some of the 3-year bonds and replace them with 10-year bonds. If the 10-year securities yield 4.5%, their duration would be 8.0. Raising the portfolio's duration to 5.0 in this way would involve selling 42% of the 3-years and replacing them with 10-year bonds. If the bid-asked spread in this market is 0.25%, this combined sale and purchase would have a transaction cost of €21,000. Extending duration using 10-year zero-coupon bonds, however, involves selling only $3.1 million of the 3-year bonds at a transaction cost of only €15,500. These two ways of extending duration do not produce identical results. The two resulting portfolios will offer slightly different yields and will perform differently to the extent that the yield curve steepens or flattens.

Third, occasionally zero-coupon bonds in certain maturities offer higher yields than the spot rate implied for that maturity by the yield curve for coupon bonds. In a market that allows for efficient stripping and reconstitution of coupon-paying bonds, market forces will generally drive market yields on zero-coupon bonds toward their theoretical fair spot rates. If yields on zeros are lower than implied spot yields — and zero-coupon prices are therefore higher than they should be, given the prices of coupon-paying bonds — bond dealers will buy coupon bonds, strip them, sell the zeros and realize a riskless profit. Conversely, if zero-coupon prices are lower than they should be, arbitrageurs will buy zeros, reconstitute the coupon-paying bond, and again realize a riskless profit.

In practice, this process does not always work as smoothly as it does in theory. Not all markets allow for efficient stripping of bonds; in fact, the process is fully developed in only a few global government bond markets. Elsewhere, misvaluations of zero-coupon bonds relative to theoretically fair prices can persist for long periods of time.

Even in markets like the U.S. Treasury bond market, where the process of stripping is well established and highly efficient, misvaluations are possible. At times, for example, zero-coupon yields are lower than implied spot levels in one range of maturities but higher than theoretically fair levels at other maturities. When this occurs, neither stripping nor reconstitution will be profitable, and the misvaluations may persist.

There has been a fairly consistent pattern in the U.S. Treasury market for very longest-maturity (25 years and more) STRIPS to yield less than "fair" levels and for STRIPS with shorter maturities to yield somewhat more. Very long-term STRIPS are unique investments in that they are the longest-duration securities available in the financial markets. Investors seeking to match very long-dated liabilities naturally gravitate toward these bonds, but the process of creating the longest duration STIPS by stripping Treasury bonds necessarily also produces shorter-maturity STRIPS for which there may be no natural buyer. As a result, the securities that are in the greatest demand, the 25+ year paper, tend to yield a bit less than theoretical fair value, while some of the shorter stripped cash flows yield a bit more than they should.

Under these circumstances, investors seeking U.S. Treasury investments with durations in, say, the 10- to 15-year range may prefer to buy zero-coupon bonds with 10- to 15-year maturities rather than buying coupon-paying bonds with 30-year maturities. The fact that these intermediate-term zero-coupon bonds are priced below their theoretically fair levels means that buying these securities is the most cost-effective, the cheapest, way to purchase securities with the desired duration.

Such misvaluations are also common in the municipal bond market, where zero-coupon bonds in some maturities offer substantially lower yields than they should theoretically, while for other maturities zeros have been the bonds to buy.

Investors who are building or managing family fixed-income portfolios should be prepared to consider zero-coupon bonds for a part of their holdings. Those few who are investing to meet a well-defined future liability should gravitate toward substantial positions in zero-coupon bonds that match future cash flow needs. Those who rely on interest income to pay living expenses should probably hold relatively few zero-coupon bonds, although even in this case some zeros might make sense if they yield more than they should, given other interest rates in the market, and to the extent that the investor's portfolio includes a large number of bonds purchased at a premium to par. The lack of income on the zero will offset the higher coupon on the premium bonds, thereby helping the investor to avoid dipping into principal by spending too much of the portfolio's periodic cash flow receipts.

Investors buying zero-coupon bonds should be aware of the level of theoretical fair spot rates. The fact that a particular zero-coupon bond's yield is higher than the fair spot rate is a good, if not necessarily decisive, argument for buying that bond rather than a coupon-paying security with comparable duration.

Likewise, if the yield offered on a zero is below the spot rate, buying a coupon-paying bond will probably make more sense.

FORWARD YIELDS AND FORWARD CURVES

All our discussions of bond transactions so far assume purchases and sales for normal settlement. As we learned in Chapter 11, standard settlement for transactions in most major government bond markets is "T + 1," one day after the trade date. For many other fixed-income securities, standard, or "regular way" settlement is T + 3. Occasionally investors may ask for faster settlement than regular way, and dealers can frequently accommodate such special requests with little or no impact on pricing. Delayed or forward settlement of transactions is also quite common, but in this case the impact on prices and yields can be substantial, particularly if the delay in settlement is for more than a few days.

Forward pricing has some importance in its own right; forward purchases and sales can be useful to family portfolio managers on occasion. In fact, though, the concept of forward pricing is one of the cornerstones of more advanced fixed-income analysis.

The most straightforward way to understand forward pricing is to evaluate two alternative investments that will provide exactly the same returns. Suppose that on January 1, 2000, an investor has the choice of:

1. Buying a bond maturing on January 1, 2005, paying an annual 5.00% coupon at par for £1 million today, or
2. A combination of:
   a. Buying a note maturing on January 1, 2001, paying an annual 4.00% for £1 million today and
   b. Committing irrevocably to purchase on January 1, 2001 a bond with an annual 5% coupon maturing on January 1, 2005.

If the issuer of all these securities is the same, the two alternatives must produce the same returns, so the pricing of the two transactions must be such that an investor would be indifferent between the two transactions. The question is: What purchase price for the 1-year forward delivery 4-year bond will make the investor indifferent? The answer is the "fair forward" price, as of January 1, 2000, of a 5% bond maturing on January 1, 2005, paid for and delivered on January 1, 2001.

Clearly, the answer to this question is not "par." If the forward purchase price were 100.00, the investor's net cash flows would be as illustrated in Exhibit 10. Under these circumstances, the investor who opted for transaction (1) would be better off. To make the investor indifferent between the two transactions, the forward purchase price of the 4-year bond must be enough less than par to make up for the fact that an investor who opts for transaction (2) will be giving up a coupon cash flow of £10,000 (= [5.00% − 4.00%] × £1 million) at the end of the first year.

Exhibit 10: Alternative Cash Flows Assuming Forward Purchase at Par

| | Net Cash Flow | |
| | Two-Year | One-Year Note + |
Date	Bond	Forward Purchase
1/1/00	−£1,000,000	−£1,000,000
1/1/01	50,000	40,000
1/1/02	50,000	50,000
1/1/03	50,000	50,000
1/1/04	50,000	50,000
1/1/05	1,050,000	1,050,000

Because in this simple example all the cash flows take place at year-end, the two transactions will produce exactly the same results if the purchase price of the 4-year bond on January 1, 2001, is £990,000. Therefore, the fair forward price of the bond in this example is 99.00, and its fair forward yield, the yield at the fair forward price, is 5.281%.

We can extrapolate from this simple example. We can calculate the fair forward price of any bond if we know:

1. The market yield on bonds delivered regular way of the same issuer with the same maturity date as the forward delivery bond, and
2. The yield on obligations of the same issuer maturing on the forward delivery date.

The forward price is the price that compensates the investor for the differential, if any, between short-term yields to the delivery date and longer-term bond yields. If, as is typical, longer-term bonds yield more than short-term instruments, the forward price will be lower than the current market (or spot) price.[1] When the yield curve is flat, spot and forward yields will be the same for all bonds, regardless of delivery date. When the yield curve is inverted, forward prices are *higher than* spot prices, and forward yields are *lower* than spot yields.

In government bond markets, where bonds with all maturities trade fairly frequently, it is generally easy to obtain the information required to calculate fair forward prices. In other markets, it may be necessary to estimate some of the information needed to compute a fair forward price. The results of this process are illustrated for the U.K. and EMU yield curves as of late April 1999 in Exhibits 11 and 12.

---

[1] Current market yields or prices are sometimes referred to as *spot rates* or *spot prices*, respectively, in contrast to "forward prices" or "forward bond yields." This can lead to some confusion because the term "spot" rate is also used to refer to the yield on a zero-coupon, as opposed to a coupon-paying bond. Which use of the term "spot" applies in any given case is usually obvious from the context of the discussion. If there is any ambiguity, however, ask for clarification.

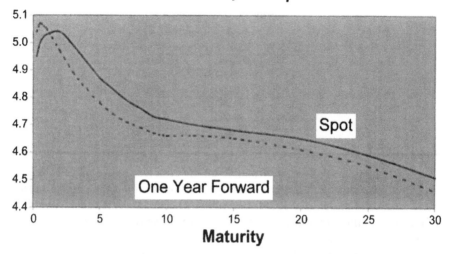

Exhibit 11: Spot and One-Year Forward Yield Curves
U.K. Governments, Mid-April 1999

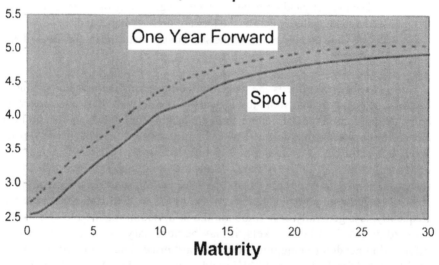

Exhibit 12: Spot and One-Year Forward Yield Curves
EMU, Mid-April 1999

The Uses of Forward Prices and Forward Curves

We have said that the concept of fair forward pricing is one of the key tools of advanced fixed-income analysis. Indeed, we refer to theoretical forward prices frequently in every chapter to follow. We begin with some of the applications of this concept.

One thing forward rates do not do is predict future interest rates with any accuracy. The 1-year forward yield of a 10-year bond as of January 1, 2000, is the fair yield at which an investor can contract on January 1, 2000, to purchase or buy this bond for delivery on January 1, 2001. This says nothing about where rates *will* be on January 1, 2001.

Fair forward rates are a function solely of short- and long-term interest rates on the date at which the forwards are calculated. In fact, forward rates are notoriously bad predictors of future interest rate levels. Because the yield curve is almost always upward-sloping, forward rates are almost always higher than current yield levels, although interest rates have been trending lower since the early 1980s. While forward rates do not predict future rates, there is an important relationship between forwards and investor expectations about future interest rate levels.

Deciding Which Views are Worth Expressing

Suppose an investor who pays no taxes and holds a portfolio of mostly 10-year bonds decides that interest rates are likely to increase over the next year.[2] Should the investor avoid market value losses and anticipate an opportunity to reinvest in bonds in 12 months by selling the 10-year bonds and buying, say, 1-year notes? The answer is: Not necessarily. It depends on whether the investor expects interest rates to rise by more than the difference between spot and forward rates.

To add some concreteness to this example, assume that we are dealing with a portfolio of *Pfandbriefe* (see Chapter 8) and that 10-year securities in this market yield 4.15% while 1-year *Pfands* yield 2.70%. By selling 10-year securities and buying 1-year obligations, the investor will be giving up 145 basis points. So this swap out of 10-year into 1-year bonds — taking into account transaction costs on the sale and the repurchase in one year — will make sense only if prices of the 10-year securities decline by more than about 1.5% over the course of the year. A 1.5% price decrease on a 4.15% 10-year bond initially priced at par and aged for one year would involve an increase in yield of 20 basis points. We say that +20 basis points is the *break-even yield change* for a the sale of a 10-year security and purchase of a 1-year security over a 1-year horizon under these assumptions.

Shortening the portfolio makes sense only if the investor expects interest rates to rise by more than 20 basis points over the course of the year. This is a relatively small increase in interest rates, so a bearish investor might want to shorten duration somewhat, although a reduction in duration from about eight years to about one year would be a fairly radical move.

The important point, however, is the observation that the calculation of the break-even yield change is exactly the same as the calculation of the yield on a nine-year bond for delivery one year forward. By the same token, if we know the forward yields on bonds of various maturities for a range of future settlement dates, we also know the break-even yield changes for sales and purchases of these bonds.

---

[2] Assuming that the investor is a non-taxpayer eliminates a great deal of complexity. See Chapter 10.

Exhibit 13: Hypothetical Market Data

Settlement		1/1/00	
Maturity	4/1/00	1/1/02	1/1/10
Coupon and Yield	4.25%	5.25%	5.75%
Duration	0.24	1.88	7.53
Portfolio I	0	100%	0
Portfolio II	77%	0	23%
3-Month Forward Price		99.75	99.625
3-Month Forward Yield		5.38%	5.80%
2-10s Spread: Spot		50 bp	
2-10s Spread: Forward		42 bp	

For example, consider the spot and one-year forward curves for the U.K. bond market illustrated in Exhibit 11. In late April 1999, the spot yield on 5-year U.K. government bonds was 4.87%, and the 1-year forward yield was 4.78%. This means that an investor who expects interest rates to decline by less than 9 basis points, and, even more so, an investor who expects gilt yields to rise, would clearly prefer a 1-year to a 5-year bond.

Assessing Relationships Among Yields

Consideration of forward rates can also help assess whether relationships among yields on different bonds are consistent with an investor's views. The yield relationships in question may be the slope of the yield curve between bonds of different maturities or credit spreads between corporate and government bonds.

With regard to the yield curve, consider the hypothetical market statistics presented in Exhibit 13. Suppose an investor holding 2-year bonds decides that the yield curve is likely to flatten, but does not wish to increase portfolio duration. The way to express this view would be to sell the 2-year paper and swap into an equal-duration portfolio consisting of 23% 10-year bonds and 77% cash. So the question is: How much flattening would be necessary for the cash/10-year portfolio to outperform the 2-year securities?

It might be possible to answer this question using scenario analysis; that is, by evaluating the portfolio at the end of three months, given a wide range of changes in 2-year and 10-year yields over the horizon. Flattening could occur with: 2-year yields rising, 10-year yields falling, some combination of these two events, both yields rising but 2-year yields rising more, and so on. It is impossible to consider all possible scenarios.

An easier way to decide whether the swap makes sense, given the investor's views, is to compare the spot and forward yield curve slopes over the horizon for the trade. In this case, the combination of cash and 10-year bonds will outperform the 2-year bond if the yield curve flattens by more than 8 basis points, regardless of what combination of yield changes in produces the result.

Exhibit 14: U.S. Treasuries and Government Agencies
Spot and Three-Month Forward Yield Curves and Yield Spreads.

Maturity	U.S. Gov't Agency		U.S. Treasury		Yield Spread (BP)	
	Spot	3-Mo. Forward	Spot	3-Mo. Forward	Spot	Forward
3 Mo.	5.09%	5.12%	4.73%	4.88%	36	24
6. Mo.	5.14%	5.20%	4.84%	5.01%	30	19
1 Yr.	5.28%	5.39%	5.08%	5.22%	20	17
2 Yr.	5.55%	5.63%	5.31%	5.41%	24	22
5 Yr.	5.93%	6.00%	5.51%	5.58%	42	42
10 Yr.	6.22%	6.28%	5.61%	5.67%	61	61

Investors can use forward analysis to evaluate yield spreads between securities of different credit quality. For example, using information from the U.S. Treasury and U.S. government agency yield curves, we can compute forward curves for both markets as in Exhibit 14. Forward yield spreads are simply the differences between forward yields in the two markets. The spot curves in Exhibit 14 imply forward yield spreads for agencies that are narrower (tighter) than spot spreads. Under these circumstances, an investor who expects yield spreads on agencies to widen, even if the anticipated widening is relatively modest, would want to sell agencies and buy Treasuries.

Evaluating Forward Sales and Purchases

The most obvious use of forward pricing analysis is in the evaluation of forward purchases and sales of securities. Most transactions in the bond market are settled regular way, but a significant minority are not, and active family portfolio managers may on occasion find it useful to enter into such forward sales or purchases.

The most common such transaction is the purchase of *when issued* (WI) bonds. Delivery of newly issued bonds typically takes place at least a week or two after the pricing date, and frequently settlement of primary market transactions can take place a month or two after the first buyer commits to buy the bonds. This lag between pricing and delivery is substantially longer than regular way settlement of secondary market transactions.

Investors who commit to buy the bonds at the initial offering may sell their securities to other buyers before the bonds are delivered. When this occurs, the bonds are said to be trading on a when issued basis. In the case of U.S. and some other government bonds, formal WI trading commences as soon as the Treasury Department announces the size of its next issue. An investor who purchases a bond on a when issued basis is, in effect, buying a security for forward delivery. For example, suppose today is May 7, 2000, and an investor with $1 million in cash is considering two alternative 10-year investments:

1. A hypothetical outstanding U.S. Treasury 6.00% of May 15, 2010, priced at 103.811 to yield 5.50%, or

2. A combination of:
   a. A short-term investment through May 17, 2000, at a yield of 3.50%, and
   b. Purchase, on a WI basis, of a newly announced new 10-year U.S. Treasury note settling on May 17, 2000.

The question is: "At what yield on the WI bond would an investor be indifferent between these two transactions?" Under these assumptions, the investor who holds a short-term investment yielding 3.50%, rather than a bond yielding 5.50%, over a 10-day period will forgo $773.48 (= [5.50% − 3.50%] × $1,000,000 × [7/181]) in interest income.[3] Therefore, in order to leave the investor indifferent between investments (1) and (2), the purchase price for the WI bond paid on the settlement date must be reduced by this amount. If the coupon on the WI bond turns out to be 5.50%, this translates into a price reduction from $1,000,000 to $999,226.52 or a price of 99.923 for the bond or a yield of 5.5099%.

In a market as efficient as the U.S. Treasury sector, such half-basis point yield differentials matter. A naive investor who was offered the choice between $1 million investments in two bonds: one settling today and priced to yield 5.500% and another trading WI for settlement in 10 days and priced to yield 5.504% might think that the latter was a better deal. But if the short-term interest rate is 3.50% at the time, the WI bond would be overpriced by about $450.

Because government bond markets are highly efficient, there is seldom a distinct advantage to buying bonds for current delivery versus buying WI issues for delayed settlement. In other markets, however, there may be such instances. The municipal bond market, for example, is notorious for mispricing bonds with non-standard settlement dates. Such mispricing can work for or against the investor. In the primary municipal market, underwriters and investors may make little distinction between new issues settling a normal two to three weeks after the pricing date and other deals that close as much as two months after pricing. This difference in the timing of settlement can have a substantial impact on fair pricing levels, especially given that the yield curve in the municipal market is usually relatively steep.

To see the magnitude of the effect, suppose an investor can purchase 20-year tax-exempt bonds for regular way settlement in the municipal market (T + 3) at a yield of 5.00%. Assume also that the short-term tax-exempt rate for all maturities is 2.50%. Under these assumptions, the fair yield for a bond delivered two weeks after regular way settlement would be 5.007%, or 0.7 basis points more than the yield on a comparable bond in the secondary market. In the municipal

---

[3] This number will not be precisely correct. The outstanding 6.00% bond will be trading with almost six months of accrued interest, or $28,826.82. A buyer who wishes to invest only $1 million in a Treasury security will therefore want to borrow that amount for the 7-day period, using the $1 million investment as collateral for the loan. The cost of borrowing these funds over the seven day period until the interest payment date on May 15, 2000, should be deducted from the forgone interest to make the comparison perfectly precise.

market, where pricing is not as precise as in the Treasury sector, a difference of less than a basis point would be considered negligible. If the delay in delivery extends over two months, though, the fair yield on the new issue would be 5.033%. This great a yield differential would be significant, even in the municipal market. In fact, the primary municipal market might not necessarily make a distinction between a normal two-week delay in the settlement of a new issue and longer lag. Investors should take note of the settlement date of a new issue and expect some compensation in terms of yield if delivery is delayed by more than a few weeks.

The mispricing of forward transactions in the municipal market can also work to an investor's advantage. On occasion municipalities find it advantageous to price bonds for delivery six months to a year or more in the future. When this occurs, the yield on the bonds for forward delivery is often *higher* than the fair forward rate. For example, suppose a municipality could price 20-year 5.00% bonds at par for normal new issue delivery (i.e., in two or three weeks) on January 1, 2000. The issuer is also offering 5.00% bonds for delivery in 18 months, that will mature 18.5 years after delivery. Assume that 18-month obligations of this municipality yield 3.50%.

We can find the fair forward purchase price of the bond to be delivered on July 1, 2001, by solving for X in Exhibit 15 so that the present value of the cash flows, discounted at 5.00%, is equal to par. At that forward price, an investor would be indifferent between:

1. Buying a 20-year bond of the issuer today, and
2. Buying a combination of
    a. An 18-month obligation of the issuer, and
    b. Committing to purchase the issuer's bond for forward delivery.

Using standard numerical techniques, we can calculate X. In this example it turns out to be $976.41, which translates into a bond price of 97.64. The yield on a 5.00% coupon bond delivered on July 7, 2001, and maturing on January 1, 2020, with a dollar price of 97.64 is 5.20%, and that is the fair forward yield in this example.

Such long-dated forward transactions have occurred with some frequency in the United States municipal bond market. When they have, the yields have typically been substantially higher than fair forward levels. In this example, the forward purchase yield might have been as high as 5.40%. Family bond portfolio managers should be prepared to take advantage of such mispricings. If a dealer offers a new bond issue for delayed delivery at any given purchase yield, investors should ask what the "fair" forward rate for the bond is. Competent dealers will, as a matter of course, know what that rate is. If the bond is offered at a yield significantly above the theoretical rate and if the bond is consistent with the family's fixed-income investment objectives, the forward purchase will make a lot of sense.

Exhibit 15: Cash Flows on a Hypothetical Forward Delivery Bond.

Date	Principal Cash Flow	Coupon Cash Flow	Total
1/1/00	$(1,000.00)		$(1,000.00)
7/1/00		$17.25	17.25
1/1/01		17.25	17.25
7/1/01	+1000 - X	17.25	17.25 + 1000 - X
1/1/02		25.00	25.00
7/1/02		25.00	25.00
1/1/03		25.00	25.00
7/1/03		25.00	25.00
1/1/04		25.00	25.00
7/1/04		25.00	25.00
.		.	.
.		.	.
.		.	.
1/1/18		25.00	25.00
7/1/18		25.00	25.00
1/1/19		25.00	25.00
7/1/19		25.00	25.00
1/1/20	1,000.00	25.00	1,025.00

Dealers will frequently require family investors who buy bonds for forward delivery to post collateral to secure the purchase price. This should not be a major problem for investors buying bonds from the dealer who holds the family's securities in custody.

CONCLUSION

Data on yields and maturities of bonds of a single issuer incorporate large amounts of information that can be useful to a family portfolio manager. By means of a fitted yield curve, information embedded in observed bond prices can be used to deduce fair yields on hypothetical bonds with different coupons and maturities. Fitted government yield curves can also serve as an unbiased indicator of the relative value of non-government bonds.

Yield curves for coupon-paying bonds can be translated into theoretical zero-coupon yields. The latter provide useful guidance as to whether purchase of zeros is attractive.

Finally, fair forward rates, which can also be derived from observed bond yields, provide guidance regarding potential sales and purchases of when issued bonds. Knowledge of fair forward prices and yield gives portfolio managers a clearer appreciation of how their own views do or do not agree with expectations that are already priced into the market.

CHAPTER 16

Fixed-Income Options

Options are an integral part of the day-to-day business of financial markets. Although a family fixed-income portfolio manager can do a perfectly adequate job without ever actually buying or selling options, some understanding of options theory and options markets is essential for successful bond portfolio management. For one thing, evaluating callable bonds involves a form of options analysis; the issuer retains the *option* to redeem the bond before maturity. Because it is difficult to build a bond portfolio in the U.S. market without holding some callable bonds, it is also difficult to avoid thinking about options.

In Chapter 17, we will apply many of the insights developed in this chapter to the issue of valuing a callable bond. Beyond this practically unavoidable involvement, investors who do use options in an informed and prudent way should, over time, enjoy somewhat better investment returns than portfolio managers who never make use of these instruments.

WHAT ARE OPTIONS?

The holder of a *call* option on a specific security enjoys the right, but not the obligation, to *purchase* the instrument at a specified price in the future. The specified security is referred to as the *deliverable* instrument. The specified price is called the *strike price*. And the last date on which the purchase right may be exercised is the "*expiration date*" of the option. The holder of a *European* call option has the right to purchase the specified security *on* a specified future "*expiration date*" while the holder of an *American* call option has the right to buy the security *on or before* the expiration date.

Put options grant the holder the right to *sell* the deliverable security at the strike price on the expiration date (European) or before the expiration date (American). The seller of a call is required to deliver the security to the option owner upon receipt of the strike price, while the seller of a put option is obliged to purchase the deliverable at the strike price if the option owner delivers the security in a timely manner. In exchange for these rights, purchasers of puts or calls pay the sellers the price of the option, referred to as the *premium*. The selling of options is also referred to as *writing* options and creates *short* positions in puts or calls.

The owner of a call option can profit from the purchase to the extent that the price of the deliverable security at the expiration date is *higher* than the strike price. In Exhibit 1 we trace the net profit, expressed as a percentage of the par value of the deliverable bond, on a call option with a strike price of 100.00 and a premium equal to 3% of par. The worst-case outcome from the optionholder's point of view is the loss of the option premium. The potential profit on the position is essentially unlimited. Because of their shape, payoff functions such as this one are referred to as "hockey stick" diagrams.

Exhibit 2 presents the hockey stick diagrams for long and short positions in puts and calls, all are struck at 100.00 and all commanding premiums equal to 3% of par.

Exhibit 1: Payoff on a Long Call Position

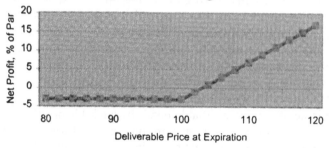

Exhibit 2: Payoff on Long and Short Call and Put Positions as a Function of Deliverable Bond Price at Expiration

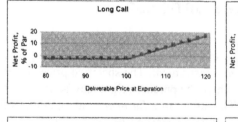
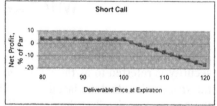
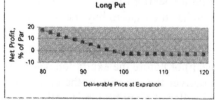
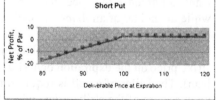

Exhibit 3: Payoff on Long and Short Put and Call Positions as a Function of Deliverable Bond Yield at Expiration

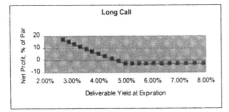

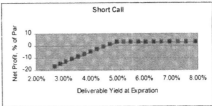

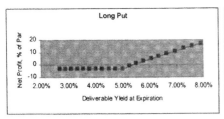

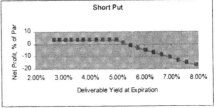

Exhibit 4: Payoff on Long Puts and Calls with Equal Strike Prices

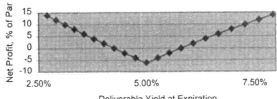

Payoff diagrams for options on fixed-income instruments can also be plotted against yield, rather than price, on the x-axis. If the deliverable bond in Exhibit 2 is a 10-year 5% security, the payoffs, as a function of yield, will be as illustrated in Exhibit 3.

We can also trace similar diagrams for the payoff functions of combinations of options positions and for combinations of options with positions in the deliverable securities. For example, Exhibit 4 shows the payoff diagram for a position consisting of a long position in a call and a long position in a put, both at a premium of 3% and struck at par. As the chart illustrates, this position will produce a profit to the holder to the extent that bond prices either rise or fall substantially. Such combinations of long call and put options with the same strike price are referred to as *straddles*. If the strike prices are different, the position is referred to as a *strangle*.

Exhibit 5: Payoff on Long the Deliverable Bond at Par and Short a Call Option Struck at Par

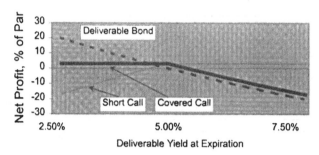

Options positions can also be combined with long or short positions in the deliverable securities, and the profit and loss of such positions, represented as a function of either price or yield at expiration can be represented in payoff diagrams. The most common such position is a long position in the deliverable bond combined with a short position in a call option. This combination is referred to as a *covered call*. Exhibit 5 shows the payoff diagram for a covered call position on the assumption that the strike price for the short call position is par and that the investor purchases the deliverable 5% coupon bond at a price of par.

ASSESSING OPTION VALUES

Using options effectively — whether through direct purchases or sales or through ownership of callable bonds — requires some understanding of option valuation. Any investor should have some sense of what makes the price of an option "cheap" or "expensive."[1]

In the previous chapter we showed how market information could be used to calculate the fair forward price of a bond. Specifically, the theoretical forward price for any given settlement date depends on two variables: the price and yield of the bond in question in the spot market and the short-term interest rate through the forward delivery date. Similarly, the fair prices of options depend on market variables. In particular, a fair premium for a put or a call on a bond will relate in a systematic way to these variables:

---

[1] Readers with some background in financial analysis may be familiar with the Black-Scholes model of option valuation, introduced by Fischer Black and Myron Scholes in a seminal article (Fischer Black and Myron Scholes, "The Pricing of Corporate Liabilities," *Journal of Political Economy*, May-June 1973). The conceptual framework presented here relies more heavily on later work by Fischer Black along with Emanual Derman and William Toy ("A One-Factor Model of Interest Rates and Its Application to Treasury Bond Options," *Financial Analysts Journal*, January-February 1990). The two approaches produce similar valuations of options, but the BDT approach has somewhat more intuitive appeal when dealing with options on fixed-income instruments.

- The "volatility" of bond prices or yields.
- The amount of time until expiration.
- Short-term ("risk-free") interest rates.
- The amount by which the option is *in or out of the money*, that is, the degree to which the strike price differs from the fair forward price of the deliverable security as of the expiration date.

We discuss how these influences impact option value.

Option Value Derives from Volatility

Options have value because buyers and sellers are *uncertain* about bond prices in the future. If we knew for certain what the market price of a bond would be at some point in the future, the right but not the obligation to purchase that security at a given price would have no meaning. If we knew with certainty that the price of a bond would be $110.00 in a week's time, then the right to buy that bond at a price of $108.00 would exactly equal the present value of $2 paid in one week, and there would be no question that the option would be exercised. Under these circumstances, the "option" would be simply a down payment on an unconditional forward purchase.

A good way to illustrate the relationship between option values and uncertainty is to begin with the simplest case of uncertainty: two and only two equally probable outcomes. Probability distributions with this structure are referred to as *binomial* distributions. Assume that we know that the price of a 10-year 6.00% coupon bond in one year (at which time it will be a nine-year bond) will be either $90.00 or $110.00 with equal likelihood, and that the relevant one-year interest rate is 5.00%. Now suppose we want to evaluate the fair value of a one-year call option with a strike price of $108.00. If the price of the bond in one year turns out to be $90.00, then the call option will expire with no value. If the price turns out to be $110.00, the option will be worth $2 (= $110.00 - $108.00). Since, by assumption, the two outcomes are equally likely, the expected value of the option as of the expiration date is $1.00 (= [0.50 × $0] + [0.50 × $2]). The fair value of the option at the beginning of the period, when the premium would be paid by the buyer to the seller, would be the present value of $1.00 received in one year discounted at the assumed short-term interest rate or $0.95 (= $1/1.05). Exhibit 6 shows the standard way of representing such a hypothetical situation.

Volatility is a percentage measure of the degree of uncertainty regarding the price of an instrument in the future. In the example illustrated in Exhibit 6, the expected value of the bond in one year is $100.00 (= [0.5 × $110.00] + [0.5 × $90.00]), but, with equal likelihood, the value will be 10% higher or lower than this expected value. Under these circumstances, we would say that the bond is subject to 10% *price volatility*. Not surprisingly, the values a bond might have in the future can be expressed in terms of yield as well as price. In our example, the market yields on the 9-year 6.00% bond will be either 4.62% or 7.55%. The yield at the expected price of par would be 6.00%. The yields at the alternative prices of $110.00 and

$90.00 are, on average, 24% different from the yield at the expected price. We thus say that the *yield volatility* of the bond in question is about 24%.[2]

Now look at the same example, but assume that the price volatility is 20%. That is, the price of the bond will be either $80.00 or $120.00. Again, the strike price of the option is $108.00, but now the value of the call at expiration will be either $0 or $12.00 with equal probability, so its expected value at expiration will be $6.00. The fair premium for this option at 20% volatility, the present value of $6.00 received in one year discounted at 5.00%, is $5.71. If the price volatility were 5%, so that the price of the bond would be either $95 or $105, the option to buy the bond at a price of $108 would have no value. Under our extremely simplified valuation model, there is no chance that the price would ever get that high.

A Better Description of Interest Rate Changes

Our characterization of price and yield volatility so far is obviously too simplistic. We can make the binomial approach more realistic by making two modifications in the simple one-period, two-outcome binomial model. First, we break the life of the option into a series of short periods, and assume that bond prices or yields move up or down with equal probabilities in small increments over each short period. If we make the time periods short enough, this approach produces a reasonably realistic description of the full range of possible option values at expiration and the probabilities associated with different outcomes.

Exhibit 6: One-Period Option Valuation with Binomial Outcomes

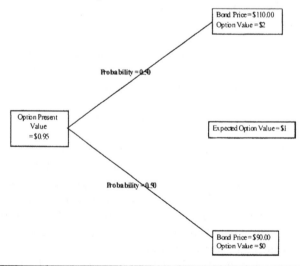

---

[2] This simple example is complicated somewhat by the fact that, because the relationship between bond price and yield is not linear, the expected yield is not the same as the yield at the expected price. In this case the expected yield is 6.09% (= [4.62% + 7.55%]/2). Suffice it to say here that this issue goes away when we undertake somewhat more detailed analysis discussed later in this chapter.

Exhibit 7: Probabilities on a Two-Period Binomial Tree

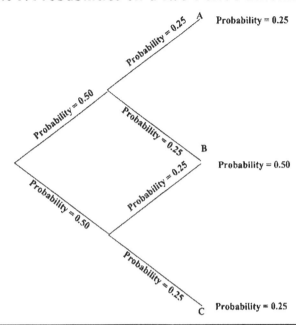

Suppose we divide a year into two six-month periods, and assume that at the end of each period the price of the bond will have one of two and only two values with equal probabilities as in Exhibit 7. Because of the shape of the diagram, this way of representing (or modeling) the process by which interest rates change over time is referred to as a "binomial tree."

In this two-period example, if we start at the beginning of the first period, the probability of winding up at point (or node) *B* by the end of the second period is 0.50; that is, there is a one-in-two chance of winding up at that node. The probabilities of winding up at nodes *A* or *C* by the end of the second period are both 0.25%: a one-in-four chance. This process of dividing the year into smaller segments can be extended indefinitely.

Exhibit 8 illustrates the binomial tree for 12 periods. The probabilities shown measure the likelihood of starting at the beginning of the first period and winding up at each respective node at the end of the relevant period. If we then plot the probabilities associated with each of the final period nodes in Exhibit 8, we can see that the resulting distribution of outcomes begins to resemble the standard normal distribution discussed in Chapter 3 (Exhibit 9).

The purpose of the second modification of the simple one-period binomial process is to make sure the changes in interest rates from period to period are consistent with other information we have about fixed-income markets. Specifically, the expected level of interest rates at any point in the future should be equal to the *fair forward* rate for that period.

Exhibit 8: Probabilities on a 12-Period Binomial Tree

Exhibit 9: Final-Period Node Probabilities for a 12-Period Binomial Tree

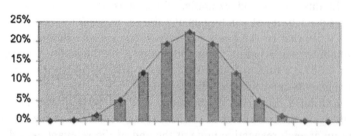

To see how this works, let's consider the one-period one-year model. Suppose that initially the yield on a one-year bond is 6.00% and the yield on a two-year bond is 7.00%, where both bonds pay annual coupons. Under these assumptions, the fair forward yield on a one-year bond for delivery in one year will be 7.14%, or the expected yield on a one-year bond in one year. If this expected yield is subject to uncertainty with 20% volatility, we can represent the situation as a binomial distribution in Exhibit 10.

Exhibit 10: One-Period Model with Expected Future Yields Equal to Fair Forward Yields and 20% Yield Volatility

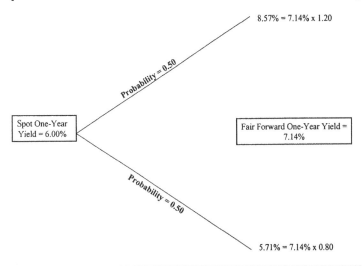

This analysis can also be extended to a multi-period process. If we observe a yield curve for each maturity, we can calculate a fair forward yield for each point in the future. With these fair forward rates as our "anchor" for each period, and with an estimate for periodic interest rate volatility, we can fill in the interest rates for each node of a binomial tree. Exhibit 11 illustrates the results of this process for a 6.00% coupon bond that begins the period with a 10-year maturity. We assume that all money market instruments with maturities between one month and one year yield 5.00%, and this gives us the fair forward rates for the (aging) 10-year bond at the end of 12 monthly periods. We also assume 15% annual volatility for the yield on this bond.[3]

This combination of assumptions allows us to compute a range of "possible" interest rates for the final period that are grounded in fair forward rates and a consistent level of volatility. Of course this is not a full accounting of all the possible yield levels for the terminal period; the actual level of yields in the final period could lie in between the levels assigned it each final period node. Again, however, the levels generated by the binomial tree process will closely approximate all the reasonably plausible outcomes to the extent that the number of periods is large.

---

[3] We can convert annualized volatility into monthly volatility by dividing the annual figure by the square root of 12. More generally, the volatility for period T is related to the volatility for period t by:

$$V_T = V_t \times \sqrt{N}$$

where V_T is the T period (e.g., annual) volatility, V_t is the t period (e.g., monthly) volatility, and N is the number of t periods in a T period (e.g., 12 months in a year).

Exhibit 11: Yield Levels Along a 12-Period One-Year Binomial Tree with 15% Annual Yield Volatility

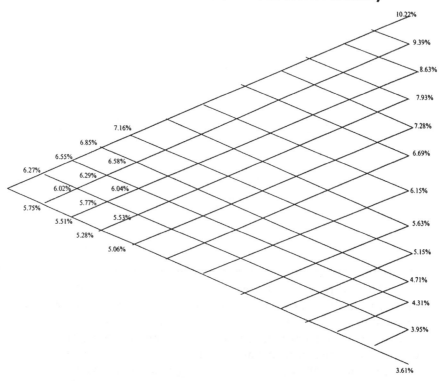

Exhibit 12: Distribution of Yields at the End of the Final Period

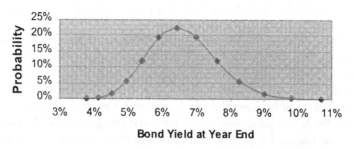

The combination of interest rate levels and probabilities for each final node produces an estimate of the distribution of yields for the final period as illustrated in Exhibit 12. The result is a normal distribution with a standard deviation equal to the (annualized) volatility used to calculate the difference between each pair of equally probable "possible" outcomes at each node of the binomial tree. Information about bond yields can be translated into bond prices, and the price and probability information can be used to compute the expected value of an option on the bond in question at the terminal period.

For example, assume that the 6.00% bond in question matures on January 1, 2010, and that on January 1, 2000, we are evaluating a one-year call option on this bond struck at par. We wish to compute the premium associated with this option at 15% annualized yield volatility and in the interest rate environment described above (that is, with short-term interest rates at 5.00%). We can combine the information on yields and probabilities to compute the expected value of the option as of the expiration date on January 1, 2001, as in Exhibit 13. The expected value of the option as of the expiration date is simply the sum of the values at each node weighted by the probabilities of each node. The final step in calculating the option premium is to find the present value as of the pricing date of the expected value as of expiration. With a 5% short-term interest rate, this will be 1.88% (= 1.97/1.05) of the par value of the deliverable bond position.

This is the method most investment professionals use to price options on fixed-income instruments.

PUT-CALL PARITY

It is useful here to delve a little more deeply into the relationship between option pricing and fair forward yields. A basic fact about options theory is that the price of a put struck at the expected price (or yield) at expiration must be equal to the price of a call struck at the same price (or yield). This rule of option valuation is referred to as *put-call parity*.

Exhibit 13: Yields, Prices, Option Values, and Probabilities at Final Period Nodes

Final Period Yield	Final Period Price	Option Value	Probability	Probability-Weighted Option Value
10.22%	75.90	0.00	0.02%	0.00
9.39%	79.99	0.00	0.29%	0.00
8.63%	84.01	0.00	1.61%	0.00
7.93%	87.93	0.00	5.37%	0.00
7.28%	91.75	0.00	12.08%	0.00
6.69%	95.44	0.00	19.34%	0.00
6.15%	99.01	0.00	22.56%	0.00
5.63%	102.59	2.59	19.34%	0.50
5.15%	106.01	6.01	12.08%	0.73
4.71%	109.27	9.27	5.37%	0.50
4.31%	112.36	12.36	1.61%	0.20
3.95%	115.29	15.29	0.29%	0.04
3.61%	118.06	18.06	0.02%	0.00
Sum			100.00%	1.97

Exhibit 14: Illustration of Put-Call Parity for Options Struck at Expected Prices

Final Period Yield	Final Period Price	98.90 Call Value	98.90 Put Value	Probability	Prob-Weighted Call Value	Prob-Weighted Put Value
10.22%	75.90	0.00	23.00	0.02%	0.00	0.01
9.39%	79.99	0.00	18.91	0.29%	0.00	0.06
8.63%	84.01	0.00	14.89	1.61%	0.00	0.24
7.93%	87.93	0.00	10.97	5.37%	0.00	0.59
7.28%	91.75	0.00	7.15	12.08%	0.00	0.86
6.69%	95.44	0.00	3.46	19.34%	0.00	0.67
6.15%	99.01	0.11	0.00	22.56%	0.03	0.00
5.63%	102.59	3.69	0.00	19.34%	0.71	0.00
5.15%	106.01	7.11	0.00	12.08%	0.86	0.00
4.71%	109.27	10.37	0.00	5.37%	0.56	0.00
4.31%	112.36	13.46	0.00	1.61%	0.22	0.00
3.95%	115.29	16.39	0.00	0.29%	0.05	0.00
3.61%	118.06	19.16	0.00	0.02%	0.00	0.00
Sum				100.00%	2.42	2.42

We illustrate how this works by using the same option on a 6.00% bond of 2010. We can see from Exhibit 13 that the expected price at expiration is approximately 99.0, or, more precisely 98.9.[4] Exhibit 14 presents the valuation of a put and a call both struck at 98.9, and shows that the values of the two options are equal. This means that the combination of a long call and a short put position where both options are struck at the expected price at expiration will have no net cost other than the bid-asked spread in the options market. But, as we note above, the combination of a long call and a short put position is the same economically as an irrevocable forward agreement to purchase the deliverable security at the expiration date of the options. If the expected price at expiration, the strike price at which put-call parity applies, is different from the fair forward price, there will be an opportunity to earn a riskless profit.

Suppose an investor could buy a call and sell a put struck at the fair forward price, and receive a net option premium (i.e., earn more on the put than paid for the call). If so, an investor could

1. Buy a call and sell a put struck at the expected price at expiration, thereby effectively selling the deliverable security for forward delivery but receive a net payment on the options transactions, and
2. Contract to sell the deliverable security at the fair forward price as of the expiration date, and
3. Thereby earn a riskless profit.

---

[4] The difference reflects the effect of rounding in the computations as well as the imprecision associated with a binomial tree of only 12 periods.

If the market price of the call struck at the fair forward is higher than the price of a put with the same strike, then the investor could buy a put, write a call, buy the bond forward, and, again, earn a sure profit: riskless arbitrage. Riskless arbitrage is not sustainable in efficient capital markets, so we should expect that put and call values will be equal when the strike price is equal to the fair forward price. For this reason, option valuation methods that set expected prices and yields at expiration equal to fair forward levels are referred to as *arbitrage-free* models.

THE ABCs OF OPTIONS TERMINOLOGY

Every field has its own professional jargon, and options dealing is no exception. In options analysis, the terms of art are generally letters of the Greek alphabet that have been assigned specific conventional meanings. Thus, financial professionals regularly refer to the *delta* (Δ), gamma (γ), *theta* (θ), and *vega* of an option.

Option Value and the Price of the Deliverable: Delta and Gamma

When the price of the deliverable security rises, the value of a call option on that security increases, while the value of a put declines. The impact of any given price change on the value of an option will vary depending on the degree to which the option is *in*, *at*, or *out of the money*. A call option is said to be *in the money* if the price of the deliverable bond is above the strike price of the option. A put option is said to be *out of the money* when the price of the deliverable is above the strike price. When the deliverable bond's price is equal to the strike price, both puts and calls are said to be *at the money*.

When financial professionals refer to the price of a deliverable security relative to the strike price of an option, they may be referring to the spot price at the time the conversation is taking place or the fair forward price as of the option's expiration date. It is best to ask for clarification if the distinction is relevant; that is, if the spot price is very different from the forward price.

In any event, the "right" way to think about whether an option is in, at, or out of the money is with reference to the *forward* price of the deliverable security. Suppose an investor buys a one-year call option on a 10-year bond struck at the spot price, and that shortly after the purchase date the spot price of the deliverable bond increases. Suppose at the same time that the yield curve steepens substantially so that the forward price of the deliverable as of the option's expiration date actually goes down. The holder of the option might see the change in the spot price of the deliverable bond and conclude that the call option is now in the money so that its market price should rise. But, all else held equal, the market value of the call option would drop because, relative to the expected value of the deliverable as of the expiration date, the option would now be out of the money.

If a call option is way in the money — i.e., if the spot price is substantially above the strike price so that it is highly unlikely that the option will not be exercised — the value of the option will reflect changes in the forward price of the deliverable security on a dollar-for-dollar basis. For example, consider a six-month call option on a 6.00% bond with an initial maturity of two years and a fair forward price as of expiration of 99.5, and suppose that the strike price of the option is 80.00. The fair forward yield at expiration is 6.355%, and for the option *not* to be exercised the yield at expiration would have to be above 22.43%! Although yields on two-year U.S. Treasury notes rose to levels nearly that high during the early 1980s, an increase of the required magnitude over such a short period of time would be absolutely unprecedented — and extremely unlikely.

Because it is essentially impossible for this option not to be exercised, the value of this call would be exactly equal to the present value of the difference between the strike price and the fair forward price. At a short-term interest rate of 5.00%, this would amount to 19.263% (= [99.50% − 80.00%]/1.05) of the par amount of the deliverable bond. If the fair forward price were to rise by 0.50% of par to 100.00, the value of the option will rise by the present value of 0.50% or 0.49%.

The *delta* of an option is defined as the change in the value of the option divided by the associated change in the value of the bond. In this case, the delta would be 0.98 (= 0.49%/0.50%) or very close to 1.00.

If an option is way out of the money, the delta will be close to zero. Suppose in the same example that the option is a put struck at 80 rather than a call. With a fair forward price of 99.50, it is highly unlikely that the put option will be exercised. The option has no value and will have no value, even if the fair forward price of the bond falls, by, say, a point or two or even by five points. Within broad limits, no matter how much the fair forward price of the bond changes, the value of the put option will not change, and the delta of the option is, therefore, 0.00.

In light of these illustrations of the extremes, it shouldn't be surprising that the delta of an at-the-money option — a put or a call for which the strike price is equal to the fair forward price — will be close to 0.50. In other words, the value of an at-the-money option will change by about half the amount by which the price of the deliverable bond changes. The more an option is in the money, the greater the delta, and vice versa.

The relationship between option delta and deliverable bond price is referred to as the option's *gamma*. As the option moves from way out of the money to way in the money, the delta of the option increases from 0.0 to 1.0. In this sense, the delta is a rough guide to the likelihood that the option will be exercised. So gamma measures the rate of change in this probability of exercise. To put it differently, gamma measures the degree of uncertainty as to whether the option will be exercised. Not surprisingly, therefore, gamma tends to peak when an option is at the money; the more an option is in or out of the money, the less the uncertainty about whether it will be exercised.

Theta and Option Time Value

Prior to expiration, the value of an option has two components: *intrinsic value* and *time value*. An option's intrinsic value is the amount, if any, by which the option is in the money. So, if the strike price of a call option is 95.00, and the spot and fair forward prices of the deliverable security are 97.00 and 95.50, respectively, we would say that the intrinsic value of this option is 2.00 points relative to the spot price and 0.50 points relative to the forward price. A put option on the same bond with the same 97.00 strike price would have no intrinsic value (an intrinsic value of zero).

At expiration, the total value of an option is exactly equal to its intrinsic value. Prior to expiration, the total value of a fixed-income option is never less than its intrinsic value.[5] The time value of an option is the difference between the option's total value and its intrinsic value.

We can make two broad generalizations about the time value of options. First, the time value depends on the amount by which the option is in the money. In our discussion of option delta, we cite two extreme examples of option valuation: calls or puts that are way in or way out of the money. In both these cases, the total value of the option is equal to its intrinsic value because there is no uncertainty about whether or not the option would be exercised. Neither of these options has any time value. In the same way, we can see that the entire value of an at-the-money option is time value. An at-the-money option has no intrinsic value — the strike price and the fair forward price of the deliverable security are equal — so any value the option has is time value.

These observations highlight the fact that the time value of an option reflects the optionholder's right to decide whether or not to exercise the option at expiration. If the option is at or out of the money — that is, if the option has no intrinsic value — the entire value of the option reflects the investor's ability to profit if the bond's price is higher than the fair forward price at expiration. If the option is in the money and has a positive intrinsic value, the full value of the option reflects the value of the protection the investor enjoys from unlimited losses if the bond's price falls below the strike price by the expiration date.

The second broad generalization is that, all else held equal, the time value of an option diminishes as the expiration date approaches. This is because the likelihood that the bond's price will rise above or fall below any given level diminishes as the amount of time left for the change to occur gets shorter. For example, consider again a 10-year 6.00% bond trading at par and a European call option on that bond struck at 105.00. Assume also that the annualized price volatility for 10-year bonds is 15 points.

Under these assumptions, the distribution of deliverable bond prices at the end of one month and at the end of one year is illustrated in Exhibit 15. There

---

[5] There are, in fact, some circumstances in which this will not be true for an option on a fixed-income security, but these cases are extremely rare. Such circumstances are slightly more common in the market for options on stocks.

is a 10% probability that the bond's price will be at or above 105 at the end of one month versus a 35% chance of closing above that level at the end of one year. This translates into a substantially higher option value for the option with the longer term to expiration. The expected value at expiration of a one-year 105 call on this bond is 3.32% of the par amount of the deliverable in comparison to 0.16% for the one-month 105 call.

The relationship between the value of an option and the amount of time remaining until expiration is referred to as the option's *theta*. The process by which the value of any given put or call tends to diminish as its expiration date approaches is referred to as the option's *time decay*.

Volatility, Vega, and Implied Volatility

We have said that options have value only to the extent that interest rates and bond prices are uncertain. The relationship between option value and volatility is referred to as the *vega* of an option. All else held equal, an increase in the level of volatility that we assume when valuing an option will increase the value of the option. We have already seen this illustrated in the simplest case of the one-period binomial tree.

In Exhibit 6 of this chapter we evaluate an option under two volatility scenarios. The call option conveys the right to purchase a bond at a price of 108. We assume in Exhibit 6 that the deliverable bond's price is subject to 10% volatility so that at expiration the bond would be worth either $90 or $110 with equal probabilities. Under these assumptions, the option's expected value at expiration is $1.00; its present value at the assumed level of short-term interest rates is $0.95. Assuming 20% price volatility, the market value of the bond at expiration would be either $80 or $120, and the value of the option would be $5.71.

Exhibit 15: Distribution of Hypothetical Bond Prices at the End of One Month and One Year

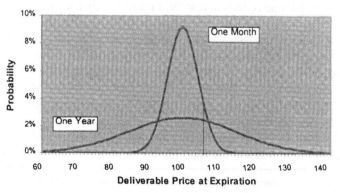

Exhibit 16: Computing Implied Volatility from an Option Price with an Option Valuation Model

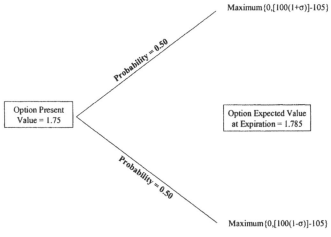

Maximum{0,[100(1+σ)]-105}

Probability = 0.50

Option Present
Value = 1.75

Option Expected Value
at Expiration = 1.785

Probability = 0.50

Maximum{0,[100(1-σ)]-105}

The vega of this option would be

Vega = Change in Option Value – Change in Volatility
     = (5.71 – 0.95)/(0.20 – 0.10)
     = 47.6

The vega of an option is always positive; the greater the volatility assumed in pricing the option, the greater the option premium.

In this simple example, we have calculated the value of an option based on an assumption about volatility. The calculation mechanism can, however, work both ways. In other words, if we know the market value of an option and the fair forward price of the deliverable security, we can use an option valuation model to compute the volatility level associated with the observed option premium.

Suppose a bond has both a spot and a forward price of par, and that the one-year discount rate is 4.00%. Assume further that we see a six-month 105 European call on the bond offered in the market at a price of $1.75. With this information and these assumptions, we can use a one-period binomial tree to compute the volatility level associated with the observed market price. In other words, we solve for σ in Exhibit 16.

Specifically, we know that the expected value of the option at expiration will be 1.785 (= 1.75 × [1.04]). We wish to find the volatility level such that the expected value of the option at expiration will be equal to 1.785. In this case, the periodic volatility level associated with a $1.75 premium for a six-month 105 call would be 8.6% for the six-month period or

12.1% (= 8.6% × $\sqrt{2}$)

annualized volatility.

Exhibit 17: Implied Annualized Yield Volatility of Three-Month Options on 10-Year U.S. Treasury Notes, July 1994–June 1999

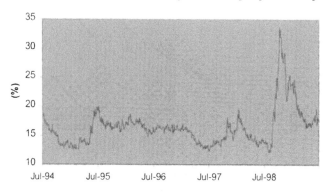

The volatility estimate derived in this way from an observed market premium is referred to as the option's *implied volatility*. Naturally the calculation of implied volatility would be much more complicated if our option valuation model were a multi-period binomial tree, but the logic of the process would be the same as in this very simple example.

Just as we use the concept of yield to compare bonds with different issuers, coupons, and/or maturities, financial professionals use the concept of implied volatility to compare options with different deliverables, strike prices, and expiration dates. And just as we speak of the level and term structure of interest rates, we also compare the level of implied volatility today with historical norms and measure the term structure of option pricing by comparing the implied volatilities of short- and long-dated options.

Exhibit 17 tracks the implied volatility of three-month options on 10-year U.S. Treasury notes from July 1994 through June 1999. While economists and market analysts attempt to understand the dynamics of interest rate changes over time, considerable effort goes into analyzing and predicting trends in implied volatility. Levels of implied volatility are affected by the recent history of realized (or historical) interest rate volatility. The spike in Exhibit 16 in the fall of 1998, for example, reflects the turmoil in financial markets that accompanied Russia's default on its domestic government debt.

Historical volatility is not the only influence on option pricing. Even in the midst of a period of stable interest rates, investors who feel highly uncertain about where interest rates will go in the future will be willing to pay relatively high prices for the protection afforded by options positions. At the same time, potential options *writers* who experience the same degree of uncertainty will be wary of selling puts and calls unless the premium is quite high. Strong demand and more tentative supply will translate into higher options premium and higher implied volatility. That is why the two lines in Exhibit 18 do not track each other precisely.

Exhibit 18: 20-Day Rolling Annualized Yield Volatility of 10-Year U.S. Treasury Notes and Implied Annualized Yield Volatility of Three-Month Options on 10-Year U.S. Treasury Notes, July 1994–June 1999

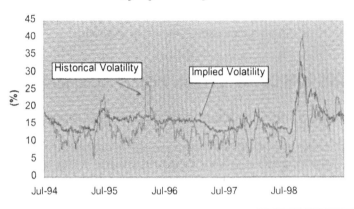

The implied volatility of options also varies depending on the option's structure. Sometimes the prices of very short-dated options will exhibit much higher implied annualized volatilities than long-dated options. This will occur, for example, when the general interest rate environment is stable within a narrow trading range (e.g., 50 bp), but a scheduled release of key economic statistics could cause bond prices to rise or fall by a point or more over a short period of time. One frequently sees noticeably higher (annualized) implied volatility for options expiring right after the release of U.S. monthly non-farm payroll employment numbers or the Japanese quarterly *Tankan* survey of business confidence than for options expiring a week after the release of these data.

Implied volatility can also vary across options on the same deliverable security with the same expiration date but with different strike prices. Specifically, we frequently see that options that are at the money are priced at somewhat lower implied volatilities than puts or calls that are way in or way out of the money. This phenomenon is referred to as the *volatility smile* because of its appearance on a graph of implied volatility versus strike price.

SUMMARY: COUNTERINTUITIVE CHANGES IN OPTION VALUES

We can summarize much of the discussion by mentioning some of the ways investors can be surprised by changes in option values. We have already noted that an increase in the spot price of the deliverable security will not necessarily lead to an increase in the fair market value of a call option if at the same time the yield curve steepens and the fair forward price goes down. Similarly, an increase in observed market volatility will not necessarily lead to an increase in the market value of options. For one thing, as we see in Exhibit 18, not all changes in actual market volatility lead to changes in the implied volatility of option pricing. Likewise, even if implied volatility does increase, an absolutely large theta may overwhelm vega — i.e., time decay may outweigh higher implied volatility — especially for an option with a short time left to expiration.

OPTIONS APPLICATIONS IN PORTFOLIO MANAGEMENT[6]

Options can play at least three important roles in a fixed-income portfolio:

1. *Enhancing investment income through option writing.* The most common type of transaction along these lines involves selling covered call options on securities the investor owns.

2. *Expressing views.* Fixed-income options provide a way for an investor to express views regarding the direction of interest rates, the degree of volatility of interest rates, or the relationship (spread) between different interest rates. Expressing views with options allows the investor to take a position with known and limited downside risk. Some market expectations cannot be expressed in practice without the use of options.

3. *Managing bond portfolio characteristics without buying or selling bonds.* Investors who have used options to reduce the risk of large single stock positions are familiar with the fact that managing portfolios in this way can be tax-efficient. Using options to manage portfolio risk can also economize on transaction costs.

Using Options to Earn the Premium
Writing Covered Calls
Covered call writing involves selling options on securities the investor holds in the portfolio. A simple example of a covered call position appears in Exhibit 19. The investor owns a five-year U.S. Treasury note on March 1, 1999, at which time the security has a spot price of 99-22 (99.6875). The investor is considering writing a one-year over-the-counter at-the-money (spot) European call option on this security. We assume that an option dealer's bid-side yield volatility for one-year at-the-money options on five-year Treasuries is 18.70%, which implies an option price of 1-08 (1.25% of the par amount). The investor will receive this

---

[6] Much of the material in this section also appears in Aaron S. Gurwitz, "Options on Fixed Income Securities: Applications for Private Clients, Part I," Goldman, Sachs & Co., March 1999, and Aaron S. Gurwitz, "Options on Fixed Income Securities: Applications for Private Clients, Part II," Goldman, Sachs & Co., July 1999.

option premium as an up-front payment, so the horizon total return will be augmented by the amount of the premium itself and earnings on this amount invested over the course of the year at, we assume, the short-term rate.

Because the investor owns the bond but has sold a call option against the position, the total return on the combined position over the life of the option will be greater than the total return on the bond itself *unless* the price of the bond increases above the strike price by more than the option premium. Thus, writing covered calls should be an attractive tactic for investors who do not expect interest rates to decline substantially.

Exhibit 19: One-Year At-the-Money (Spot) Covered European Call on a Five-Year U.S. Treasury Note

Term Sheet

Pricing Date	3/1/99
Deliverable Bond	
Issuer	U.S. Treasury
Coupon	4.75%
Maturity	2/15/04
Spot Price	99-22
Repo Rate	4.80%
Spot Yield	4.8211%
Forward Yield	4.8270%
Forward Price	99-23
Option	
Type	European Call
Expiration	3/15/00
Strike Price	99-22
Option Premium	01-08
Implied Yield Volatility	18.70%
Implied Price Volatility	3.93%

Payoff Diagram

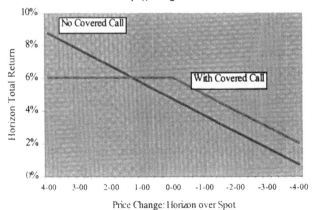

Price Change: Horizon over Spot

Writing Caps

An *interest rate cap* is an option contract that makes a periodic payment equal to the amount, if any, by which a floating interest rate index exceeds a specified level, multiplied by a *notional principal amount*. Suppose an investor owns an interest rate cap with characteristics as follows:

- Notional principal amount = $10 million
- Reset period = Quarterly
- Interest rate index = One-month US$ LIBOR
- Strike yield = 4.5%
- Term = Two years

Suppose that during the first quarter after the initiation of this contract, one-month US$ LIBOR averages 4.25%. If so, no payment would be due the holder of the cap. Then suppose that one-month US$ LIBOR averages 4.85% during the second quarter. For that period, the holder of the cap would receive a quarterly payment of $8,750 [= (4.85% − 4.50%) × $10,000,000/4].

This two-year quarterly cap contract is equivalent to a series of eight separate "caplets," each of which is a put option on a three-month investment struck at 4.50%. In fact, the analytical models that deal with caps (and floors and collars) on floating rates treat these contracts simply as the sum of the individual put options of which they are composed.

An investor who confidently expects to hold a substantial volume of short-term or floating-rate investments for a specified period is in a position to write a "covered cap" on that position. For example, assume a German investor fully expects to hold euro 10 million in highly liquid short-term assets for the next two years. At present, three-month EURIBOR is 3.125%.[7] Assume that the investor believes it is possible that core European interest rates will decline over time and very unlikely that they will rise. Under these assumptions, the investor might want to extend the average maturity of the euro 10 million, but suppose this is precluded by, say, a loan covenant or an established investment policy. An alternative in these circumstances is to write a two-year EURIBOR cap, as illustrated in Exhibit 20.

The investor who writes the cap in this example will owe the holder of the option the amount, if any, by which EURIBOR in any quarter exceeds 3.25% multiplied by euro 10 million divided by four. This obligation is "covered" in that the investor will be receiving EURIBOR multiplied by euro 10 million on a quarterly basis as a return on short-term investments. Therefore, absent any adverse credit event affecting the short-term investments, the funds will certainly be available to meet the cap writer's obligations. The covered short cap position has created an investment that will pay a higher yield than a standard floating-rate

---

[7] EURIBOR, the European interbank offered rate, is emerging as a standard short-term interest rate index for the European Economic and Monetary Union (EMU).

note unless EURIBOR rises above 3.53%. Above that level, market EURIBOR will exceed the combined value of the investor's maximum net yield on the cash investments after cap payments of 3.25% plus the periodic value of the cap premium (0.28%).

Using Options to Express Views

Investors who hold strong views regarding the direction of interest rates or the relationship between different bond yields will frequently find that options provide the best vehicle for expressing these opinions. Long options offer three distinct advantages in this regard: leverage, limited downside, and nearly unlimited flexibility in design. When option prices are high— that is, when implied volatility is high— investors may prefer other ways of expressing opinions. There are other ways to leverage fixed-income investments and to limit the downside potential of such positions.

Assume an investor believes that bond yields in the U.S. are likely to decline substantially over the next month and wishes to invest $500,000 in the position that will perform best if this view is correct. Suppose also that the investor's bond dealer permits 10-to-1 leverage of Treasury note positions through repurchase agreements. We compare the return on two investments: (1) purchase of a call option on the U.S. Treasury 5.25% of February 2029 with a $500,000 premium, and (2) purchase of $5 million market value of zero-coupon U.S. Treasury principal securities ("STRIPS") maturing in November 2027, financed through a repurchase agreement. We present the particulars of these two positions in Exhibit 21.

Exhibit 20: Writing a Cap on a Euro LIBOR Floater

Pricing Date	3/1/99
Index Terms	
Index	EURIBOR
Term	Quarterly
Reset Period	Quarterly
Current Yield	3.125%
Option	
Type	Quarterly Cap
Expiration	3/1/01
Strike Yield	3.25%
Notional Amount	Euro 10 million
Option Premium	0.48%
Implied Yield Volatility	25.0%
Combined Investment	
Cash Yield	EURIBOR
Implied Spread	28 bp
Maximum Net Yield	3.53%

Exhibit 21: A Call Option versus a Leveraged Purchase of STRIPS

Option		Zero	
Pricing Date	3/1/99	Pricing Date	3/1/99
Deliverable Bond		Bond	
Issuer	U.S.A.	Issuer	USA
Coupon	5.25%	Coupon	0
Maturity	2/15/29	Maturity	11/15/27
Spot Yield	5.69%	Spot Yield	0.05865
Repo Rate	4.42%	Repo Rate	4.42%
Forward Yield	5.70%	Spot Price	19.026
Spot Price	93.655	Cash Requirement	10%
Forward Price	93.560	Par Amount	26,279,928
Duration	14.40		
Option			
Type	Call		
Expiration	4/1/99		
Strike	93.6554		
Premium	1.428%		
Implied Yield Vol.	16.20%		
Implied Price Vol.	13.30%		
Par Amount	35,000,000		
Premium Paid	499,844		
Premium @ 24%	2.125%		
Par Amount	23,500,000		
Premium Paid	499,375		

Payoff Diagram

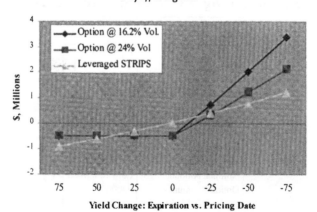

Yield Change: Expiration vs. Pricing Date

To analyze this situation, we compare the leveraged purchase of Treasury STRIPS with call options priced at two different levels. The lower premium, 1.428% of the par value of deliverable bonds, reflects market conditions as of March 5, 1999. At that time the implied volatility of one-month at-the-money options on 30-year Treasuries was 16.2%. The higher premium, 2.125%, reflects peak implied volatility levels of 24% experienced during the global market turmoil of late summer 1998.

The payoff diagram illustrates the general differences between options and leveraged long positions. First, the maximum loss on the options position is limited to the premium paid, while the maximum loss on a leveraged long position held until the horizon date is essentially unlimited. This difference should not be overemphasized, however, because an investor can establish an individual maximum loss simply by determining that the long position will be liquidated as soon as mark-to-market losses reach a predetermined level. Of course, it may not be possible to unwind a position at exactly the specified level, but in a market as liquid as the Treasury market, the extent of such "liquidation errors" will probably be small. Further, if interest rates rise above the leveraged investor's "stop loss" level, so that the position is unwound at the maximum loss, but bond yields subsequently fall to a level at which the trade is profitable, the optionholder would realize a profit while the leveraged investor would be left with a loss.

More important, the leveraged long position performs better if interest rate moves are relatively small, while the option outperforms if realized interest rate volatility exceeds the level implicit in the option's pricing. In choosing between the option and the leveraged long position, the bullish investor must decide whether to establish a leveraged long position in anticipation of a relatively modest move in the expected direction or to buy a call option in expectation of a more substantial move. In this context, the pricing of the option becomes important.

In this example, the less expensive option will perform better than the leveraged STRIPS position if yields decline by more than about 12.5 basis points. A 25 bp move would be required for the more expensive option to do better than the leveraged long position.

Using Options to Manage Portfolio Risk

When an investor wishes to change the risk characteristics of a bond portfolio — to lengthen or shorten duration, to change the yield curve exposure, or to modify call risk — the most efficient way is usually simply to sell the bonds that no longer fit and replace them with different securities. In a frictionless and tax-free world with no transaction costs and where all bonds are readily available at all times, such straightforward transactions would almost always make sense.

The real world does not accommodate us, however. Cash transactions are not costless, particularly if the sale of a security involves the realization of a taxable gain. And not all types of bonds are readily available in all maturities at all times. So an investor who likes the AT&T credit but wishes to reduce portfolio duration may find it difficult to sell 30-year AT&T bonds and replace them with five-year obligations of the same issuer. In the real world of taxes and market imperfections, the use of derivatives in general and options in particular is frequently the best way to accomplish a particular portfolio management goal.

Using options to manage the risk of — or hedge — real-world portfolios of corporate or municipal bonds, while potentially quite effective, can become quite complicated. When this type of hedging is called for, a family portfolio manager should work closely with a competent fixed-income specialist.

A somewhat oversimplified example will illustrate how options can be used to change the return characteristics of a bond position. Suppose an investor owns $10 million face amount of the U.S. Treasury 4.75% of November 15, 2008, priced at 91.27 to yield 5.98%, and decides that interest rates are substantially more likely to rise than to decline in the near term, but, in any case, to be quite volatile. The way to express this outlook would be to purchase, say, a three-month at-the-money put on the investor's bond position. At 15% yield volatility, such an option would cost about 1.5 points or $200,000.

Exhibit 22 depicts the total return on the combined bond and put position over the three-month life of the option as a function of the bond's yield on the expiration date. The exhibit compares three alternative strategies: (1) holding the 2008 bond on an unhedged basis, (2) holding the bond and buying an at-the-money put, and (3) selling the bond and investing in a three-month Treasury bill.

The three alternatives produce very different return profiles. The Treasury bill produces the best result if rates rise, and the long position performs best if the bond market rallies. The hedged strategy is never the best performer, but will do better than the bill if rates decline by more than about 25 basis points and better than the unhedged bond position if rates rise by more than the same amount. Given expectations, the investor might reasonably conclude that the hedged (bond plus put) position is the best alternative.

Exhibit 22: Returns on Three Investment Strategies as a Function of Bond Yield at the End of Three Months

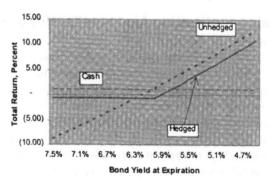

This example illustrates the simplest possible use of options to manage the risk of a bond position. The investor has a very specific point of view and could make use of a hedge vehicle — a put on the bond he happens to own — that is perfectly matched with the investment. While such situations may arise from time to time, most investors find themselves in much more complex situations. Their feelings about the market outlook are much less defined, and none of the available financial contracts provide a perfect hedge. At these times, highly qual-ified assistance should come in handy.

CHAPTER 17

Evaluating Bonds with Embedded Options

A t various places in this text we have had occasion to discuss callable bonds. In Chapter 2 we note that bond issuers frequently retain the right to redeem, or "call," bonds before their maturity date. The same chapter introduces the concepts of yield to call and yield to worst and advises investors to seek clarity with respect to which yield is being quoted in any given situation. Chapter 5 focuses on differences in the price performance of callable and non-callable bonds as interest rates change and introduces the concept of bond and portfolio convexity.

Part of Chapter 7 deals with the fundamental dilemma that callable bonds present to investors. All other characteristics held equal, callable bonds typically offer higher yields than non-callable bonds. If interest rates are volatile over the investment horizon, however, a portfolio with a large percentage of callable bonds will underperform a more convex portfolio consisting entirely of non-callable securities. Chapters 8 and 9 note that callable securities are much more common in the U.S. bond market than in Europe. Finally, the examples of portfolio construction and management presented in Chapter 13 show how callable bonds can complicate the process of monitoring and managing portfolio duration.

All the discussions of callable bonds to this point have, of necessity, been somewhat imprecise. We know that callable bonds generally offer higher yields than otherwise comparable non-callable securities. We know that an investor must judge whether the additional yield is sufficient compensation for the disadvantages of callable bonds. We also know that the presence of callable bonds in a portfolio creates some uncertainty as to how the market value of the portfolio will change as interest rates vary. We have not so far addressed ways of judging how much additional yield provides sufficient compensation for any given set of call provisions. Further, we have no precise way of knowing exactly what kind of non-callable bond is "otherwise comparable" with any given callable bond. Finally, we have no convenient measure of the duration of a portfolio that includes callable bonds.

Now that we have introduced the basic concepts of fixed-income option valuation, we have the tools needed to develop a more precise understanding of the investment characteristics of callable bonds and their effect on portfolio performance. Family investors will be able to build and manage perfectly adequate bond portfolios without making use of these concepts. Reasonable judgment as to whether any given yield pickup compensates an investor sufficiently for any given call provision will not lead investors too far astray, provided the portfolio is not overloaded with too many callable bonds. Similarly, few family portfolio managers require highly precise estimates of their portfolio's duration; a "high" and "low" estimate of duration, where the difference between the two depends on whether bonds are called or not, will be sufficient in most cases.

Family portfolio managers who understand the concepts discussed in this chapter will be prepared to make more effective use of callable securities in their portfolios and should, over time, produce better investment results and experience fewer surprises.

VARIETIES OF EMBEDDED OPTIONS

Callable bonds are not the only type of fixed-income security with an embedded option, although they are by far the most common variety. A smaller, but significant, proportion of bonds are "putable," in that they are issued with embedded put options. In addition to these basic types, there are an endless variety of securities incorporating more complex combinations of puts and calls.

Callable Bonds

The structure of a callable bond is detailed in the prospectus or official statement for the issue. Call provisions will typically include the first call date, the first call price, and a schedule of subsequent call prices and dates. Occasionally the bond will be subject to "one-time call," but more often the issuer will have the right to call the bond periodically after the first call date. Exercise of calls tends to be limited to interest payment dates after the first call date.

Traditionally, the first call price has included a premium over the par value of the bond, and many municipal bonds are still callable at, for example, 102% of par. If there is a premium on the initial call price, it will usually decline in steps on each subsequent call date until the call price reaches par. The call price of zero-coupon bonds will be expressed as a percentage of the bond's compound accreted value.[1]

---

[1] For example, suppose a zero-coupon bond maturing on January 1, 2010, is initially issued on January 1, 2000, and priced at 55.368 to yield 6.00%. Suppose further that this bond is callable starting on January 1, 2005, at a price equal to 102% of the compound accreted value (CAV). The CAV of the bond on the first call date would be 74.409 (the price at a yield of 6.00% of a zero-coupon bond maturing on January 1, 2010, as of January 1, 2005), and the call price would be 77.386 (= 1.02 × 74.409).

The typical option embedded in a callable corporate or municipal bond can be described as a European option that becomes an American option after the first call date with a strike price that declines for a period of time and then remains constant until the bond matures and the option expires.[2] The conceptual framework for analysis of this type of option is the same as that for a simple one-time call, but, as a practical matter, the analysis of the options embedded in callable bonds is a much more complex computational undertaking.

Putable Bonds

Bonds with embedded put options are much less common than callable bonds, but they do exist, and they can be an attractive addition to a well-managed fixed-income portfolio. A putable bond is usually a relatively long-term security that grants the investor the right to sell, or "put," the bond back to the issuer at some point during the life of the instrument.[3] Most such puts are straightforward, one-time European options. For example, a corporation might issue a bond with a 20-year final maturity and a 6.50% coupon, and grant investors the right to put the bond back to the issuer on the fifth anniversary of the bond's dated date. A rational investor will exercise this right on the put date if, at that time, yields on the issuer's 15-year obligations are higher than 6.50%. In other words, the put will be exercised if a non-putable 15-year bond of the issuer with a 6.50% coupon would be trading at a discount.

In the case of a callable bond, the investor is short the call option and is entitled to receive a higher yield than on an "otherwise comparable" non-callable bond. Investors who purchase put bonds are long the embedded option — the investor has the right but not the obligation to sell the security back to the issuer at the strike price — and must expect to pay a premium for this right. The premium for the embedded put is paid through a lower yield on a putable bond than on an otherwise comparable non-putable security.

---

[2] Options that allow the issuer to exercise on specific dates, but not continuously, are referred to as Bermuda options. Many embedded calls allow exercise only on interest payment dates after the period of call protection has ended. It is most correct to refer to such structures as European calls converting to Bermuda calls.

[3] Securities structured in this way are frequently referred to as "put bonds." Using this term may create some confusion between the "putable" fixed-rate *corporate* bonds under examination here and a common type of security in the U.S. tax-exempt municipal bond market that may also be referred to as a "put bond." Municipal put bonds are variable-rate securities with an interest rate that resets periodically, usually every seven days. Indenture provisions grant the investor who holds the security the right to put the bond back to the issuer at a price of par on any interest rate reset date. This type of put option assures the investor who holds these securities liquidity on a weekly basis, and guarantees that the interest rate will be reset at an appropriate market level so that few securities will be put and those that are will find ready buyers at a price of par. Municipal "put bonds" are also referred to as "variable-rate demand notes" or "VRDNs." In effect, from the investor's point of view, each put date is a maturity date. It is safe to assume that if the "put bond" in question is a corporate bond, then it is the kind of "putable security" under analysis in this chapter. If the security is a municipal bond, then it is almost certainly a variable-rate demand note.

Other Types of Embedded Options

Callable and putable bonds are the standard option structures, but the variations on these two themes that have appeared on the market seem to be endless. One common elaboration is a bond that is both callable and putable. For example, a bond with a 30-year final maturity might grant the investor the option to put the bond back to the issuer at par on one occasion five years after the security's dated date and provide the issuer with the option to call the bond on the tenth anniversary of issuance and at any time thereafter.

FLOATING-RATE NOTES WITH EMBEDDED OPTIONS

Most of the discussion in this chapter focuses on the valuation of options embedded in fixed-rate bonds, although floating-rate notes may also incorporate embedded option structures. Chapter 16 analyzes an interest rate cap as a portfolio of call options. Such caps are frequently embedded in floating-rate notes. So a particular FRN might have a 5-year final maturity and pay a semiannual coupon equal to LIBOR + 50 bp *or* 7.50%, whichever is less. Purchase of such an instrument can be decomposed into buying a straight floating-rate note and writing a LIBOR cap with a strike yield of 7.00%. The investor who has purchased such a floater must be compensated for writing the cap. Compensation is paid in the form of a wider spread over LIBOR for the floating-rate formula than the same issuer would pay on an uncapped FRN with the same maturity. So, in this example, the issuer of the capped floater paying LIBOR + 50 bp might issue an uncapped 5-year FRN with a coupon of LIBOR + 25 bp.

FRNs may also incorporate "floors." The issuer might sell a 5-year floater that pays a coupon of LIBOR flat or 6.00%, whichever is greater. An investor who purchases an FRN subject to a floor has, in effect, purchased a combination of a straight floating-rate note and a portfolio of put options.

STRUCTURED NOTES

Whether or not a call or put embedded in a fixed-rate bond will be exercised depends on the market value of the bond in question. If the market value is above the strike price, the issuer will likely exercise a call; if the market price of the bond is below par, an investor who holds a putable security will likely exercise the option. The "exercise" of caps and floors embedded in FRNs is automatic — it is incorporated in the trustee's computation of the periodic interest rate payment due — and depends solely on the interest rate index and the particular bond's coupon formula. Issuers, however, can and do embed puts and calls in bonds where the option payoff has nothing at all to do with the security in question. Such instruments are referred to as "structured notes," and the variety of such securities is endless.

Exhibit 1: Hypothetical Bonds of a Single Issuer

Bond	A	B	C	D	E
Maturity	1-Jan-05	1-Jan-10	1-Jan-20	1-Jan-10	1-Jan-20
Coupon	6.000%	6.500%	6.750%	6.375%	6.000%
First Call Date	N.A.	N.A.	N.A.	1-Jan-05	N.A.
First Call Price	N.A.	N.A.	N.A.	100.00	N.A.
Put Date	N.A.	N.A.	N.A.	N.A.	1-Jan-05
Put Price	N.A.	N.A.	N.A.	N.A.	100.00
Market Price	100.00	100.00	100.00	?	?
Yield	6.000%	6.500%	6.750%	?	?
Yield Measure	Maturity	Maturity	Maturity	?	?
Spread	25 bp	30 bp	55 bp	?	?
Treasury Benchmark	5-Year	10-Year	10-Year	?	?
Modified Duration	4.3	7.3	10.9	?	?

For example, an issuer might offer a 1-year zero-coupon note in which the payment the investor receives at maturity depends entirely on the level of the S&P 500 stock index on a specified determination date. Or, the payoff may be keyed to a currency exchange rate or an interest rate that may have nothing to do with the market value of the bond in question. For example, the payoff on a U.S. dollar-denominated 2-year structured note may be keyed to the average level of 10-year Japanese government bond yields over the life of the security.

Valuation of structured notes is beyond the scope of this chapter, but the options embedded in these securities can usually be analyzed using the tools presented in Chapter 16.

THE VALUATION OF BONDS WITH EMBEDDED OPTIONS

Consider the hypothetical bonds of a single issuer listed in Exhibit 1.

To value bonds with embedded options, we need to fill in the question marks in Exhibit 1. We want to find the prices for bonds D and E — the callable and putable issues — that are consistent with the information we have about the option-free "bullet" bonds of this issuer. We also want to know how the purchase of bonds D and E might affect the performance of a bond portfolio, so we need a reasonable estimate of the duration and convexity of the bonds with embedded options.

We have already presented one rough-and-ready approach to answering these questions. We know that the callable bond will perform like the '05 non-callable issue if interest rates decline and like the '10 non-callable if interest rates rise. Since rates might go either up or down, the right yield on the security should lie somewhere between the yields on the two bonds. Because 6.375% is closer to the yield on the 10-year bullet than on the straight 5-year issue, the bond seems like a reasonable purchase at a price of par. Further, as in Chapter 13, we can assume that the duration of the callable bond will lie somewhere between that of the 5-year and the 10-year. So we won't go too far wrong if we assume that the duration of the callable issue will probably lie somewhere in the 5-year to 6-year range and peg 5.5 years as a reasonable estimate.

We can go through a similar exercise with the putable bond and assume that its yield should be somewhat less than that of the 5-year. The put bond position can be thought of as holding a 5-year bond but having the right to exchange it for a 15-year issue on the put date. An investor might reasonably conclude that giving up 25 bp of yield relative to the straight 5-year bond is an attractive trade-off so that buying the putable bond at par is a good idea. An investor might also "guesstimate" that the duration of this put bond is somewhere between that of a 5-year and a 20-year security. It would not be a huge mistake to assume that, on average, adding this bond to a portfolio will have the same effect on overall duration as adding a non-callable issue maturing in 2010.

This kind of thinking will not lead an investor very far astray. As we have said, one can build and manage a fixed-income portfolio quite adequately without doing any more "embedded option valuation" than this. Indeed, until about 15 years ago such ballpark analysis was the only approach available to portfolio managers to help evaluate callable issues.

Still, these are rough estimates. To be sure, the yield on the Bond D issue should lie somewhere between those of Bonds A and B. But a 50 basis point yield difference is a very wide range; a yield differential of that magnitude translates into about a 5% difference in bond prices. Paying five points too much for a bond counts as a pretty serious mistake in fixed-income management. Even if we can use our seat-of-the-pants estimation method to narrow the issue down somewhat, an investor using crude valuation techniques will still be vulnerable to paying 1% or 2% too much for a bond or missing out on an opportunity to pick up an undervalued security.

VALUING BONDS WITH EMBEDDED OPTIONS — USING MATHEMATICAL MODELS

Going beyond rules of thumb in the valuation of callable bonds requires the use of option valuation models. Investment dealers began developing such models in the mid-1980s when increases in the speed and power of computers made it possible to meet the demand for more rigorous valuation techniques from institutional money managers. At first the valuation models tended to be proprietary; each major firm had its own unique approach to embedded option valuation, and a great deal of energy was devoted to figuring out why one dealer's model concluded that a particular callable bond was "cheap" at its market price while another dealer's model pegged the same bond at the same price as "overvalued." By the late 1990s, the techniques of embedded option valuation had become standardized so that disagreements about the value of typical embedded option structures have become rare.

Embedded option valuation models currently in use all work in roughly the same way. The inputs to the calculation include (1) the characteristics of the bond being evaluated including its maturity, coupon, issuer, and call or put schedule, and (2) the benchmark yield curve for the currency in which the bond is denominated. Given these inputs, the model calculates one of three measures of the bond's value. These include:

1. The price of the bond.
2. The interest rate volatility level used to value the embedded options.
3. The bond's option-adjusted spread.

Besides these three basic outputs, valuation models can also report the value of the embedded option, the bond's option-adjusted duration, and the bond's option-adjusted convexity.

Option Adjustment

The goal of the valuation process is to decompose the value of a bond with an embedded option into two components: (1) the value of the embedded option, and (2) the value of the hypothetical "host bond" in which the option is embedded. Take, for example, Bond D in Exhibit 1. Suppose this bond has a market price of 98.00 so that its yield to the 2010 maturity is 6.652%. In Exhibit 1 Bond B yields 6.50%, which is 30 bp more than the 2010 benchmark, so the yield on the benchmark bond maturing in 2010 is 6.20%. At 6.652%, Bond D would be trading at a spread of 45.2 basis points over the 10-year benchmark. The key valuation question, therefore, is whether the additional 15.2 basis points the investor earns on the callable bond provides sufficient compensation for the call option.

Now suppose that we apply our valuation model and conclude that the value of the call option embedded in this hypothetical bond is 2.5% of the bond's par value. If so, we can say that the investor has implicitly purchased a non-callable bond from the issuer and sold a call option back to the issuer. If the investor had not sold a call option on the bond, the all-in purchase price of the non-callable bond would, therefore, have been 100.50 (= 98.00 + 2.50). At a purchase price of 100.50, the yield to maturity of a 10-year bond with a coupon of 6.375% would be 6.307%. At this price, the yield spread over the 10-year benchmark would be 10.7 basis points. This figure — the yield spread of the theoretical non-callable "host" bond — is referred to as the bond's *option-adjusted spread*.

In this example, the option-adjusted spread of Bond D — assuming the callable bond is priced at 98.00 and the value of the embedded option is 2.50 points — is narrower (tighter) than the spread on a non-callable bond with the same maturity, we would say that the callable bond is expensive. Its yield to maturity is higher than that of the non-callable bond, but not enough higher to compensate the investor fully for both the credit risk on the bond and the value of the call option.

Next assume that market participants wake up to the fact that a price of 98.00 is too high for this callable bond, and the price falls to 96.974. At this level, the value of the callable bond plus the value of the call option equals 99.474, and at that price the yield to maturity of the non-callable "host" bond is 6.50% and its spread is 30 bp over the 10-year benchmark. In other words, at a price of 96.974, the price of the callable bond is consistent with the price of the same issuer's non-callable obligation. At this price, the yield to maturity of the bond would be 6.797%.

A dealer offering this bond to an investor at this price might quote the yield as 6.797% to maturity because the bond's price is below the call price. At that yield, the bond's yield spread over the 10-year benchmark bond would be about 60 basis points. The dealer should also indicate that the option-adjusted spread on the bond is 30 bp.

Now suppose interest rates instantaneously rise by 100 basis points across all maturities. If this happens, it becomes unlikely that the bond will be called; the option loses almost all of its value; and it will make sense to evaluate the 6.375% of 2010 as if it were a non-callable bond. The price of a non-callable 6.375% of 2010 as of January 1, 2000, at a yield of 7.50% would be 92.183. So if interest rates rise by 100 basis points, the price of this bond will decline by about 4.79 points (= 96.974 − 92.183).

What, then, would happen to the bond's price if interest rates decline by 100 basis points instantaneously, across the board? At this point it becomes highly likely that the bond will be called, and the market will be pricing the bond as if it were a non-callable issue with a maturity of 2005. If the yield curve shifts downward by 100 basis points across the board, the yield on bonds maturing in 2005 will be 5.00%. The price of a 6.375% bond maturing in 2005 and yielding 5.50% as of January 1, 2000, would be 106.017. So if interest rates decline by 100 basis points instantaneously, the price of this bond would increase by 9.04 points.

If we take the average of these two price changes and express the result as a percentage of the bond's initial price, we find that the average percentage price change for a 100 basis point change in interest rates would be 7.13% (= [4.79 + 9.04]/[96.974 × 2]). Now recall that this is the definition of the modified duration of a bond. Modified duration calculated in a way that takes into account the fact that the bond has an embedded option is referred to as *option-adjusted duration*. Note that the option-adjusted duration of the callable bond is somewhat shorter than the duration of the non-callable 10-year bond (7.13 versus 7.30 in this example). This reflects the possibility that the bond will not remain outstanding for 10 years but will be called before maturity. In this particular example, however, the option-adjusted duration is substantially greater than the average of the durations of a 10-year and a 5-year bond. An investor who uses a rough estimation method such as simply averaging duration to maturity and duration to call would underestimate the potential price volatility of this security.

This computational process can be carried a step farther. Now we calculate the duration of Bond D after interest rates have declined by 100 basis points so that Bond D is now yielding 5.00% to its first call date. Again, after this change in rates, it becomes likely that the bond will be called, so duration to the '05 call will be a reasonably accurate measure of how this much this bond's price will change if its yield to call changes by small amounts around 5.00%. The duration as of 1/1/2000 of a bond with a 6.375% coupon yielding 5.00% to a 1/1/2005 "maturity" is 4.27 years. The duration of the same bond yielding 7.50% to its 2010 maturity would be 7.16 years. Now recall that the option-adjusted duration of the bond at its initial yield to maturity of 6.797% is 7.13 years.

Exhibit 2 compares the effects of interest rate changes on the duration of Bonds B (6.50% of 2010, NCL) and D (6.375% of 2010/2005).

The convexity statistic measures the change in duration as the bond's price increases. The non-callable bond exhibits a small positive convexity; each increment of price increase raises duration slightly. As the callable bond's price increases from 92.183 to 96.974, its option-adjusted duration decreases slightly from 7.16 to 7.13, a 0.4% decrease. Then as the price rises from 96.974 to 106.017, the bond's option-adjusted duration declines by 40%. The average of these two percentage changes gives the bond's option-adjusted convexity at the initial price of −0.20. The callable bond's convexity is "negative." And because our calculation of convexity takes into account the fact that the bond is callable, we can refer to −0.20 as the bond's option-adjusted convexity.

Computing Option Value

We have assumed so far that we know the embedded option is worth 2.5% of the bond's par value. How can we draw such a conclusion?

The computational process of option valuation can become very complicated, particularly when dealing with long-term bonds, combinations of puts and calls, and variable strike prices. The basic framework for evaluating embedded options and computing option-adjusted spreads and durations, however, is a straightforward extension of the models introduced in Chapter 16.

To illustrate how these valuation models work, we explore the simplest possible case of a callable bond: a 2-year zero-coupon government bond that is callable at the end of one year. Specifically, suppose we know that the yield on a 1-year zero-coupon government bond today is 6.00%, and the yield on a non-callable 1-year government zero one year forward is 6.125%. Under these assumptions, the price of a non-callable 2-year zero would be 88.90 (= $100/\{[1.06] \times [1.06125]\}$). At this price, the yield on a 2-year zero-coupon bond would be 6.063% because

$$88.90 = 100/1.063^2$$

Exhibit 2: Duration of Two Hypothetical Bonds at Different Interest Rate Levels

Statistic	Duration	
Bond	B	D
Post Rally Level	7.13	7.16
Initial Level	7.27	7.13
Post Sell-Off Level	7.41	4.27
Convexity	0.02	−0.02

Exhibit 3: Binomial Tree of Yields on One-Year Zero-Coupon Government Bonds

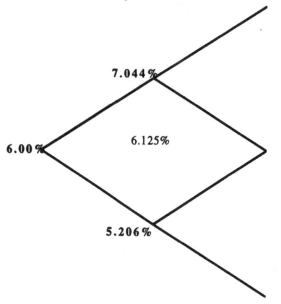

At this yield, the accreted value of the bond at the end of the first year would be 94.284 (= 88.90 × 1.063).

Now suppose the bond is callable at the end of the first year at a price of 94.5; that is, at a call price of 100.229% of compound accreted value. We know from Chapter 16 that, in order to analyze an option, we have to assume some degree of interest rate volatility and decide on some way of modeling the process by which interest rates change over time. Let us assume that annualized volatility of yields on 1-year zero-coupon bonds is 15% and use a two-period binomial tree as our model of the interest rate fluctuations.

A two-period binomial tree based on these assumptions is represented in Exhibit 3. In this particular application of the binomial tree model, interest rates at the end of the second period are irrelevant because at that point the bond under analysis will have matured. Now we can use the interest rates on this tree to calculate the market value of a non-callable zero-coupon bond under examination at each node of the tree with the results as illustrated in Exhibit 4.

As the numbers in the exhibit indicate, if interest rates decline over the first period and the market yield on the bond is now 5.206%, the bond's price will be 95.051, above the strike price of the call. We can therefore assume that the issuer will likely sell a new zero-coupon bond at a price of 95.051, use 94.500 of the proceeds to redeem to old bond, and earn a profit of 0.501% of par net of transaction costs. If so, the values of the bond from the investor's point of view will be as depicted in Exhibit 5 rather than Exhibit 4.

Exhibit 4: Bond Prices Implied by Yields in Exhibit 3

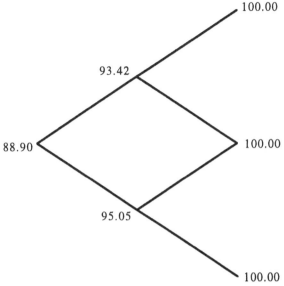

Exhibit 5: Binomial Tree of Prices of a Bond Callable in One Year at 94.50

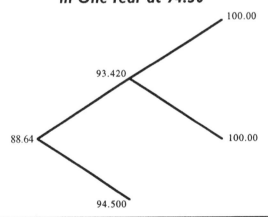

The non-callable security will be worth either 93.42 or 95.05 in one year's time. The expected value, therefore, is 94.24 (= [93.42 + 95.05]/2). The present value of this amount, discounted at the 1-year zero-coupon rate of 6.00%, is 88.90, the value of the instrument at the beginning of the first period.

At the end of period 1, the callable security will be worth either 93.42 or 94.50; its expected value will be 93.96; and the present value of this amount discounted to the beginning of the first period will be 88.64. So, at the beginning of the first period the non-callable bond is worth 88.90, and the callable bond is worth 88.64, or 0.26 points less. As the only difference between these two hypothetical securities is the embedded call, the value of that option must be worth 0.26% of the par value of the bond.

In practice, the computer models developed by dealers and data vendors are much more complex than this simple two-period example. But the basic analytical framework — comparing the value of the callable bond under examination and a hypothetical non-callable issue — is common to all the embedded option valuation techniques in use today.

The same framework can be used to analyze putable bonds. Suppose that instead of being callable at 94.5 at the end of the first period, the two-period zero is putable at a price of 94.00. Under these assumptions, the binomial tree would appear as illustrated in Exhibit 6. In this case, the expected value of the bond at the end of the first period is 94.53 (= [94.00 + 95.05]/2), with a present value of 89.176. This is 0.276 points higher than the price of the bond with no embedded options, so we can conclude that the value of the embedded 94 put is 0.28% of the par value of the bond.

Estimating the Option-Adjusted Spread

Now suppose the bond under examination is not a government bond but a corporate zero-coupon issue. If we knew the yields on coupon-paying or zero-coupon bonds of this issuer across all relevant maturities, we could adopt the method we have just used to evaluate the option value. As a practical matter, however, few corporate issuers have obligations outstanding all across the yield curve. Most embedded option valuation models therefore use information about the benchmark government yield curve in combination with information about the callable bond under examination to derive separate estimates of the value of the embedded option and the implied pricing of the hypothetical non-callable bond in which the option is embedded.

Exhibit 6: Binomial Tree of Prices of a Bond Putable in One Year at 94.00

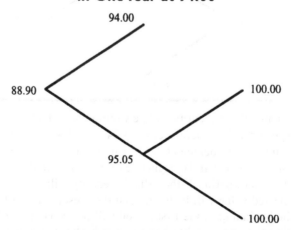

Exhibit 7: Binomial Tree for Calculating the Option-Adjusted Spread on a Callable Corporate Zero-Coupon Bond

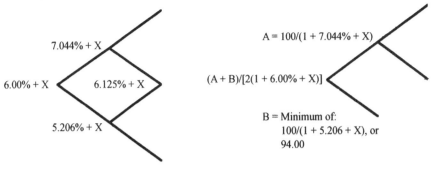

An extension of the example will illustrate how this process works. Suppose that spot and 1-year forward yields on 1-year zero-coupon government bonds are still 6.00% and 6.125%, respectively, and that interest rate volatility is still 15%. Consider a 2-year corporate zero callable at the end of one year at a price of 94.00, and assume that the market price of this bond is 87.50. Under the two-period binomial tree model, we assume that the market price is the discounted expected value of the bond in one year, and that the market yield on this bond in one year will be at one of two possible levels. Given the volatility estimate of 15% and the spot and forward 1-year zero-coupon government yields, we know the two possible levels of government bond yields at the end of one year, but we do not know what the yields on this particular corporate bond might be.

We can answer this question by making one additional assumption about the relationship between corporate bond yields and government bond yields. Most embedded option valuation models assume constant credit spreads; that is, that the yield spread between any given non-government bond and its "matching" government bond is the same for all bond maturities and durations.[4] Under this assumption, the job of the option valuation model is to find the number of basis points, X, so that the pair of binomial trees in Exhibit 7 produces an expected present value of 87.50.

Once the problem is set up this way, the job of the computational model is to find X so that

$$87.50 = (A + B)/[2(1 + 6.00\% + X)]$$

In this simplest of examples, we can solve for X algebraically. In more realistic situations, the computational process will be one of trial and error. In any case,

---

[4] Some options models make the more realistic assumption that credit spreads increase with maturity. In order to specify such models completely, we must make some assumption about the term structure of credit spreads. Provided these additional assumptions are a good description of reality, these more general models will produce better results. Standard practice in the financial services industry today is to assume constant credit spreads across maturities.

the solution in this case is X = 0.735% = 73.5 basis points. One can characterize this solution by saying that the option-adjusted spread (OAS) on the 2-year, non-call 1-year, zero-coupon bond of this issuer priced at 87.50 is 73.5 basis points. One might also observe that the nominal yield to maturity of this bond priced at 87.50 is 6.90% or 84 bp over the 6.06% yield on a non-callable 2-year government zero-coupon bond. The 84 basis point figure includes 10.5 basis points compensation for the call option the investor has implicitly sold to the issuer. The relevant figure is the OAS.

The model can also be used to calculate the value of the embedded option. We know that the credit spread on this bond is 73.5 basis points. So, a consistently priced non-callable zero-coupon bond of this issuer would yield 6.795% (= 0.735% + 6.06%). This yield would produce a price of 87.68. If we compare this price with the 87.50 price of the callable bond, we find that the value of the embedded call option is 0.18% of the security's par value.

Although we have illustrated the use of the model to compute the bond's OAS, given its price, the computation can also be run in reverse. Suppose we know from other sources of information that the appropriate credit spread for this issuer is 95 basis points rather than 73.5. If so, we can plug the appropriate discount rates into the binomial tree illustrated in Exhibit 7, and find that 87.298 is the price that is consistent with an OAS of 95 bp.

Using the Model to Calculate OAD and OAC

We can also use embedded option valuation models to estimate the option-adjusted duration (OAD) and convexity (OAC) of callable bonds. Specifically, consider the impact of instantaneous 100 basis point shifts in interest rates. Suppose that the change in market yield levels has no effect on the level of interest rate volatility, which remains at 15%, or on the issuer's credit spread, which we assume remains at 95 basis points. Exhibit 8 illustrates the effect of such interest rate shifts on the binomial tree.

The model allows us to calculate the prices for the bond after 100 bp changes in interest rates assuming constant OAS and 15% annualized yield volatility. A 100 bp decrease in yields results in a 0.628% (= [88.592 − 87.30]/87.298) price increase relative to the initial price for the bond at a 90 bp OAS. A 100 bp yield increase is associated with a 2.54% price decrease from 87.298 to 85.802. On average, this comes to a 1.58% change for a 100 basis point change in interest rates, so the model would report 1.58 as the option-adjusted duration of this security.

We will not carry this methodology further to calculate the option-adjusted convexity of the bond. Such a computation would parallel what we have already done, and would involve calculating the effect of small interest rate changes around the higher and lower yields illustrated in Exhibit 8. Suffice it to say that this bond is highly negatively convex: the bond's downside, given a 100 basis point interest rate increase, is much greater than its price improvement if rates decline by the same amount.

Exhibit 8: Impact on Bond Pricing of 100 bp Shifts in Rates Volatility and OAS Held Constant

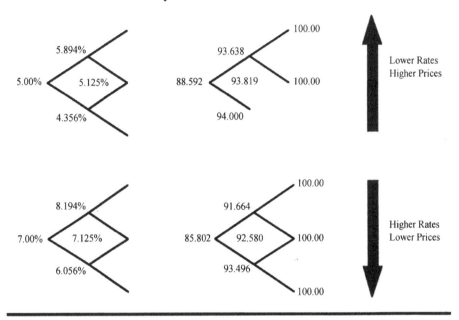

USING OPTION-ADJUSTED BOND CHARACTERISTICS

Bond portfolio managers use the results of embedded option valuation models in two broad ways: (1) to allow "apples to apples" comparisons of bonds with different option structures, and (2) to anticipate how the market value of individual bonds and bond portfolios will change as interest rates change.

Suppose an investor concludes that the credit quality of Albertson's, Inc., a U.S. supermarket chain, is likely to improve, and wishes to purchase some of this issuer's bonds. Suppose also that the investor wishes to buy bonds with durations between seven and nine years. A bond dealer reports that two Albertson's issues are available in the market with characteristics and offering prices as listed in Exhibit 9.

If we naively compare the nominal yields on the two offerings on either a yield to maturity or yield to put basis, the option-free bond looks like a better deal. However, if, after July 30, 2012, yields on 16 year bonds (i.e., bonds with 2028 maturities) are below 6.10%, an investor who chose the higher-yielding non-putable issue would be sorry about the choice. The value of the putable bond is that it offers the investor the opportunity to continue earning a yield to maturity of 6.653% until 2028, *if* that yield is higher than market yields on comparable bonds on the put date. The investor must pay for this option, and the payment comes in the form of a lower yield on the putable bond.

Exhibit 9: Hypothetical Offerings of Two Real Bonds of Albertson's, Inc.

Characteristic		Putable Bond	Option-Free Bond
Settlement		September 9, 1999	
Maturity		April 10, 2028	July 30, 2012
Coupon		6.10%	6.81%
Embedded Option		• One time put • April 10, 2008 • @ 94.75	None
Offered Price		92.958	97.830
Option-Adjusted Duration	@ 12% Volatility	8.40	8.31
	@ 15% Volatility	8.43	8.31
Yield	To Maturity	6.653%	7.07%
	To Put	6.730%	N.A.
Option-Adjusted Spread	@ 12% Volatility	112.9 bp	104.9 bp
	@ 15% Volatility	121.2 bp	104.9 bp

So a true comparison of the two offerings must incorporate an evaluation of the embedded option. Option valuation models allow us to make this comparison, and the results of one such evaluation also appear in Exhibit 9.[5] Once we take the value of the embedded option into consideration, we see that the putable bond is a better deal than the option-free issue.

The exact value of the put depends on the volatility assumption incorporated into the calculation. In Chapter 16 we saw that yield volatility for "10-year bonds" — that is, bonds with roughly this investor's target duration — ranged from the low teens to the high teens through most of the 1990s.[6] Although there have been volatility spikes higher than that during occasional market crises, we can be fairly safe in saying that 12% is a relatively low level of yield volatility while 18% is a high level.

The higher the volatility, the greater the value of the option, and the lower the yield the buyer of a putable bond should be willing to accept, the yield of an option-free bond held constant. In this example, even at 12% volatility, the putable bond offers an OAS that is 8.0 basis points greater than that of the option-free bond. At a more normal 15% volatility, the OAS differential is 16.3 basis points.

An investor might reasonably believe that interest rate volatility is likely to be quite subdued in the future and conclude that an 8 basis point pickup in OAS does not provide adequate compensation for the put bond's likely relative illiquidity. These would constitute sound reasons to buy the option-free bond rather than the putable issue, but the simple fact that the nominal yield on the former is higher is not a good reason.

---

[5] All option valuation models in current use produce roughly similar results, especially when the option under consideration is as straightforward as this case of a single embedded option (a one-time put). The lognormal option valuation model provided by Bloomberg Financial Markets generated the particular OAS estimates reported in Exhibit 9.

[6] See, in particular, Exhibits 16 and 17 in Chapter 16.

Exhibit 10: Hypothetical Offerings of Two Federal Farm Credit Bank System Bonds

Characteristic		Callable Bond	Option-Free Bond
Settlement		September 9, 1999	
Maturity		March 22, 2004	April 20, 2003
Coupon		6.10%	5.31%
Embedded Option		• Non-call until March 22, 2000 • Callable at any time thereafter	None
Offering Price		96.972	96.189
Yield	To Maturity	6.89%	6.51%
	To First Call	12.03%	N.A.
Option- Adjusted Duration	@ 12% Vol.	3.32	
	@ 15% Vol.	3.17	3.16
	@ 18% Vol.	3.03	
Option- Adjusted Spread	@ 12% Vol.	94.6	
	@ 15% Vol.	87.9	71.0
	@ 18% Vol.	79.5	

In the case of a put bond the investor is long the option and pays a premium in the form of a lower yield. An investor who owns a callable bond is short the option and receives a higher yield as compensation. A manager can use option valuation techniques to determine whether the additional yield provides sufficient compensation.

Compare the two issues of the U.S. Federal Farm Credit Bank System described in Exhibit 10. In this example, the naive initial reaction of buying the bond with the higher yield would be the correct choice for most investors. Unless interest rates are extremely volatile, the callable bond will prove to be the better investment.

Few family portfolio managers will actually run embedded option valuation models themselves, but private investors who understand how these models work will be much better informed consumers. The main lessons should be clear. Nominal yield to maturity, yield to call, or yield to put are not the best decision making tools for investors considering alternative bond purchases with different option structures. The right numbers to consider in such cases are the option-adjusted spread offered by the bond and the interest rate volatility assumption used to evaluate that bond.

A dealer who is offering an investor a callable or putable bond should be prepared to provide the potential buyer with an estimate of the bond's option-adjusted duration and spread and an indication of what volatility assumption is used to compute the OAS estimate. An astute investor will be prepared to use this information, in the context of other facts about the bond, to decide whether this particular offering (1) is consistent with the particular portfolio management objectives at the time and (2) is attractively priced.

Exhibit 11: Duration and Convexity of a Portfolio of Callable and Non-Callable U.S. Government Agency Bonds

Issuer	Coupon	Maturity	Next Call Date	Next Call Price	Market Price	Yield To Maturity	Yield To Call	Modified Duration To Maturity	Modified Duration To Call	Option-Adjusted	OAS (bp)	Conv.
FFCB	6.0%	1/24/05	1/24/01	100	96.229	6.850%	8.995%	4.5	1.3	3.8	88.5	-0.47
FHLB	5.9%	5/10/06	5/10/02	100	95.373	6.753%	7.839%	5.3	2.4	4.6	79.1	0.05
FNMA	7.8%	3/29/05	3/29/00	100	100.309	7.729%	7.198%	4.3	0.5	1.7	102.0	-1.30
FFCB	5.7%	1/18/05	NCL	N.A.	96.117	6.571%	6.571%	4.5	4.5	4.5	77.1	0.24
FNMA	7.4%	3/28/05	NCL	N.A.	103.401	6.603%	6.603%	4.7	4.7	4.7	80.6	0.24
FHLMC	5.9%	2/21/06	NCL	N.A.	96.191	6.585%	6.585%	5.2	5.2	5.2	79.3	0.33
Wtd. Avg.								4.7	3.1	4.1	84.5	-0.16
Cash Flow Method*										3.9		-0.16

* Source: Bloomberg

MEASURING PORTFOLIO CHARACTERISTICS

Recall that in Chapter 13, when we were working through an example of building a U.S. dollar bond portfolio, we had to use an imprecise and somewhat complicated approach to dealing with callable bonds. The method involved computing each callable bond's duration in two different ways. First, we calculated the bond's duration to worst: i.e., duration to maturity for any bond trading below its call price or duration to call for any bond trading above a call price. The second measure was more subjective and was equal to duration to call for any bond trading substantially above its first call price and duration to maturity for bonds that were less certain to be called.

This method was adequate for our purposes in the example because there were relatively few callable bonds in the portfolio, and it was fairly clear how to handle each of the callable issues. Investors who hold relatively few bonds with embedded options or confine their purchases to issues that are trading at large premiums or discounts — that is, bonds incorporating embedded options that are either way in or way out of the money — can be satisfied with that methodology. Investors who hold substantial proportions of callable bonds in their portfolios or who frequently buy putable or callable bonds trading close to par should instead use embedded option valuation techniques to measure portfolio duration and convexity.

We illustrate the application of this type of analysis to a portfolio consisting entirely of a combination of callable and non-callable U.S. government agency securities. Such a portfolio would not be optimal; it is not diversified across bond market sectors. Consideration of an all-agency portfolio, though, allows us to consider the application of embedded option analysis in isolation from the other issues related to portfolio construction discussed in Chapter 13.

Assume that each position in Exhibit 11 and has a par value of $1 million. The portfolio consists of callable issues of the Federal Farm Credit Banks

(FFCB), the Federal Home Loan Bank System (FHLB), and Fannie Mae (FNMA); and bullet issues of FFCB, and Freddie Mac (FHLMC).

There are two ways of calculating the duration and convexity of a portfolio of bonds. One way is simply to calculate the weighted average durations and convexities of the individual bonds in the portfolio, where each position is weighted by its market value. The second approach is to treat all of the cash flows generated by the portfolio as if they were payments made by a single bond investment and calculate the duration and convexity of this complex single bond. When the portfolio in question includes callable bonds, some of these cash flows will be received with certainty, as long as the issuer does not default, while others will be contingent payments that depend on the level of interest rates. As long as the securities in the portfolio are not too complex and are independent of one another, the two methods will produce similar results, as they do in Exhibit 11.

The exhibit also highlights a number of characteristics of callable bonds. Note that the securities differ in their option-adjusted spreads. The "cheapest" security, the one with the widest spread, is the FNMA 7.80% of '05 callable in 2000. This is also the bond with the greatest "negative convexity." Put differently, this is the security that creates the greatest problem for a manager who is trying to maintain a steady portfolio duration. The bond is priced close to par, and there is a significant difference between its maturity and first call dates. The wide OAS on this bond indicates that investors demand compensation, over and above the theoretical option value, for holding a bond that makes the portfolio management process particularly difficult.

This example illustrates the use of embedded option valuation analysis in the easiest possible case. The hypothetical portfolio consists entirely of taxable securities that are either not callable or incorporate relatively straightforward call structures.[7] In this case, embedded option analysis gives clear answers regarding option-adjusted duration, option-adjusted spread, and convexity. The results of embedded option analysis in other sectors of the bond market are much less clear-cut.

SPECIAL CONSIDERATIONS FOR SPECIFIC BOND MARKET SECTORS

This discussion in this chapter relates most directly to the analysis of corporate and government agency bonds. Evaluating municipal and mortgage-backed securities requires further analysis. Extensive treatment of mortgage-backed securities is not worthwhile in a volume devoted to family investing, because MBS do not play an important role in individuals' portfolios. Municipal bonds, however, do. Available embedded option valuation models are not entirely adequate when it comes to dealing with tax-exempt securities.

---

[7] The Federal Home Loan Bank and Federal Farm Credit Bank bonds are exempt from state income taxes. Interest on all the bonds in Exhibit 11 is taxable on the Federal level.

Municipal Bonds

Two unique characteristics of municipal bonds — advance refunding and the tax treatment of any market discount — complicate their analysis in the context of embedded option valuation.

Advance Refunding

An investor who owns a callable corporate or agency bond will not know with absolute certainty whether the security will actually be redeemed on any given call date until the issuer actually sends out the notice. For example, consider an agency bond with a 10-year final maturity that is callable at par in two years and priced at 108.00. An investor seeking a bond with a duration close to two years might buy such a security on the assumption that the bond will be redeemed on the first call date. If so, the investor would be exposed to *extension risk* in the event that interest rates rise before the call date by enough to eliminate the issuer's incentive to refund the issue. The pricing of the bond will reflect this risk, and the bond's yield to call will be higher than that of an agency security with a definite 2-year final maturity. Suppose that an option-free 2-year agency bond with the same coupon as the callable issue would be priced at 110.00. If so, the value of the extension risk is two points. The investor knows that this extension risk will never be entirely eliminated until the bond is actually called.

Municipalities frequently advance refund their bonds before the first call date by issuing new, lower-coupon securities and using the proceeds of the new issue to purchase a portfolio of U.S. Treasury securities sufficient to meet interest payments on the bond, and then redeem the security on the first call date. By depositing this "escrow" with the bond's trustee with instructions to redeem the outstanding issue, the issuer has, in effect, eliminated the possibility that the bond will remain outstanding after the call date. An investor who purchases a prerefunded municipal bond thus has no extension risk. Further, an investor who purchases a non-prerefunded municipal bond that qualifies for advance refunding at a premium price knows that, at some point before the call date, the extension risk associated with the investment may be eliminated.

A complete option valuation model for municipal bonds must take the possibility of advance refunding into account because the value of a premium bond may be significantly different, depending on whether or not the extension risk might be eliminated before the call date. A number of the option valuation models in use for municipal bonds do incorporate this consideration in their computations. Operating these models requires both information about whether or not the bond qualifies for advance refunding and an assumption regarding the circumstances under which the issuer will prerefund the bonds.

Market Discount Taxation

While some option models in current use deal with the advance refunding problem, none of those available as of late 1999 deal with the second complication affecting the evaluation of municipal bonds: the tax treatment of market discount bonds. This aspect of bond valuation is not, strictly speaking, a variety of option valuation; there is no embedded option associated with the way the government taxes municipal bonds purchased at a market discount. The tax treatment, however, affects the value of the bond in a way that is quite similar to the impact of an embedded option.

Suppose an investor buys $10 million par amount of 10-year municipal bonds for $9.5 million. Assume also that the bonds were originally issued at par. If the investor then holds the bond to maturity, the $500,000 difference between the purchase price and the redemption value will be taxed as ordinary income when the bond matures. A potential purchaser's valuation of such a market discount bond must take into account the fact that the part of the return generated by the security, the coupon income, is tax-exempt and part, the accretion to par, is taxable.

Exhibit 12 illustrates how the tax treatment of market discount bonds affects the price of municipal securities. Here are two bonds with identical coupons and maturities but different dollar prices, because the one originally issued at par is now a market discount bond and will generate taxable income for the purchaser, while the other is an original issue discount bond, which, if held to maturity, produces returns that are fully tax-exempt.

Now suppose an investor had purchased both of these bonds sometime previously at a yield to maturity of 4.50% so that both of the securities were priced at par. Since that time interest rates have risen by 100 bp. This increase has led to a 7.6% (= 100 − 92.386) decline in the price of Bond A, the OID issue, and a 9.9% (= 100 − 90.110) decrease in Bond B, which is now a market discount bond. We can say, therefore, that the effective modified duration of Bond B is 9.9, which is more than 30% greater than the effective modified duration of the OID Bond A.

If the yield on the two bonds, instead of rising from 4.50% to 5.50%, falls to 3.50%, the prices of both bonds would rise to 108.376. Under these circumstances, the identical performance of the two bonds would lead us to conclude that they have identical modified durations of 8.4.

Exhibit 12: Market Prices of Two Hypothetical Tax-Exempt Bonds

	Bond A	Bond B
Issue Date	6/1/00	9/5/98
Settlement	6/1/00	6/1/00
Coupon	4.50%	4.50%
Maturity	6/1/10	6/1/10
Initial Yield	5.50%	4.50%
Initial Price	92.386	100.000
After-Tax YTM	5.50%	5.50%
Market Price*	92.386	90.110
Nominal YTM	5.50%	5.82%

* Assumes 39.6% tax rate.

Because of the tax treatment of market discount, the duration of municipal bonds increases as their price drops below par. In technical terms, unless the bond is priced at a substantial premium to par, all municipals are "negatively convex." We have seen that embedded call options can render a bond negatively convex — so the impact of market discount taxation is similar to the effect of an embedded option.

A thorough analysis of effective duration and convexity of a municipal bond must take these considerations into account. Yet none of the embedded option valuation models currently in use incorporates this aspect of tax-exempt bond performance into the calculation. Therefore, portfolio managers must use estimates of the duration and convexity of municipal bond portfolios with extreme caution until the available analytical tools capture all the determinants of tax-exempt bond price performance as interest rates change.

Mortgage-Backed Securities

In the case of a simple callable corporate or government agency bond, the owner of the embedded option is the issuer of the bond. In such cases, it is relatively easy to predict whether and when the option will be exercised. If the bond's period of call protection has expired and if the issuer can save money, after paying the cost of issuing new bonds, by refunding the callable issue, the security will almost certainly be redeemed very soon. This certainty allows us to specify an option valuation model quite precisely. In Exhibit 5, for example, there is no uncertainty that if the market value of the bond at the end of the first period is greater than 94.50, the bond would be called at that time.

The options embedded in mortgage-backed securities represent the right of the borrowers whose home loans are bundled into a passthrough security to prepay their loans ahead of schedule. Unlike a corporate or agency bond, therefore, each MBS incorporates a large number of separate options "owned" by a variety of individuals. A homeowner's decision to prepay a mortgage does depend in part on the level of interest rates; if interest rates drop substantially, many homeowners will refinance.

It is much more difficult to predict when a mortgage loan will be prepaid than to predict when a corporate or agency bond will be called. For one thing, interest rate changes are not the only consideration that might induce a homeowner to prepay a mortgage. Mortgages may be paid down when homeowners sell their house and move, or by insurance payments if the home is destroyed by a fire or other catastrophe. Nor do all homeowners respond to interest rate changes in the same way. Some borrowers with small remaining balances due on their mortgages may find that it does not pay to incur the closing costs involved in refinancing a mortgage. In other cases, if home prices have declined substantially after the mortgage was taken out, mortgagees may not be able to meet the equity requirements for refinancing. This may be why prepayments on California mortgages were much lower in 1993 than one would have expected, given the low level of interest rates at that time; California real estate values dropped substantially in the early 1990s, and some homeowners may not have been able to obtain approval for refinancing loans. Finally, some homeowners may simply remain unaware of refinancing opportunities when they do arise.

For all these reasons, embedded option valuation models for MBS require an additional analytical component. In addition to a model of how interest rates might change in the future, the analysis also requires a prepayment model predicting what proportion of the outstanding mortgages in a pool will be paid down at any given level of interest rates. Prepayment models are complex because they take into account a wide range of characteristics of the mortgages in a pool. These include not only the weighted average coupon (WAC) and weighted average maturity (WAM) of the pool, but also the history of interest rates since the mortgages in the pool were issued, the geographic distribution of the properties, and the average size of the loans. The modeling process becomes even more complex when the security in question is not a straightforward Fannie Mae, Freddie Mac, or Ginnie Mae passthrough but a collateralized mortgage obligation tranche. Determining how quickly or slowly a specific CMO will pay down requires not only the framework of an option valuation model and a prepayment model, but also detailed information about the passthroughs that constitute the collateral for the CMO and about the structure of the deal that created the particular issue.

Different option valuation models produce similar results in terms of OAD and OAS for specific securities, but only for corporate and agency securities with relatively straightforward option structures and for recently issued mortgage passthroughs. At the other end of the complexity spectrum, different option valuation methods based on different prepayment models may produce radically different evaluations of uniquely structured CMO tranches.

Even the most astute professional managers of large portfolios of highly structured mortgage-backed securities have been unhappily surprised by the performance of their holdings because they relied too heavily on a single option valuation model. The degree of uncertainty about the value of CMOs is one of the primary reasons that most family portfolio managers avoid heavy involvement in this sector of the fixed-income market.

CHAPTER 18

Fixed-Income Derivatives

■■■■■■■■■■■■■■■■■■■■■■■■■■■■■■■■■

F ixed-income derivatives are financial contracts whose value depends on — is *derived from* — the market value of one or more fixed-income securities. Chapter 16 focuses in some detail on one class of derivative contracts: over-the-counter (OTC) options on fixed-income securities. The value of a put or a call is derived from the value of the deliverable security; hence, an option is a *derivative* contract. This chapter introduces the full array of fixed-income derivatives.

We cover this topic not because family fixed-income portfolio managers make frequent use of such contracts. In fact, individual investors rarely enter into derivative contracts. As with much of the material presented in Part III, an understanding of fixed-income markets is incomplete without some basic knowledge of how derivative contracts and derivatives markets work. Indeed, by the late 1990s, the market in one type of fixed-income derivative contract — interest rate swaps — had begun to rival the U.S. Treasury market as the most important sector of the global bond market.

VARIETIES OF DERIVATIVE CONTRACTS

There are six types of derivative contracts:

1. Over-the-counter forward rate agreements.
2. Over-the-counter options.
3. Exchange-traded futures contracts.
4. Exchange-traded options on futures contracts.
5. Interest rate swaps.
6. Options on interest rate swaps ("swaptions").

All these contracts are traded in active markets as separate instruments. In addition, bond dealers frequently create hybrid instruments consisting of a fixed-income security coupled with one or more derivative contracts. Such securities are referred to as *structured notes*.

In this chapter we focus most on the last four of these types of contracts. Forward pricing and over-the-counter options are covered in Chapters 15 and 16, respectively.

The main distinction between the exchange-traded and over-the-counter (OTC) contracts on this list is that, in the case of the latter, the two parties to the contract know each other's identity. An investor or dealer who enters into an OTC transaction must make a judgment about the ability of the counterparty to perform the obligations of the contract. Under these circumstances, a prudent market participant will undertake a considerable amount of due diligence regarding the counterparty's financial condition and will negotiate specific collateral requirements designed to guarantee performance. The process of vetting a counterparty can be time-consuming and costly, but, as we will see, the benefits of OTC contracts, in terms of convenience and flexibility of design, will often make this effort worthwhile.

In the case of exchange-traded contracts, the buyer and the seller of the futures or the options do not know each other's identity. Performance is guaranteed by the exchange, its members, its rules, and the contract specifications. Buyers and sellers of exchange-traded contracts are required to post cash or very high-quality collateral as *margin* to assure performance. Two types of margin are required: *initial margin* and *variation margin*. The initial margin is a small percentage of the face amount of the contract and serves to collateralize the buyers' and sellers' obligation to pay variation margin. The variation margin — which must be made current at the end of each business day — is equal to the full amount by which the buyer's or seller's obligation has changed in value since the position was initiated. Through this mechanism, the futures and options exchanges guarantee participants that funds are available to meet all contractual obligations.

Exchange-traded futures are standardized forward sale and purchase contracts that trade on an organized, regulated financial exchange. The contracts are standardized in all respects: the deliverable security or securities, the formula for determining the delivery price or value of the contract at expiration, the forward delivery date, the security arrangements that guarantee the performance of each party to the contract, the trading hours, and so on.

EXCHANGE-TRADED FUTURES INVOLVING PHYSICAL DELIVERY

The Euro Bund contract traded on the German EUREX has the specifications listed in Exhibit 1. Suppose that on January 5, 2000, the June 2000 EUREX Euro Bund futures contract is trading at a price of 94.39. The buyer of a single futures contract at that price agrees to two contract terms. First, the buyer agrees to make or receive variation margin payments while the contract is outstanding. When the price of the contract goes down, the buyer pays the amount of the decline. When the price goes up, the holder of a long futures position will receive margin payments through the futures exchange; in this latter case, it is the seller who is obligated to make a variation margin payment. Second, the contract buyer agrees to purchase a deliverable bond at contract expiration at a price determined by the closing price of the contract.

By means of these two mechanisms, the buyer of a futures contract locks in a purchase price for the bond that is related to the price at which the contract was purchased. A seller of the same contract at the same price is agreeing to deliver on the bonds within the deliverable maturity range, to make (if the contract price goes up) or receive (if the contract price goes down) variation margin payments while the contract position is open, and to sell the delivered bond at a price related to the closing price of the contract on the last trading day.

Because settlement of the Euro Bund futures involves actual purchase or delivery of a security — rather than simple cash settlement based on a specific interest rate or an index — this contract belongs to the category of futures vehicles referred to as *physical delivery contracts.*

Each of the bonds in the *deliverable universe* will, in general, have a different coupon and maturity, and will be priced at a different yield to maturity. The contract terms must thus specify the method for calculating the purchase and sale price of each of the deliverable bonds as of each contract's settlement date. Specifically, we need a method for calculating a delivery *factor* for each bond. The actual purchase price of each bond, if it is delivered to close out a short position in the futures contract, will be the closing price of the contract multiplied by the delivery factor for that particular bond.

The contract's notional coupon — 6.00% in the case of the Euro Bund contract — provides the key for calculating each bond's factor. The factor is equal to the price of the bond in question that will produce a yield to maturity of 6.00% divided by 100.00. If one of the deliverable bonds for the EUREX Bund contract actually has a coupon of 6.00%, the factor for that bond would be 1.00; the factor for the 4.00% Bund of July 4, 2009, as of the delivery date for the March 2000 Euro Bund contract would then be 0.860 (= 86.01/100.00). So, if the March 2000 contract settles at 107.65, the purchase price of 4.00% Bunds of '09 with a face value of €100,000 would be €92,579 (= 107.65% × 0.860 × €100,000) plus accrued interest.

Exhibit 1: Specifications for the EUREX Euro Bund Contract

Contract Provision	Specification
Notional Size	€100,000
Notional Coupon	6.00%
Deliverable Bonds	German Government Bonds with between 8.5 and 10.5 years remaining to maturity.
Trading Hours	8:00 am - 7:00 pm on Frankfurt business days.
Contract Settlement Months	March, June, September, and December
Delivery Date	10th of settlement month or next business day.
Last Trading Day	Two business days before settlement.
Tick Size (Minimum Price Move)	0.01 points = €10

Exhibit 2: Hypothetical Purchase and Sale Prices of Two Bonds Eligible for Delivery into the March 2000 EUREX Euro Bund Contract

Settlement	3/10/00	
Maturity	7/4/09	1/4/09
Coupon	4.00%	3.75%
Factor	0.860	0.849
Market Price	92.52	91.22
Deliverable Amount Purchase Price	€92,520	€91,220
Closing Contract Price	107.65	107.65
Sale Price	€92,590	€91,415
Profit	70	195

The Cheapest To Deliver and the Delivery Option

The seller of a futures contract has the right to deliver any of the bonds in the deliverable universe and need not decide which bond to deliver until shortly before the settlement date. At that time, the seller will generally find that the cost of fulfilling the delivery obligation will vary across the bonds in the deliverable universe and that one of the bonds will be the cheapest to deliver. Compare the two bonds in Exhibit 2, for example. Again we assume that the contract settles at a price of 107.65. Given the factors for the two bonds and the market prices of the two securities, a seller of the March 2000 Euro Bund contract would find that there is a slight advantage to delivering the 3.75% of January 4, 2009, rather than the 4.00% of July 4, 2009. Of these two bonds, the shorter, lower-coupon issue is the cheaper to deliver.[1]

We can repeat these calculations for all the bonds in the deliverable universe to identify the particular issue that is the cheapest to deliver. At any point during the life of a futures contract, it will be possible to calculate which of the bonds in the universe would be cheapest to deliver at expiration assuming that the relative prices of the bonds in the contract do not change substantially before expiration.

The contract seller's right to choose which bond to deliver is referred to as the contract's *delivery option*. The value of this option increases to the extent that the universe of deliverable bonds is large and varied and to the extent that the relative values of deliverable bonds are volatile. Since all the bonds deliverable into the EUREX Euro Bund contract are German government obligations, the relevant distinctions among the various issues are their durations and, because of the way the German tax system calculates interest income, their coupons.[2] Therefore,

---

[1] Do not confuse the small profit earned in this example on the difference between the market prices of the deliverable bonds and the contract delivery price with the overall profit or loss the seller of the contract may realize. The latter will depend primarily on movements in the price of the contract between the investor's sale date and the last day of trading. Additional profits or losses associated with delivering a particular bond will usually be very small in comparison.

[2] See Chapter 12 for a description of the German tax system as it affects fixed-income investments.

the delivery option built into the EUREX Euro Bund contract will be most valuable when the euro yield curve is near 6.00% throughout the 8.5-year and 10.5-year maturity range, when the yield curve slope is volatile, and when there are a wide range of coupons and maturities of the deliverable bonds.

Deriving Contract Value

Exchange-trade fixed-income futures contracts are derivatives; their value is derived from the value of bonds and other fixed-income securities. One can understand futures if one understands the process by which this derivation takes place and how the relationship between the price of the derivative and the prices of the "cash" securities that determine its value is maintained.

Since futures contracts are standardized forward contracts, it should not be surprising that one of the key considerations that enters into the determination of contract prices is the relationship between spot and forward yields. Imagine a futures contract with one and only one deliverable bond: a 6.00% issue maturing on January 1, 2010. Suppose that the spot price of this bond today (January 14, 2000) is par, and that we wish to evaluate a futures contract that settles on March 31, 2000. Finally, assume that the yield on three-month securities of the same issuer as the deliverable bond, calculated on the same basis, is 3.50%. These assumptions provide everything we need to know to calculate the "fair" price of the futures contract because it is the same as the fair forward price of the deliverable bond.

Recall from Chapter 15 that the fair forward price will equal the spot price adjusted for the "cost" of carrying the bond rather than the three-month investment over the period until settlement. In this case, under the assumption that the accrual convention for the bond in question is actual/actual, the fair futures and forward price will be:

$$99.473 = 100 - [(6.00 - 3.50)(77/365)]$$

and the fair forward yield as of the settlement date would be 6.068%.

Arbitrage activity in the futures market assures that the actual prices of these contracts will be very close to the theoretically fair price. Suppose, for example, that the price of the hypothetical contract is 99.90 instead of the fair price of 99.473. Under these circumstances, an arbitrageur could purchase the deliverable bond at par through a leveraged transaction using other investments as collateral and sell the futures contract. At the settlement date the investor would deliver the bond into the futures contract, receiving 90.900. Over the period between the purchase of the bond and the settlement of the futures contract, the arbitrageur would receive coupon income on the long bond position of 1.266 points (= 6.00 × (77/365) and owe 0.738 points of interest on the borrowing incurred for the leveraged purchase. So, on the settlement date the arbitrageur will have:

Proceeds on Futures Settlement	99.900
+ Interest Income on the Bond	1.266
− Repayment of Loan Principal	100.000
− Interest on the Loan	0.738
= Total	0.422 points

The investor who executes this transaction takes no risk — he or she is long and short the same instrument — and, by assumption, put up no incremental cash, so the 0.422 points is a risk-free arbitrage profit. Arbitrageurs would execute such transactions until the selling pressure on the futures contract brings the price down to its fair value. Likewise, if the contract is trading below its fair price, arbitrageurs would buy the contract and sell the deliverable bond short through a leveraged transaction (see Chapter 14) and, again, earn a free arbitrage profit.

Note that if market conditions remain unchanged — that is, if the spot price of this bond remains at par — the fair futures price will gradually rise to 100.00 as the amount subtracted from 100 on the right side of the equation gets smaller and smaller. Indeed, whatever happens to the spot price over time, the differential between spot and futures prices will tend to shrink. There may be some volatility along this path; a decrease in the short-rate with the bond yield held constant will have the opposite effect for a period of time, but the tendency toward convergence of futures and spot prices is inexorable.

Fair futures and fair forward prices are identical for futures contracts with a single deliverable bond or for cash-settled futures contracts. Most futures contracts, however, provide for *physical delivery* of more than one specific bond.[3] In this case, the fair value of the contract would depend on the spot and forward prices of the particular bond that is cheapest to deliver into the contract *and* the value of the delivery option. The seller of the futures contract holds the delivery option, and the buyer of futures is short this option. Therefore, the fair price of a physical delivery futures contract should be slightly lower than it would be if the cheapest to deliver bond were the only deliverable bond. The greater the value of the delivery option, the greater the difference between the fair price of the futures contract and the price based solely on the fair forward value of the cheapest to deliver bond.

The valuation of delivery options can become quite complex, particularly when there is a large number of deliverable securities and their characteristics are varied. Discussion of the models used to evaluate delivery options and to determine whether futures contracts are rich, cheap, or fairly priced is beyond the scope of this book. Family investors who wish to use futures contracts to manage their portfolios should work closely with investment professionals who are familiar with the use of these models and their practical applications.

---

[3] The term "physical delivery" is somewhat out of date in that futures traders with open short positions at expiration seldom, if ever, actually deliver physical bonds. Today, all deliveries are electronic, and the term physical delivery refers to the fact that a specific bond (issuer, coupon, maturity) is being "delivered."

Exchange-Traded Options on Futures

Investors can also buy and sell puts and calls on exchange-traded futures contracts. The security provisions that guarantee market participants' performance under these options contracts — initial margin and variation margin — are the same as for exchange-traded futures. Also, as with exchange-traded futures, options on futures are uniform contracts. All options expire on certain predetermined dates, and exchange rules specify a limited number of strike prices. In most respects, the analysis of exchange-traded options on futures is the same as the analysis of over-the-counter options presented in Chapter 16; the value of the option depends on the price of the futures contract, volatility, and short-term interest rates.

Two differences between the analysis of OTC options on cash securities and exchange-traded options on futures are worth highlighting. First, the analysis of options on futures does not need to take into account the difference between spot and forward prices of the deliverable instrument; the futures price is the forward price. Second, the analysis of options on futures must incorporate consideration of the delivery option embedded in the futures contract. The latter could prove to be an additional source of volatility in the price of the futures contract, independent of the general level of interest rate volatility. In light of these observations, it should not be surprising that deriving a precise estimate of the fair value of a call or a put on a futures contract can become a very complex undertaking. Even a cursory description of how that analysis works is beyond the scope of this book.

The Uses of Bond Futures and Options on Futures

All derivative contracts have three broad uses: hedging, speculation, and arbitrage. The specific uses of bond futures mirror the applications of leveraged long and short bond positions discussed in Chapter 14. In fact, except for the delivery option and the rules regarding margin, the economics of a futures contract and that of a leveraged investment in the cheapest to deliver bond are identical. An investor can use a long or short futures position to extend or shorten portfolio duration, respectively, without actually selling bonds in the portfolio. Long and short futures positions can be used to generate very large percentage returns on correct beliefs that interest rates will fall or rise.

Finally, in Chapter 14 we point out that there are occasional opportunities to buy bonds for forward delivery at prices substantially lower than the theoretically fair levels. Participants in the futures market can occasionally find similar opportunities. For example, an investor considering using cash on hand to buy a Treasury note or bond will occasionally find that futures are "undervalued" relative to their theoretical fair price, and that the best thing to do is to buy short-term Treasury bills and the "cheap" futures contract. Similarly, an investor considering selling a bond or note to reduce portfolio duration may conclude that a futures contract is "expensive" relative to fair value, and that the best trade is to keep all the bonds and notes in the portfolio and to sell futures contracts instead.

In both these cases, the investor would continue to monitor the relative value of futures and cash instruments and, when the futures contracts return to fair value, reverse the derivatives trade and buy or sell cash bonds as appropriate.

CASH-SETTLED INTEREST RATE FUTURES

The majority of fixed-income futures contracts stipulate physical delivery, but a number of contracts, including the most actively traded interest rate futures contract, are *cash settled*. Under a cash-settled contract, the seller of the futures contract does not deliver, nor does the buyer take delivery of, any actual security at settlement. Instead, the contract settles through a cash payment that is proportional to the difference between the price at which the contract is purchased or sold and the level of a specific interest rate or bond price index on the last day of contract trading. A market participant who sells a cash-settled futures contract at a price of, say, 94.50 will receive a net payment at settlement if the level of the index underlying the contract on the last day of trading is below 94.50 and will make a payment if the index closes higher than 94.50.[4] It is somewhat easier to analyze cash-settled futures contracts than contracts stipulating physical delivery because there are no delivery options to consider.

The most important by far of the cash-settled, exchange-traded futures contracts, in terms of both volume of open interest and impact on other financial markets, is the Eurodollar contract traded around the clock on various futures exchanges. The specifications for these contracts are listed in Exhibit 3. Settlement for these contracts is in cash — no securities are delivered or purchased — on the last trading day of each contract month and is based on the level of three-month LIBOR on that day determined by a systematic survey of large commercial banks in London. Specifically, the settlement price of the contract is equal to 100.00 minus the level of LIBOR determined by the survey.

Exhibit 3: Terms of Eurodollar Futures Contracts

Term	Specification
Underlying Instrument	Three-month Eurodollar time deposits
Contract Size	US$1 million face value
Last Trading Day	Two London business days before the third Wednesday of March, June, September, and December
Settlement	Last Trading Day
Minimum Price Change	0.01 points = US$25
Settlement Price	100 – LIBOR

---

[4] The actual two-way payments at settlement are usually very small, because most of the funds to be paid or received will already have already been paid or received as variation margin under the rules of the futures exchange.

So the price of, say, the March 2003 Eurodollar futures contract reflects the forward yield on a large three-month U.S. dollar deposit in a large international bank initiated on March 17, 2003, and maturing three months later. A futures price of 92.85 for this contract reflects a forward yield of 7.15% on such deposits. The settlement price is based on an *annualized* yield on a three-month deposit. The $25 value of minimum changes in the contract price reflects the fact that this annualized rate is earned for only three months or one quarter of the year and that the day count convention for calculating interest on bank deposits is 30/360. That is:

$$\$25 = \$1,000,000 \times 0.01\% \times (90/360)$$

Eurodollar futures were originally a vehicle for commercial banks to hedge their cost of borrowing money. To see how this can work, suppose it is early in the year 2000 and a bank wishes to lock in its cost of borrowing three-month funds — that is, lock in three-month LIBOR — for loans negotiated in March of 2001. Assume further that the bank wishes to lock in its cost of funding for $10 million and that March '01 eurodollar futures are trading at 93.25. This price is consistent with a level of LIBOR in March of 2001 of 6.75%. To accomplish its goal, the bank would sell ten March '01 eurodollar futures and maintain the position until the contract expires.

Now suppose we get to March 2001 and find that three-month LIBOR is at 7.38%, so the settlement price of the eurodollar futures contract expiring at that time will be 92.62. The bank's profit on the transaction will be $15,750 (= $25 \times 10 \times [(93.25 - 92.62) \times 100]$). If invested at LIBOR, this amount will grow to $16,040.59 (= $15,750 \times [1 + (7.38\%/4)]$). Interest due on the $10 million loan at the end of the three-month period will be $184,500 (= $10,000,000 \times 7.38\% \div 4$). The profit on the futures position plus interest on that gain can be used to offset the interest payment on the loan, bringing the net payment to $168,459.41. Expressed as a percentage of the amount borrowed and converted to an annual rate, this comes to 6.74% (= $100\% \times 4 \times \$168,459.41 \div \$10,000,000$).

So by selling eurodollar futures short, the bank has been able to lock in three-month LIBOR for borrowings commencing in the future. Similarly, investors who hold cash balances to be invested in LIBOR in the future can use long eurodollar futures positions to lock in investment yields in the future. Alternatively, a borrower with a future three-month liability at a predetermined interest rate can convert that obligation into a liability that will depend on the level of LIBOR at the time by taking a long position in Eurodollar futures.

As a straightforward extension of this single-period example, borrowers with floating-rate loans outstanding, or who expect to be rolling over a borrowing at frequent intervals over a period of time, can use short positions in a series ("strip") of eurodollar futures to convert such floating-rate obligations into a fixed-rate loan. This latter application became one of the primary uses of the eurodollar futures contract, and through an extension of the process of buying and selling strips of futures contracts, the eurodollar futures market facilitated the growth of the largest and most liquid fixed-income derivatives market — perhaps the largest and most liquid fixed-income market, bar none — the interest rate swap market.

INTEREST RATE SWAPS

To see how a strip of Eurodollar futures can effectively "fix" a floating-rate liability, assume that in October 1999 a financial institution issues a $10 million two-year FRN with a three-month reset at LIBOR flat and wishes to eliminate the uncertainty associated with this obligation. Suppose further that at the beginning of this period the borrower finds that eurodollar futures contracts are trading at the prices listed in Exhibit 4. The investor can sell ten of each of these contracts, and lock in the approximate financing costs listed in column C of Exhibit 4.[5] A two-year $10 million loan with this particular series of predetermined but different interest costs has an annualized internal rate of return of 6.516%.

Therefore, a borrower should be indifferent between the two obligations:

1. A floating-rate borrowing with each quarterly LIBOR reset locked in using Eurodollar futures contracts.
2. A fixed-rate borrowing with interest payable quarterly at an annualized interest rate of 6.516%.

Exhibit 4: Futures Prices and Cash Flows on a Two-Year Floating-Rate Borrowing at LIBOR Flat

Year	Expiration Month (A)	Futures Price (B)	Interest Cost on $100 Million (C)	Fixed Rate Equivalent Cost (D)
1999	December	93.895	152,625	162,907
2000	March	93.955	151,125	162,907
	June	93.670	158,250	162,907
	September	93.495	162,625	162,907
	December	93.345	166,375	162,907
2001	March	93.320	167,000	162,907
	June	93.250	168,750	162,907
	September	93.200	170,000	162,907
	December	93.120	172,000	162,907

[5] The computed borrowing cost is only approximate because, until we know the actual level of LIBOR at the beginning of each three-month period, we are unable to calculate the interest earnings on the profits or losses from expiring futures positions. Also, the borrower would actually sell slightly under ten each of the contracts expiring in 2001, because discounting reduces the present value of the future cash flows.

To put it differently, *the series of futures prices listed in Exhibit 4 implies that a series of quarterly floating-rate payments of LIBOR flat over this period of time have the same market value as a series of equal payments made over the same period based on a fixed annual rate of 6.516%.* The Eurodollar futures market thus provides a way for borrowers and lenders to convert a series of floating-rate payments into the equivalent of a series of constant fixed-rate payments (and vice versa). Investors converted floating-rate investments into "synthetic" fixed-rate holdings by buying strips of Eurodollar futures or converted fixed-rate bonds into synthetic FRNs by selling Eurodollar futures.

You might well ask why a borrower would want to convert a variable-rate obligation into a fixed-rate liability. Isn't it easier simply to repay the floating-rate debt and replace it with a fixed-rate bond? In fact, certain types of borrowers find it much easier to raise funds in the variable-rate market, while others have a comparative advantage as fixed-rate borrowers. Borrowers with credit ratings at the lower end of the investment-grade scale usually find that a floating-rate financing combined with derivatives transactions locks in a lower all-in borrowing cost over a period of time than the straightforward issuance of fixed-rate bonds. Borrowers with credit ratings of double- or triple-A will frequently find the opposite: that issuance of fixed-rate bonds combined with a strip of eurodollar futures produces a lower variable-rate borrowing cost than direct issuance of floating-rate debt.

So the derivatives market provides a mechanism by which lower-rated borrowers can create fixed-rate obligations on the best possible terms, and higher-rated borrowers can create the most efficient variable-rate debt. Indeed, both types of issuers have used the eurodollar futures market for just this purpose.

Managing strips of eurodollar futures contracts is a somewhat complex undertaking, particularly for borrowers and investors not in the financial services business and for borrowers and lenders who seek different floating rate reset periods or indexes from those mandated by the futures exchanges. The first interest rate swap contracts were created as a convenient package for borrowers and lenders wishing to convert fixed-rate debt to floating-rate debt or vice versa for arbitrary choices of floating-rate reset and maturity dates and indexes.

What are Interest Rate Swaps?

An interest rate swap is a contract between two counterparties. In Exhibit 5, A agrees to pay B a stream of periodic fixed payments over a defined period of time, expressed as a fixed percentage of a notional principal amount. Party B agrees to pay A a variable payment determined by multiplying the notional principal amount by a floating interest rate index. At the end of the contract period, the agreement simply expires and payments cease. In general, no actual principal payments are exchanged between the parties; this is why the multiplicand in the payment formulas is referred to as *notional principal.* The most common index used to calculate variable rate payments is LIBOR.

Exhibit 5: Schematic of an Interest Rate Swap Contract

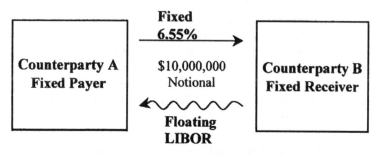

The schematic in Exhibit 5 illustrates the terms of an interest rate swap contract that produces the same general result for counterparty A as the strip of eurodollar futures contracts in Exhibit 4. Recall, however, that in the example the borrower is able to lock in the equivalent of a 6.516% fixed borrowing cost by selling a strip of eurodollar futures. With the interest rate swap contract, the borrower locks in a slightly higher cost of 6.55%. The additional 3.4 basis points represents the price of convenience.

Variations on the Theme

The first interest rate swaps may have been little more or less than convenient over-the-counter packages of eurodollar futures contracts. The financial product then quickly evolved beyond its origins. After all, there is no requirement that the contract illustrated in Exhibit 5 be equivalent to a strip of eurodollar futures. All that's needed for this interest rate swap to go into effect is two willing counterparties: one who wants to make quarterly payments at a rate of 6.55% on $10 million for two years in exchange for receiving three-month LIBOR, and another who wants to do the opposite. As the 1980s and 1990s progressed, derivatives dealers realized that there are willing counterparties on both sides of a wide variety of interest rate swap contracts. Variations on the original theme include

1. Different payment and interest rate reset frequencies, such as monthly or semiannually rather than quarterly.
2. Alternative floating indexes, such as sterling LIBOR, the prime rate, or a floating-rate tax-exempt bond index.
3. Floating-to-floating swaps (pay LIBOR flat, receive Federal Funds plus some number of basis points).
4. Longer terms (as much as 30 years).
5. Cross-currency swaps (pay U.S. dollar LIBOR, receive EURIBOR plus or minus a spread).
6. A variety of customized structures, such as floating rates with caps and floors.

Exhibit 6: Schematic of Offsetting Interest Rate Swaps

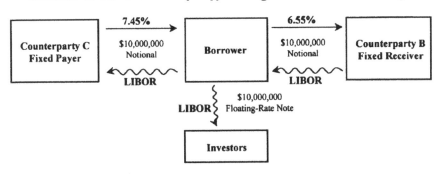

Throughout the 1980s and 1990s, an active secondary interest rate swap market developed. Suppose the financial institution that enters into the two-year interest rate swap contract illustrated in Exhibit 5 decides to create a synthetic fixed-rate liability at 6.55% in anticipation of a rise in interest rates. Now assume that this expectation proves to be correct, and that prices of eurodollar contracts quickly decline by 1.00 points across the board; that is, forward LIBOR for the next eight consecutive three-month periods increase by 100 basis points. This shift would also lead to a 100 basis point increase in the fixed rate, which could effectively be locked in by selling a strip of eurodollar futures, and to a similar upward shift in the fixed payments on two-year interest rate swap contracts. Suppose that the borrower now wants to reverse the swap transaction and go back to paying a floating rate on the original liability. One way of accomplishing this objective is to enter into a new swap transaction, this time as a fixed receiver. The result is as illustrated in Exhibit 6.

Although the general level of interest rates has risen by 100 bp, the fixed rate the borrower receives on the second interest rate swap transaction (7.45%) is only 90 bp higher than the rate on the first swap (6.55%). This differential reflects the bid-asked spread in the interest rate swap market. The 10 bp figure probably overstates the size of the bid-asked spread on a two-year LIBOR-based interest rate swap, but it does illustrate the fact that swap dealers must be compensated for making a market in these contacts.

The impact on the borrower of the combined swap transactions is that the effective cost of financing the $10 million loan will be LIBOR minus 90 basis points (= LIBOR − 6.55% + LIBOR + 7.45% − LIBOR). The initial cost of borrowing was LIBOR flat. The 90 bp savings relative to the initial cost is the profit earned by the borrower for correctly anticipating the rise in interest rates.

A borrower who wants to reverse the effect of an initial interest rate swap transaction can enter into a new, offsetting swap contract with another counterparty as illustrated in Exhibit 5. Alternatively, the borrower could simply agree with the initial counterparty (counterparty B in Exhibits 5 and 6) to cancel the original swap contract. This cancellation would involve a lump-sum payment by counterparty B to the borrower equal to the present value of 90 bp paid quarterly over two years. Financial institutions and other institutional investors, the most active users of interest rate swaps, enter into these types of initial and offsetting transactions with aggregate notional principal amounts totaling many billions of dollars and euros and trillions of yen on a daily basis. Trading and market making in the swap market has begun to rival the government bond sector in terms of both activity and liquidity.

This development has progressed so far that dealers have begun on occasion to quote yields on government agency and corporate bonds and mortgage-backed securities as a spread to fixed payments on LIBOR-based interest rate swaps. For example, suppose that five-year U.S. Treasury notes yield 6.50%, fixed payments on five-year swaps versus LIBOR flat are at 6.95%, and five-year U.S. government agency notes are yielding 6.85%. Standard operating procedure would still be to quote agency as yielding 35 basis points over Treasuries. Investors might then compare this spread with the average relationship between agencies and Treasuries over some historical period to decide whether the agencies are attractively priced. By the late 1990s, however, active market participants would be equally interested in the fact that agencies are trading 10 basis points below the yield ("10 basis points through") on interest rate swaps, and compare this 10 basis point with the "normal" spread between agency notes and interest rate swaps.

A securities dealer might also characterize the same set of yields by saying that five-year agencies can be swapped to "LIBOR − 10 bp." This would be what market participants call an *asset swap*. An asset swap is an investment combining a fixed-income security and an interest rate swap contract. In this case, for example, an investor might purchase a five-year, fixed-rate government agency note and simultaneously enter into a five-year interest rate swap contract as a fixed payer. The result is illustrated in schematic form in Exhibit 7. The effect of the combination of the investment in the agency note and the interest rate swap is that the investor receives a floating-rate yield of LIBOR − 10 bp.

Exhibit 7: Schematic of an Asset Swap

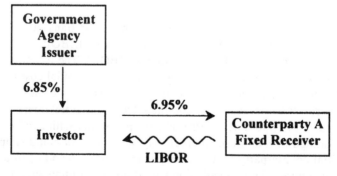

Swaptions

An option to enter into an interest rate swap contract is referred to as a *swaption*. Because investors and issuers may be equally likely to be fixed payers or fixed receivers, the terms "put" and "call" can be confusing in the case of swaptions. It is easier to say that an investor who is long — has paid a premium to purchase — a fixed-payer option has the right, but not the obligation, to begin making fixed-rate payments at a predetermined rate in exchange for receiving a floating rate on the option expiration date and for a predetermined period of time thereafter. For example, a borrower might purchase a two-year option to pay 7.25% on a five-year swap. This options contract would be referred to as a "two-year into a five-year fixed-payer swaption." The polar opposite of this long position in a fixed-payer option is a short position in a fixed-receiver option. A party who enters into such a contract will receive an option premium from the option buyer, and will be obliged to receive fixed payments at the strike rate and make LIBOR payments, should the owner of the option choose to exercise the right to pay a fixed rate.

We analyze swaptions just like we analyze fixed-income options; the value of a swaption depends on the relationship between the strike fixed rate and the forward fixed rate for the appropriate swap term, the short-term interest rate to swaption expiration, and the volatility of interest rates. Each swaption contract can be characterized by its

- Delta, the change in the swaption premium per unit of change in the forward fixed-payer rate.
- Gamma, the rate of change in delta as the forward fixed-payer rate changes
- Theta, the change in option value as the expiration date approaches.
- Vega, the change in value as the implied volatility of swaption pricing changes.

Just as the interest rate swaps have begun to rival the government bond market as the benchmark for all fixed-income prices and markets, the swaptions market is emerging as the benchmark for all options on term interest rates. If you ask for a indication of market-implied volatility, the representative of a major bond dealer is more likely to quote the "midmarket" implied volatility of options on interest rate swaps — half way between the implied volatility of dealer bids for and offers of swaptions — than the implied volatility of any other variety of options contract.

The Uses of Interest Rate Swaps

Family investors hardly ever participate directly in the interest rate swap market; as of the late 1990s, the market was still entirely institutional. Yet because developments in the swap market have begun to drive value shifts across all bond market sectors, family portfolio managers who participate actively in the fixed-income market must have some understanding of how this market works and how it is used.

Institutions use interest rate swap contracts to manage the effective duration of liabilities and assets. We have seen how fixed-payer swap positions can be used by borrowers to convert fixed- to floating-rate liabilities or vice versa. Indeed by the late 1990s, the use of interest rate swaps in this way had become routine for financial institutions and other active borrowers. Ten or fifteen years ago an institution seeking to structure a five-year floating-rate liability would automatically issue a five-year FRN at, say, LIBOR + 25 bp. Today, such an institution will consider a wide variety of alternative structures combining bond issuance and derivatives contracts to determine whether any of them produce a lower all-in cost of funds than LIBOR + 25 bp.

The simplest such alternative would involve issuing five-year fixed-rate bonds and entering into a five-year fixed-receiver interest rate swap contract. Suppose the fixed rate paid on the bonds is 6.85%, and the fixed rate received on the swap is 6.65%. If so, the combined transactions will produce an all-in floating-rate cost of LIBOR + 20, which is lower than the cost of the FRN. Under the circumstances, the issuer will offer fixed-rate bonds and enter into a swap.

By the same token, an issuer aiming to create a fixed-rate liability will consider the possibility of issuing an FRN or just rolling short-term borrowing and fixing the rate with an interest rate swap. The choice might go either way, depending on the yield on the particular issuer's fixed-rate bonds and FRNs, and on the level of fixed-payer swap rates.

The alternatives an issuer may consider are not necessarily straightforward combinations of fixed- or floating-rate bonds and interest rate swaps. A slightly more complex alternative for an issuer seeking a floating-rate liability might include issuance of a *callable* fixed-rate bond, a fixed-receiver interest rate contract, and a short position in a fixed-payer swaption. The fixed-rate bond and the fixed payments received on the swap will cancel out, leaving the issuer with a floating-rate liability. By issuing a callable bond, the borrower will in effect be buying a call option from the investor, and this long options position will be offset by the sale of the swaption. If fixed-rate bond yields, fixed swap payments, embedded option values, and swaption prices are configured appropriately, the combination of transactions will produce the lowest all-in cost of floating-rate financing for the issuer. This structure may seem elaborate, but in fact this mix of callable bonds, swaps, and swaptions has become one of the most common borrowing vehicles in the U.S. market.

Interest rate swaps also have uses on the asset side of institutions' balance sheets. Consider, for example, an investor who expects the credit quality of certain corporations to improve and wishes to buy these issuers' bonds, but who also expects interest rates to rise. Such an investor might want to buy floating-rate notes of these issuers, but an alternative is to buy *fixed-rate* bonds of these issuers and enter into fixed-payer swap contracts. The idea behind this "asset swap" combination is that, if interest rates do increase, the rising market value of the fixed-payer swap position will offset mark-to-market losses on the bonds. If this works as expected, the market value of the combined positions will reflect only the changes in the relative yields on the corporate bonds and interest rate swaps. If, as expected, the credit quality of the particular corporate borrowers improves, yields on these securities will decline relative to fixed-payer swap rates, and the investor will enjoy a mark-to-market profit.

In effect, the investor has used fixed-rate bonds and swaps to create a "synthetic" floating-rate note. Investors will choose the simpler strategy of buying FRNs or the more complex synthetic structure, depending largely on which produces the widest spread over LIBOR on the floating-rate investment.

These uses of interest rate swaps to manage assets and liabilities have become so routine in institutional fixed-income markets that fixed swap rates and corporate bond yields have become closely linked. If corporate bond yields — or yield spreads over Treasuries — get too high relative to swap rates, issuers will stop offering fixed-rate bonds and begin creating synthetic fixed-rate liabilities by combining floating-rate issues with fixed-payer swaps. A reduced supply of fixed-rate bonds will eventually have the effect of reducing corporate yields, while the increased interest in acting as a fixed-payer in swaps should push up fixed-payer swap rates. Yield spreads will adjust in the two markets until great numbers of issuers are indifferent between straightforward fixed- or floating-rate liabilities, on the one hand, and synthetic structures, on the other.

Because borrowers and investors constantly compare straight and synthetic structures, there is a tendency for swap rates (and spreads) and corporate bond yields (and spreads) to move in tandem (see Exhibit 8). This tendency has become so pronounced that yield spreads between interest rate swap contract fixed rates and comparable-maturity government bond yields have emerged as the most visible benchmark for yield spreads in general in the fixed-income markets. A sudden, sharp widening of swap spreads is taken as symptomatic of a problem in the fixed-income sector, and may be worrisome to investors in all financial markets, including the stock market. At the same time, narrow, stable swap spreads tend to be taken as indicators of clear sailing for all financial assets.

Exhibit 8: Spreads over Five-Year Treasury Yields, LIBOR-Based Interest Rate Swaps, and Double-A Rated Financial Corporate Obligations

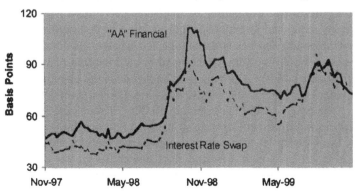

Exhibit 9: Implied Volatility of Five-Year Swaptions on Five-Year Swaps and Yields Spreads on 10NC5 U.S. Government Agency Securities

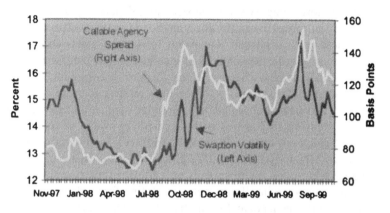

Similarly, implied swaption volatility has emerged as the benchmark for all long-dated options markets. For family portfolio managers, the most important use of a long-dated volatility benchmark relates to the valuation of callable bonds. Investors evaluate callable bonds by estimating the option-adjusted spread (OAS) paid by these securities and comparing it with yield spreads paid on non-callable bonds of the same issuers. Portfolio managers who include callable bonds in their holdings use estimates of option-adjusted duration (OAD) to monitor interest rate exposure. Computing OAS and OAD requires some assumption about interest rate volatility. A given callable bond might appear attractive — that is, it might offer a wide OAS — under a low volatility assumption but appear expensive at a higher implied volatility. Likewise, the OAD of a portfolio might appear appropriate to the manager at a low volatility but too long or too short at a higher volatility.

Increasingly, investors seeking a benchmark, market-based volatility input for purposes of evaluating an embedded call option will look to pricing of comparably structured swaptions and, depending on that implied volatility, decide whether the bond's OAS is wide enough and whether its duration is appropriate. As more and more investors have looked to the swaption market for guidance in pricing callable bonds, the pricing of callable bonds has begun, more and more, to reflect volatility levels in the swaption market. Exhibit 9 reflects this tendency.

The graph relates the implied volatility of five-year into five-year swaptions to the nominal (not option-adjusted) yield spread on U.S. government agency issues with 10-year maturities and five years of call protection. When swaption volatility is high, investors have demanded greater compensation in the form of wider spreads for buying callable agency securities rather than (non-callable) Treasuries.

CHAPTER 19

Putting it All Together: Building and Managing a Private Fixed-Income Portfolio

W e are now in a position to tie together all the material presented in this volume by summarizing the process of building and managing a family fixed-income portfolio. We can also indicate how the more sophisticated concepts and techniques presented in Part III can fit into this process.

BUILDING THE PORTFOLIO: A TWO-TRACK TOP-DOWN PROCESS

Chapter 7 characterized constructing a bond portfolio as a top-down process. That is, the portfolio manager begins by designing the portfolio's broad characteristics and only then starts searching for suitable individual bonds to buy.

Exhibit 1 summarizes the steps in a two-track top-down process of building a fixed-income portfolio. The process has two tracks: one for designing the portfolio's bond holdings, and one for shaping the net currency exposure. As discussed in Chapter 6, these two processes are separable in principle and in practice. Of course, for investors who confine their holdings to one national bond market — a large majority of U.S. taxpayers — a one-track process will be adequate.

The first task is to estimate the approximate size of the bond portfolio. Given the family's total liquid net worth — total net worth less real estate, restricted stock positions, and other illiquid positions of wealth — sizing the bond portfolio is an exercise in asset allocation. On the most basic level, as we learned in Chapter 3, the greater the investor's degree of risk tolerance, the smaller the allocation to fixed-income investments. It is also true that substantial holdings of such non-traditional investments as market-neutral hedge funds or commodities, which may be quite volatile in their own right but reduce overall portfolio risk through their low correlation with the stock market, will similarly reduce the need for substantial fixed-income holdings. Families who find it strange that such uncorrelated but highly volatile investments can make sense for risk-averse investors may instead want to limit their overall risk simply by holding a relatively large fixed-income portfolio. The process of building the fixed-income portfolio begins only after the family has determined the allocation of its liquid net worth across the full array of available asset classes.

Exhibit 1: The Top-Down Process of Building a Fixed-Income Portfolio

SIZE MATTERS

The target size of the fixed-income portfolio has an immediate implication with respect to the approach the family should take to managing its bond investments. If the size of the portfolio is to be less than several hundred thousand dollars, then it is not advisable for the family to buy individual bonds. In the U.S. municipal bond market and other "retail" oriented fixed-income sectors, blocks of bonds of more than $100,000 are substantially more liquid than "odd lots." In "institutional" sectors such as the U.S. corporate or mortgage-backed securities markets, the smallest liquid block size is much larger: as much as $1 million in the corporate market, for example. That is, the bid-asked spread on these small positions will be much wider than on larger blocks.

So, an investor trying to build a small portfolio of individual bonds will be faced with three choices: (1) buying a number of inefficiently sized positions in order to achieve credit diversification, (2) confining investments to government bonds, obviating the need for credit diversification, or (3) accepting a small number of concentrated credit positions. A better alternative than all of these will probably be to use one or more bond mutual funds as the family's principal fixed-income investment vehicle.

It is not possible to identify a level below which families should always use mutual funds and above which more families should hold bonds directly. Each specific case is different. Investors with complex tax situations who intend to invest in markets that are "retail friendly" may decide to build a portfolio of individual bonds with a total market value of, say, $250,000. At the same time, a family with $10 million to invest in bonds may decide that a few well-managed, no-load mutual funds meet their needs quite adequately.

Selecting bond market sectors and targeting portfolio duration and convexity are important both for families deciding to use mutual funds and those intending to buy a portfolio of individual bonds.

SELECTING SECTORS

Part of Chapter 13 focuses on the process by which investors should identify the right primary and principal alternative fixed-income sectors in which to invest. To review: The decision should be based on tax considerations, familiarity, liquidity, availability of information, and consistency with fundamental investment objectives. In Chapter 13 we assume that the investor's choices are limited to the "cash" markets: government, government agency, corporate, and municipal bonds in both mature and emerging national markets. At this point, we can add a variety of derivatives as possibilities.

It would be unusual, even for an institution, to allocate a portion of a fixed-income portfolio to "derivatives" in the same way as one might choose to invest regularly in U.S. municipals or eurodollar corporates. As outlined in Chapters 16 and 18, the most common use of derivatives is to help manage the interest rate exposure of portfolios of cash securities. Still, investors must decide whether to make use of these tools on a regular basis.

This decision, like all the others discussed in this book, involves a trade-off. Judicious, well-informed use of derivatives can enable a portfolio manager to achieve portfolio objectives more quickly and efficiently than would be possible if investments were confined to cash investments. Yet use of derivatives requires more time and attention than simply working with cash investments.

Under normal circumstances, investors who confine their involvement to the cash markets can feel comfortable reviewing their portfolios once a quarter or once a month. (Abnormal circumstances requiring more immediate attention to the bond portfolio might include surprising economic events leading to a change in the long-term economic outlook or changes in an investor's personal or tax situation.) Investors who use derivatives do not have the luxury of leaving the portfolio unattended for as long as a month or two. Most derivative contracts expire after relatively short periods of time, and even if they don't it is necessary to review positions frequently to determine whether they are still appropriate or require some "rebalancing." Furthermore, effective use of derivatives requires deeper understanding of fixed-income analytical concepts. After considering these trade-offs, most family portfolio managers decide that use of fixed-income derivatives is not cost-beneficial.

Currency Hedging: Forwards versus Options

At this point, we can make two additional points regarding sector selection. First, building an international investment portfolio and hedging the currency risk involves some use of derivatives in the form of forward foreign exchange transactions. In its most basic form, a hedged foreign currency bond investment involves the purchase of enough foreign currency in the spot market to buy the bond and the forward exchange of the foreign currency for the investor's base currency. While futures contracts are available for various common key exchange rates (e.g., dollar-yen, euro-dollar, euro-sterling, and so on), markets for over-the-counter currency forwards are so deep and liquid that the use of exchange-traded contracts offers little benefit to compensate for their relative inflexibility.

Active international investors may, however, benefit from the use of foreign exchange options rather than forwards. Investors can use exchange rate options in a variety of ways to control risk or to add exposures. For example, suppose the exchange rate is ¥110/$ in the spot market and ¥104/$ one year forward. A Japanese investor with a $10 million portfolio of U.S. dollar-denominated bonds might be willing to accept some degree of exposure to the dollar-yen exchange rate but still want to limit risk. One way to do this would be to sell only $7 million forward for yen at the ¥104/$ rate. This would leave the investor fully covered on 70% of the U.S. dollar exposure, but exposed to an unlimited currency loss or gain on US$3 million. An alternative is to buy an out-of-the-money option to sell $10 million for yen at an exchange rate of, say, ¥95/$. The option would place an absolute limit on the currency-related loss. Which of these alternatives is best will depend on the size of the option premium and the investor's objectives and outlook. Frequently, the option solution to partial hedging will be the best alternative.

The basic premise of the two-track, top-down, process of portfolio construction is that investors should consider currency exposure and bond market allocations separately. So far we have focused on only one aspect of this distinction — the fact that investment in a foreign bond market does not necessarily require significant exposure to that country's currency. The opposite is also true; an investor seeking exposure to a particular foreign currency does not necessarily have to invest in that country's asset market.

Exposure to the currency of a country in which one holds no assets may seem speculative, but for a U.S. dollar-based investor there is really no conceptual difference between, on the one hand, leaving part of an investment in U.K. gilts unhedged and, on the other, simply buying sterling forward. As with hedging transactions, such stand-alone currency positions can take the form of forward purchases or options. However, because such stand-alone investments do have some lingering speculative flavor, many investors prefer to express currency views through long options positions with the downside limited to the option premium paid.

Callables and Putables

The second point regarding sector selection relates to the role in the portfolio of bonds with embedded options. Chapter 17 outlines the methods used to estimate the option-adjusted spreads and durations of callable bonds. Understanding of these concepts empowers investors to make astute decisions about buying callable bonds and mortgage-backed securities and to manage portfolios including large proportions of these instruments effectively.

A corollary of this observation is that investors who do not feel comfortable with the concepts of OAS and OAD should probably limit callable bonds to a relatively small proportion — say, 10%-20% — of the fixed-income portfolio and focus on "call-protected" rather than "call-vulnerable" securities. The former include bonds with optional call dates close to their maturity dates — a bond with a 12-year maturity that is callable after 10 years, for example — and bonds that are trading at prices well above or well below their call prices.

TARGETING PORTFOLIO DURATION AND CONVEXITY

Chapter 7 ties together the materials in Part I by providing some broad guidelines for selecting a target duration for a bond portfolio. The conclusion of that discussion is that the most reasonable duration target for most families is something close to the market average. For most bond markets, the weighted average duration of all bonds lies within a range between 4.0 and 6.0. Investors who suspect that interest rates are more likely to increase than to decline might want to gravitate toward the shorter end of that range, while more bullish investors or families seeking steady investment income might build portfolios with durations closer to 6.0 than to 5.0.

There are a number of good reasons for some families to build portfolios outside the 4.0 to 6.0. range For one thing, managers holding very strong views regarding the direction of interest rates might want to express their opinions by building portfolios of all money market instruments or all very long-term bonds. Also, investors aiming to match a very specific liability may want to build portfolios matching the duration of that liability. Thus, an investor who has taken out a 10-year "balloon" loan — one that requires interest payments only for 10 years and then a single principal payment at the end of the period may want to build a portfolio of 10-year bonds. Such a portfolio would have a duration somewhat greater than 7.0.

This market-neutral approach to portfolio construction also applies to targeting portfolio convexity. Unless a portfolio manager has a very strong view regarding the degree of interest rate volatility in the future, a portfolio with slightly positive convexity will be most appropriate. As a practical matter, for a large majority of family investors, who are unlikely to monitor such portfolio statistics as option-adjusted convexity very closely, this means that the portfolio should include a modest proportion of call-vulnerable bonds. Investors who expect interest rate movements to be very subdued in the future may wish to build portfolios including more than 50% call-vulnerable securities. Investors who anticipate wide swings in rates will not want to buy any call-vulnerable securities. But for most families, the proportion of 10%-20% call-vulnerable bonds will make sense.

Investors who wish to use the embedded option valuation techniques presented in Chapter 17 will be able to go beyond these rules of thumb and manage their purchases and sales of callable bonds in a more precise way. Such investors will be able to earn the higher yields paid on callable bonds without inadvertently taking more volatility risk than they intend. Investors willing to take the time to become comfortable with the most sophisticated portfolio management techniques may also be comfortable using putable corporate bonds to help manage portfolio convexity in a cost-effective way.

MATURITY STRUCTURE

Investors can achieve any given target duration in one of three broad ways:

- A bullet portfolio in which most of the bonds have individual durations close to the portfolio average, or
- A barbell portfolio consisting of a combination of bonds with durations that are shorter and longer than the portfolio average duration, or

- A ladder portfolio of approximately equal amounts of bonds maturing each year, with the longest maturity set so that the weighted average duration of the holdings is at the target level.

Maturity structure has much less of an influence on portfolio total return than duration or sector selection. Still, a choice must be made, and it is better to make the right choice.

Under most market circumstances — that is, when the yield curve is upward-sloping and has a bowed shape — the bullet portfolio will produce the highest return in terms of both yield and price change. The only common circumstances in which this is not the case are when the yield curve flattens substantially and/or interest rates are volatile. More precisely, unless the yield curve flattens by more than forward rates imply, and absent a very large (100+ basis point) change in interest rates, a bullet portfolio with any given duration will outperform both barbell and ladder portfolios with equal durations. If the yield curve does flatten by more than forward rates imply and/or interest rates do shift substantially, a barbell will outperform both a bullet and a ladder.

A ladder portfolio will never produce the best return of the three alternative structures, but this structure offers two advantages over either barbells or bullets. First, the ladder will seldom be the worst performer of the three. Second, a ladder is relatively easy to manage. Because the investor will have at least some bonds maturing each year, it will be relatively easy to make adjustments to the portfolio on an annual basis, whether to shift the asset allocation from bonds to other asset classes or to adjust the duration of bond holdings.

Faced with these trade-offs, most family investors wind up compromising; they build portfolios that look like a cross between a bullet and a ladder. That is, the portfolio will include some bonds maturing each of a series of sequential years, but there will be a concentration of securities in the middle of the ladder. When an opportunity presents itself, families may purchase barbell structures, but such holdings will reflect more of an opportunistic "trade" than a stable portfolio structure over a long period of time.

CREDIT QUALITY AND DIVERSIFICATION

Two more decisions complete the top-down process of determining the desired shape of a fixed-income portfolio. Investors who have decided to participate in "credit-sensitive" sectors such as the corporate or municipal bond markets must define two related portfolio characteristics: the average credit quality of holdings, and the minimum credit quality of holdings.

With respect to average credit quality, Chapter 10 highlights two common mistakes investors make in this regard. The first is to avoid credit risk entirely by confining purchases to government or government-guaranteed paper.

The second is to take too much concentrated credit risk in a small number of corporate bond positions.

There may be times that avoiding all credit risk makes sense; an investor building a very small bond portfolio and unwilling to use a mutual fund will not be able to diversify credit risk and should probably limit investments to government bonds or triple-A rated issues for reasons of credit quality and liquidity. Substantial family investors, however, will be in a position to take advantage of the fact that portfolios of corporate and municipal bonds have outperformed government bond portfolios over long periods of time. To be sure, there have been and will be times when credit spreads widen by enough to reduce corporate bond returns below government bond results, but such periods are the exception rather than the rule.

So an average credit quality of triple-A is probably unnecessarily high for most substantial family investors. Whether the target should be in the double-A, single-A, or triple-B range will depend on three considerations. The first of these is the size of the portfolio. Size matters in this regard because, as noted previously, the portfolio should be sufficiently diversified for its credit quality while individual bond positions should be large enough to be liquid. If an investor plans to build a $5 million portfolio in a market where any block of bonds smaller than $500,000 is considered an odd lot, it would be inefficient to hold more than 10 different positions. Under the circumstances, the investor should probably aim to build a portfolio with a minimum rating of A1/A+ and an average rating well within the double-A range.

An investor aiming to build a $20 million portfolio in the same market will certainly meet the size qualification for a more aggressive bond portfolio, and could reasonably target an average rating of A2/A and set the minimum credit quality at Baa3/BBB- or even a bit lower. Whether an investor would set average and minimum credit quality this low depends on whether the portfolio will be large enough to allow sufficient diversification. It will also depend on the investor's degree of risk tolerance and willingness to devote time to portfolio management.

A portfolio with an average rating in the double-A range and a minimum rating of A1/A+ can reasonably be termed a "low credit risk" bond portfolio. The relative performance of such a portfolio will depend on what happens to corporate or municipal credit spreads in general; if spreads widen substantially, the portfolio will underperform government bonds. Serious adverse credit surprises for bonds rated A1/A+ or better, while not impossible or unprecedented, are unlikely. And the likelihood of unanticipated bad news lessens as the issuer's credit rating rises from A1/A+ to Aaa/AAA.

At the other end of the investment-grade spectrum, it would be a mistake to think of a portfolio with a minimum credit rating of Baa3/BBB- and an average rating of A2/A as "highly risky." "Moderately risky" is a better description, although the probability of adverse credit developments in this ratings range is much higher than for the low-risk portfolio. An investor planning to build a $20 million portfolio who could build a well-diversified, highly liquid corporate bond portfolio but who would not feel comfortable holding weaker investment-grade issues would be perfectly justified in targeting an average rating of double-A and a minimum of A1/A+ or even higher.

The lower the average and minimum credit quality, the more time the manager should devote to monitoring the portfolio. To the extent that large, double-A rated companies or municipalities account for all of the holdings, the portfolio manager can reasonably take a fairly passive role with regard to tracking the credit quality of individual holdings. If, however, the portfolio includes obligations of more obscure triple-B issuers — even if each one accounts for a relatively small proportion of the total holdings — the manager should be prepared to scrutinize individual credits proactively and frequently. Again, an investor planning a $20 million corporate portfolio who could "afford" to buy weaker credits but who is unwilling to spend time monitoring credits should build a low credit-risk portfolio.

All these points regarding moderately risky portfolios apply to an even greater extent to subinvestment-grade ("high yield," or "junk bond") portfolios. Adverse credit developments are not just possible but, in fact, highly likely in even the most well-selected and well-managed portfolios of bonds rated double-B or lower. For this reason, such portfolios require extensive prepurchase research and more or less constant surveillance by the portfolio manager.

Occasional and temporary purchases of specific high-yield issues may make sense, provided the investor is willing to monitor the position as closely as one would a similarly opportunistic equity investment. Over longer periods of time, some routine participation in the high-yield bond market can make a great deal of sense for investors with a reasonable degree of risk tolerance. For this purpose, however, most family investors will find that here mutual funds make the most sense.

BUYING SPECIFIC BONDS

In the stock market, the transition between the portfolio planning process and the actual accumulation of the portfolio is seamless. Once the portfolio manager has decided which companies he or she wants to own, it is a simple matter to enter the market and place orders for the specific securities. The manager may decide to accumulate the portfolio gradually over a period of time as a tactical matter, but, unless the portfolio is extremely large, it will be possible to buy the individual positions instantaneously.

The process in the bond market is quite different. For one thing, even after the portfolio design process is complete, the manager will, in general, have no idea which specific bonds will fill the various categories in the portfolio structure. It will depend on which particular bonds happen to be available at the time the cash is going to work.

Second, the considerations that influence the timing of purchases are different in the stock and the bond markets. As in the stock market, a manager must decide how quickly to try to complete the process of accumulating the portfolio. Two considerations go into this decision. First, a portfolio manager may have a view about near-term trends in interest rates. Suppose an investor aims to build a portfolio with a five-year duration but believes that bond yields are more likely to rise than to fall over the next few weeks. Such an investor might want to buy the bonds slowly, thereby increasing the portfolio's duration to 5.0 gradually. Likewise, an investor who is near-term bullish on bond prices would want to get the bonds bought as quickly as possible.

At most times, however, investors in the fixed-income market should have a bias in favor of buying bonds sooner rather than later. The fact that the yield curve is usually upward-sloping means that investors are giving up yield while they wait to buy their bonds. Unless interest rates rise to above fair forward rates by the time the bonds are actually purchased, the cost of staying short will reduce the investor's return. So an investor who is neutral on the near-term direction of interest rates would want to buy bonds quickly.

The second consideration that affects the timing of purchases is practical. In some markets it is easy to accumulate a portfolio of any given duration nearly instantaneously. In the U.S. Treasury market, for example, investors can purchase portfolios totaling several $100 million or more with durations ranging from zero out to 30.0 in a matter of seconds. Investors who use leverage or short positions can extend this range of possible portfolio durations into negative numbers and well beyond the duration of a 30-year zero-coupon bond. The same is true of other government bond markets.

In other markets, it can take much longer to build a portfolio with a specific target duration. An investor seeking, for example, to build a portfolio of double tax-exempt Minnesota municipal bonds with a duration between 5.0 and 5.5 might find that it takes several weeks or even months to accumulate the right positions. While the investor is waiting for the right bonds to show up in the market at acceptable prices, the funds reserved to build the bond portfolio will be sitting in money market instruments usually earning relatively low yields.

An investor in this situation will be faced with three choices: (1) incurring the opportunity cost of keeping the funds invested in money-market instruments, (2) compromising the portfolio management objectives by buying something other than Minnesota double tax-exempt paper, or (3) using more sophisticated or aggressive portfolio management techniques. Most family portfolio managers will opt for one of the first two alternatives, and the results will be perfectly adequate. Yet this is one of the circumstances in which a slightly more active approach to management should produce a slightly better outcome in terms of average portfolio returns over time.

SOPHISTICATED PROCESS MANAGEMENT

One relatively straightforward yet sophisticated option is to purchase whatever suitable Minnesota (or Puerto Rico) bonds are available in the market immediately and invest the rest of the portfolio in U.S. Treasury securities of the appropriate durations. The Treasuries are not the most tax-efficient investment in this situation, because the interest on them is not exempt from federal taxes. The Treasuries are highly liquid, however, and interest on them is exempt from state income taxes. Over time, as double tax-exempt securities become available, the investor can sell the Treasuries and use the proceeds to buy the municipals.

This approach is not guaranteed to produce better results than simply holding money market instruments until the Minnesota bonds become available. Yet unless interest rates rise by more than the slope of the yield curve implies, and assuming minimal transaction costs of buying and selling the Treasury securities, temporary purchase of governments will produce a better outcome than the money market alternative.

One of the disadvantages of the approach of buying Treasury securities as an interim expedient is that interest on these investments will be subject to federal taxes. A somewhat more tax-efficient alternative would be to continue to invest the funds to be used for purchase of the bond portfolio in tax-exempt money market instruments while adding duration to the portfolio through the use of leveraged or derivative transactions. There are three techniques an investor could use to accomplish this objective: (1) using some of the cash reserves as collateral for a leveraged purchase of Treasury securities through a repurchase agreement, (2) buying Treasuries for forward delivery, or (3) buying bond futures contracts. The futures contract might be one of the U.S. Treasury note or bond futures contracts or the Municipal Bond Index futures contract.

Which of these approaches would be the most efficient depends on all the facts and the circumstances of the investor's situation and the relevant markets. Using leverage or derivatives offers the greatest potential efficiency, but purchases and sales of leveraged or derivative contracts require a considerable amount of expert knowledge as well as more time and attention than most family portfolio managers are willing to commit to.

MANAGING THE PORTFOLIO

Chapter 13 lists three broad varieties of bond portfolio management activity: maintenance management, restructuring, and opportunistic trading. At that point in the text, we illustrated all three types of activity, but limited the hypothetical transactions to the market for cash bonds. At this point, we can review the processes of portfolio management while mentioning some of the ways in which the techniques presented in Part III can play a role in the process.

Maintenance Management

The purpose of maintenance management is to hold portfolio characteristics in a steady state. As time goes by, portfolio duration will drift lower; as the economy evolves, individual issuers' credits will improve or deteriorate; as interest rates rise or fall, option-adjusted duration will rise or fall, and currency hedges, by their nature, will expire and need to be rolled over. An investor who wishes to maintain more or less constant portfolio structure must review the portfolio periodically and, when characteristics move out of an acceptable range, execute maintenance transactions.

In Chapter 13 we illustrate this process by showing how a hypothetical portfolio's duration would shorten after the passage of a year and a decrease in interest rates. Specifically, the passage of 12 months and a 75 basis point decline in interest rates reduce the portfolio's duration (to worst) from 6.4 to 5.3. We assumed then that the investor wishes to maintain a constant duration close to 6.5 and a deviation of 1.2 (= 6.5 − 5.3) from this target duration is too great. The remedy was to sell the three shortest-duration bonds and to replace them with three longer duration issues. For most family investors, this scenario would produce perfectly adequate results. A more aggressive or more involved investor might want to consider a broader array of management techniques.

One reason to consider somewhat more active maintenance management is that one year is a long time to wait to manage portfolio duration, especially if interest rates have declined by as much as 75 basis points over the period. To put it differently, while many family investors with a target portfolio duration of 6.5 would not be particularly concerned if actual duration falls to 5.3 before adjustment, some families, like most institutions, might view this deviation from target duration as far too great. Such families would want to refresh duration calculations much more frequently than annually. For example, a family might decide to monitor portfolio duration at least quarterly or whenever a given benchmark interest rate changes by more than 50 basis points, and to make adjustments whenever duration to worst falls below 6.0 or rises above 7.0. Committing to this type of management schedule will guarantee that the portfolio's characteristics remain close to target levels.

Another reason for more frequent maintenance is that changes in market values can affect currency exposures. Recall that in the examples of currency-hedged bond investments in Chapter 6 the portfolio manager sold an amount of foreign currency forward equal to the bond's purchase price plus interest that would accrue over the forward period. This hedging approach leaves any change in the bond's market value unhedged with respect to exchange rate risk.

For example, consider a Japanese investor holding a hedged investment in the U.S. dollar bond market. Any substantial rally in U.S. bond prices would increase this investor's exposure to the dollar-yen exchange rate. An investor in this situation might want to adjust currency hedges, especially if the portfolio manager is somewhat bearish on the dollar versus the yen.

More frequent portfolio management will probably mean more frequent bond and currency market transactions, though, and any such transaction necessarily involves selling at the market's bid side price and buying on the offered side. The barest minimum for a combined sale and purchase of government securities will be about 1/8%. In the municipal market or for blocks of less than $1 million corporate bonds, the cost of the two-way transaction could rise as high as 1% or more. So, as for most other investment choices, a family's decision about how frequently to manage its bond portfolio involves a trade-off. In addition, active trading can involve realization of taxable short-term gains.

The benefit of frequent reviews and narrow target ranges for characteristics is that these guarantee that the portfolio will perform as expected, given general market conditions. The cost of running a tight ship in the fixed-income markets is paid in the form of capital gains taxes and transaction costs, and can be particularly onerous in relatively illiquid markets. Faced with this trade-off, many families opt to invest in the markets that best meet their long-term needs — municipals for U.S. taxpayers, euro governments and corporates for European families — and set portfolio maintenance schedules and tolerance bands that do not require frequent transactions. In the extreme, investors may intend to buy and hold bonds until the securities mature.

One of the principal uses of the techniques and instruments discussed in Part III is to reduce the transaction costs involved in managing a bond portfolio. Use of leverage, short sales, and certain derivatives can enable investors to adjust portfolio duration without actually buying or selling relatively illiquid bonds.

For example, suppose an investor finds that, after the passage of a few months and in the wake of a substantial rally in bond prices, portfolio duration should be extended by half a year. Suppose further that the portfolio consists largely of municipal bonds from a high tax state where double tax-exempt paper is hard to find, and that the current and target maturity structure of the portfolio is a "bullet." At best, adjusting duration by selling individual securities and replacing them with somewhat longer bonds would involve substantial transaction costs. At worst, transaction cost will be high, and it might take several months to find replacement bonds. The investor could avoid hefty transaction costs and illiquidity problems by holding a portion of the portfolio in U.S. Treasury securities, but this would make sense only for a very active trader; it would take a lot of transaction cost savings to compensate the investor for the fact that the interest on Treasuries is taxable while interest on municipals is tax exempt.

An alternative to either trading scarce and illiquid municipal bonds or holding Treasuries at low after-tax yields is, as a temporary expedient, buying enough Treasury notes on a leveraged basis to bring total portfolio duration up to the target range. Alternative transactions might include buying Treasury or municipal futures contracts, or buying call options on Treasuries. These leveraged or derivatives positions could be kept in place until market conditions change or until suitable in-state bonds appear in the market.

Restructuring

The goal of maintenance management is to hold portfolio characteristics — bond sector allocation, duration, convexity, maturity structure, and credit quality — as constant as possible. The goal of restructuring is to *alter* portfolio characteristics in response to a change in the investor's fundamental objectives, life situation, or market outlook. A change in an investor's tax status, occasioned, for example, by realization of a large gain or loss or a change of residence, will frequently require substantial restructuring. Sale of a family business, divorce, retirement, and various phases of estate planning may also require substantial shifts in the structure of an investor's portfolio. Such occasions for portfolio restructuring are inevitable during the course of a wealthy family's life cycle. This is the primary reason why the buy-and-hold strategy seldom makes sense over long periods of time.

Restructuring in response to changes in market outlook is not inevitable. Indeed, a well-respected school of finance theory — the efficient markets hypothesis in its strongest form — holds that it is impossible, except by pure luck, to outperform the market as a whole on a consistent basis. If so, a family investor seeking to include a fixed-income component in a diversified, balanced investment portfolio would be quite justified in consistently maintaining portfolio characteristics close to the average for the markets in which he or she is involved.

The efficient markets hypothesis, however, is a hypothesis not a forgone conclusion. Many investors, quite reasonably, hold the opposite view: that careful attention, focused thinking, and good instincts along with just average luck can enhance investment returns substantially over time. Members of this school will want to restructure their bond portfolios as frequently as their market outlook changes, and this may occur as often as several times a day and as infrequently as once every several years.

Investors who anticipate restructuring bond portfolios more often than once or twice a year should take this expectation into account when selecting bond market sectors. An active trader's portfolio should include a substantial proportion of highly liquid instruments such as government bonds. In addition, active managers will find that the use of leverage and various types of derivatives will enhance the efficiency of restructuring transactions. In fact, an investor who intentionally changes target portfolio duration by more than 1.0 more than twice a year but executes all these restructuring transactions through unleveraged transactions in the cash market is probably making a mistake.

Opportunistic Investing

Our subject matter has been portfolio management. The primary purpose has been to guide the process of designing, building, maintaining, and, on occasion, restructuring a relatively stable portfolio of bonds. The goal is to provide an investor with the basic benefits of fixed-income investments: relative return stability and risk diversification. In other words, although investors can and should expect comfortably positive real after-tax returns from their bond portfolios, this material is not intended as a guide to making lots of money in the bond market. Nevertheless, situations offering a particularly attractive risk-return trade-off do arise in the bond market from time to time. Most family investors will decide to leave such opportunities to be exploited by institutional specialists. Performance-oriented family fixed-income managers, who are willing to devote the time and attention required to understand these situations and to structure appropriate transactional responses, should be prepared to consider such opportunities.

Successful opportunistic trading in the fixed-income market presupposes the use of leverage and/or derivatives. With a few exceptions, the impact of an expected change in interest rates on the price of an unleveraged, cash security will be small relative to the amount of time and effort required to analyze and structure a transaction. In most cases, the transaction will be worth the effort only if the potential profitability can be amplified through leverage or the use of derivatives.

Five varieties of opportunities occur in the fixed-income markets. These relate to market direction, carry, spread changes, individual credit changes, and volatility changes.

Market Direction

Predicting changes in interest rates over any period of time is extremely difficult at best. It may, in fact, be impossible. All the same, individual investors may on occasion conclude that the bond market has clearly overreacted to a piece of economic news, and that a near-term correction is inevitable.

The chapters on leverage, futures, and fixed-income options illustrate efficient ways in which investors can express views regarding market direction. Given the difficulty of predicting interest rate changes, family portfolio managers with a taste for directional trading would be well advised to control risk by expressing these views through long options positions or with very tight stop loss triggers.

Carry

Buying bonds with borrowed money usually produces positive carry, especially if the financing is efficient. Therefore, when the yield curve is steeply upward-sloping, an aggressive investor who does not necessarily expect interest rates to decline but is fairly confident that rates will not rise substantially might reasonably buy long-term bonds with funds borrowed pursuant to a repurchase agreement.

As in the case of speculative positions, investors who position carry trades should impose strict loss limits and liquidate transactions quickly if the market begins to head in the wrong direction.

Spread Changes

Changes in relative value — that is, changes in the spreads between different interest rates — may be a bit easier to predict than the general direction of interest rates. One reason is that some yield spreads follow consistent seasonal patterns. Yields on municipal bonds, for example, have a strong tendency to decline relative to Treasury bond yields during the last few weeks of each year and through the first weeks of the subsequent year. One would expect such a seasonal pattern to disappear as more and more investors catch on to the pattern and buy municipal bonds against short positions in the Treasury securities in November. Yet this pattern has not disappeared, and municipals-over-bonds (MOB) fairly consistently make money over the late-fall through late-winter period.

Relative value shifts may also reflect short-term supply and demand imbalances. A rush of issuance in the corporate bond market in the wake of a sharp decline in interest rates can push yield spreads over Treasuries wider for a period of a few weeks. Investors who purchase corporate bonds at such times and take duration-matched short positions in Treasuries are not guaranteed to make money. The economy might sink into recession and corporate spreads might continue to widen. Spread trading based on primary market congestion has been a fairly consistent source of enhanced returns, however.

The general level of corporate credit spreads also reflects economic conditions. An investor who concludes that the economy is emerging from a recession but that this outlook is not yet fully reflected in the bond market might also want to buy corporate bonds and sell U.S. Treasury securities short. Expressing the opposite point of view would be more difficult because selling corporate bonds short can be difficult for a family portfolio manager.

Other yield relationships worth looking at include yield curve spreads between bonds of different maturities. Changes in some yield curve spreads — for example, the spread between 2-year and 30-year maturities — may be as inherently difficult to predict as the general direction of interest rates. At the same time, careful observers of government bond yield curves may find, for example, that the slope between two- and five-year maturities is too steep relative to the slope between two- and 10-year notes. The thing to do under these circumstances is to buy five-year bonds and sell twos and 10s. If a transaction along these lines is leveraged, and the analysis turns out to be correct, the returns to a relative value investor can be worthwhile.

Individual Credit Changes

Active traders in the stock market typically engage in detailed research on the near- and long-term prospects for individual companies. Trading opportunities arise when an investor reaches correct conclusions about a company's near-term prospects that are different from the market consensus. Analysis may lead an investor to either a long or a short position in the company's stock.

Similar opportunities can arise in the bond market. Changes in market perceptions of companies' credit quality affect yield spreads in both the investment-grade and high-yield bond markets. In this case, the potential price impact of changing credit views on bonds rated triple-B or better will be modest. And since family investors' ability to leverage corporate bond positions is limited, it is unlikely that extensive credit analysis of investment-grade companies will produce many worthwhile trading opportunities.

By contrast, detailed research on companies or emerging market governments with high-yield bonds outstanding — the lower-rated, the better — can be highly rewarding if the analysis leads to conclusions that differ from the market consensus, if the market comes to the same conclusions, and, especially, if the investor is able to lever the position. As in the investment-grade corporate market, it is much more difficult for family portfolio managers to take short positions in the high-yield corporate bond market.

Volatility Changes

Investors who anticipate that interest rates will remain in a narrower range than the pricing of options implies can profit from this view by selling straddles and strangles. Investors who anticipate greater than implied volatility should buy straddles or strangles.

Expectations regarding volatility can be combined with views on other market variables. So, an investor who believes rates are likely to decline and that market volatility will be substantially greater than the market implied level might choose to express this directional view by buying call options.

CONCLUSION

A small number of family investors will want to use the material presented in Part III to structure opportunistic transactions. The vast majority will not. For most individuals, the fixed-income portfolio is intended as the family's "sleep well money." Indeed, any family with a large portfolio of high-quality bonds should not be losing sleep over its financial circumstances. The night should be even more restful if the family is confident that no major mistakes are being made in the design, construction, and maintenance of its bond portfolio.

Managing a portfolio with attention to the concepts and information in this book will not guarantee superior performance. It will, however, provide considerable assurance that the portfolio's performance will not surprise the investor and that no major mistakes have been made.

In other words, the goal of this book is met if it enables family investors in the bond market to sleep better.

Index

Printed and bound by CPI Group (UK) Ltd, Croydon, CR0 4YY

16/04/2025

14658444-0005